H O T E L A S H O M E

HOTEL AS HOME

THE ART OF LIVING ON THE ROAD

GARY CHANG

PRINCETON ARCHITECTURAL PRESS
NEW YORK

Published by
Princeton Architectural Press
37 East Seventh Street
New York, New York 10003

For a free catalog of books, call 1.800.822.6657
Visit our website at www.papress.com

Printed and bound in China
09 08 07 06 5 4 3 2 1 First Edition

Originally published in Chinese by MCCM Creations, Hong Kong in 2004

Design and editorial: MCCM Creations
Translation: Sunny Pang

For Princeton Architectural Press:
Editor: Nicola Bednarek
Cover design: Paul Wagner

Special thanks to Nettie Aljian, Sara Bader, Dorothy Ball, Janet Behning, Becca Casbon, Penny (Yuen Pik) Chu, Russell Fernandez, Pete Fitzpatrick, Sara Hart, Jan Haux, Clare Jacobson, John King, Mark Lamster, Nancy Eklund Later, Linda Lee, Katharine Myers, Lauren Nelson Packard, Scott Tennent, Jennifer Thompson, Joseph Weston, and Deb Wood of Princeton Architectural Press —Kevin C. Lippert, publisher

Library of Congress Cataloging-in-Publication Data
Chang, Gary, 1962–
Hotel as home : the art of living in transit / Gary Chang.
p. cm.
Includes bibliographical references and index.
ISBN-13: 978-1-56898-603-6 (alk. paper)
ISBN-10: 1-56898-603-3 (alk. paper)
1. Hotels—Decoration. 2. Hotels—History. 3. Chang, Gary, 1962– I. Title.
NK2195.H6C53 2006
728'.5—dc22

2006015583

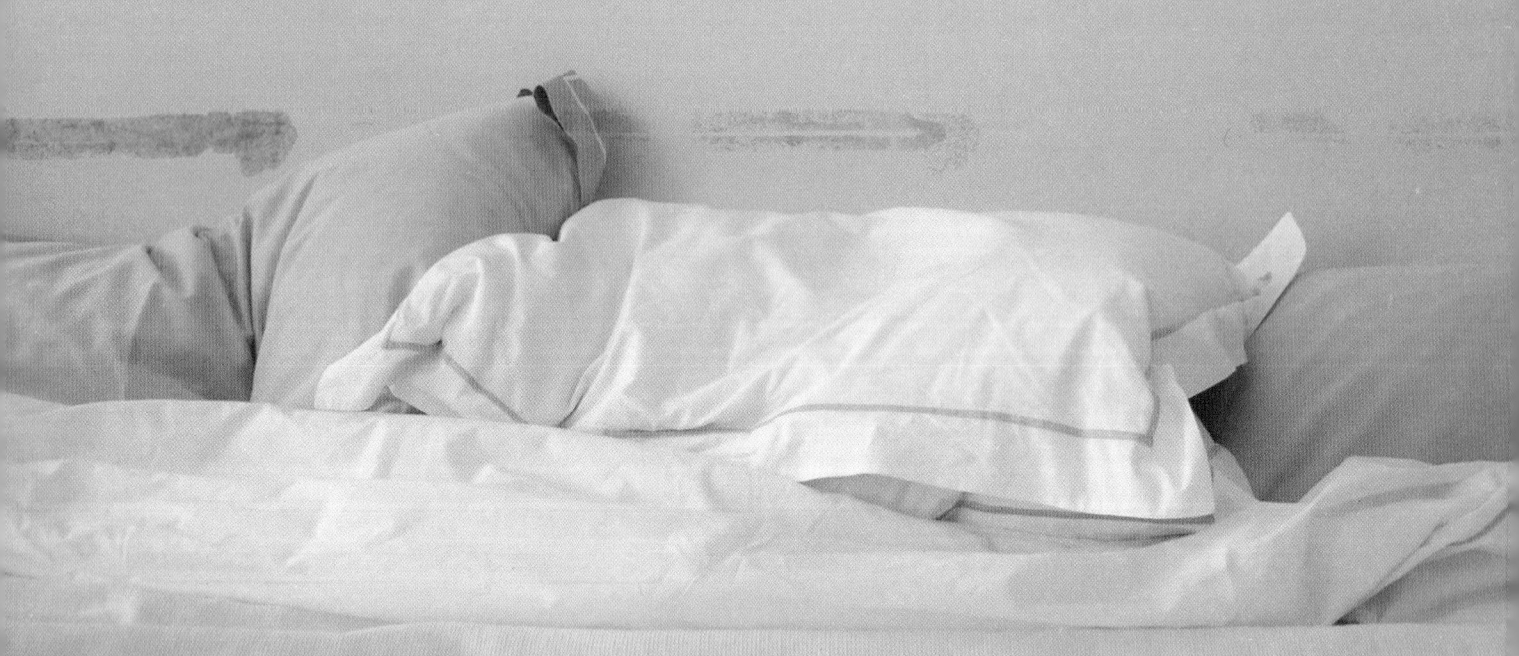

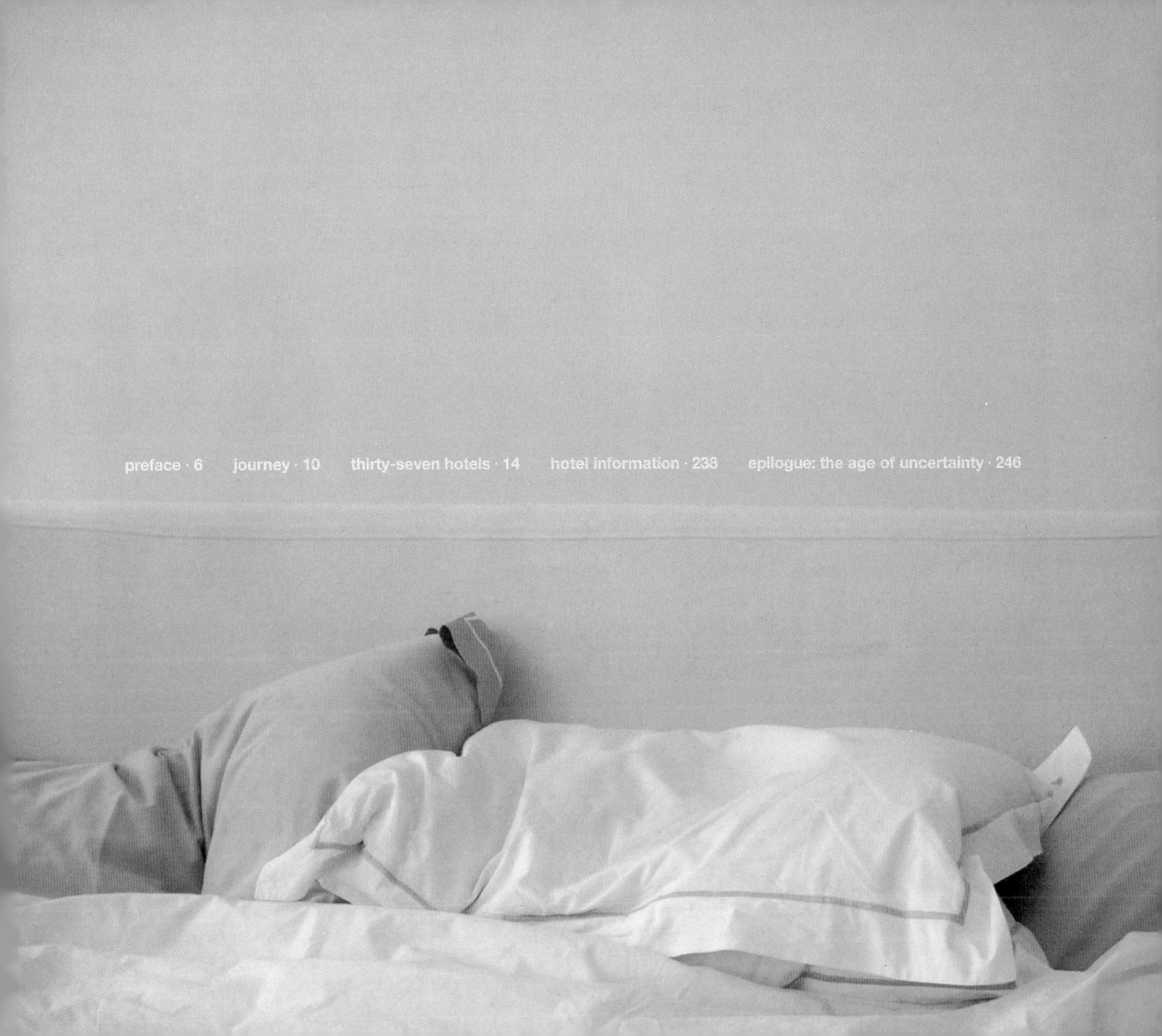

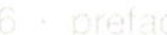

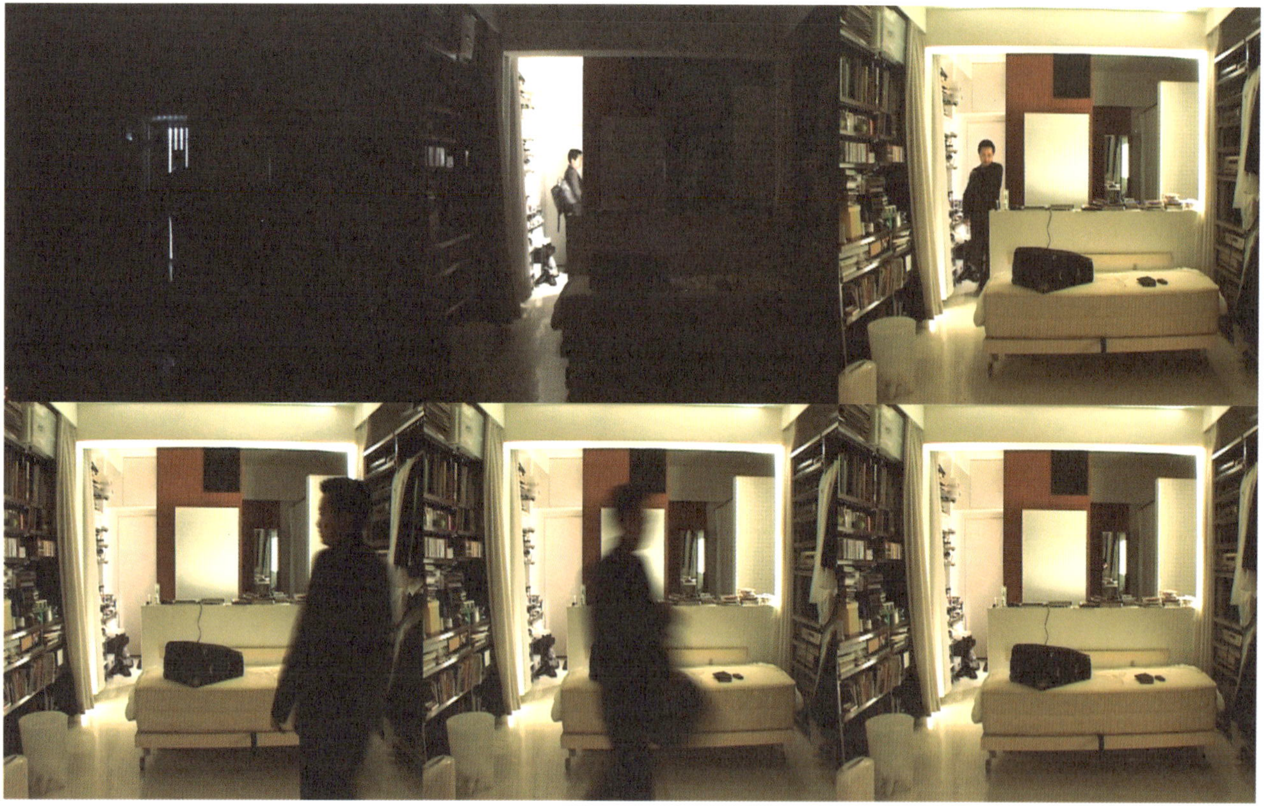

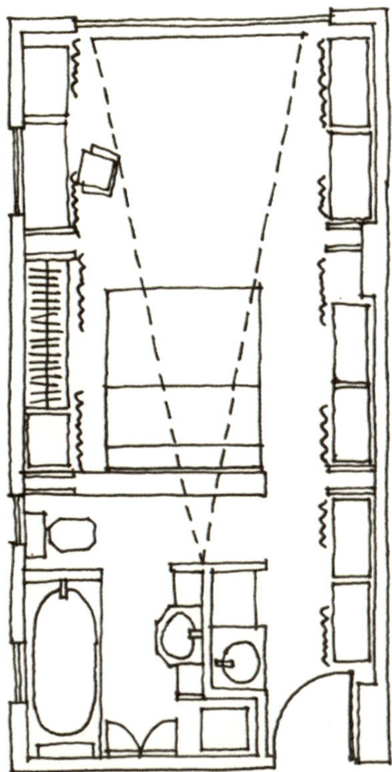

Why Another Book on Hotels?

Here's a realization that took me by surprise: it turns out that on average I spend about 120 days a year staying in hotels. While living just two-thirds of the year in the small pad I call home has made me unusually attached to it, it has conversely led me to look at hotels with relatively exacting standards. This is also the reason why these days I tend to decline the good intentions of my hosts or friends to arrange hotel accommodation for me. In fact, I have become somewhat of a fiend for anything and everything "hotel"—books, magazines, you name it—and finding the perfect hotel has become an obsession. Whenever I travel, as soon as I'm settled, and regardless of the fact I might have hardly any free time, I scour the town for hotels I may have missed but which I think might be of interest, or for that newly opened one I have read about in some publication. I even go as far as changing hotels, or rooms in the same hotel, every night. All this has made me something of a "know-it-all" expert on hotels to my friends and clients. They come to me for advice and insider information when they want to book hotels, sometimes down to *which* room to request in a particular hotel. After all, I even have photographs of the emergency exit plans!

Considering our increasingly cosmopolitan lifestyles, *Hotel as Home* might actually just as well be called *Home as Hotel*. After all, the boundaries between the categories of home, service apartments, and hotels have become fuzzier these days—perhaps another testimony to our age's insistence on adaptability. As my addiction to hotels continues to be fed by my constant

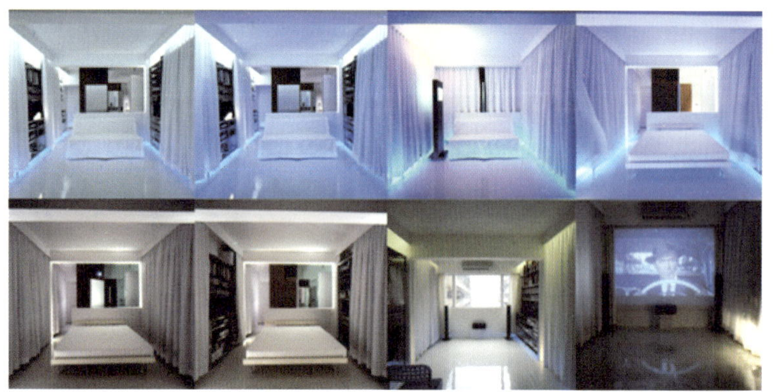

business trips, a rather strange metamorphosis has taken place in my own home: it has come to increasingly resemble a standard hotel room. Its inherently compact size of thirteen by twenty-six feet doesn't help (or does, depending on how you look at it), and it is furnished with various trophy-freebies from my sojourns—toiletries, stationery, mementos, and laundry bags—as well as souvenir items specially bought—a bathrobe from New York's Soho House Hotel, a cup from Rotterdam's Hotel New York, a clothes brush from the Park Hyatt in Tokyo, slippers from Melbourne's Prince Hotel, and CDs of the in-house music of various "happening" hotels. But above all, apart from my near-fetishism, what my home and a hotel room have in common are their convenience and practicality.

Come to think of it, many people treat their homes as if they were transient way stations. Quite a few Hongkongers buy their apartments with a view to eventually resell them. As a result, they furnish their homes with salability rather than their own needs in mind. Neither the layout nor the décor should be too personal or individualistic, which of course coincides with the philosophy of hotel chains. Like the transitory hotel guest, these people have become urban nomads in their own apartments, which have lost all the traditional characteristics of home.

These days, books on hotels often seem to make it onto various bestseller lists, and books on hotel design are all too numerous to keep tabs on. But when you take a closer look, many of these publications are nothing more than blurbs about recently opened hotels, filled mainly with pictures (many of which haven't even been taken by the author) and the obligatory but vacuous preface. The hotels become blurry and start resembling each other. No matter how fine the packaging and printing, most of these books turn out to be about the leading hotel chains. It's all quite frustrating and infuriating in a love-hate kind of way to an "über-fan" of hotels like myself.

My motivation for writing this book then was to provide a first-person perspective based on my personal experiences as a hotel guest and as an architect. The selection of these thirty-seven favorites of mine was a rather dynamic process, as I was constantly tempted to revise my list when I discovered new surprises. There is certainly no shortage of the latest and the newest, and yet I haven't shied away from the tried and true either: good design is not the exclusive prerogative of the new. Besides, such is the regrettable wont of modern urbanite amnesia that it renders some of the most talked-about hotels of the year all but out of the in-crowd's collective memory twelve months later. It does no harm to remind people of the exquisite designs of some of the grand houses of old that have survived the test of time.

The hotels in this book are ordered according to the date of my stay at them during the last seven years. As such, *Hotel as Home* is also a kind of personal journal, including my photographs and descriptions of the layout and furnishings of each room I stayed in. Also noted are the room number, the date of my first night of stay, and the room rate. Some of the rates might seem amazingly low, but keep in mind that I stayed at some hotels during their pre-opening trial period. I must extend my sincerest gratitude to Jessica Wong for patiently listening to all my hotel stories during the past six months and for helping me to transform them into a text after my own heart.

Finally, the book is also a reflection and exploration of what hotel design is about, which of course leads back to the fundamental question: what is design? My hope is that the book will confirm my long-held tenet that there are no clear-cut boundaries in our world; I believe that we can find meaningful connections between seemingly unrelated things by looking at them from different angles.

GARY CHANG

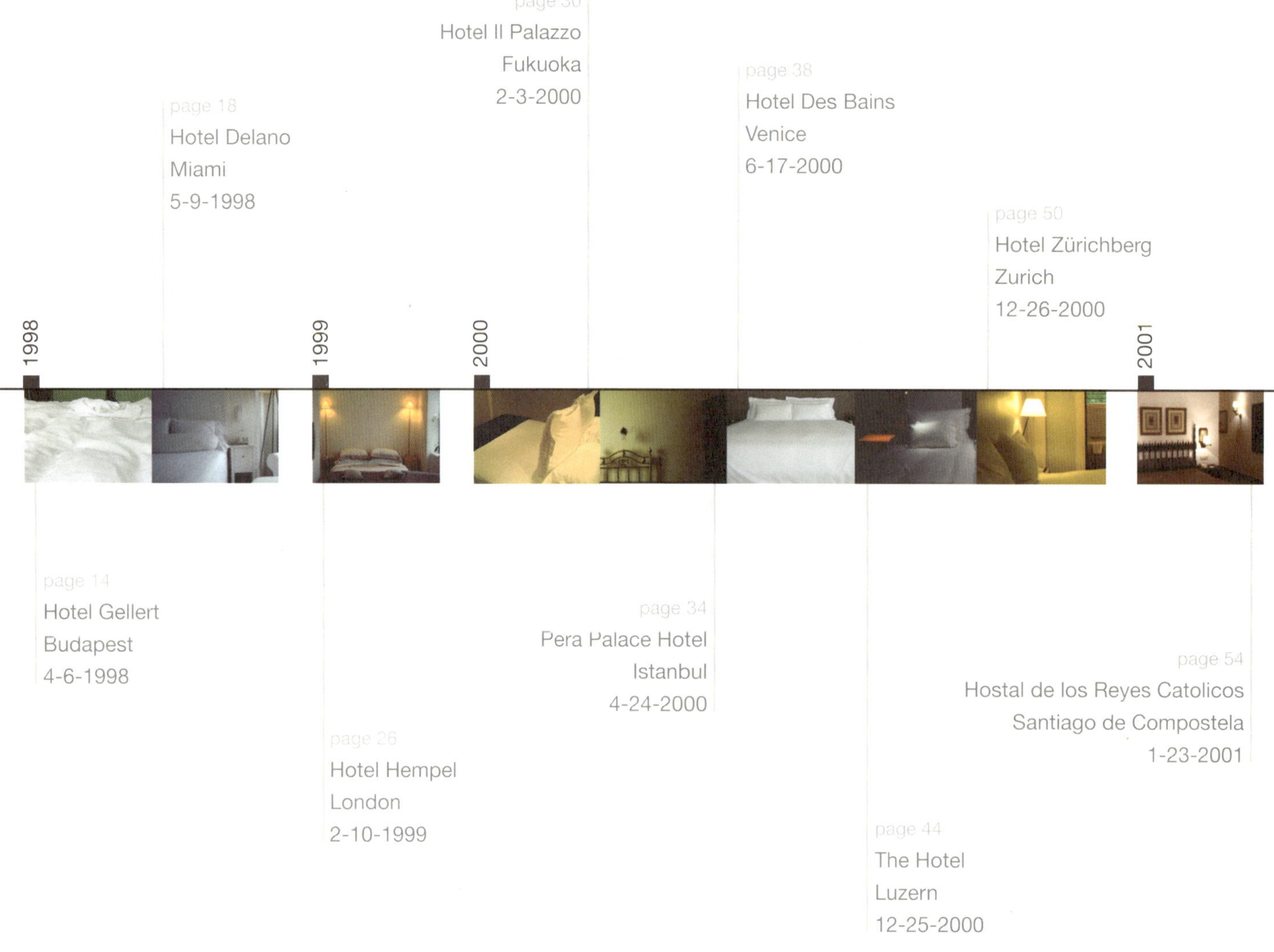
1998
1999
2000
2001
page 14
Hotel Gellert
Budapest
4-6-1998
page 18
Hotel Delano
Miami
5-9-1998
page 26
Hotel Hempel
London
2-10-1999
page 30
Hotel Il Palazzo
Fukuoka
2-3-2000
page 34
Pera Palace Hotel
Istanbul
4-24-2000
page 38
Hotel Des Bains
Venice
6-17-2000
page 44
The Hotel
Luzern
12-25-2000
page 50
Hotel Zürichberg
Zurich
12-26-2000
page 54
Hostal de los Reyes Catolicos
Santiago de Compostela
1-23-2001

page 58
Radisson SAS Royal Hotel
Copenhagen
4-13-2001

page 62
Hotel Standard West Hollywood
Los Angeles
7-7-2001

page 66
The China Club
Beijing
7-15-2001

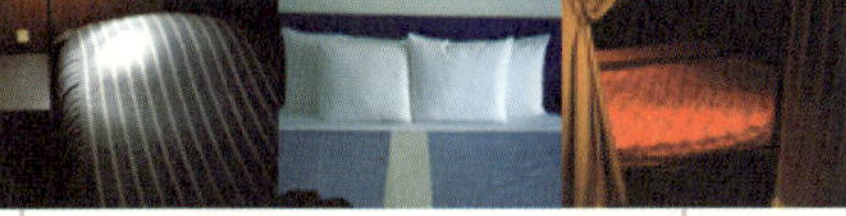

2002

page 72
Four Seasons Hotel at Sayan
Bali
2-3-2002

page 76
Hotel Begawan Giri
Bali
2-5-2002

page 82
Hotel Parco dei Principi
Sorrento
3-30-2002

page 88
ES Hotel
(now Radisson SAS)
Rome
9-10-2002

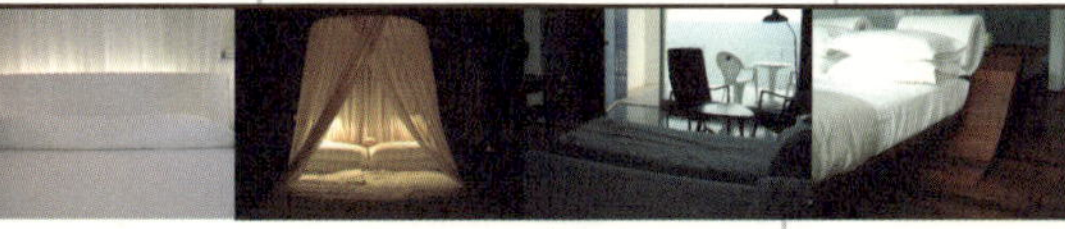

2003

page 92
Hotel 3 Rooms
Milan
4-13-2003

page 102
Northern Light Inn
Grindavik
4-14-2003

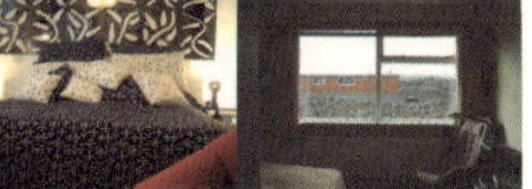

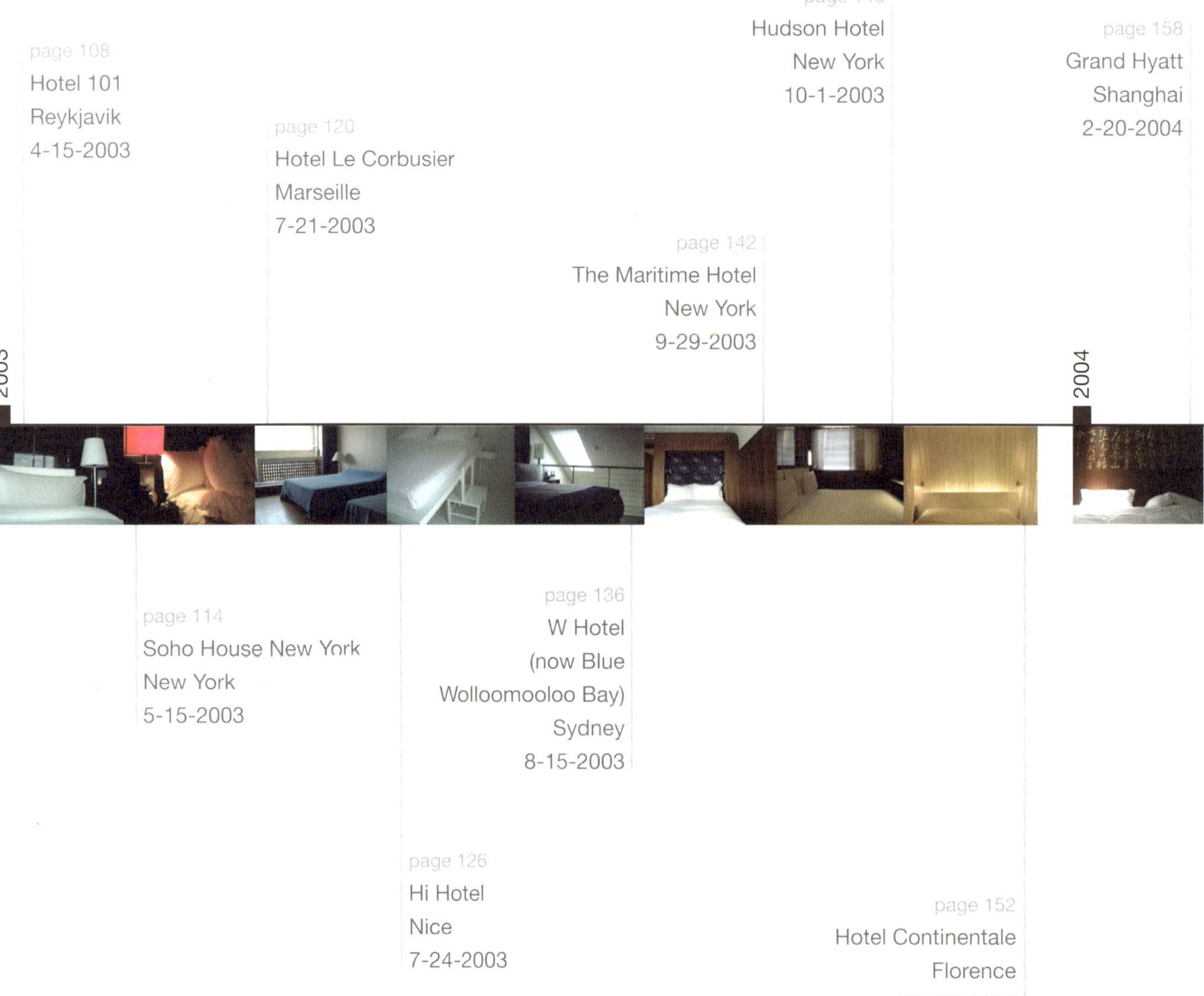

2003

page 108
Hotel 101
Reykjavik
4-15-2003

page 114
Soho House New York
New York
5-15-2003

page 120
Hotel Le Corbusier
Marseille
7-21-2003

page 126
Hi Hotel
Nice
7-24-2003

page 136
W Hotel
(now Blue
Wolloomooloo Bay)
Sydney
8-15-2003

page 142
The Maritime Hotel
New York
9-29-2003

page 146
Hudson Hotel
New York
10-1-2003

page 152
Hotel Continentale
Florence
11-27-2003

2004

page 158
Grand Hyatt
Shanghai
2-20-2004

page 162
Four Seasons Hotel at Marunouchi
Tokyo
3-6-2004

page 166
Westover Hall Hotel
Milford-on-Sea
6-13-2004

page 172
Babington House
Somerset
6-16-2004

page 182
Hotel Vigilius Mountain Resort
Vigilius
9-29-2004

page 190
Hotel Therme Vals
Vals
10-1-2004

page 200
The Metropolitan
Bangkok
10-17-2004

page 208
Hotel New York
Rotterdam
12-5-2004

page 220
Lloyd Hotel
Amsterdam
12-6-2004

page 226
5 Rue de Moussy
Paris
12-10-2004

2005

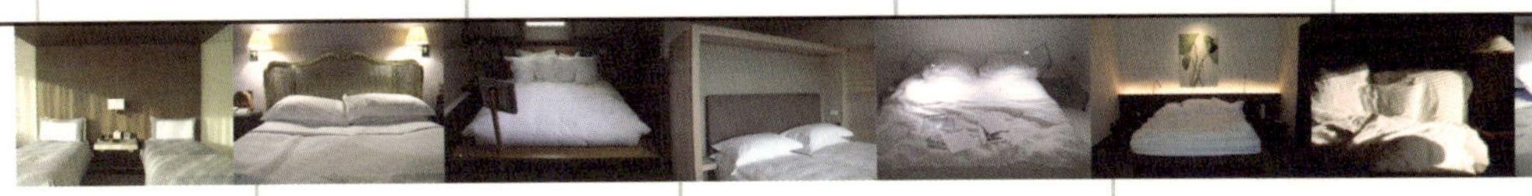

page 232
Mercer Hotel
New York
3-18-2005

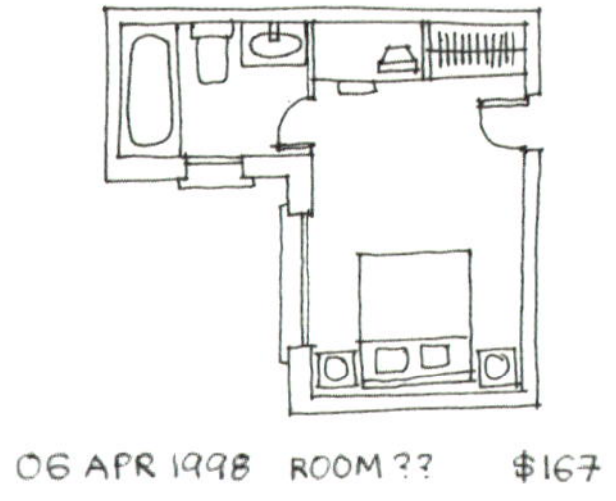

Hotel Gellert

A TASTE OF COMMUNISM

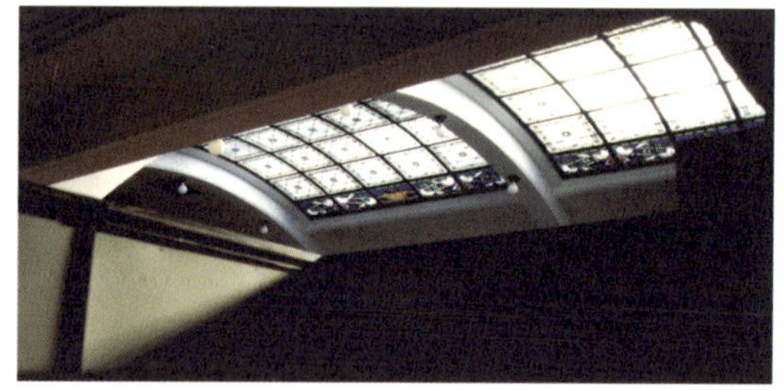

Let's face it: no matter how much you strive to adhere to the original design, once an old architecture is refitted to suit new purposes, the original *genius loci* is gone forever, and it's never the same again. Witness, for instance, the Peace Hotel of Shanghai. Fortunately, that's not the case with Budapest's Hotel Gellert. Built in 1900, it has survived both counts and commissars, yet its elegant classicism still evokes the remote, romantic past of a *czardas*-loving people. Budapest was once a significant economic center of Europe, a fact reflected in its people's appreciation for quality living despite the city's recent Spartan Communist past.

Today spa hotels or hotel spas are all the rage, when in fact they have been around for decades. The Gellert, which comprises the Gellert Hotel and the Gellert Spa, is a prime example. Its Turkish spa is a memento to Hungary's encounter with the Ottoman Empire. While the original unisex changing room was abandoned with the passing of Hungary's old Soviet-style government, a certain atmosphere of melancholy reminiscent of that era still seems to linger in the air. The country's Communist past also remains visible in the largely unaltered guest rooms. History permeates the bricks and mortar of the Gellert.

HOTEL-GELLÉRT-GYÓGYFÜRDŐ

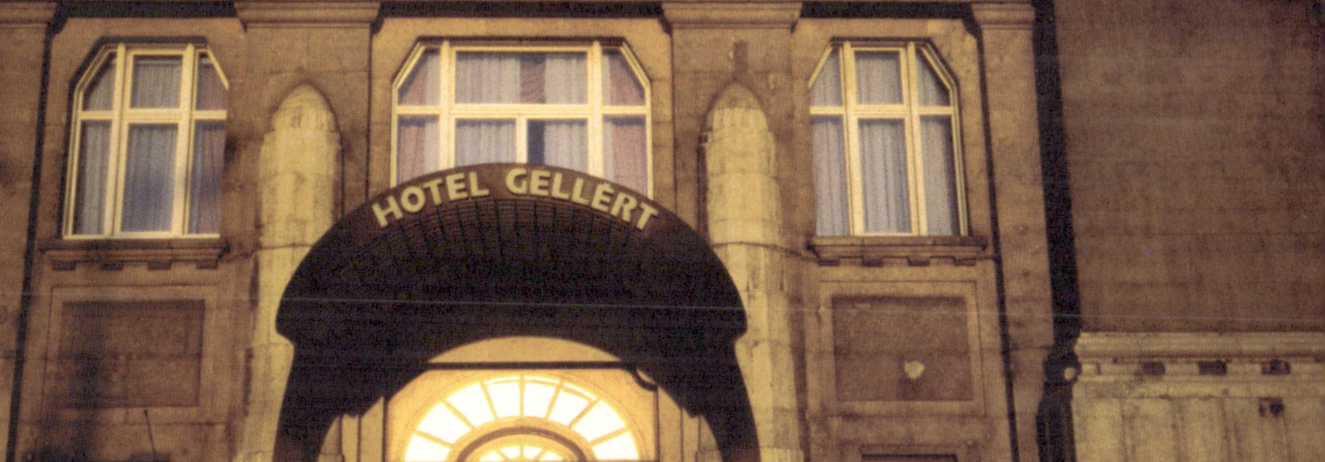
HOTEL GELLÉRT GYÓGYSZÁLLÓ
HOTEL GELLÉRT

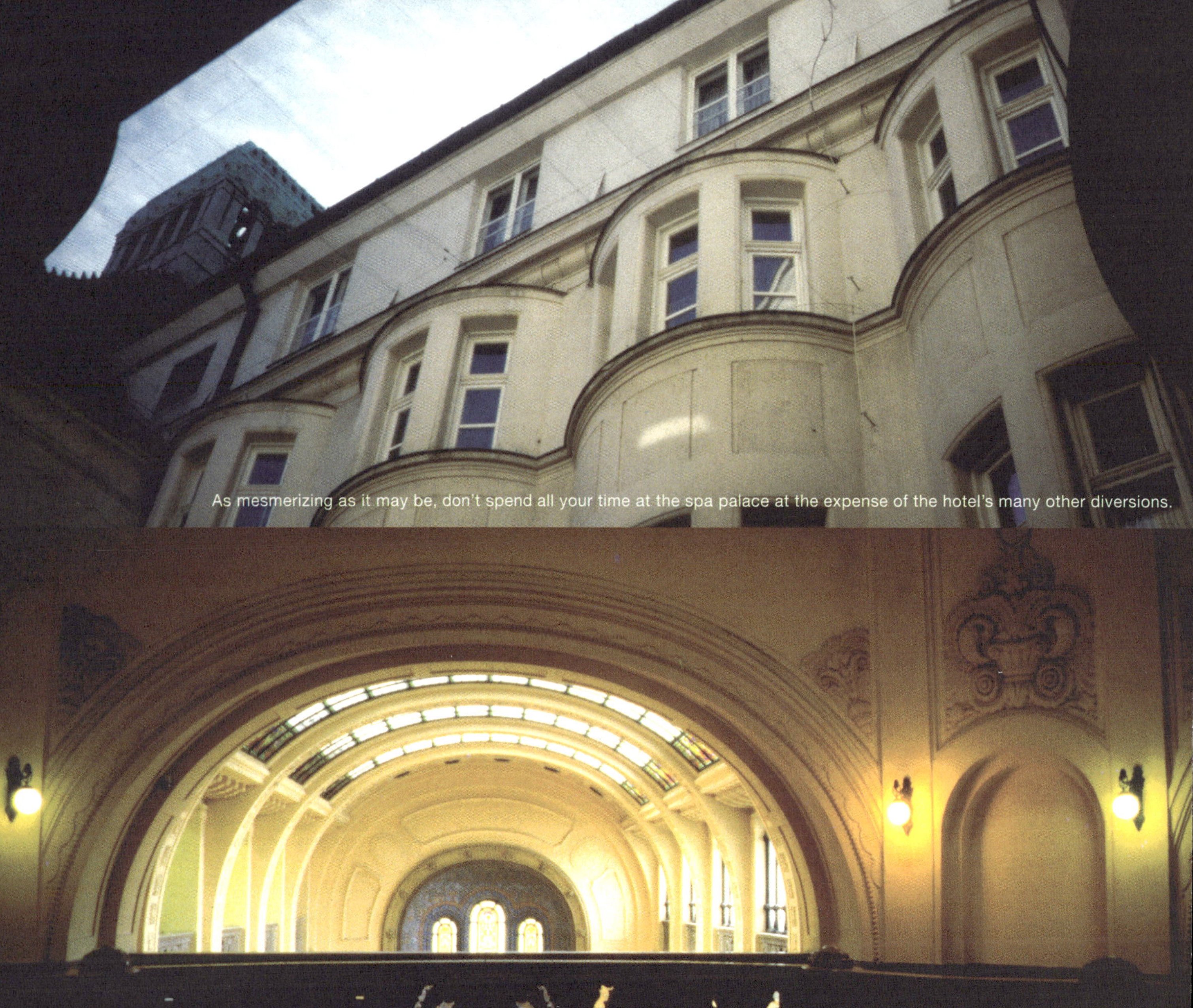

As mesmerizing as it may be, don't spend all your time at the spa palace at the expense of the hotel's many other diversions.

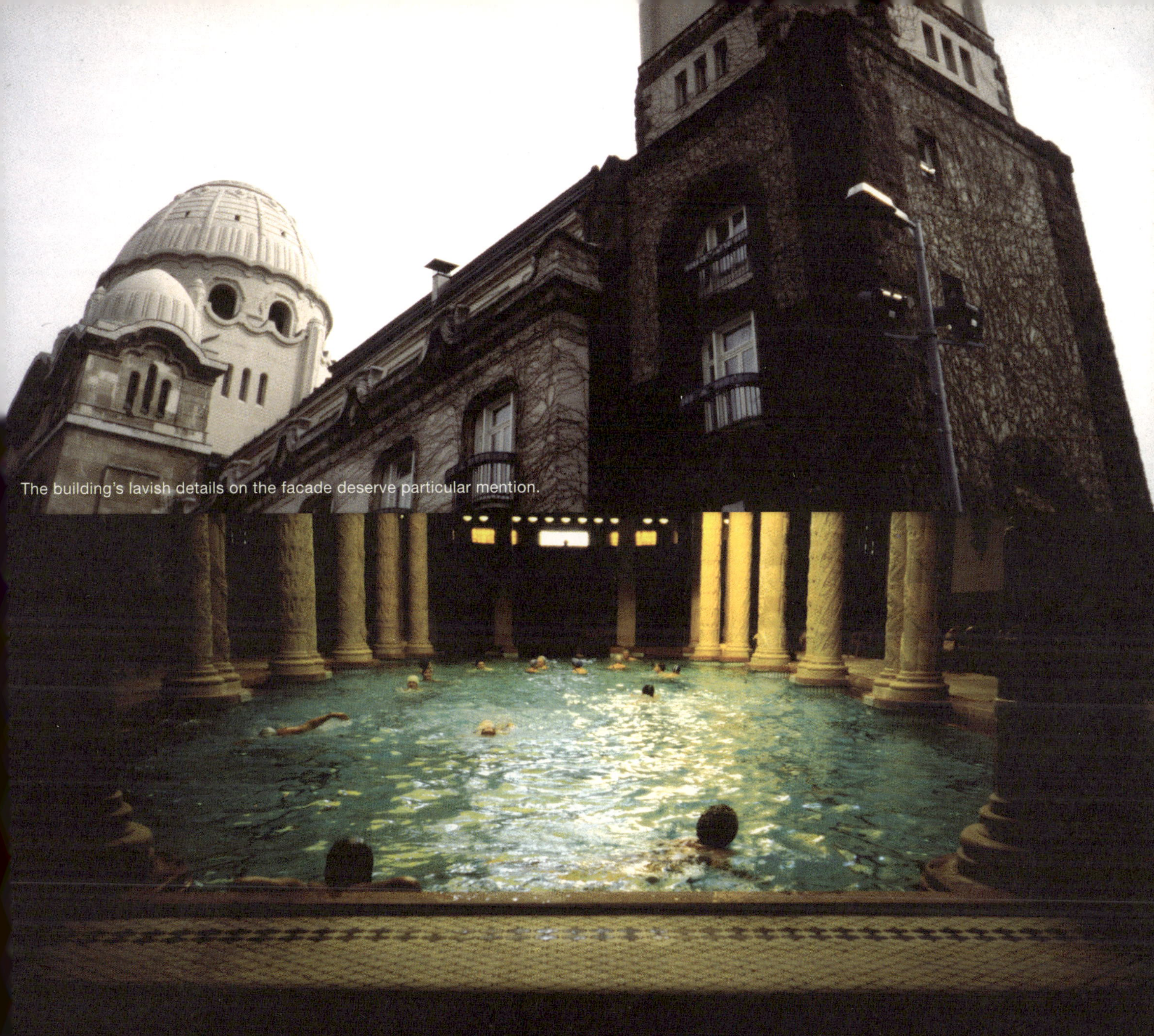
The building's lavish details on the facade deserve particular mention.

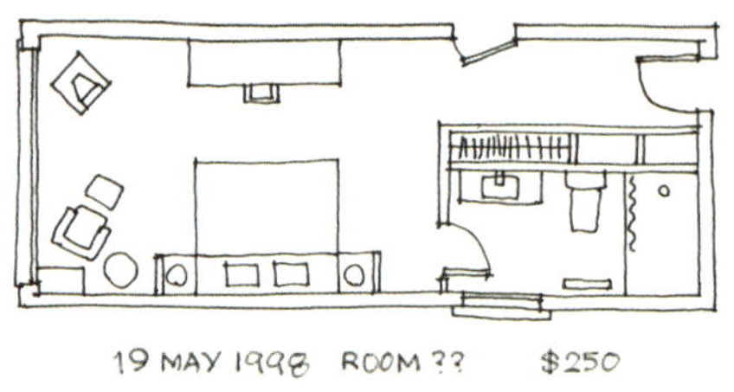

Hotel Delano

REVERIE IN WHITE

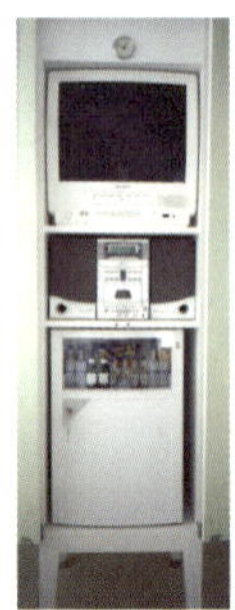

All those layers of drapes, billowing like the white-crested waves of the ocean outside, have turned what seemed so lucid and well-defined just a moment ago into a dream. The plane ride, which lasted close to twenty hours, has taken a toll on the traveler's body, while the sun simply refuses to let up. He wants to go out for a stroll, but when he is almost outside, he decides to head back into the whited-out Hotel Delano. As he passes the entrance, his muddled mind seems to mumble: "Look at that door! So small, so low-key . . . "—Starck's joke of an entrance. Back in his hotel room, closing his eyes, he tries to fall asleep. And when he awakes, it is already the following day. Or is it? His bleary eyes make out a mysterious white door beside the bed, beckoning to be opened. He gingerly obliges, only to be taken aback by the ray of light streaking in. The door turns out to connect his room to his neighbor's. His heart skips a beat, and he closes the door before anyone on the other side notices. Right away he regrets his curiosity, feeling sheepish and embarrassed. Or has he just imagined all that?

Collecting his thoughts, he scans the room. Starck's ingenuity never ceases to amaze. The room is completely white, as white as a hospital ward—a white TV set, a white minibar, a white stereo, white orchids, and of course, the obligatory white upholstery and drapery. The different shades of white make the blue and green landscape outside all the more pristine. Sinking into the white sofa, he notices the towel in the bathroom draped nonchalantly on a wooden rack in a "lived-in" sort of way. And the hotel brochure is printed on copier paper! All this white freshness and fresh whiteness have lessened his headache somewhat, and once again, he decides to go out. From his last visit he still remembers the Aqua Spa on the roof with its view of the sea, but instead he decides to go down to the lobby, which resembles a movie set with its thick white columns. He sits down at a table, joining other guests who have come here to see and be seen, to know and be known, and to make their exits and entrances. Dream and reality converge. He is in my dream. *I'm* in my dream. And I see myself engulfed in a sea of layer upon billowing layer of white drapes. It doesn't get any more David Lynch than this.

MIAMI

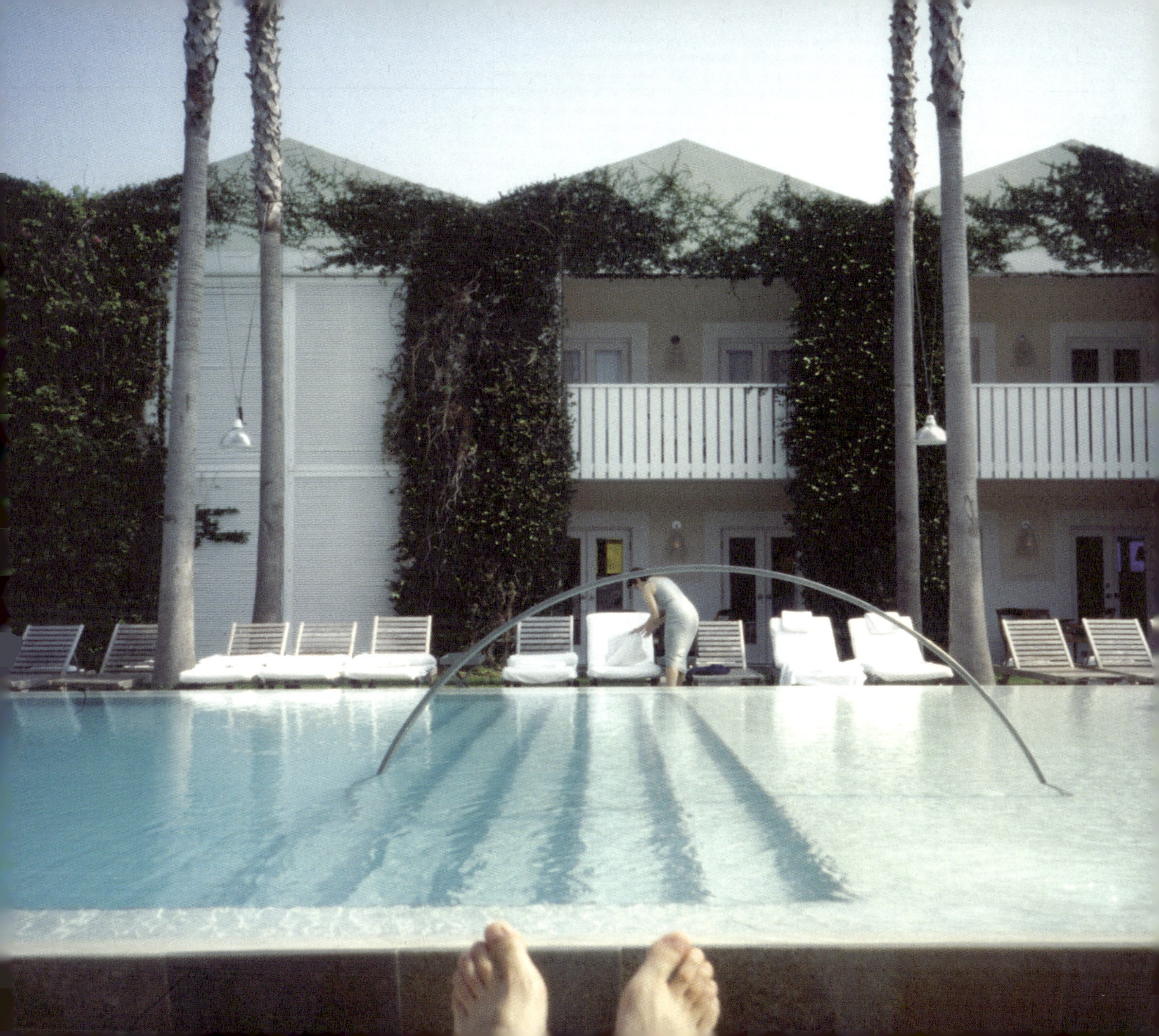

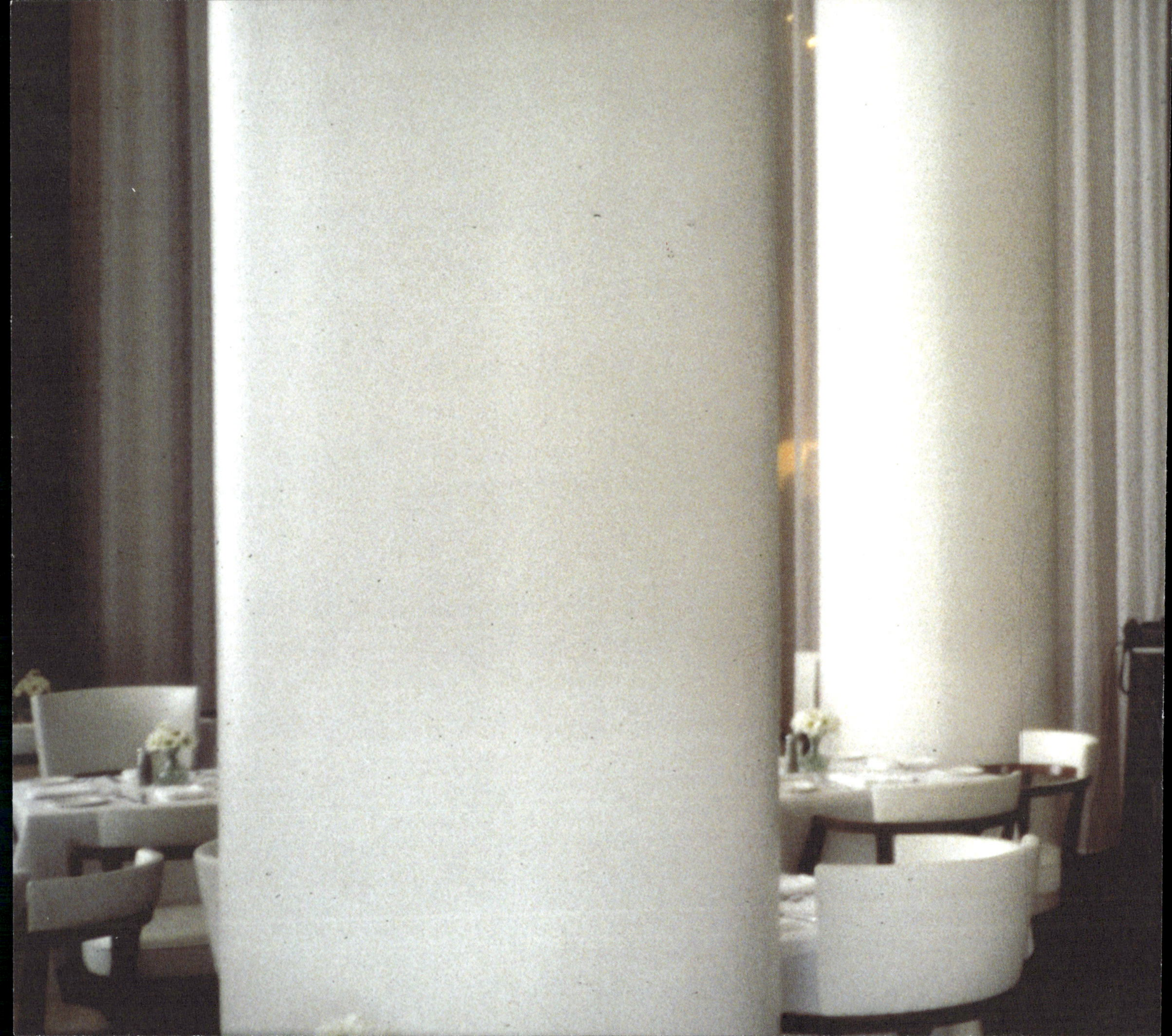

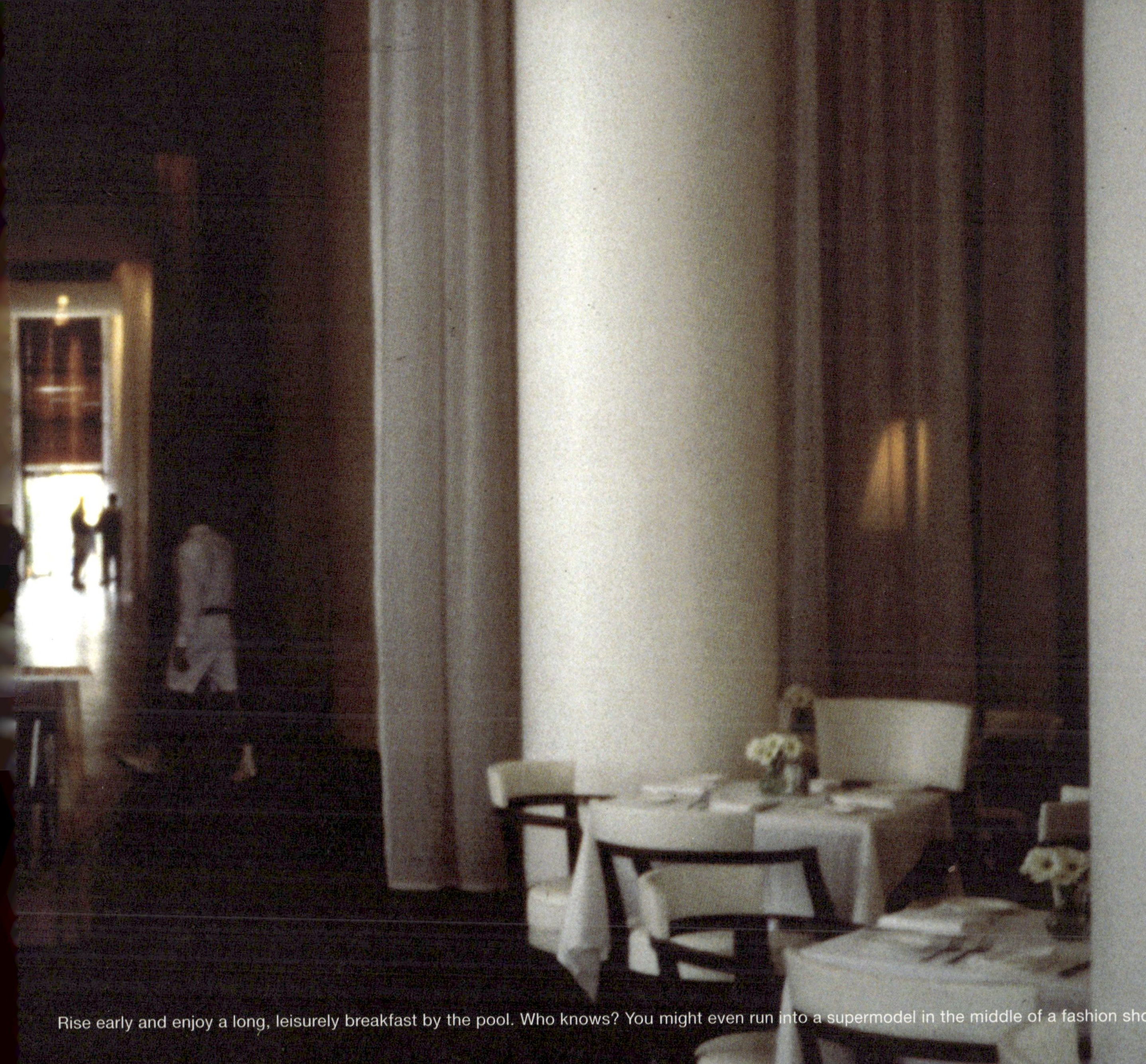

Rise early and enjoy a long, leisurely breakfast by the pool. Who knows? You might even run into a supermodel in the middle of a fashion shoot.

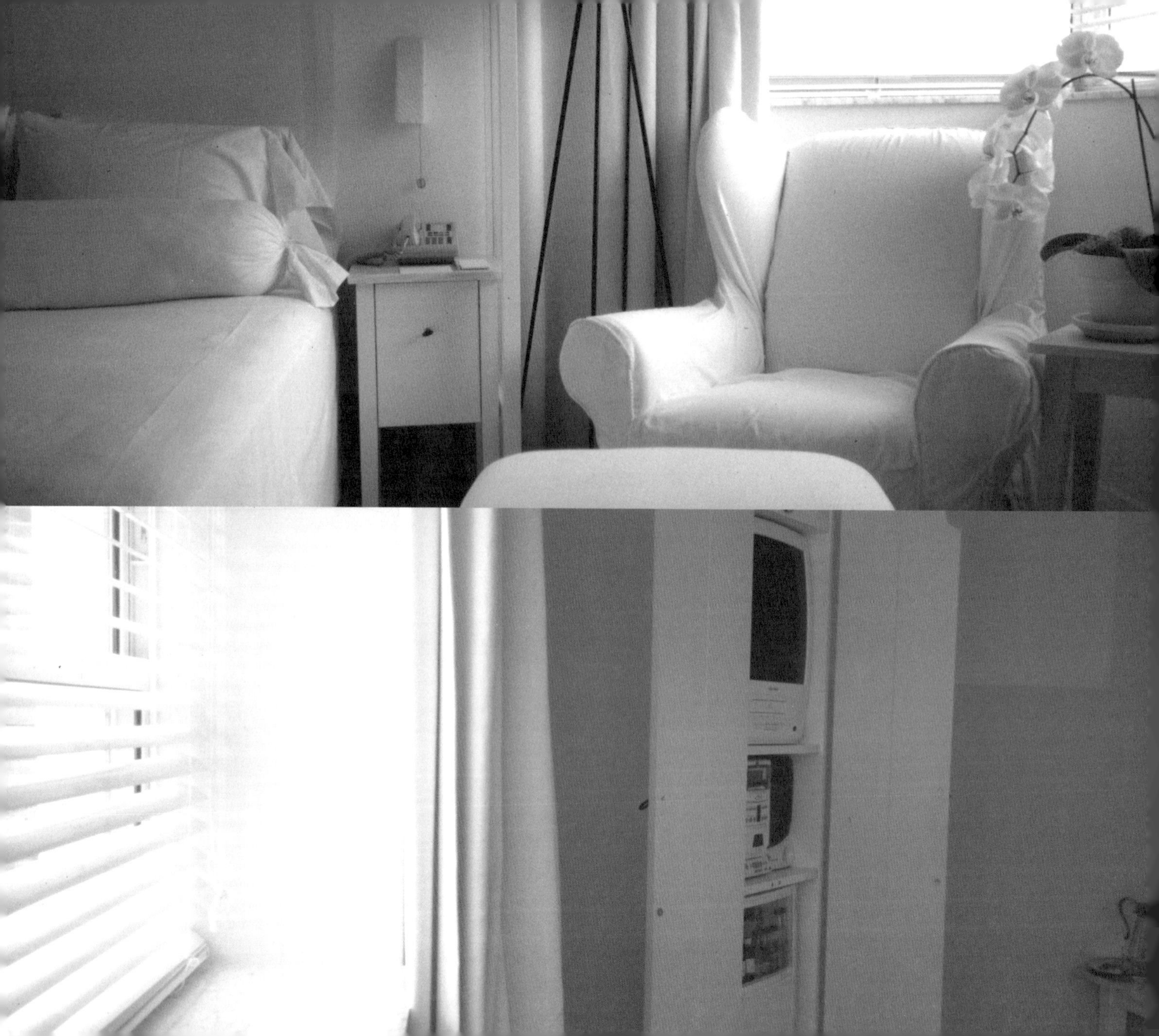

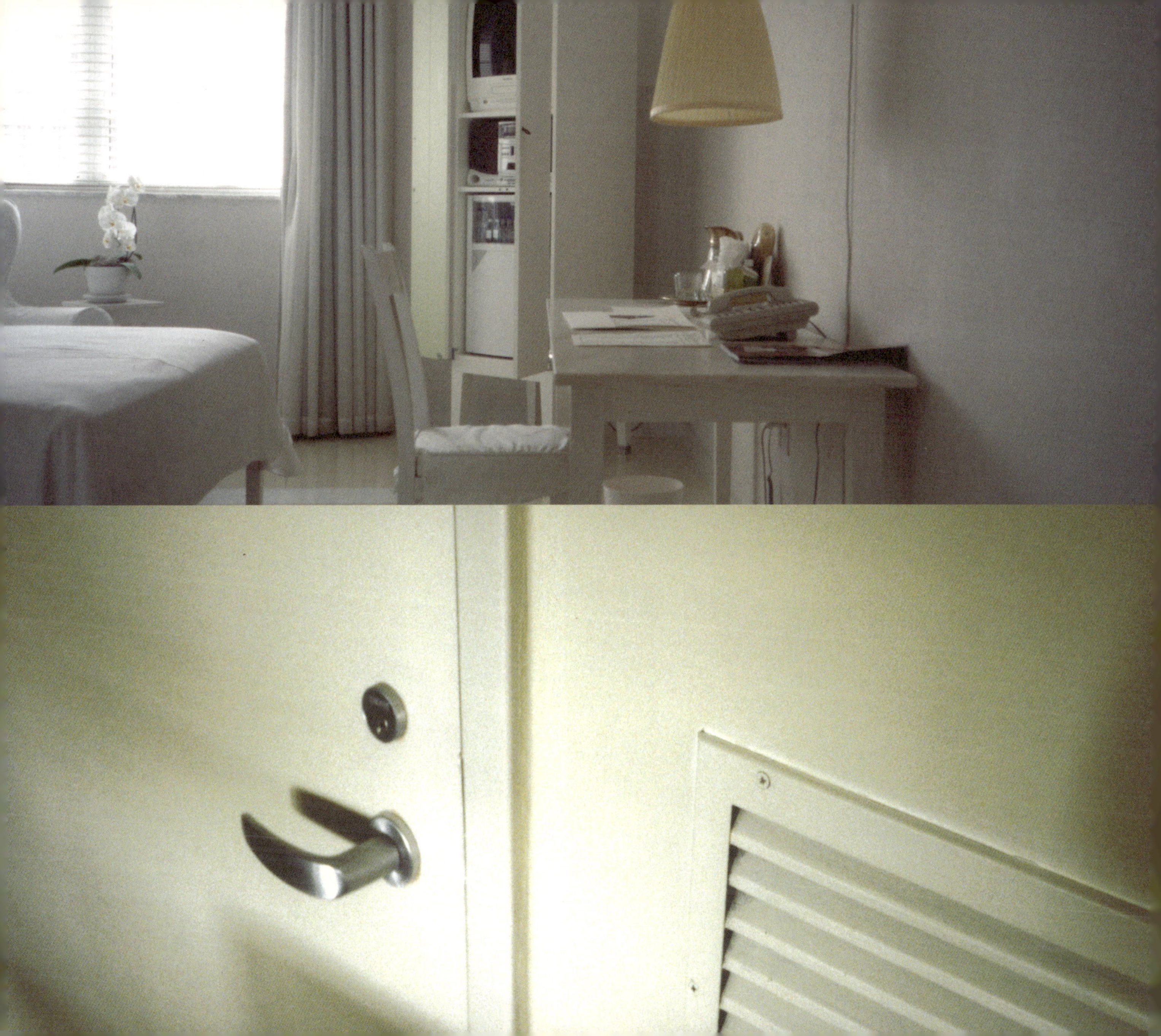

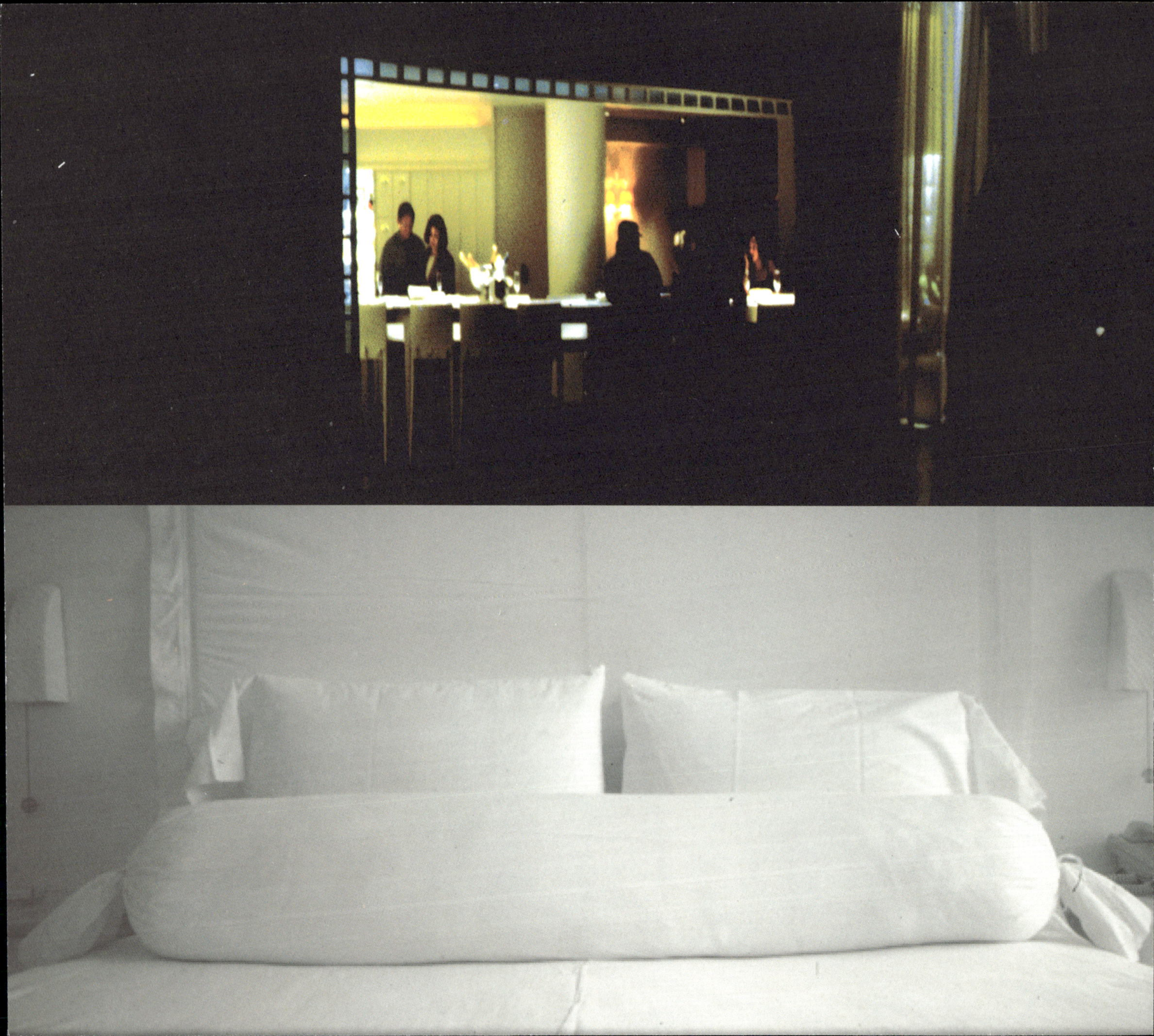

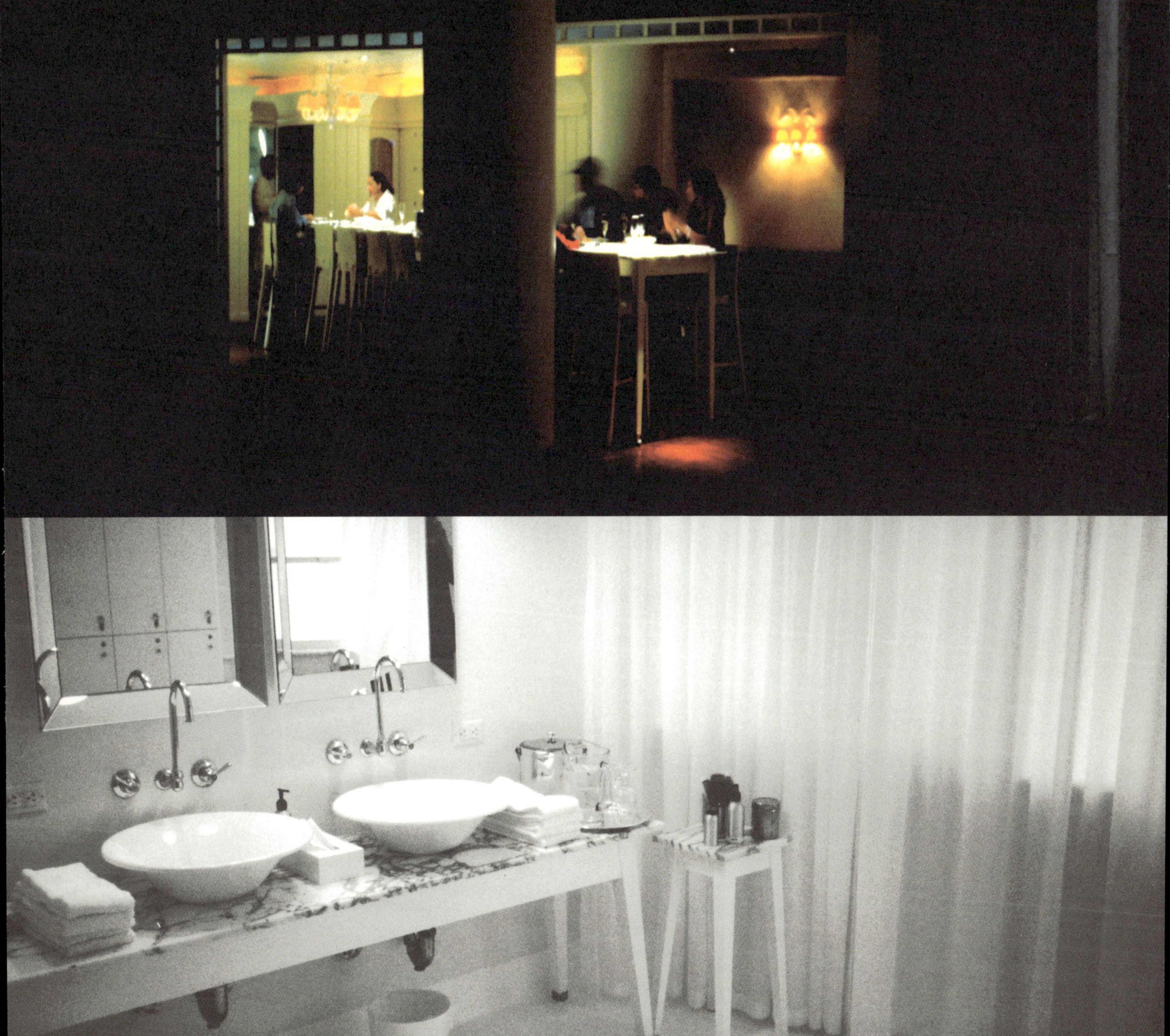

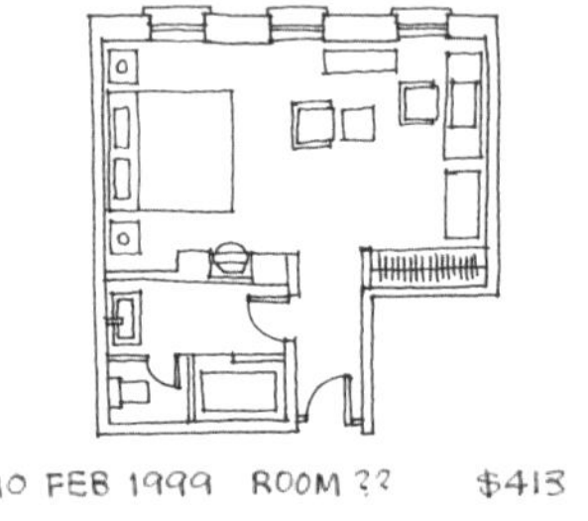

Hotel Hempel

LOST IN NOTHINGNESS

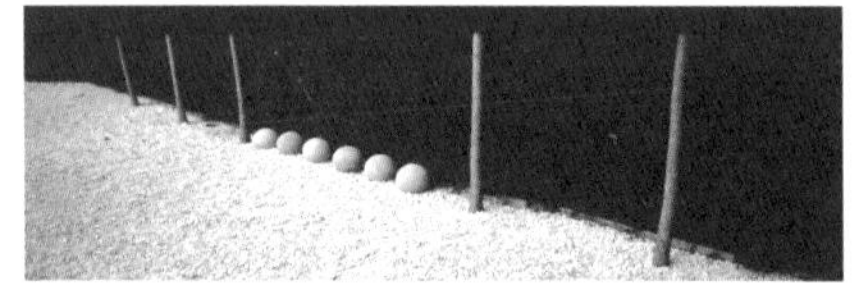

The location for the 1994 movie *Four Weddings and a Funeral*, this most minimalist of hotels doesn't even boast a banner or sign. Located north of London's Hyde Park, Hotel Hempel is named after its architect, Anouska Hempel. In its design, Hempel has infused her personal eclecticism of Eastern and Western philosophy. The garden consists only of whites and greens in a simple formation of squares, so that anyone who enters it instantly becomes the subject of the tableau. The hotel's white facades are constantly transformed by the rich shadow play of branches and foliage swaying and morphing in the sun. The lobby, as big as a standard-sized swimming pool and supported only by a few geometrically shaped beams, greets the guest with a magnificent serenity and sense of purity that is reminiscent of a sacred temple. My room has three large windows, inviting the garden's play of shadows to continue inside—all very Zen and modern at the same time. Minimalism is not mere quantitative subtraction. It is refinement through distillation, so that all that is extraneous is whittled away, leaving only the most essentially beautiful. Hempel's approach is so disciplined that every detail is perfectly coordinated, right down to the smallest square ceramic plate on the table.

A word of caution, however: the all-white detailing requires considerate and thoughtful guests. The hotel is already showing various signs of wear and tear, especially inside the guest rooms.

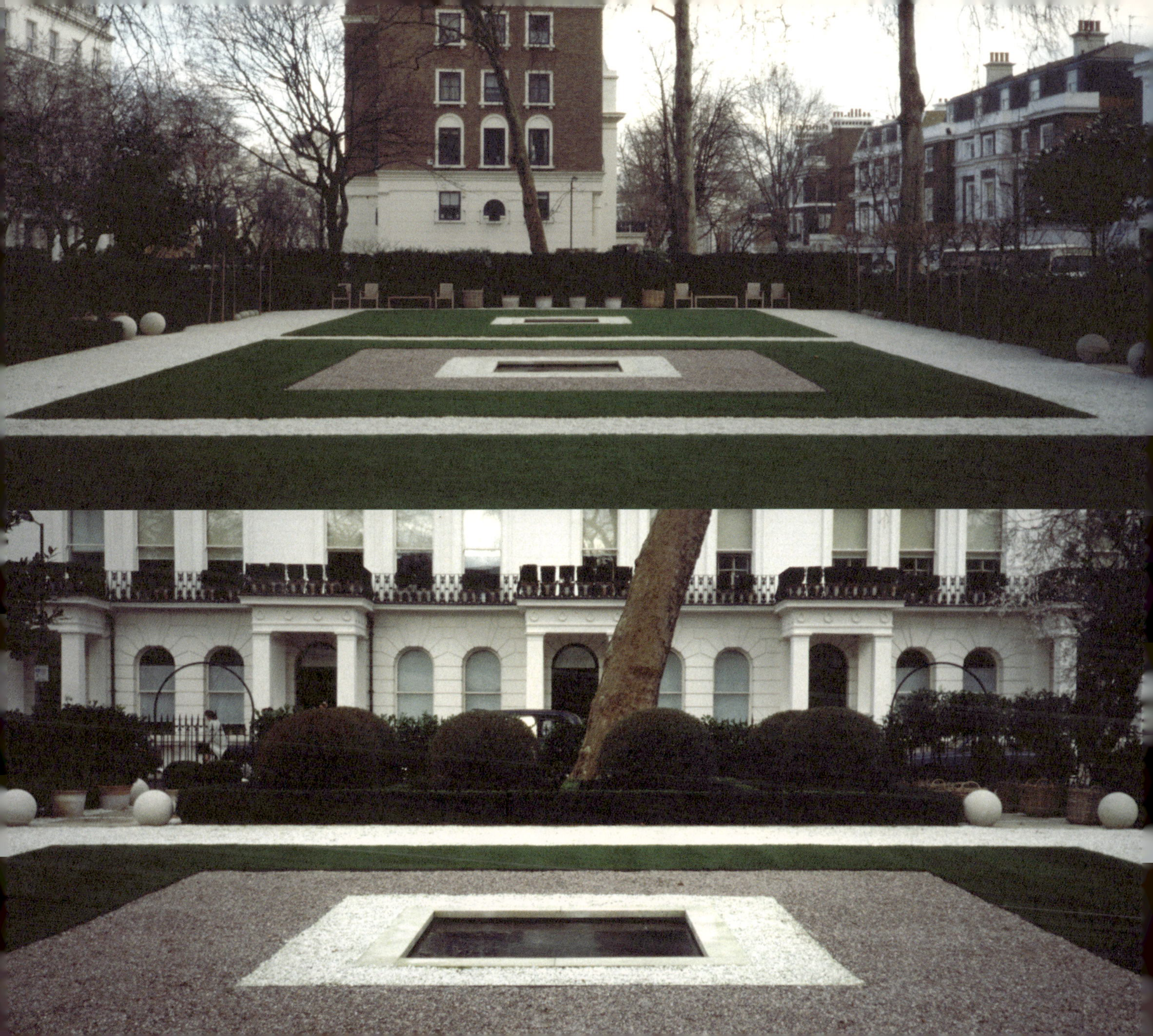

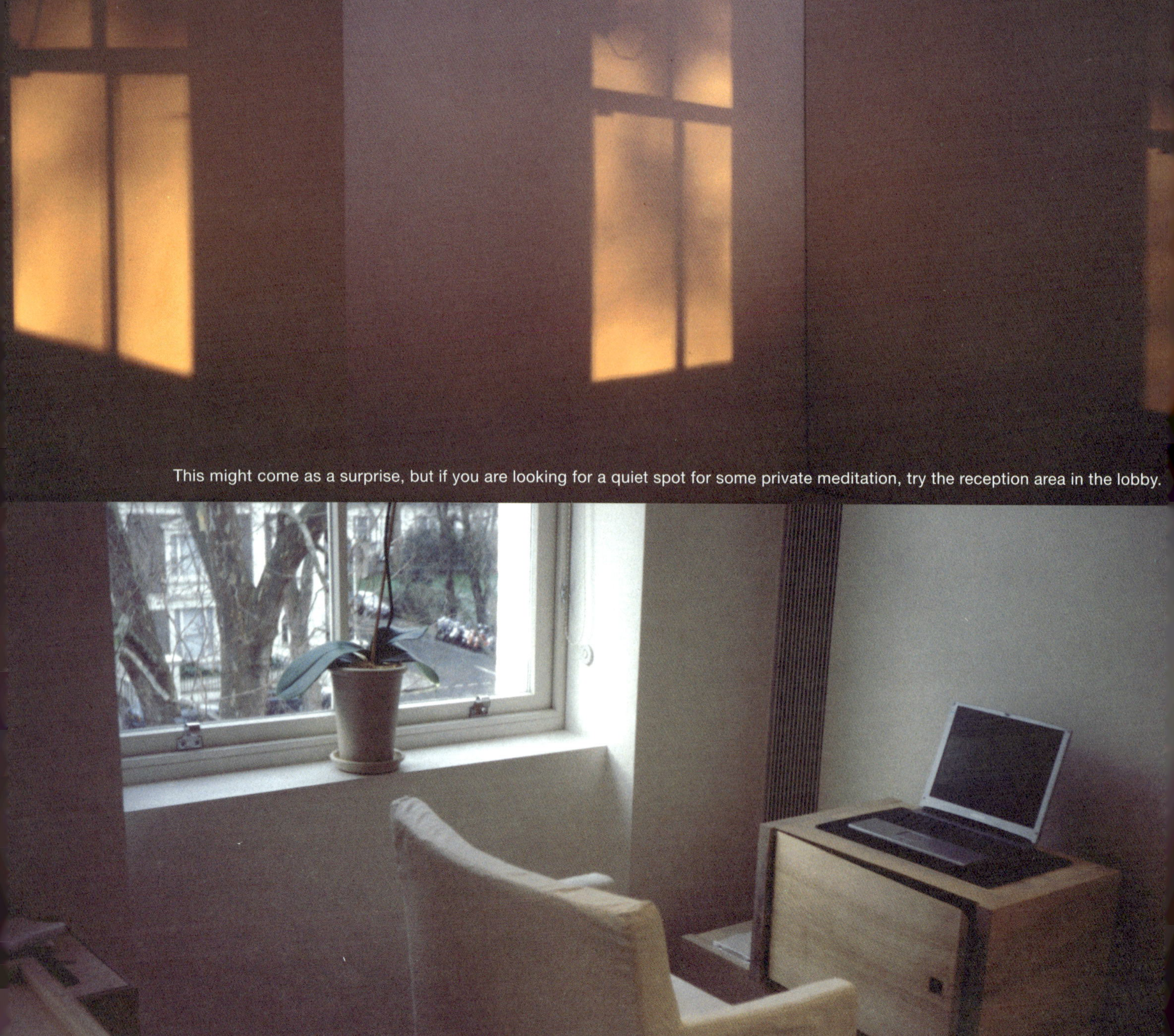

This might come as a surprise, but if you are looking for a quiet spot for some private meditation, try the reception area in the lobby.

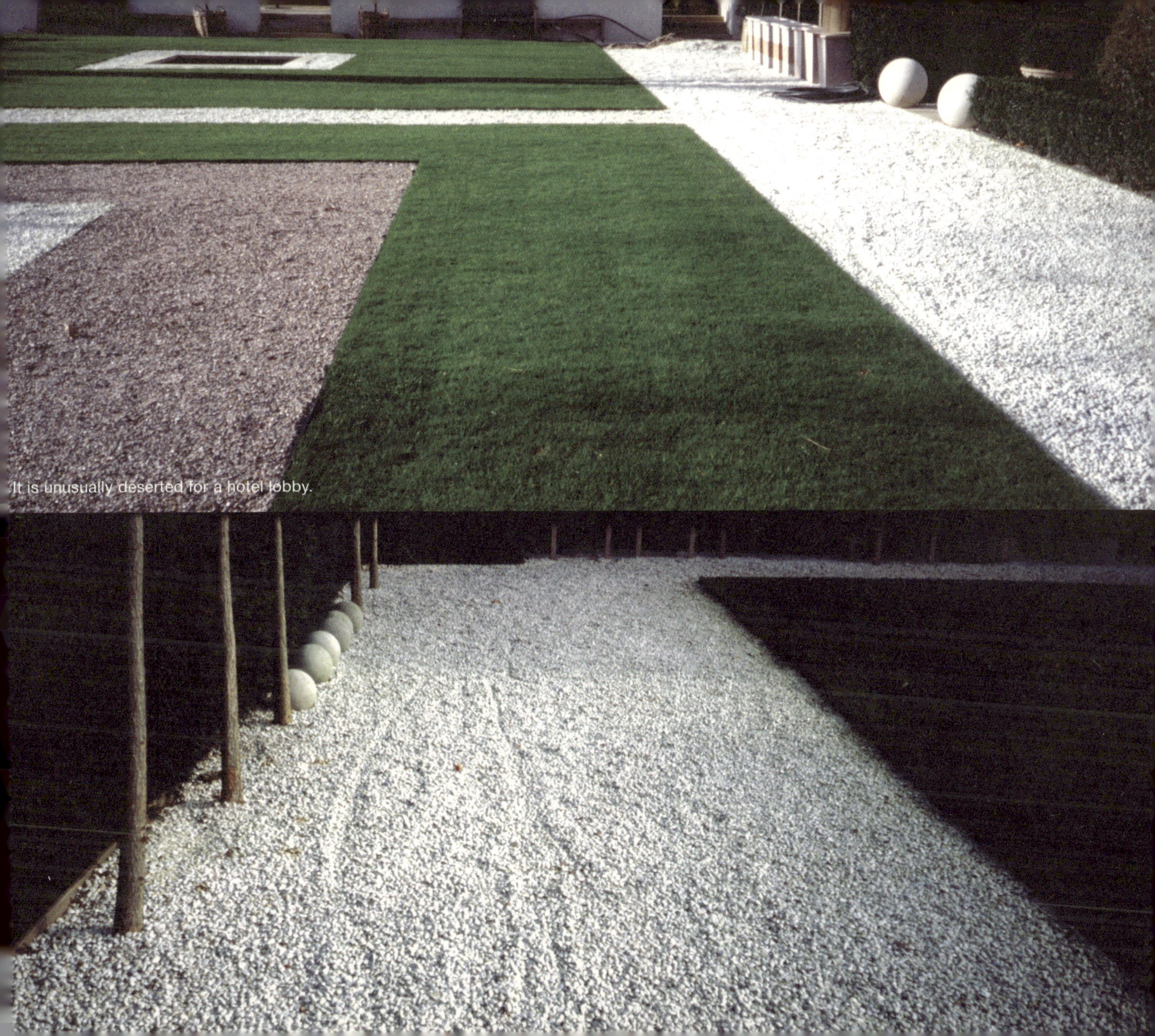

It is unusually deserted for a hotel lobby.

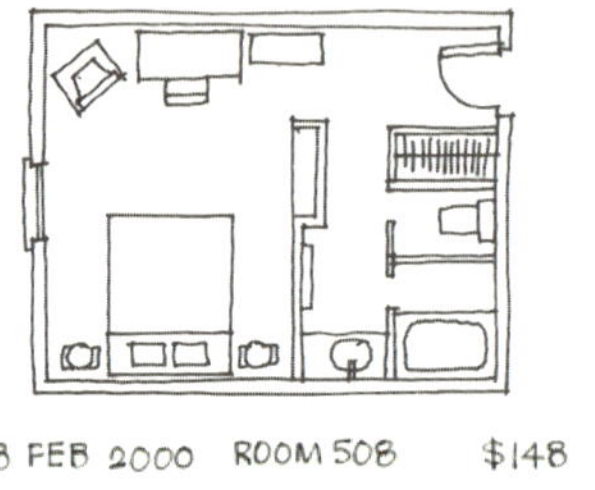

Hotel Il Palazzo

A MICROPOLIS

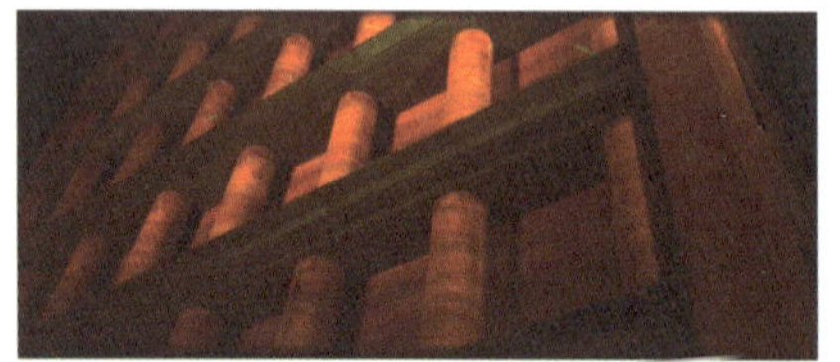

I've liked Aldo Rossi ever since I was at school, so I was thrilled when I finally made it to this twenty-odd-year-old hotel, in which Rossi coalesced the ideas of various designers. Actually, Hotel Il Palazzo is more like a micropolis or a miniature city than a simple building. The "streets" of this micropolis are lined with various miniature free-standing structures, including six restaurants designed by different architects. Standing in the middle of the lobby is an anachronistic, temple-like structure, flanked by the bar and the convention center. The miniature buildings form harmonious parts of the large complex, which is best viewed from a focal, stage-like plaza in the center. The hotel's location may be Japan but the Italian architect stresses the country's commonalities with his native Europe in his design. Fukuoka perhaps reminded him of his hometown Venice, similarly criss-crossed with lazy, meandering alleyways and canals—in front of one, Rossi has placed the most striking feature of the hotel: a windowless facade.

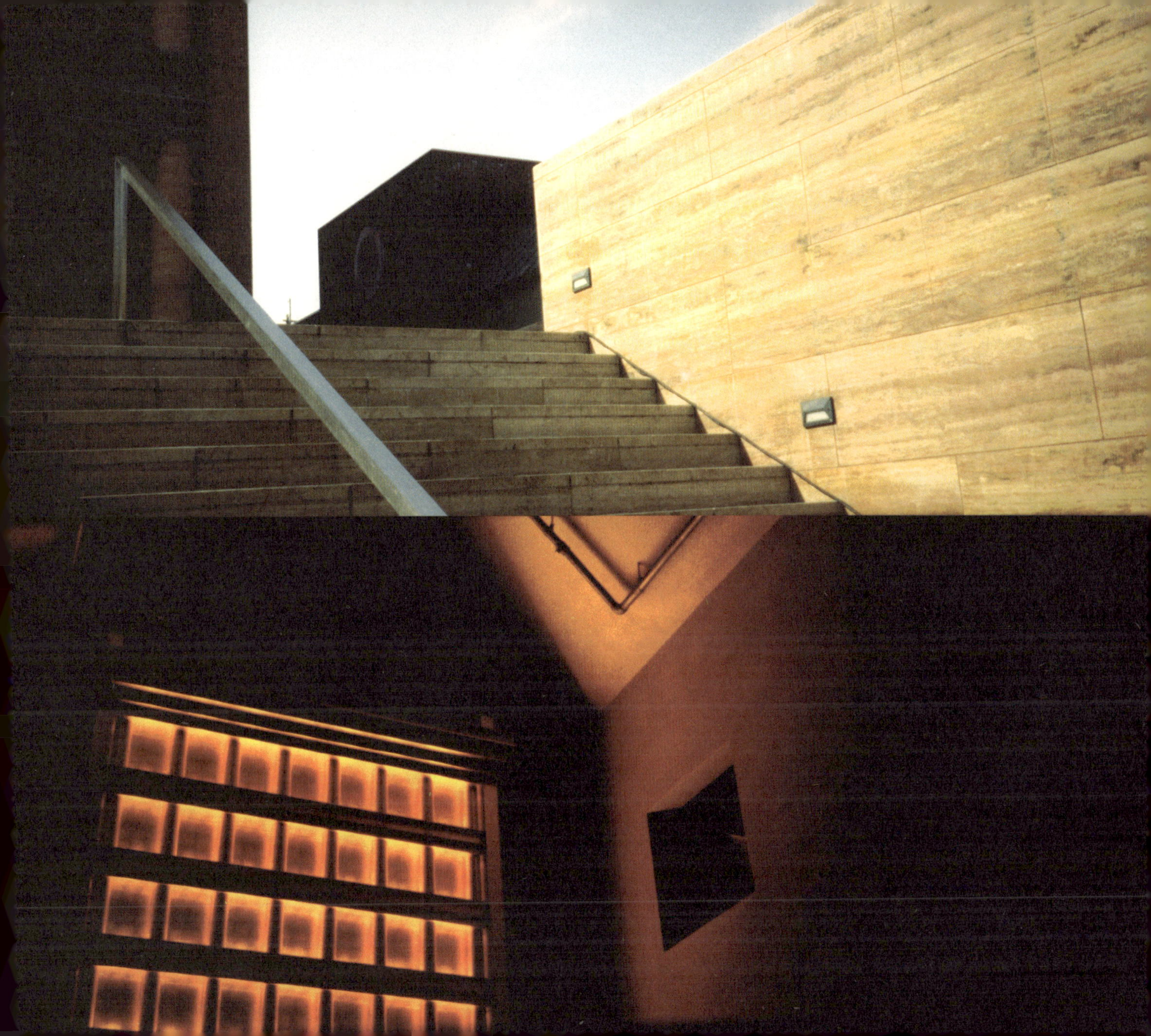

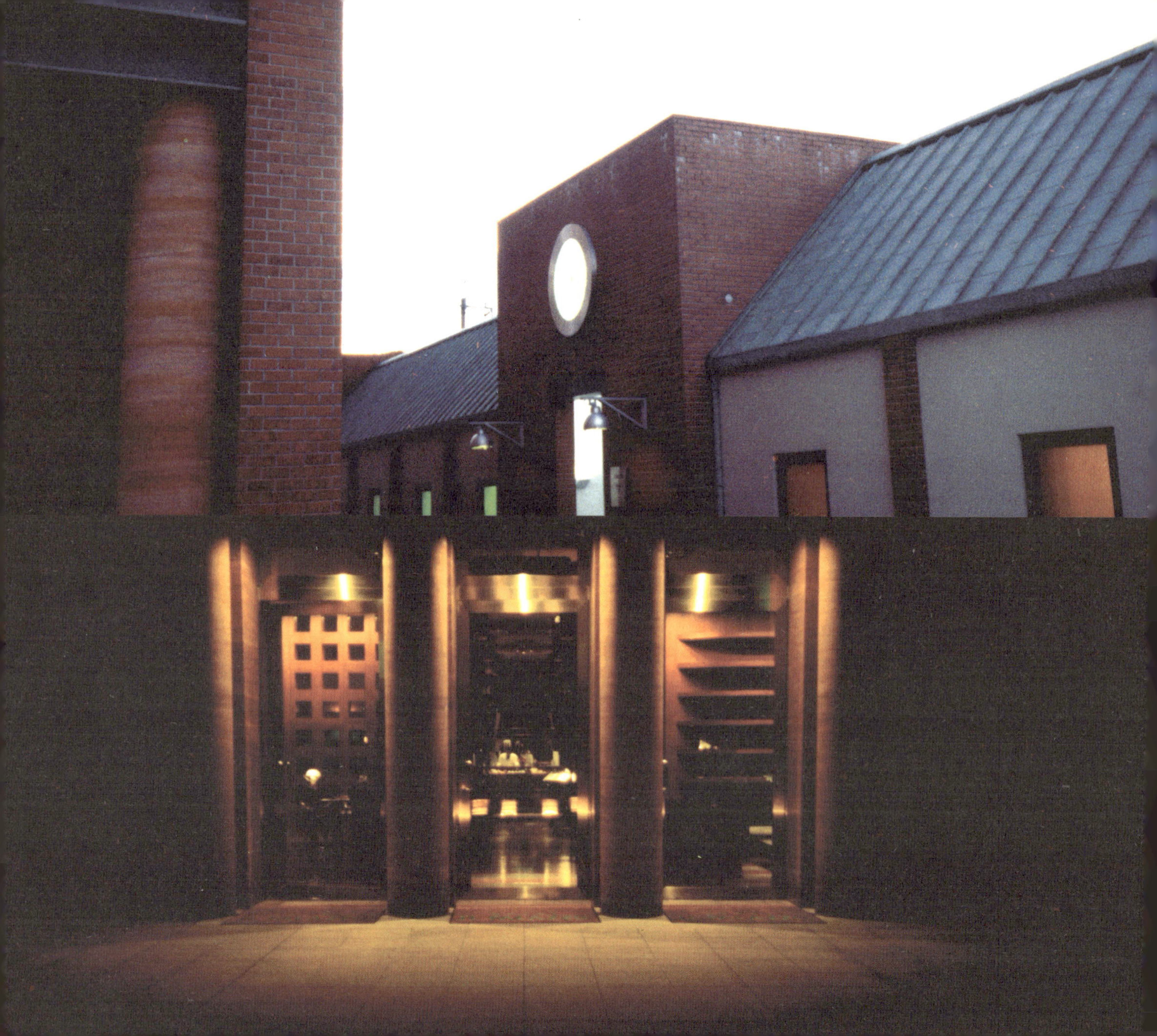

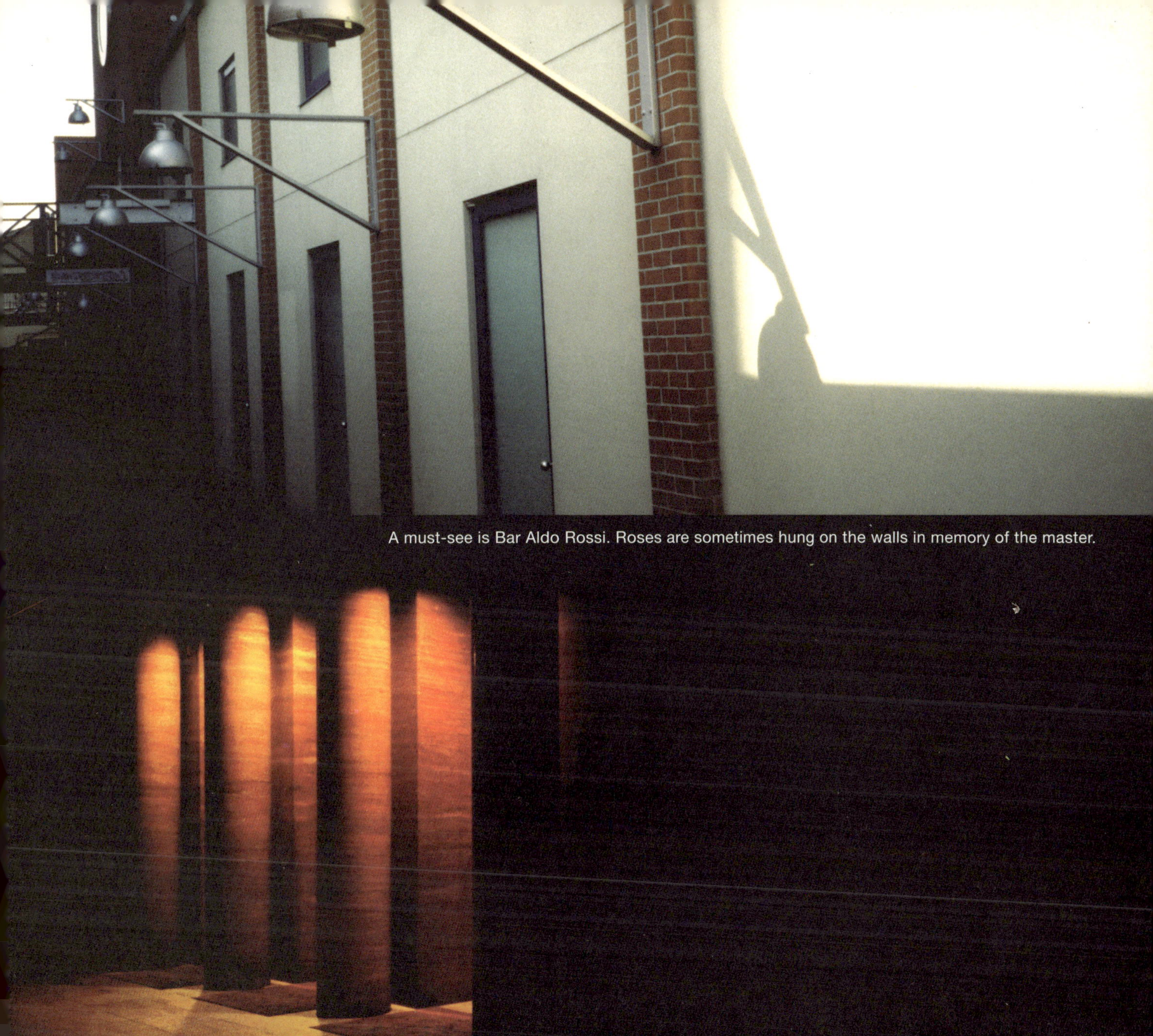

A must-see is Bar Aldo Rossi. Roses are sometimes hung on the walls in memory of the master.

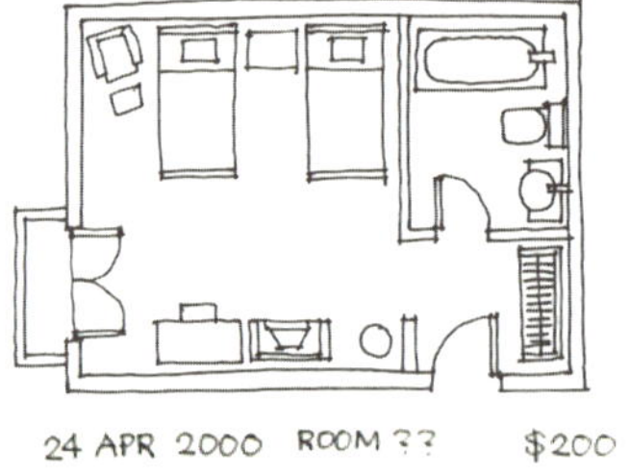

Pera Palace Hotel

SHADES OF THE ORIENT EXPRESS

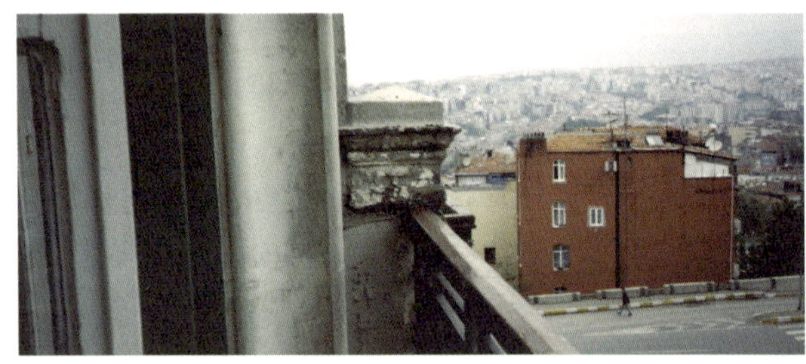

It was here where Agatha Christie wrote her famous novel *Murder on the Orient Express*. And it was here where the enigmatic Greta Garbo chose to stay when she was in town. As Constantinople, Istanbul was the meeting point of East and West, and Pera Palace, a grand and sumptuous hotel designed in 1892, still stands proud today after more than a century. The building also stands apart from other hotels in the city, which were updated with veneer and plaster makeovers. In fact, it is one of the few hotels remaining that has kept most of its original fittings and furnishing unaltered and in good (or perhaps acceptable?) working condition. Yet its shadows of antiquity do not intimidate. Rather, they have years and years of narratives to tell to those who are ready to listen. Its design is archetypal with its glazed elevator, the big brass bed tucked into a dark corner, the low-hanging chandeliers, and the burgundy-colored carpet. But above all, what Pera Palace has to offer is a reflection on the meaning, significance, and humanity of history.

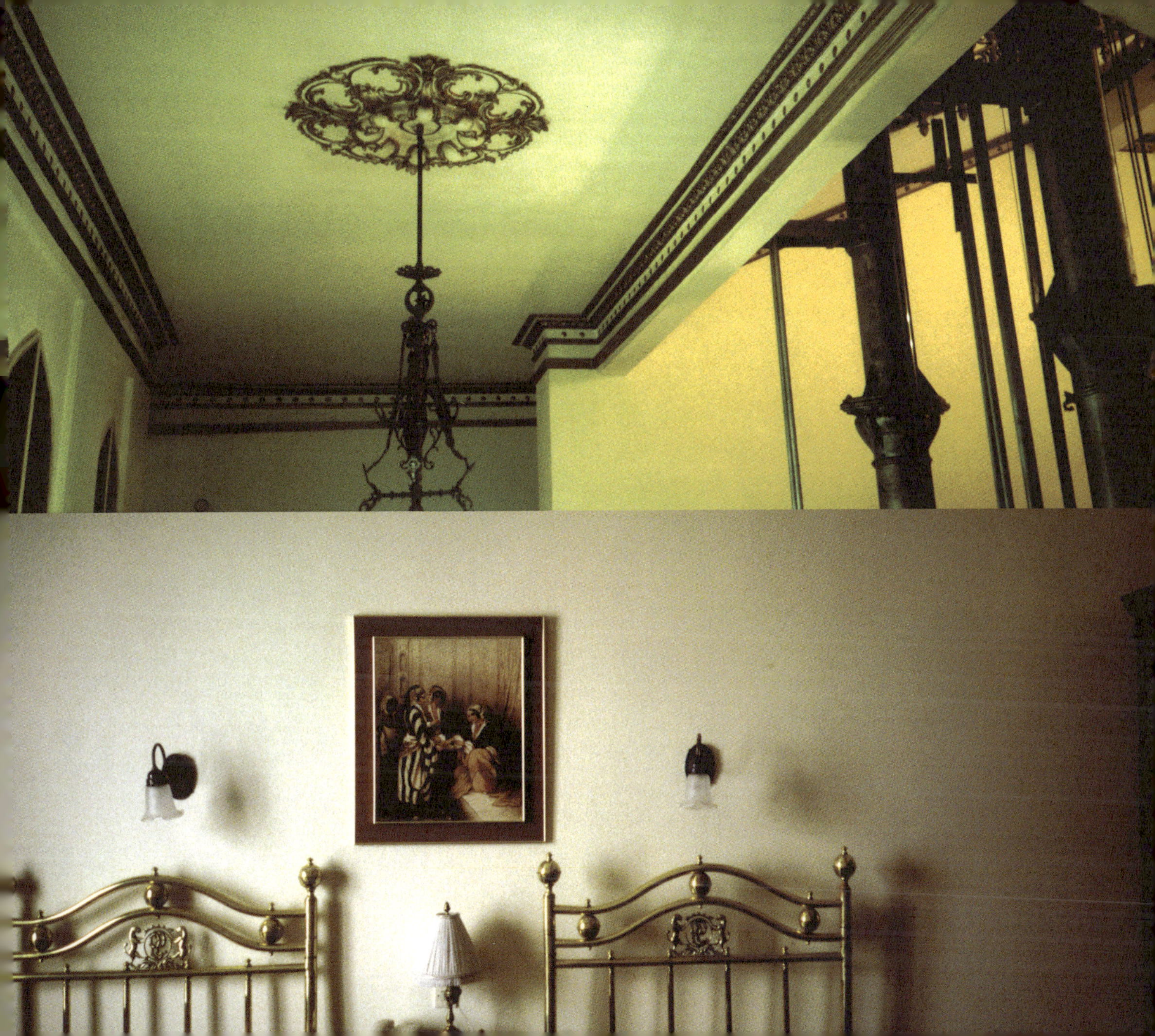

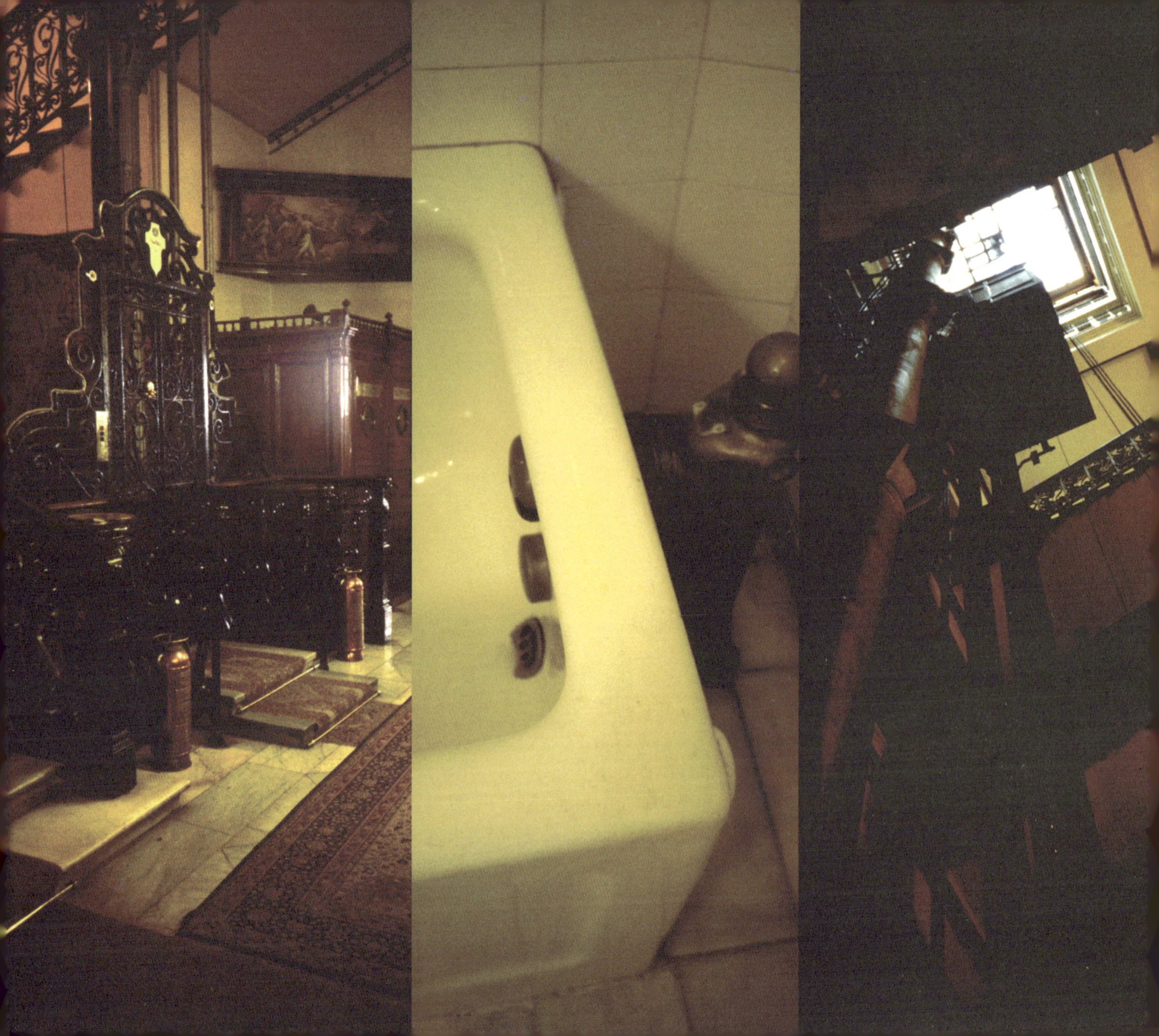

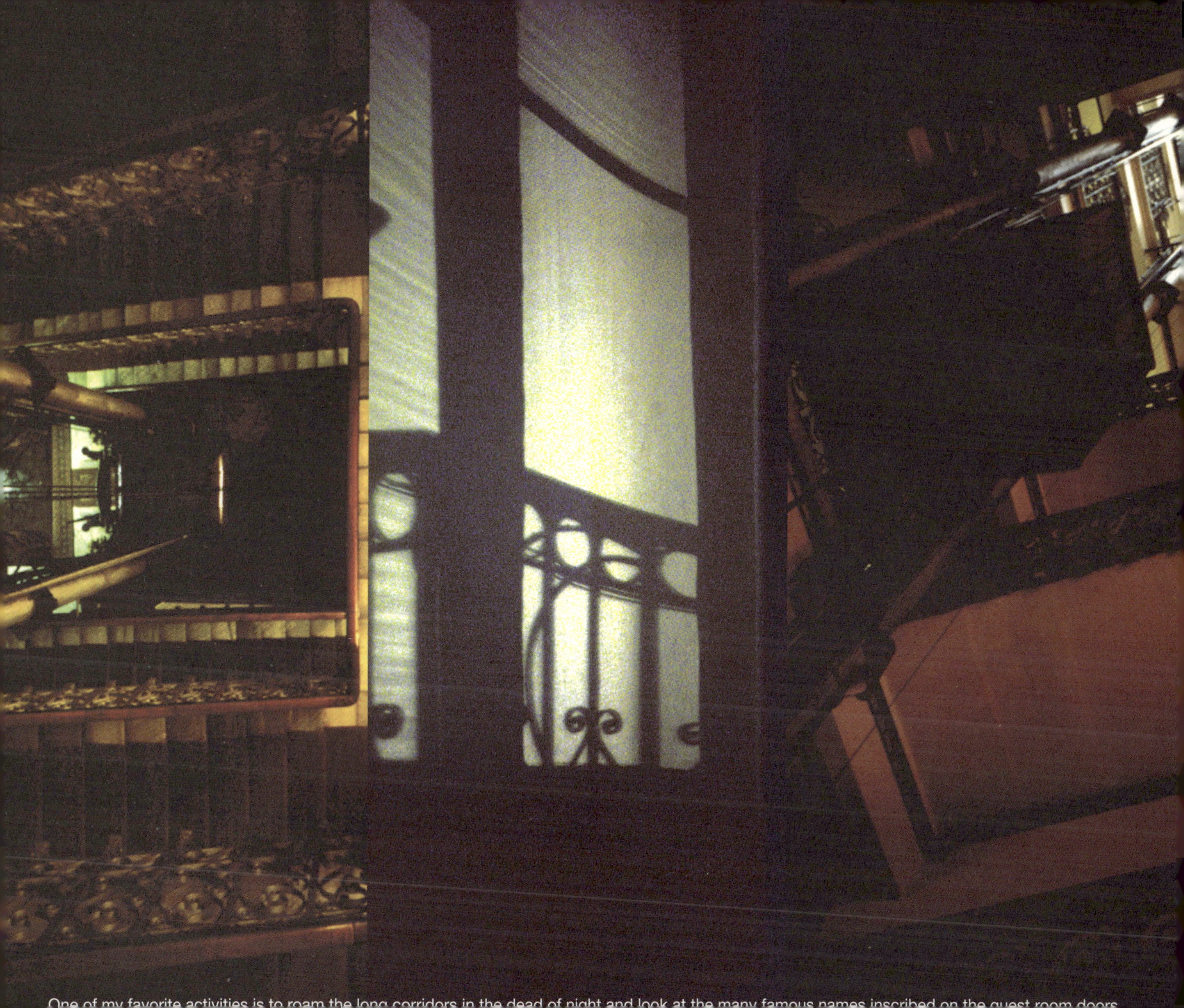

One of my favorite activities is to roam the long corridors in the dead of night and look at the many famous names inscribed on the guest room doors.

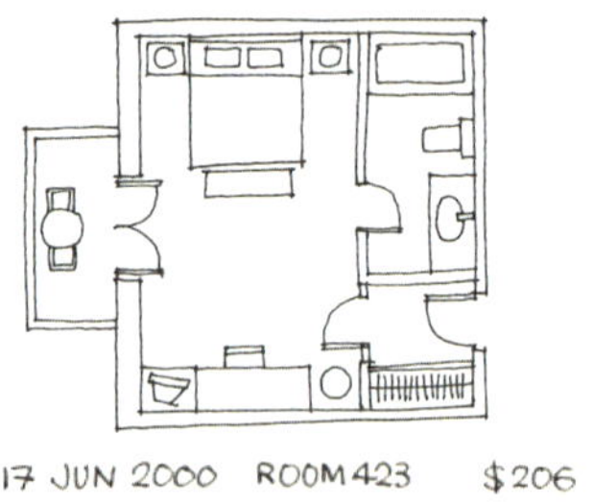

Hotel Des Bains

ON AND OFF THE SET

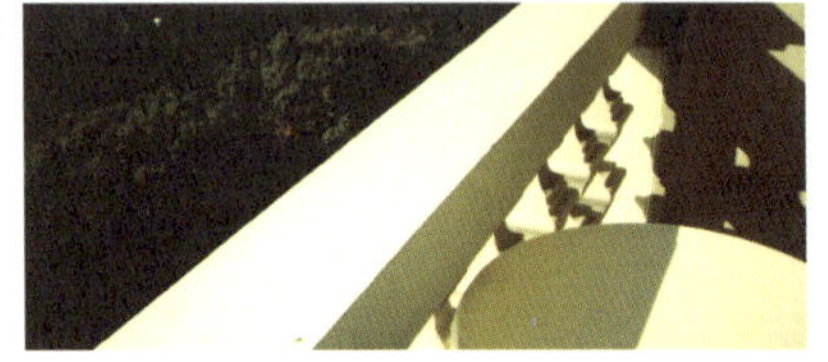

It is perhaps because of Visconti's *Death in Venice* that I feel as if I've always known the town: Lido, the writer with his white panama hat, his meeting with the surreally beautiful youth, and the light dancing on the water of the Mediterranean at dusk. His eyes riveted on the youth, the writer gives chase . . .

Here I am in Venice again, in the year 2000. The courtesy water-taxi provided by the hotel ferries me, in just half an hour, away from Piazza San Marco, drowning in hordes of tourists and pigeons, to the very hotel that once played host to the panama-hatted, linen-suited old writer. Extravagant hotels in Venice are abundant, but none caught my eye, which made the simple and reasonably priced (for Venetian standards, that is) Hotel Des Bains such a pleasant find. In Venice's Lido, every hotel has its own private beach outfitted with vaguely African-looking beach cabins—just like in the old days. Hotel Des Bains's seaside location makes it an imperative to insist on a beach-facing room with a balcony and to spend a lot of time doing nothing. What made Visconti decide to film his classic here? Could it have been for the *Belle Époque* aura that the hotel seems to exude so unceremoniously? What it lacks in grandeur, it more than makes up for with its turn-of-the-century vitality: anything is possible here. *Cinema Paradiso* once brought me to Sicily, to see that decrepit white wall with its specters of sight and sound. I am here now because of Visconti.

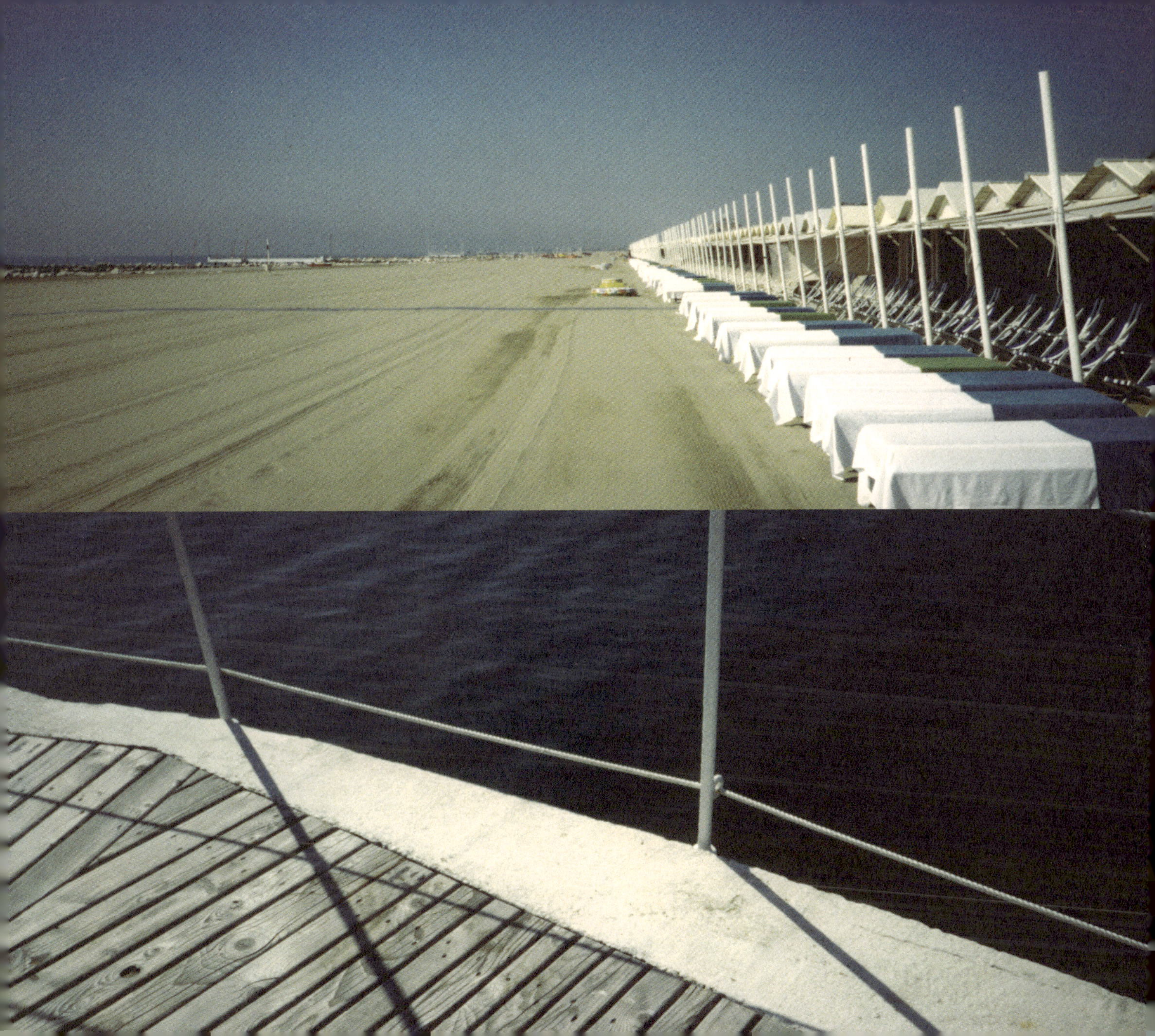

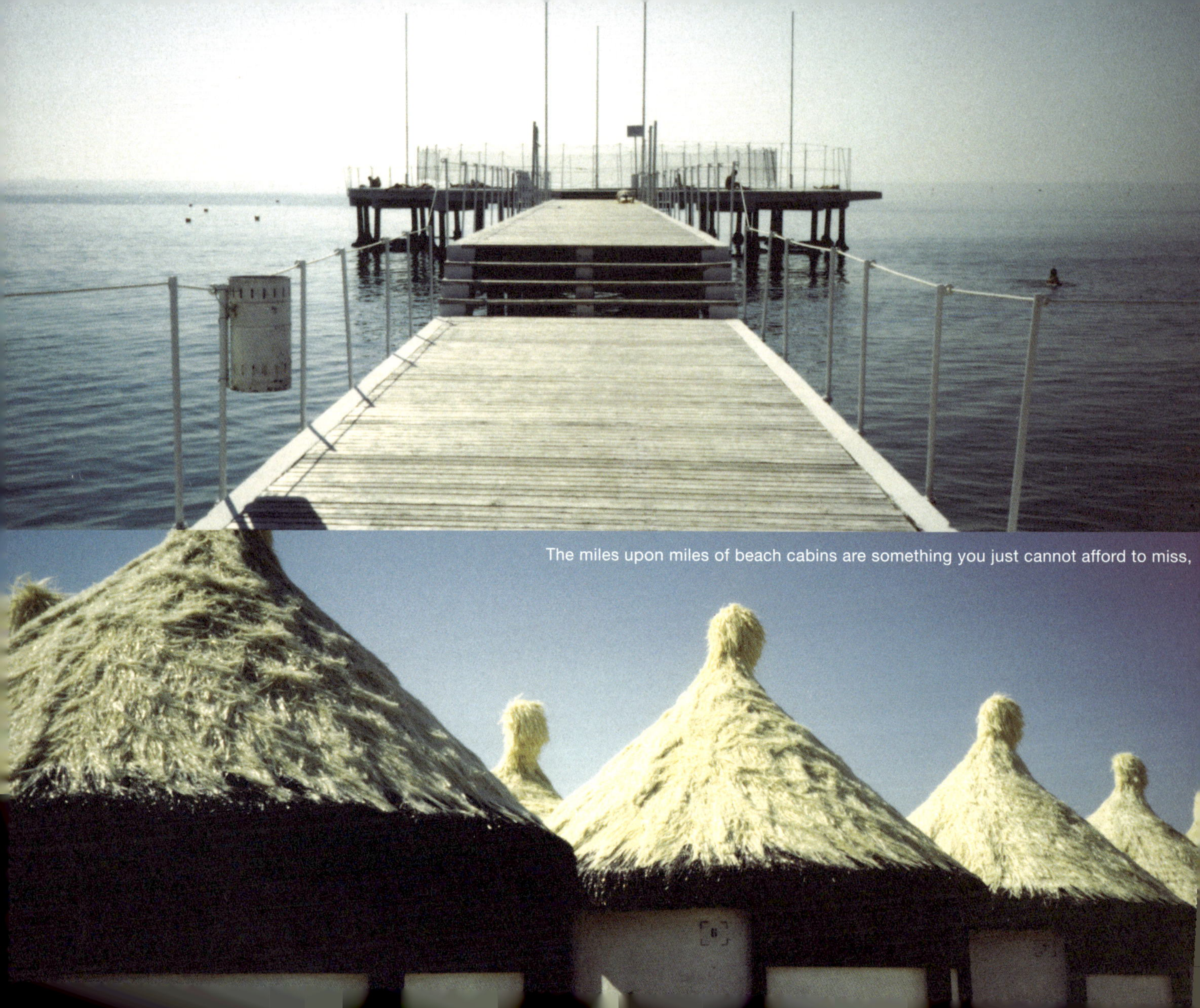

The miles upon miles of beach cabins are something you just cannot afford to miss, but be prepared to pay up to half your daily hotel room rate to rent one of them.

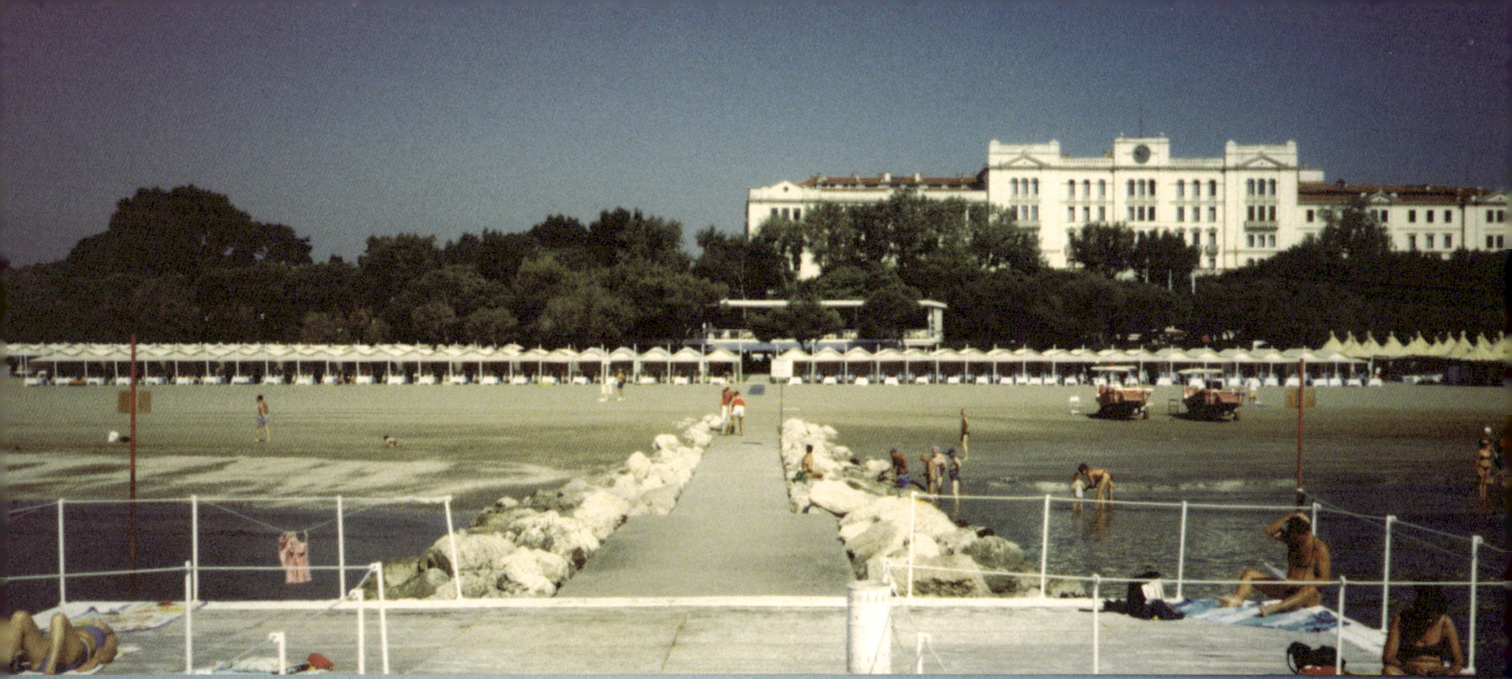

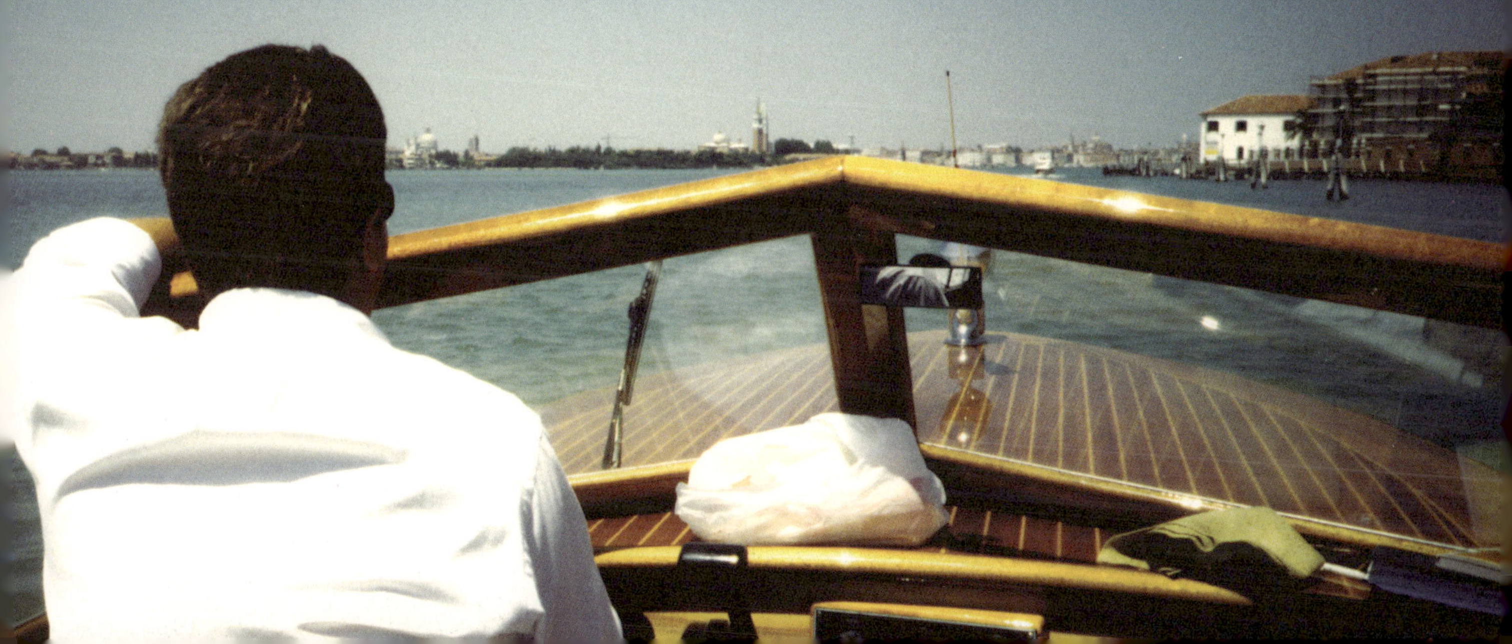

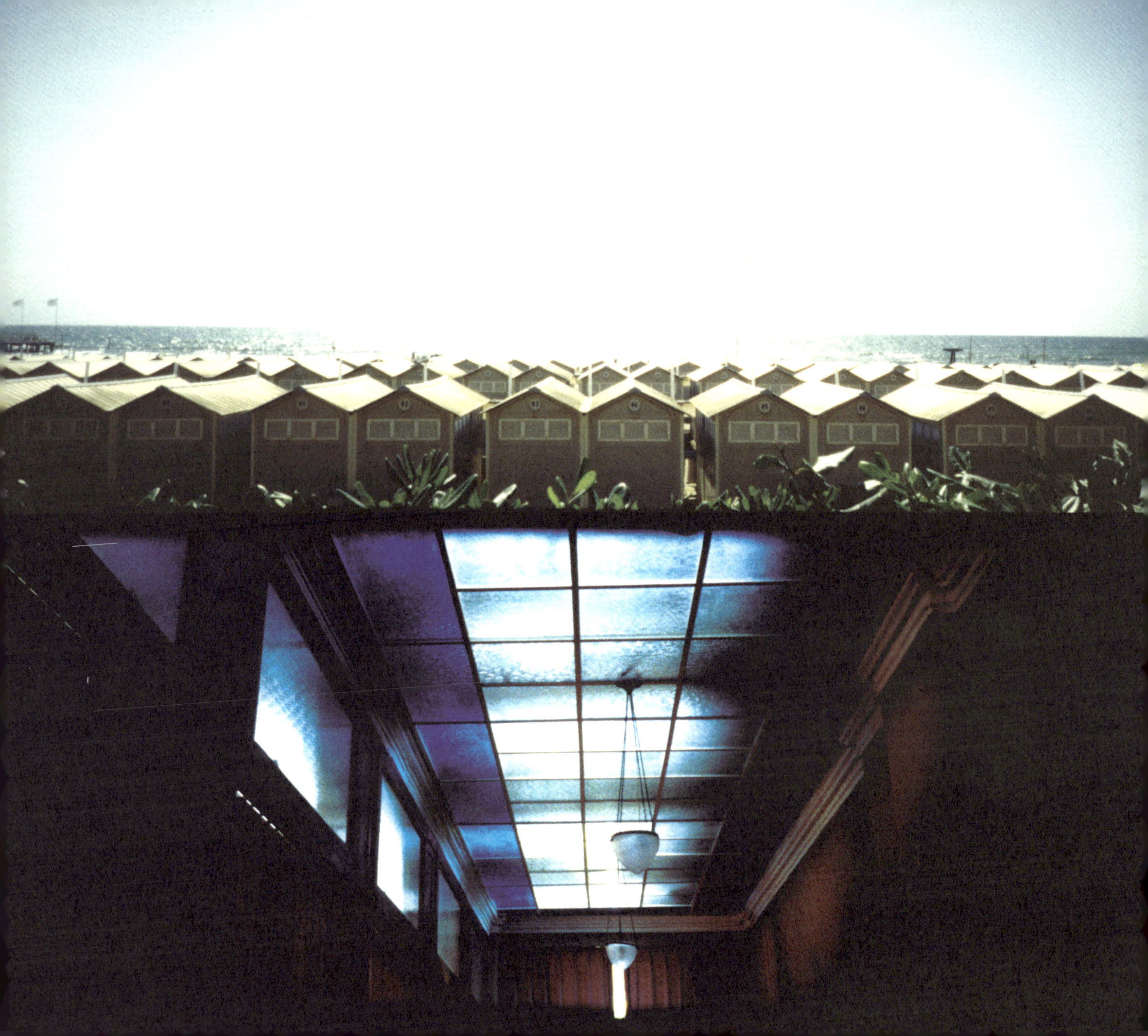

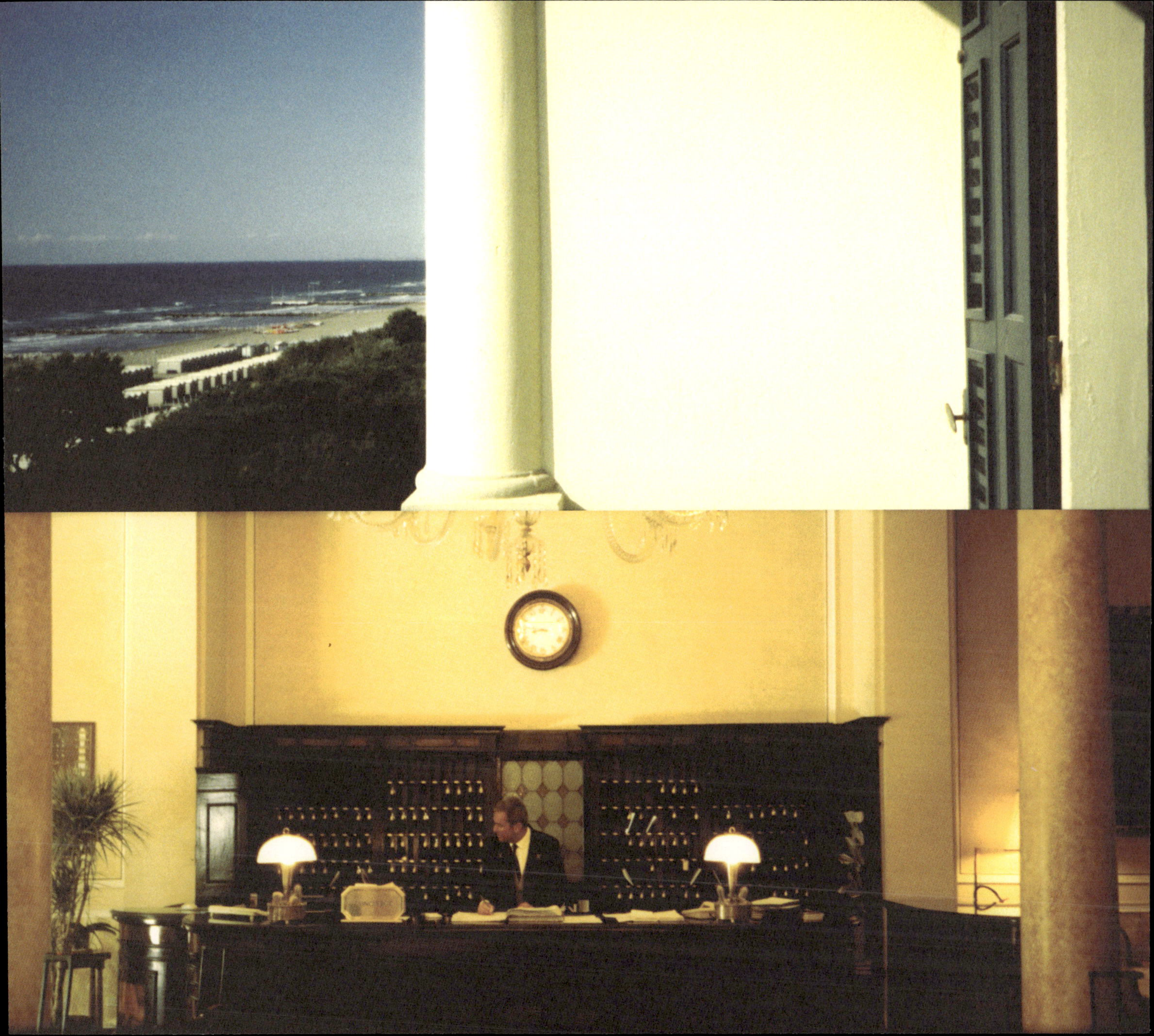

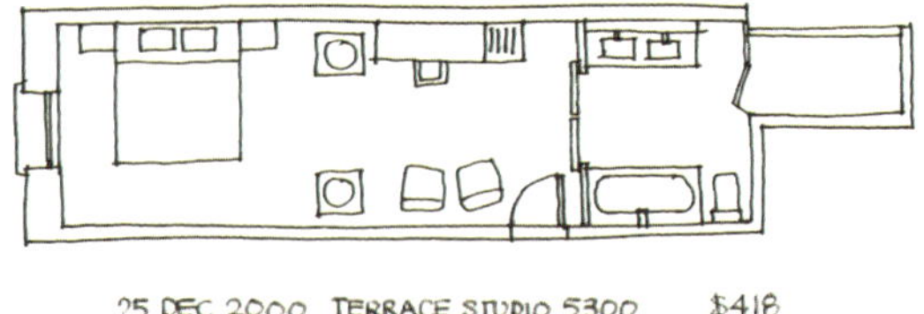

The Hotel

ELUSIVE NARRATIVES

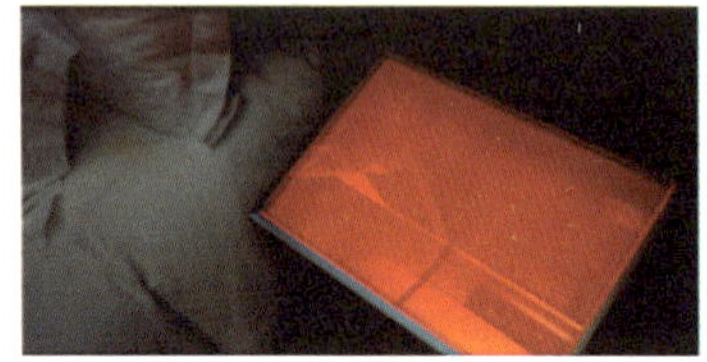

Similar to film directors, Jean Nouvel, my most-admired architect, narrates with illusions. The rooms in The Hotel (the name betrays its proprietor's belief that this is *the* hotel) are basically unfathomable expanses of darkness, but the darkness is rife with insuppressible sensuality emanating from the prints of film stills that are mounted on the ceilings: Oshima's *Realm of Senses*, Antonioni's *Beyond the Clouds*, Lynch's *Lost Highway*, Bertolucci's *Last Tango in Paris*, and numerous others by Fassbinder, Wenders, Buñuel, Fellini, Almadovar, and Greenaway. Looking in from the outside, the rooms resemble dark theaters in which the characters from these films come back to life to play out their elusive and illusive narratives. The sensuous hallucination the ceilings evoke is a far cry from the God-fearing piety inspired by the Sistine Chapel. I must say that this is the only hotel I can think of in which you'd rather focus on what is happening on the ceiling than on the banalities below, in the room itself.

Jean Nouvel is a master of lights. Like the guest rooms, even the lobby is unusually dimlit. Of course, this makes one ache all the more to find out where the light and colors come from—the TV, the desk, the wardrobe, or perhaps even the stainless-steel chair.

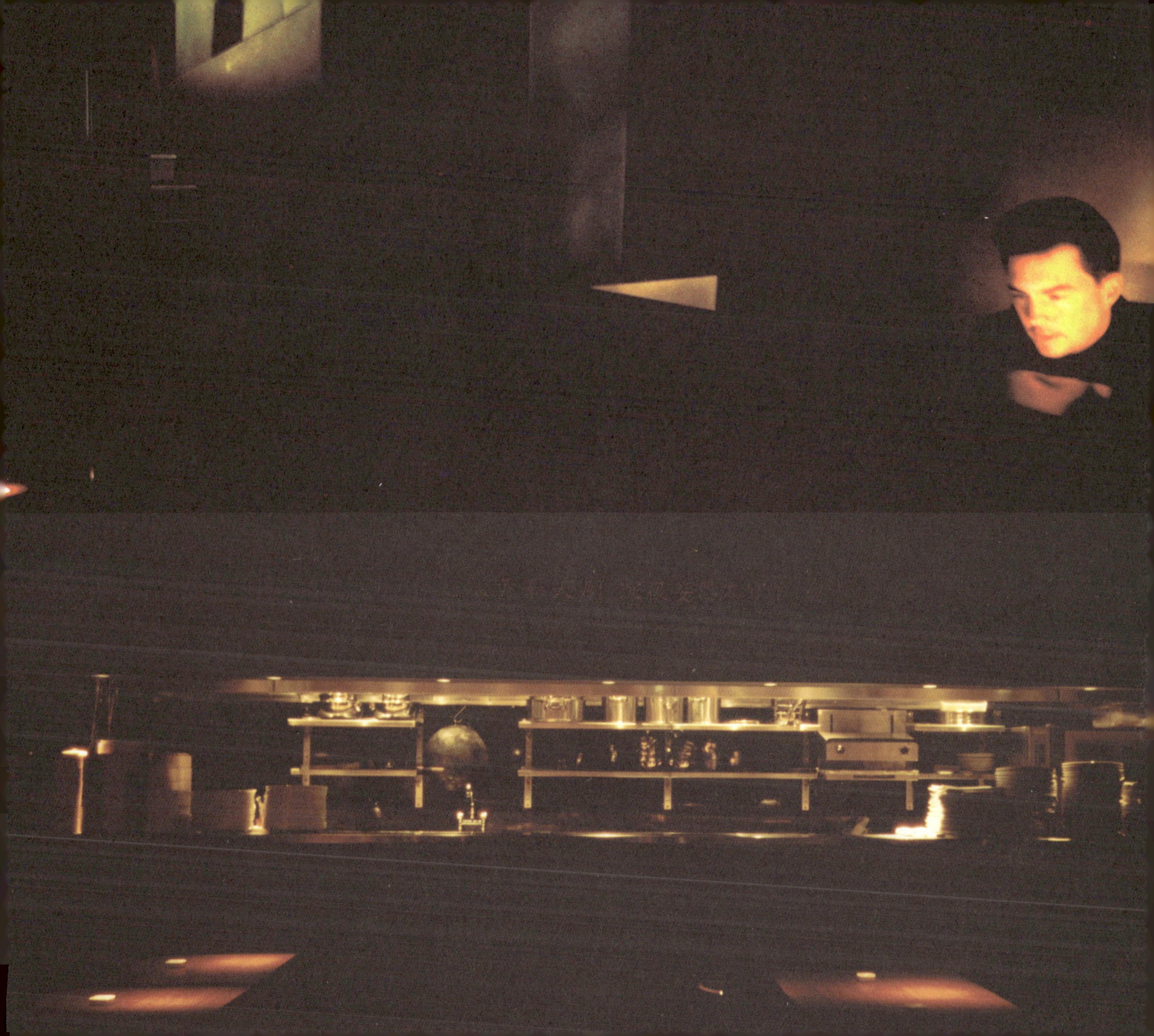

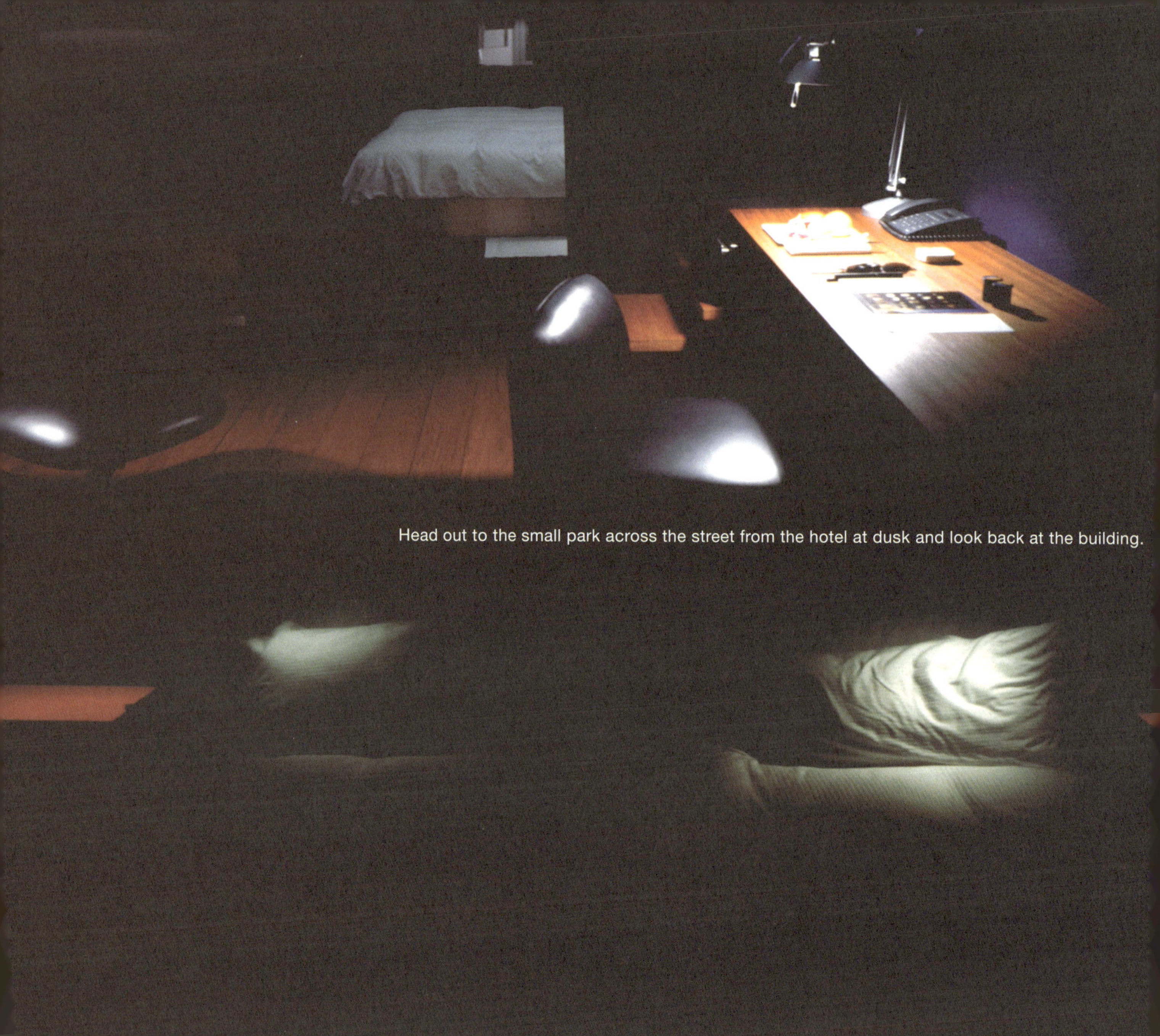

Head out to the small park across the street from the hotel at dusk and look back at the building.

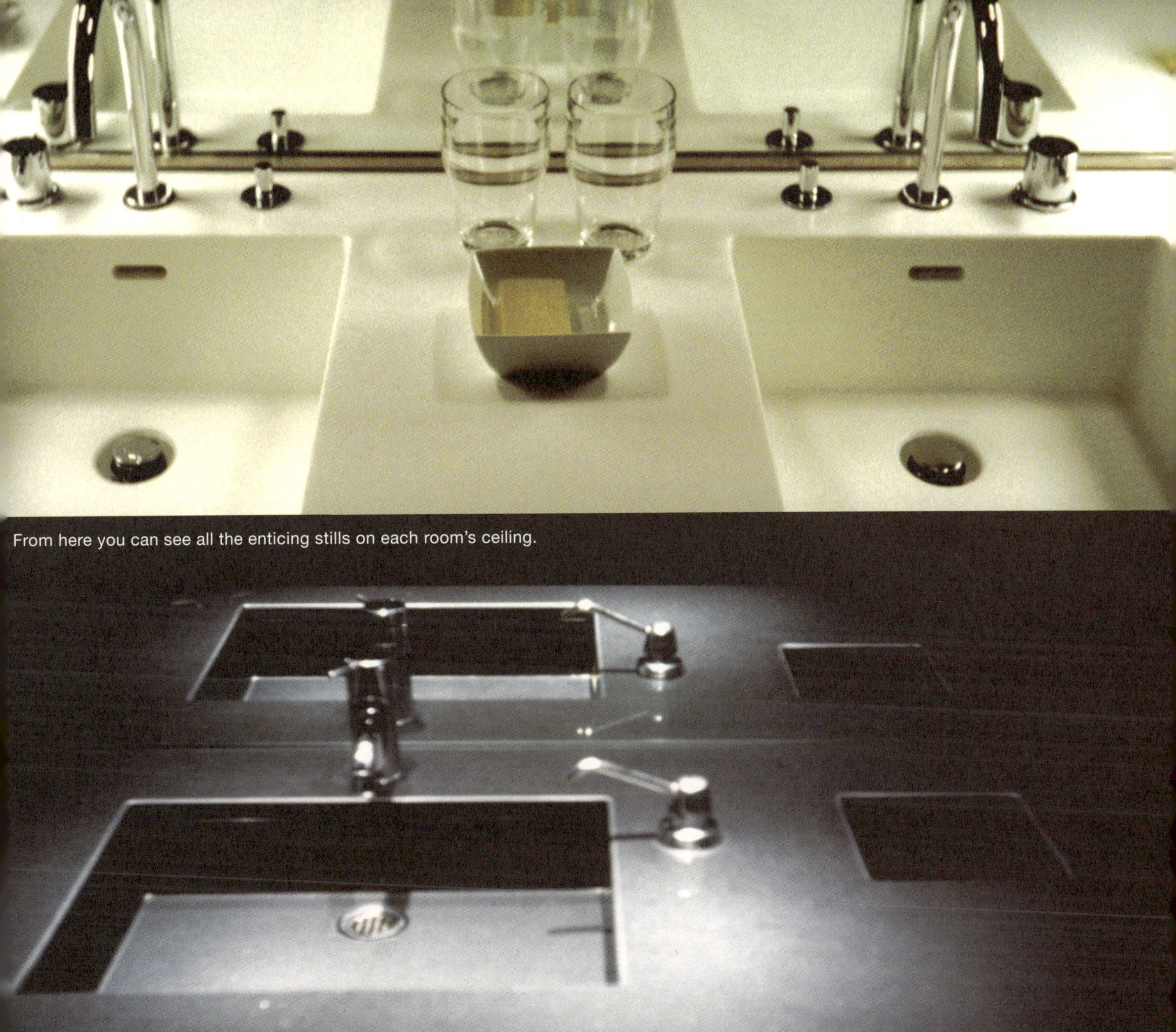

From here you can see all the enticing stills on each room's ceiling.

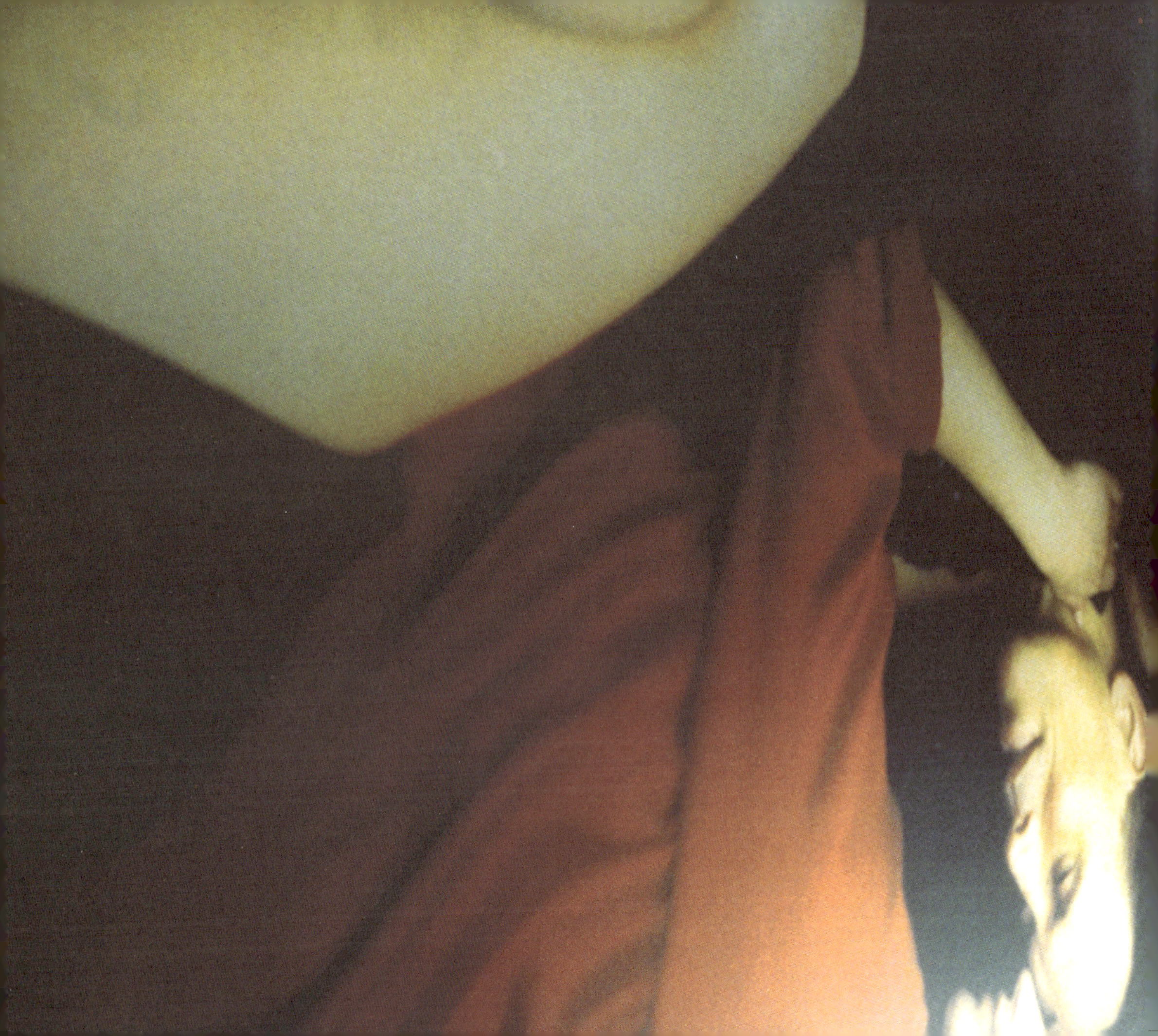

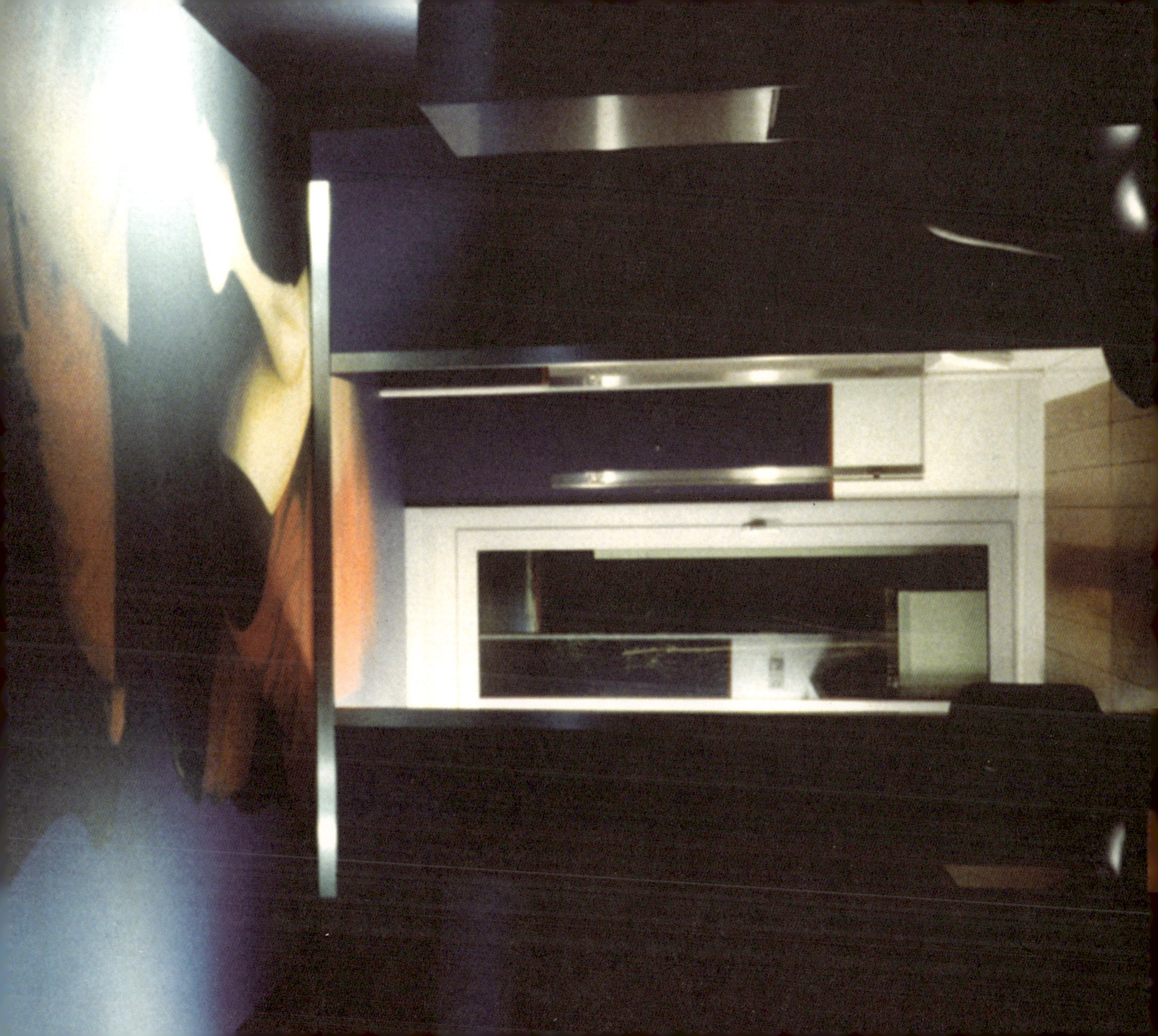

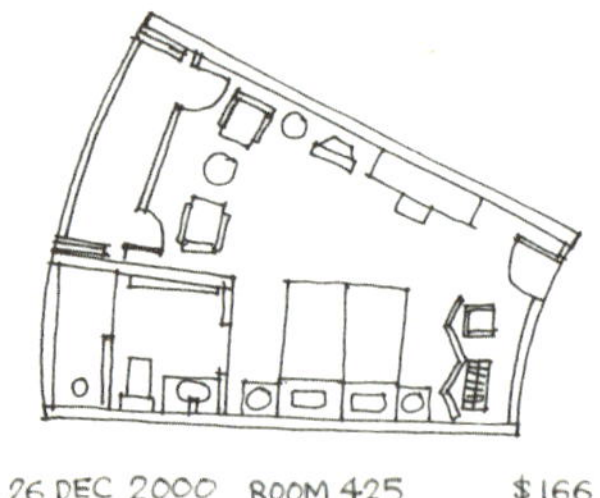

Hotel Zürichberg

SPIRALS THROUGH THE HILLS

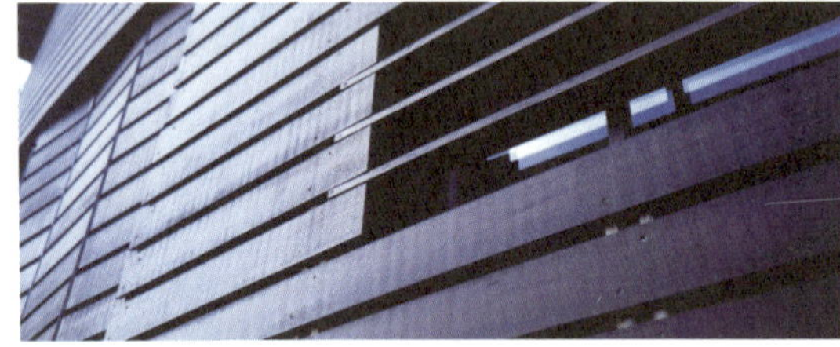

It was a Hotel Zürichberg enveloped in a romantic veil of mountain mist that I found when I arrived. In a mere fifteen minutes, the No. 6 tram had brought me here from the busy train station of downtown Zurich, along streets lined with shops and banks. Up here on the lush, green hilltop, there is nothing else besides the hotel save a zoo, a cemetery, and trees. The hotel itself opens out onto a large lawn. The guest rooms' picture windows look out on the woods, and skylights afford a thought-provoking view of the starry sky at night.

The hotel's original building has retained the classic elegance of old houses, while the new extension sports a striking contemporary look. Designed as a rotunda with rounded wooden slats on the exterior, it gives the impression of a large spiral. Even the windows seem to have been caught up in its swirl. A somewhat symbiotic relationship exists between the old and the new: an underground passage connects the two buildings, which otherwise have no common point of access.

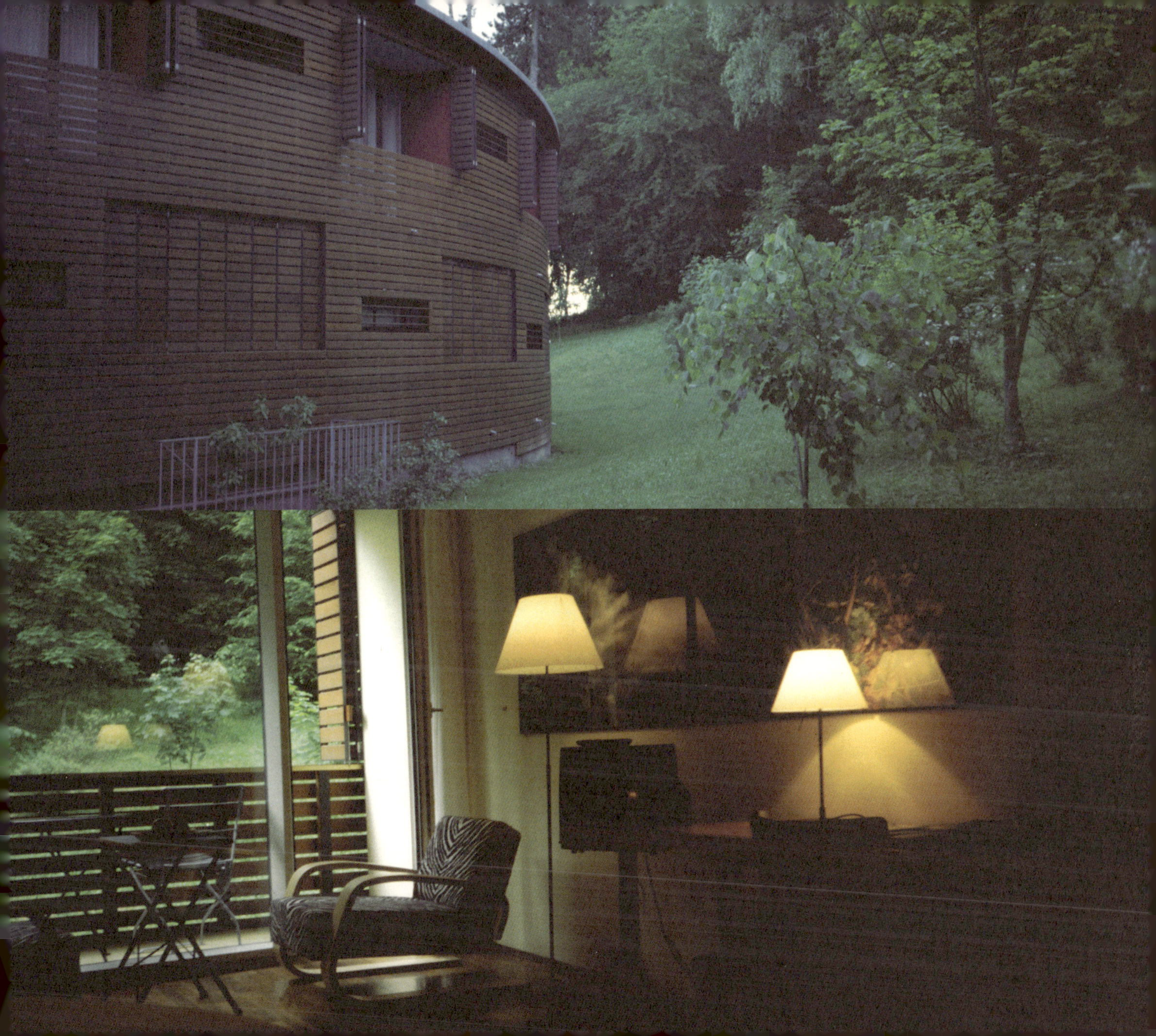

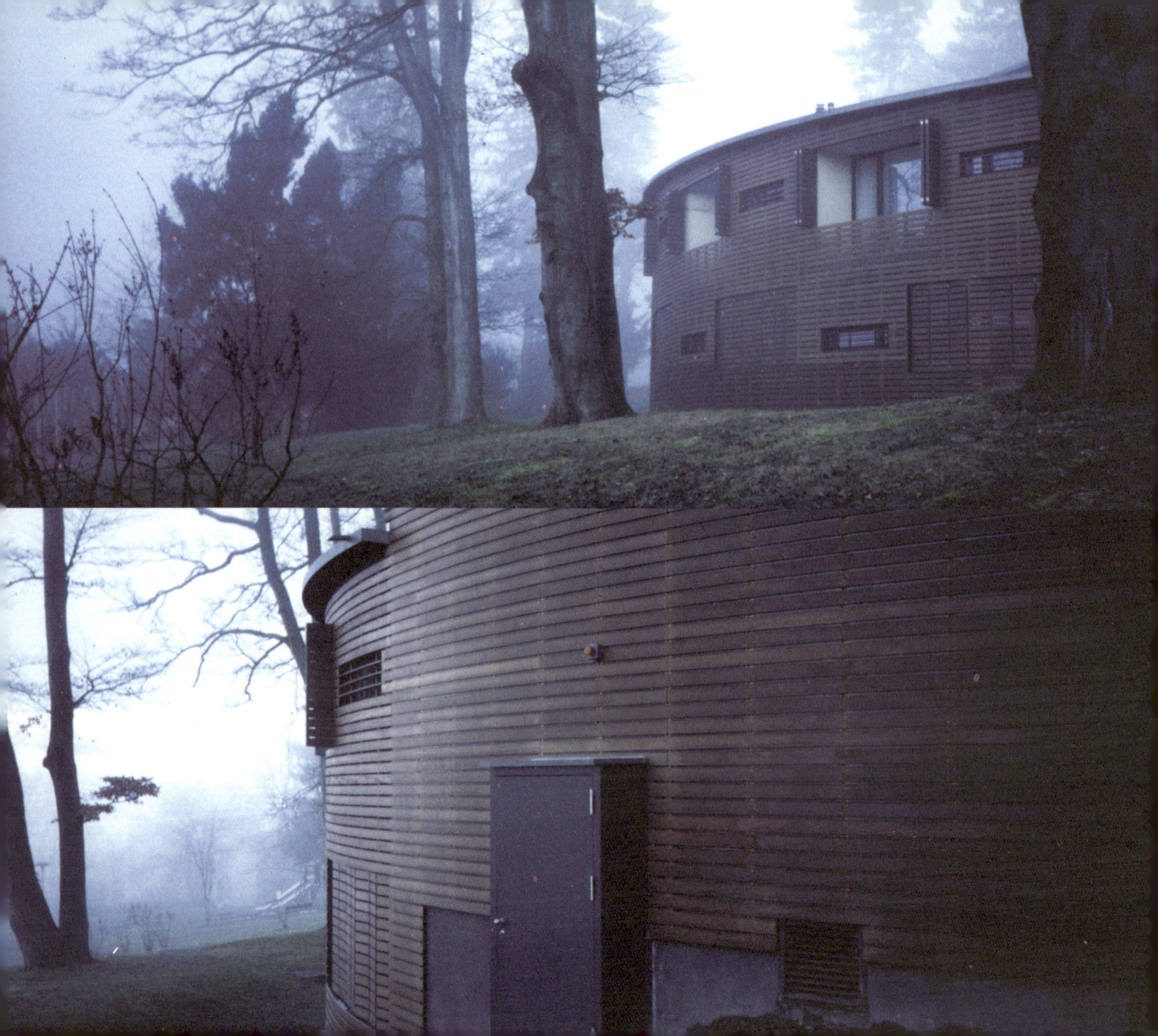

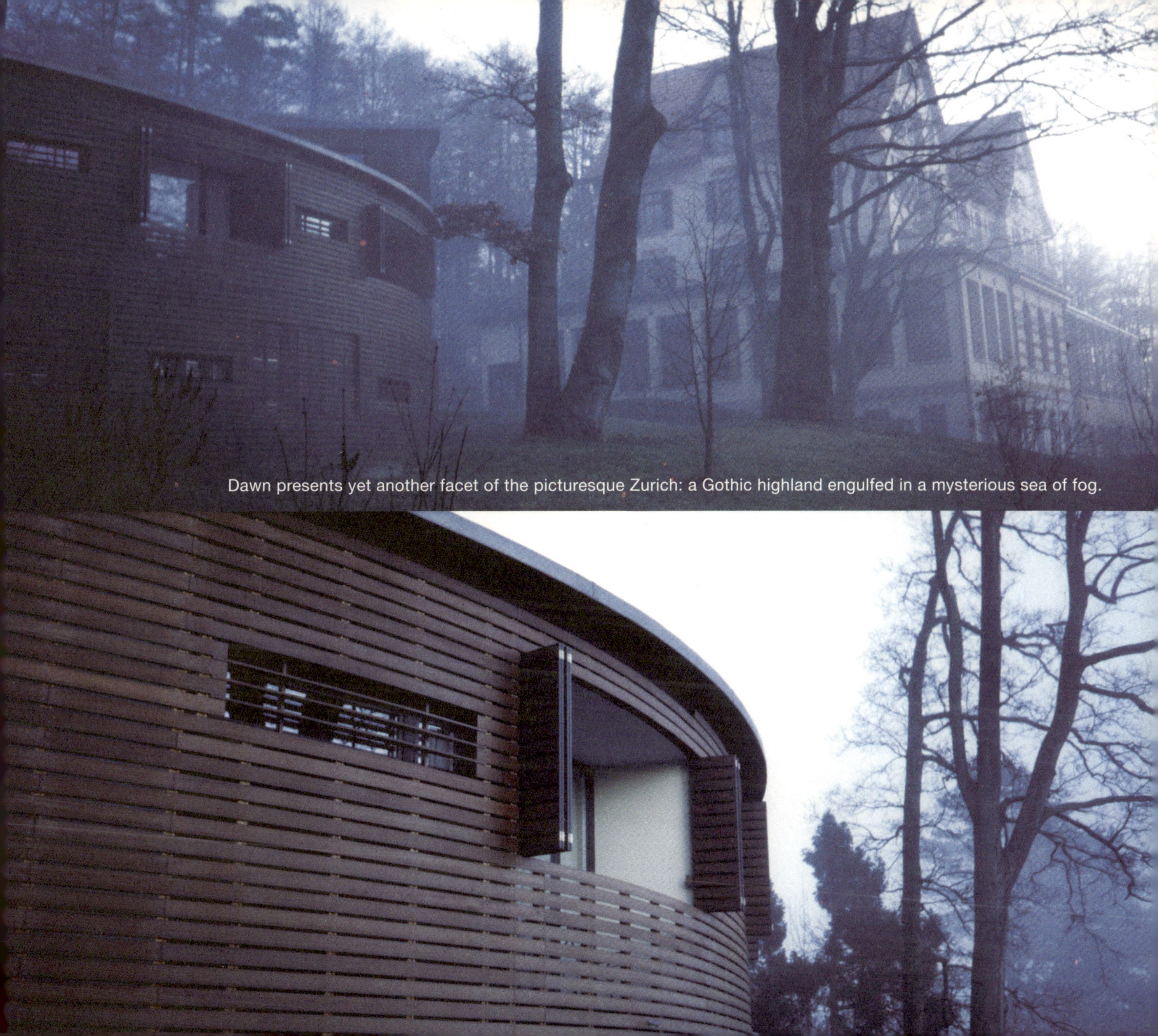

Dawn presents yet another facet of the picturesque Zurich: a Gothic highland engulfed in a mysterious sea of fog.

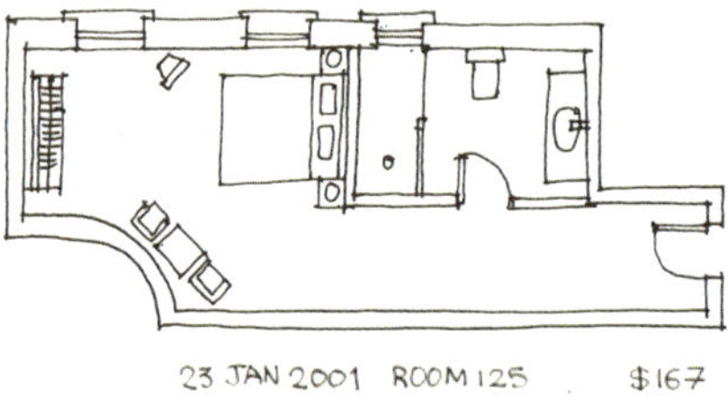

Hostal de los Reyes Catolicos

IN A MEDIEVAL TOWN

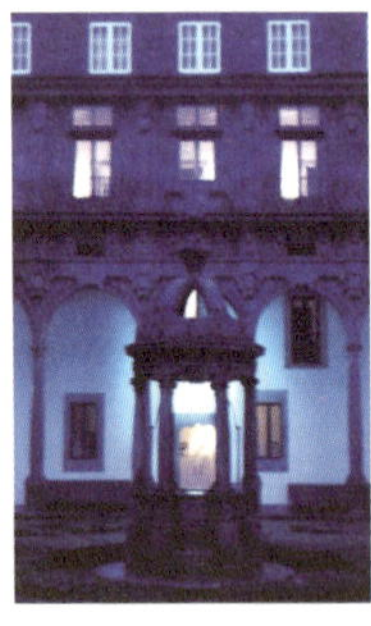

I arrived at Santiago in the north of Spain in the midst of a heavy rain shower and checked into a monastery—a monastery that was once a hospital and is now a hotel. One can become lost in time in the Hostal de los Reyes Catolicos's open courtyard, its seemingly endless corridors, and its many archways. The state-run hotel still stands tall in the center of the old town square, next to the old cathedral, just as it has done for centuries. But instead of meditative recluses, it now hosts pilgrims of the touristy kind. The interior has also retained much of its original design and layout; the most captivating element is the series of serene yet nostalgic colonnades surrounding the central courtyard. Everything seems to have been designed with largesse in mind—a bathroom here is bigger than my entire apartment back home.

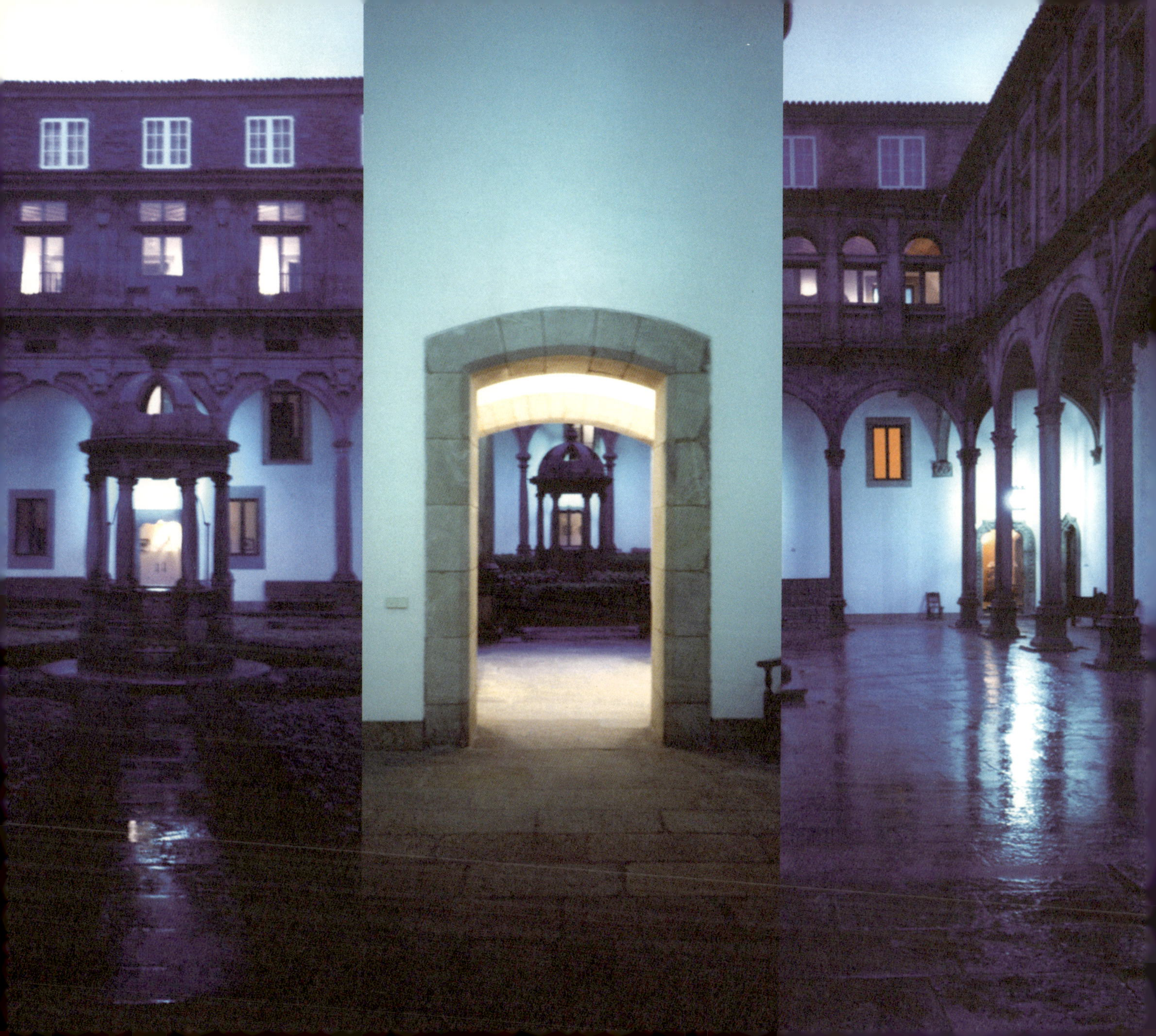

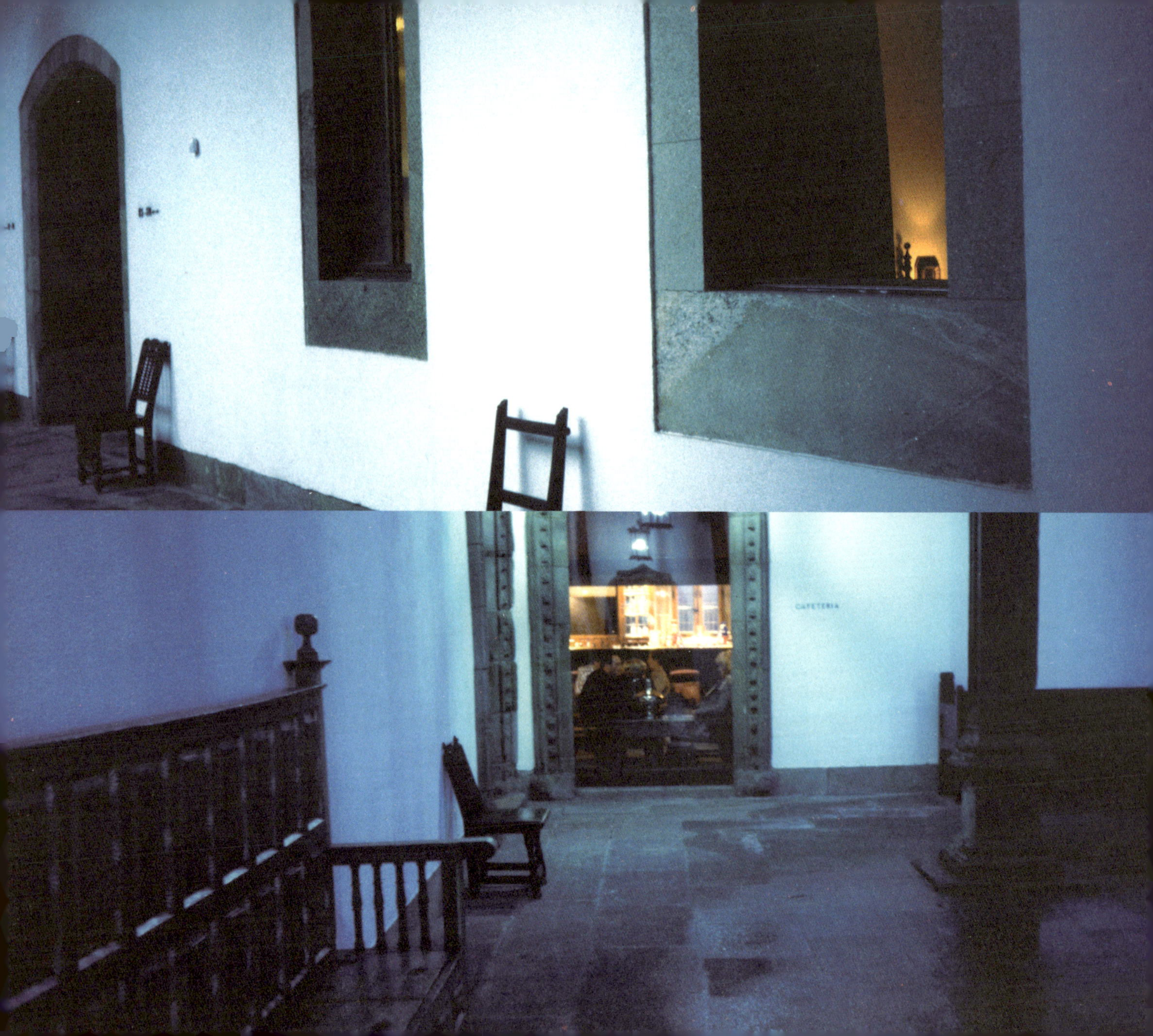
CAFETERIA

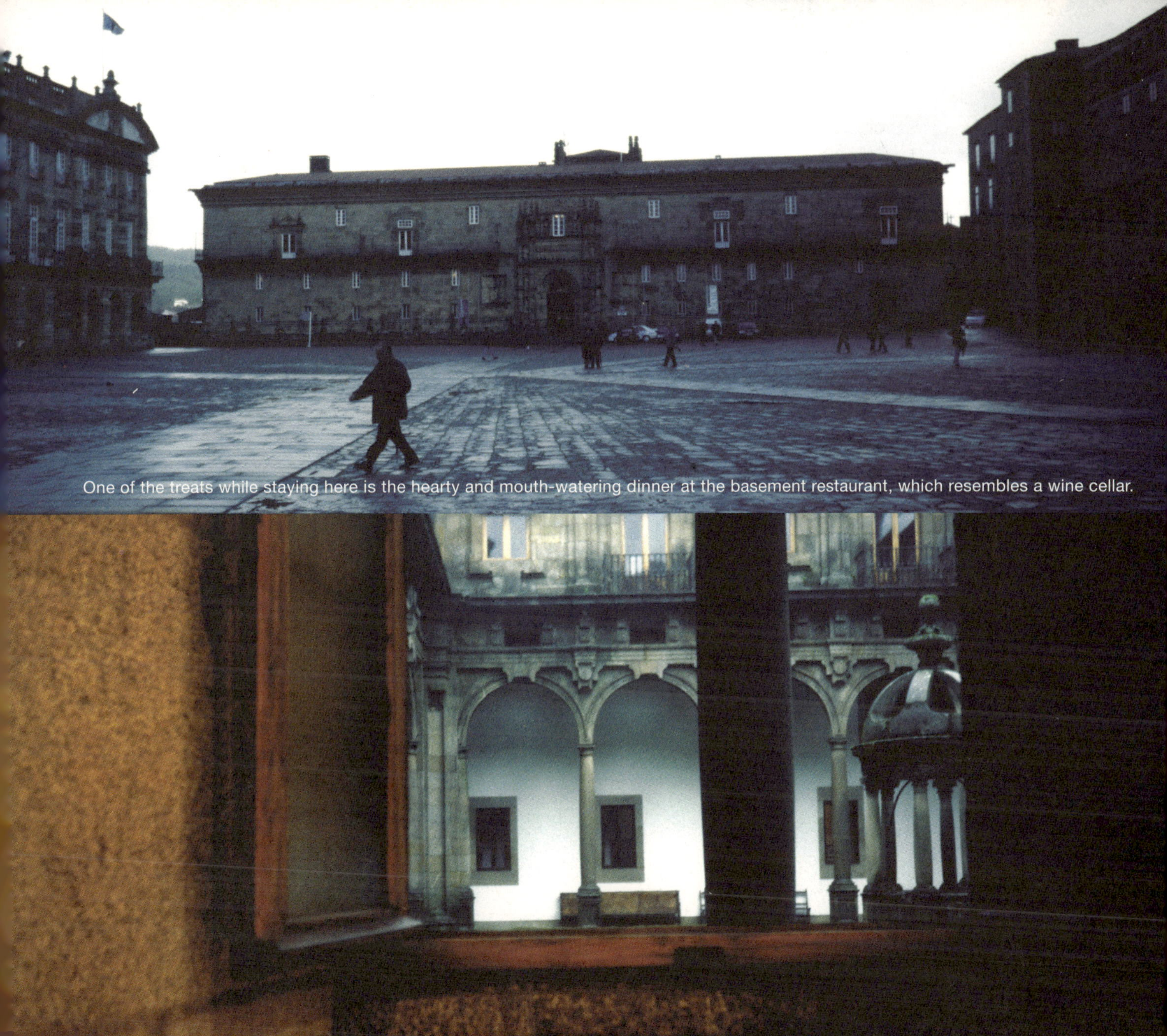

One of the treats while staying here is the hearty and mouth-watering dinner at the basement restaurant, which resembles a wine cellar.

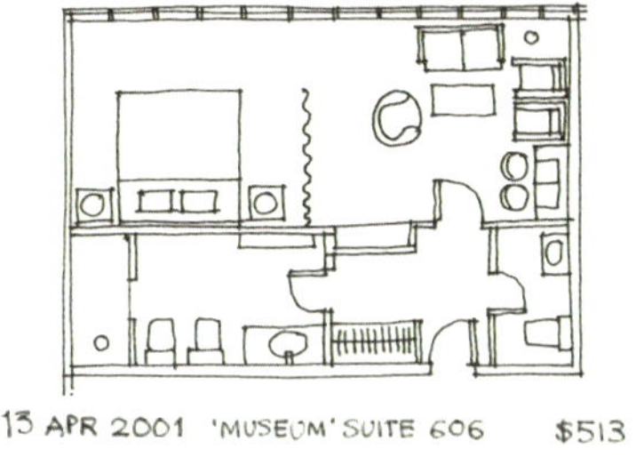

RADISSON SAS Royal Hotel

TELESCOPING A METROPOLIS

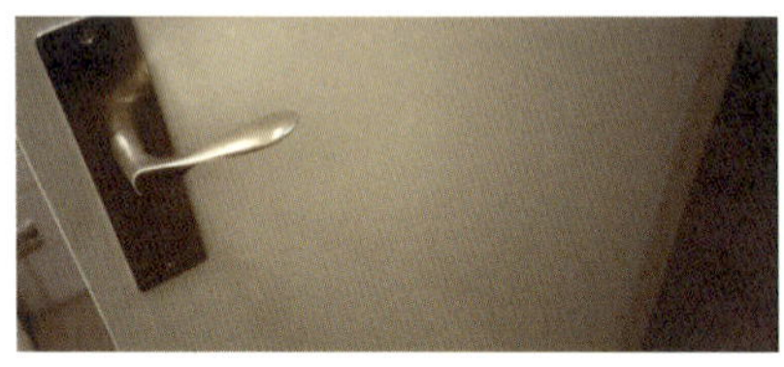

Until we think about it, the fact that Arne Jacobsen, the Danish master architect-designer, has had a tremendous influence on our lives easily escapes us. His Hotel SAS Royal from the 1960s is deemed a landmark of the Jet Age; its twenty-two-story structure was once the tallest in Scandinavia. The hotel is connected to the SAS airline office and almost looks more like a business building than a hotel. The metropolis of forty years ago has been telescoped and preserved in the hotel's Room 606, the "museum room," which is still furnished with all the original Jacobsen artifacts: the apple-green walls (the same calming apple-green that used to grace Hong Kong's many public housing estates and hospitals); the iconic Swan Chair; the Drop Chair; the 3300 aqua-colored sofa that resembles three people in a *tête-à-tête*; the desk that transforms into a vanity which looks like a jewelry box; the pure white, utilitarian bathroom; the blue-striped bedding. All these items have made their way into our collective memory through, among other things, the films of Audrey Hepburn, Rock Hudson, Marcello Mastroianni, and Catherine Deneuve. The world would be a very different place without them.

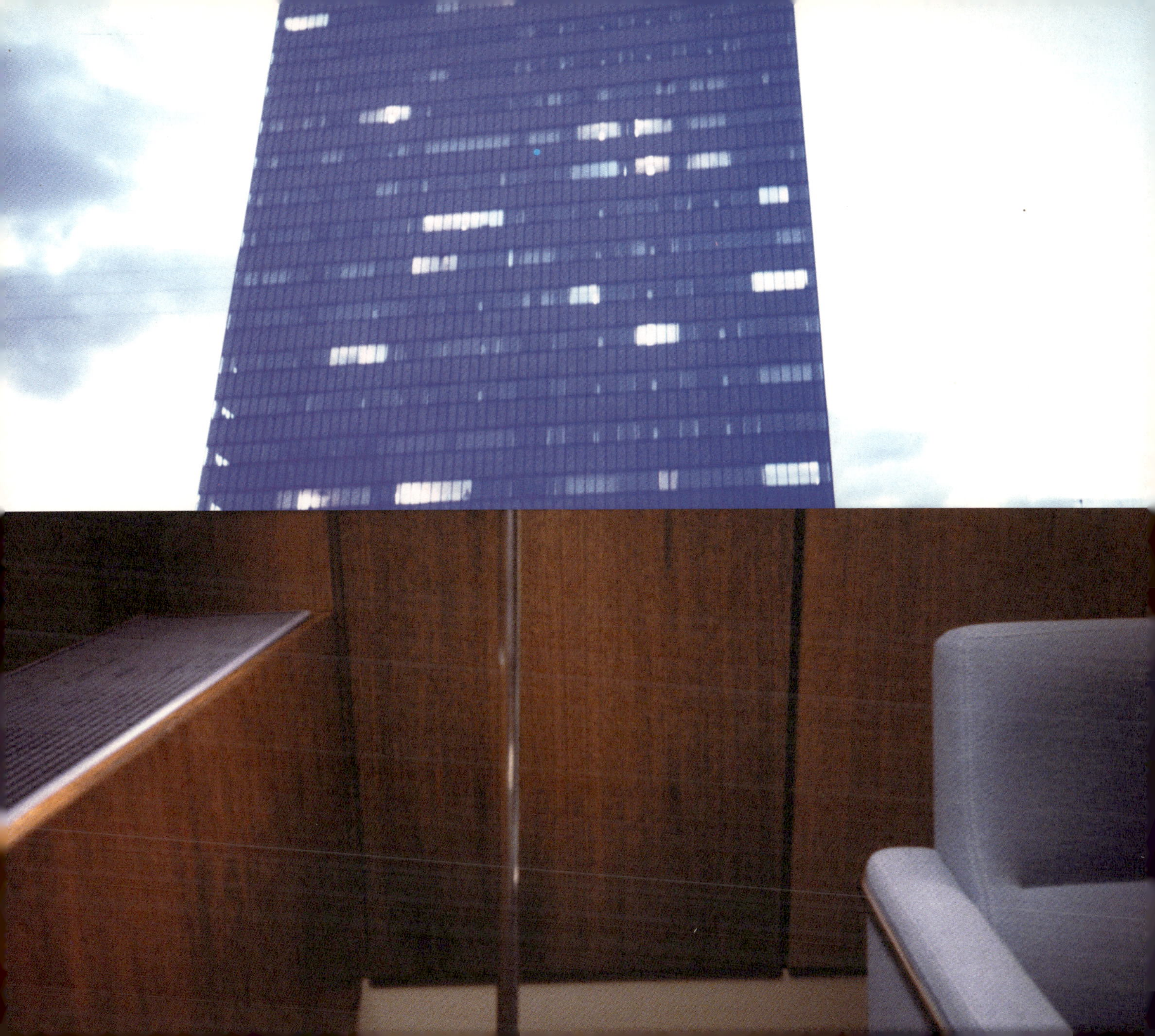

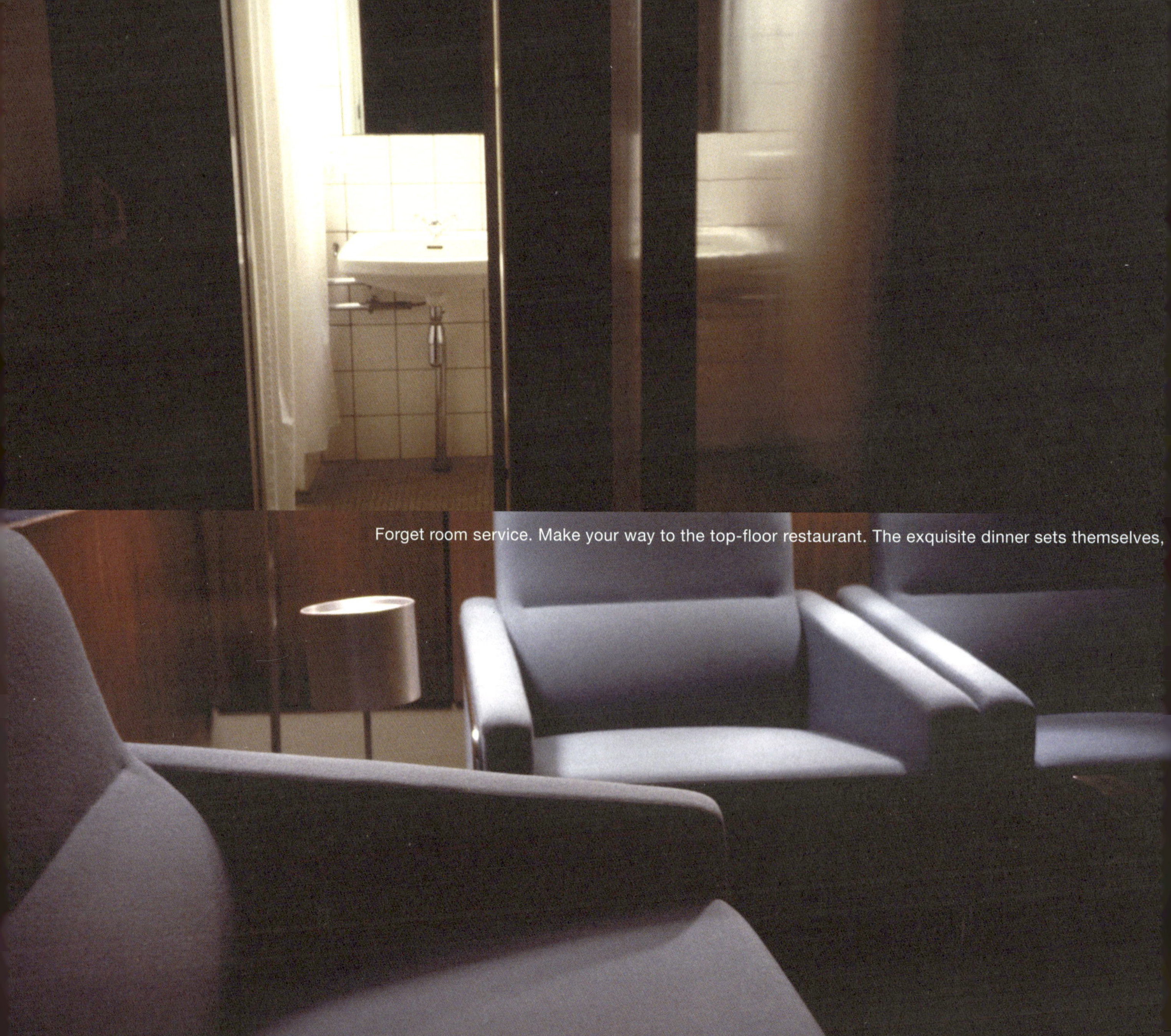

Forget room service. Make your way to the top-floor restaurant. The exquisite dinner sets themselves,

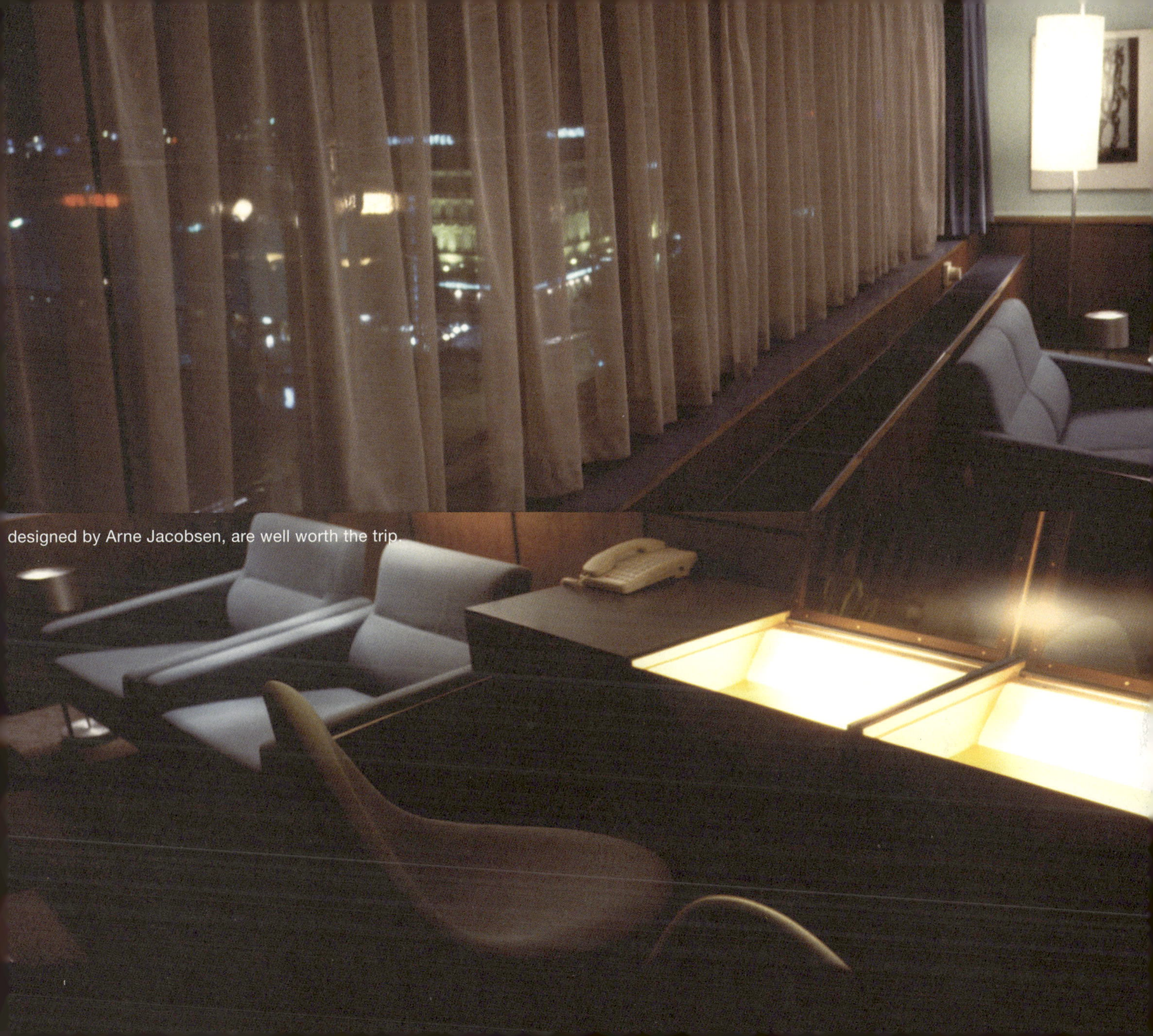

designed by Arne Jacobsen, are well worth the trip.

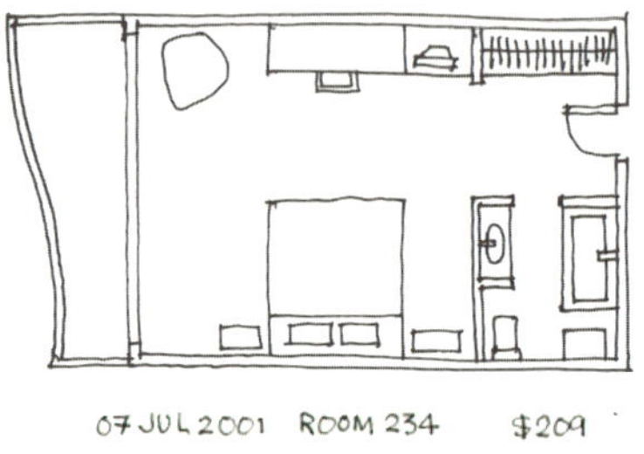

Hotel Standard West Hollywood

SETTING A NEW STANDARD

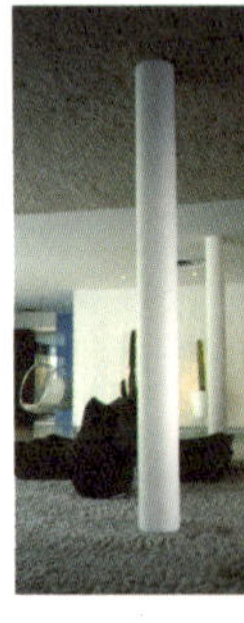

Right from the outset, the upside-down sign that says "The Standard" sets the standard for this hotel in West Hollywood; or should I say, anti-standard. The upendedness continues in the shag carpet that covers the wall and the ceiling of the lounge, while the wallpaper with its desert-and-cactus motif and the fish that is suspended in mid-air conspire to create a 1960s virtual reality, which strangely reminds me of the landscape wallpaper in my childhood home.

Converted from a 1963 rest home, the hotel has unusually large rooms, and its lobby, which features a fish tank with live models, has turned into a fashionable spot on Sunset Boulevard. The blue-and-white terrace with its deck chairs and table tennis tables attracts a largely young, hopeful, and aspiring clientele. After dark, the place becomes a cacophony of party noises. A hotel isn't always just for accommodation.

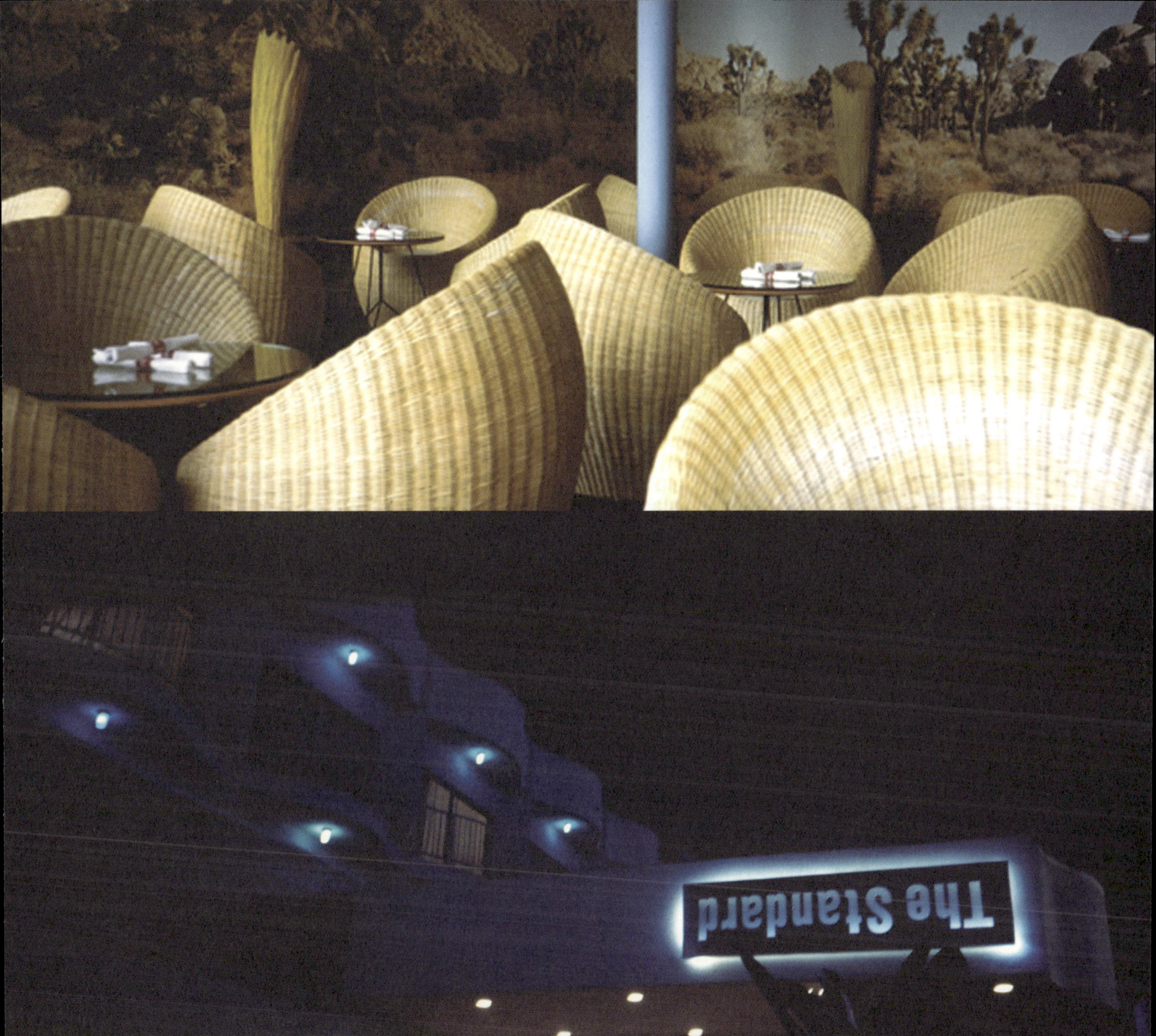
The Standard

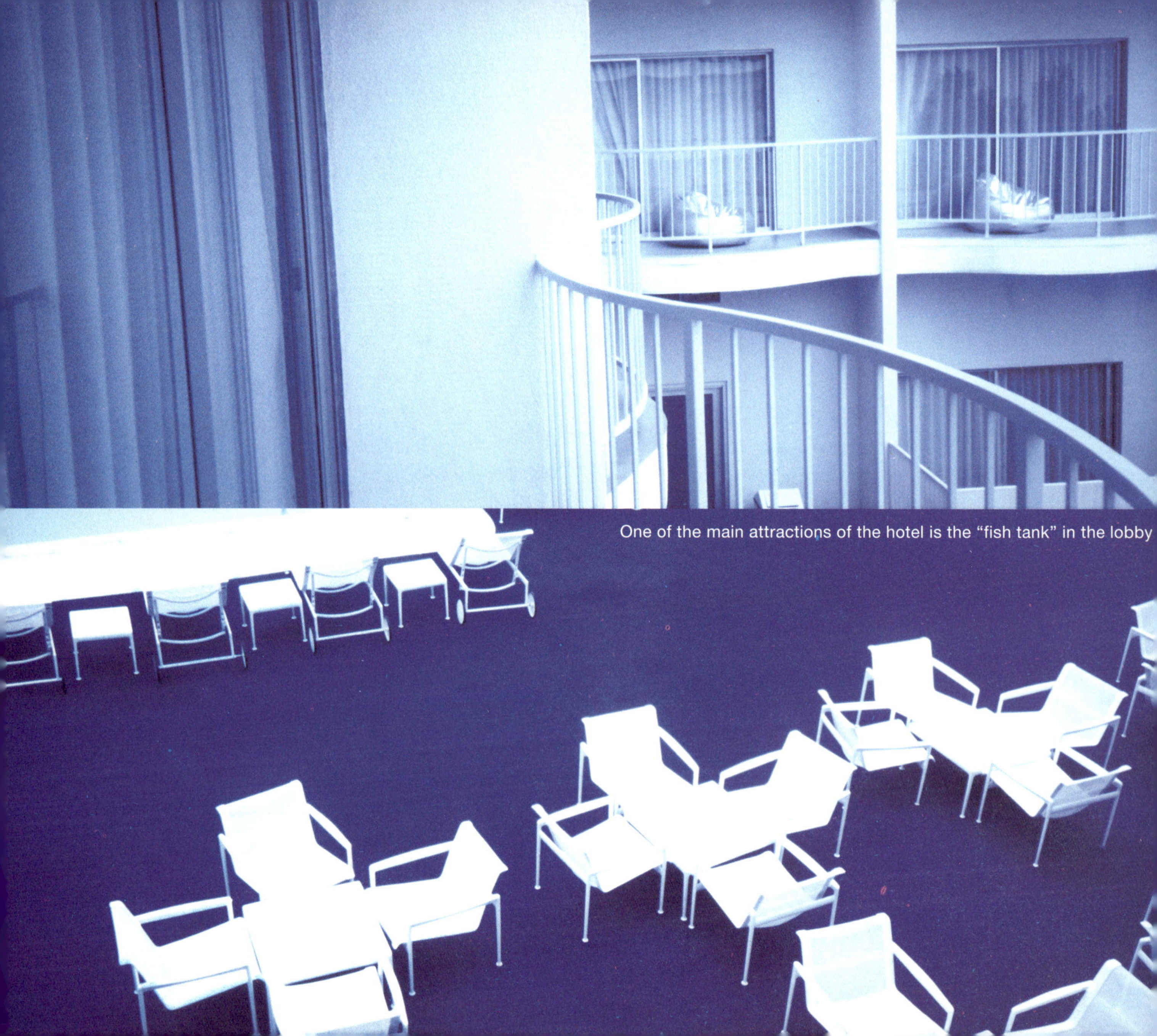

One of the main attractions of the hotel is the “fish tank” in the lobby

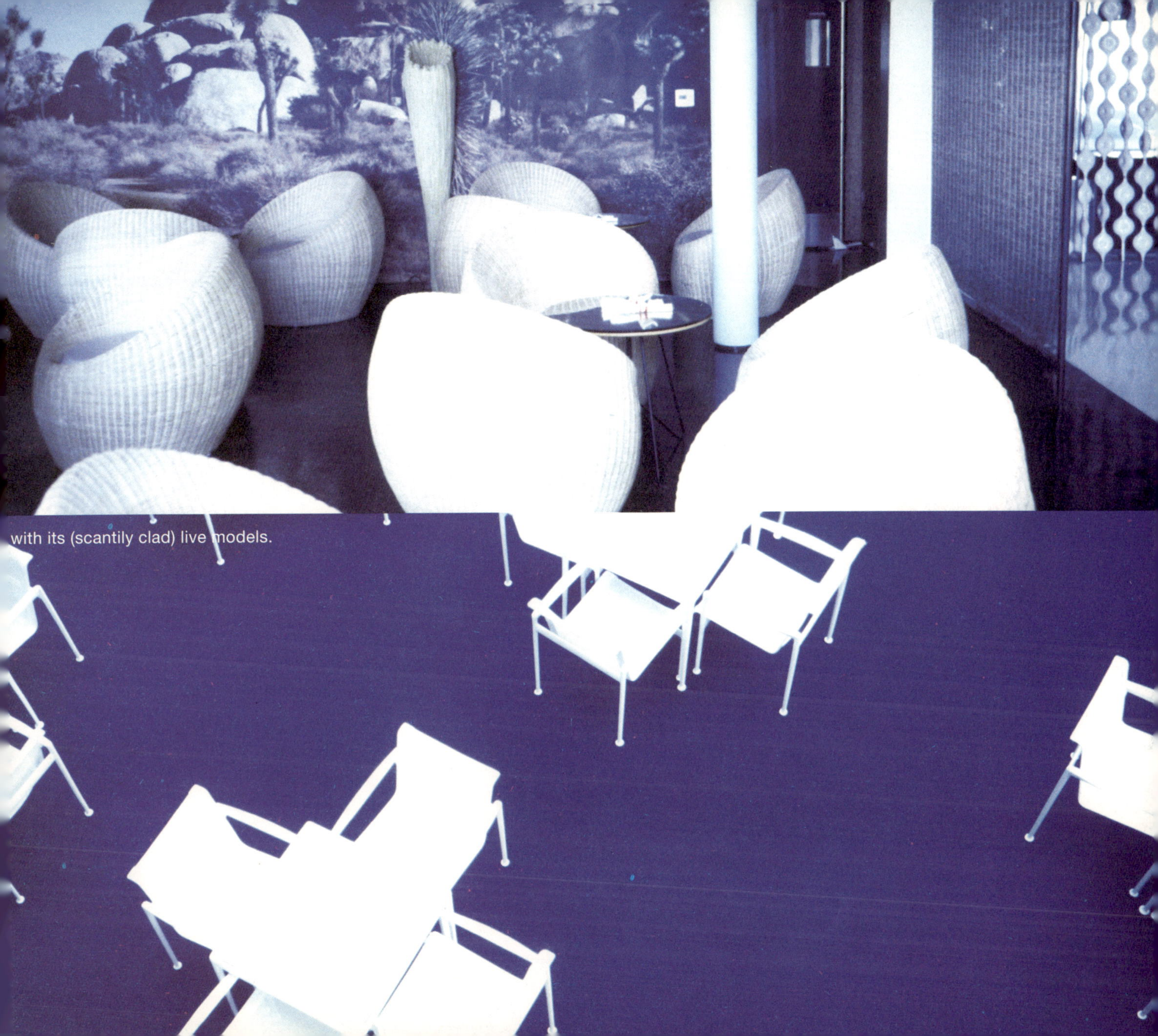

with its (scantily clad) live models.

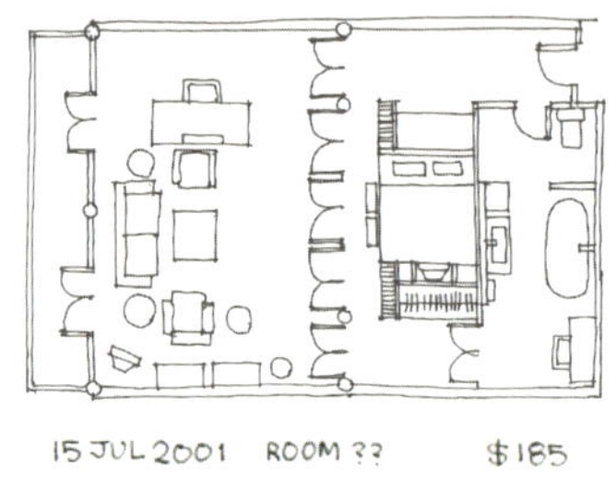

The China Club

NEW MEMORIES OF AN OLD ACQUAINTANCE

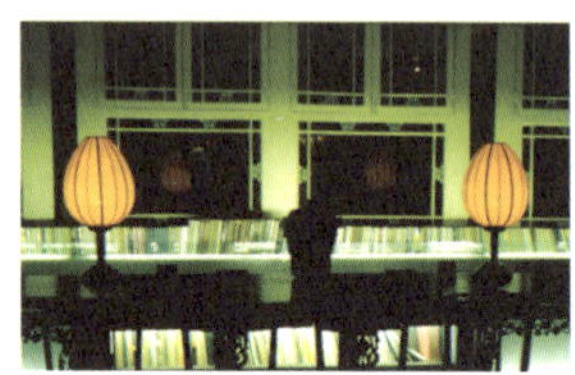

Way back in the 1980s I made it a habit to dine at the Sichuan Restaurant in Xi-rongxian-hutong whenever I was in Beijing. Then in the 1990s, in the course of the overall transformation of the city itself, the Sichuan Restaurant became The China Club, escaping the unfortunate fate of destruction, which beset many of Beijing's old *hutong* (alleys). The hotel's rooms, four large and four small, are located in a century-old quadrangle courtyard house. Thanks to careful maintenance, it has retained much of its original charm. The rooms' balconies look out onto a sea of classic tiled roofs of neighboring houses and the greenery in their courtyards, while the interior design is a marriage of classic folk art and pre-revolutionary Shanghai-style francophilia: the immense but snug bed, the soft velvet maroon sofa decked with white lace, the faded parquet floor with its gentle gleam, the daring but apt fuchsia towels, and the wooden windows and screens decorated with relief-work. There is something very new in this old structure.

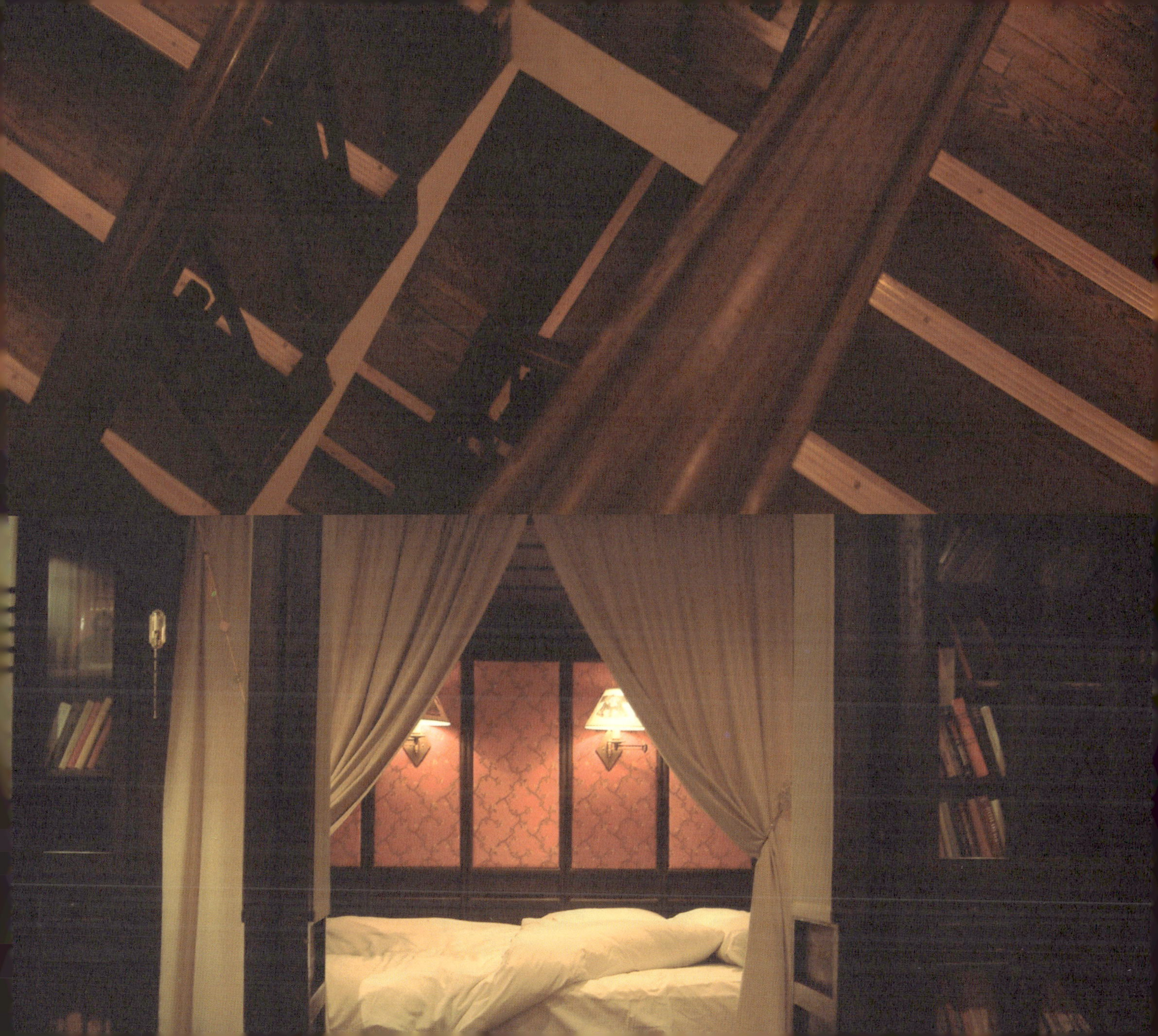

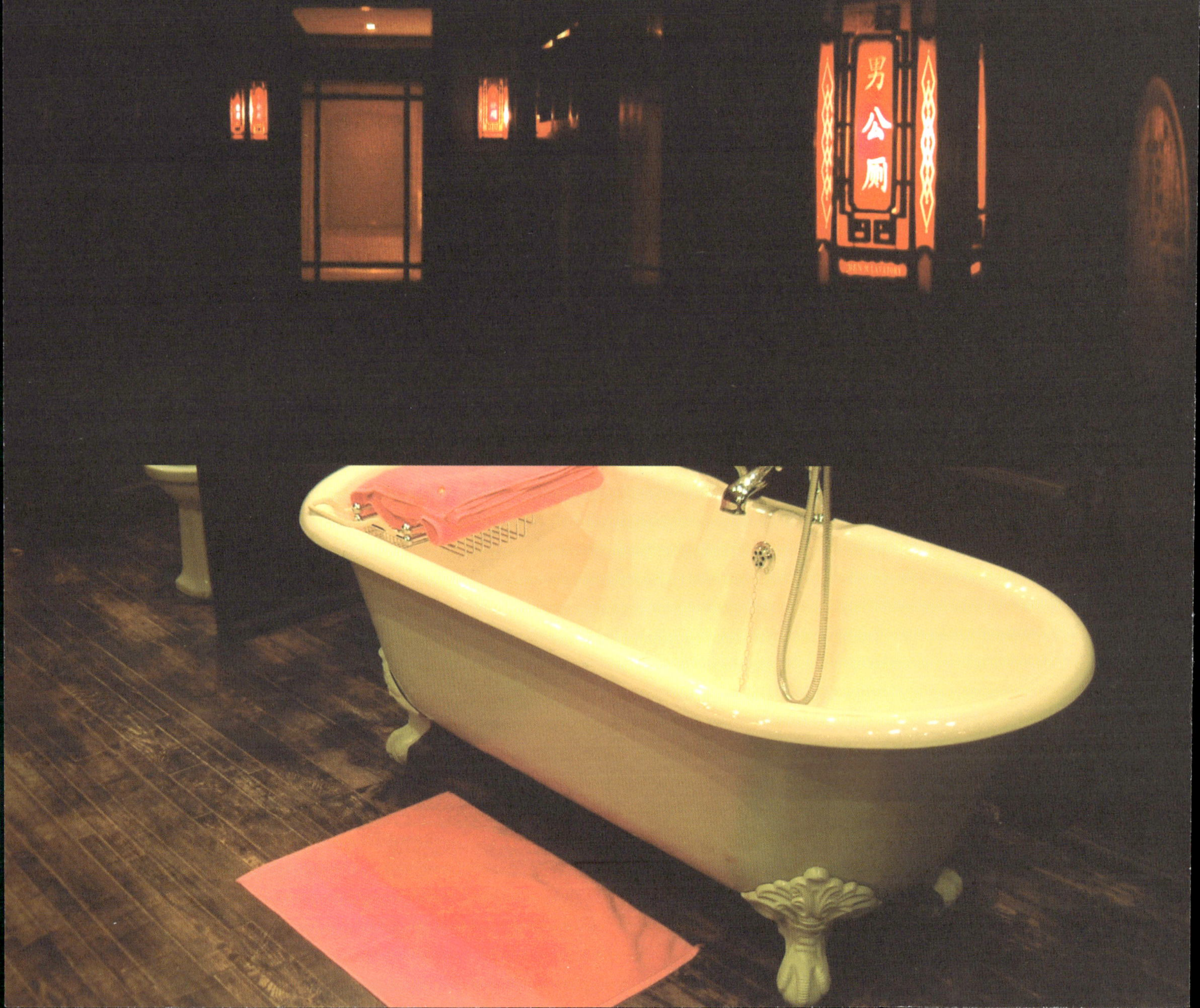
男公厕

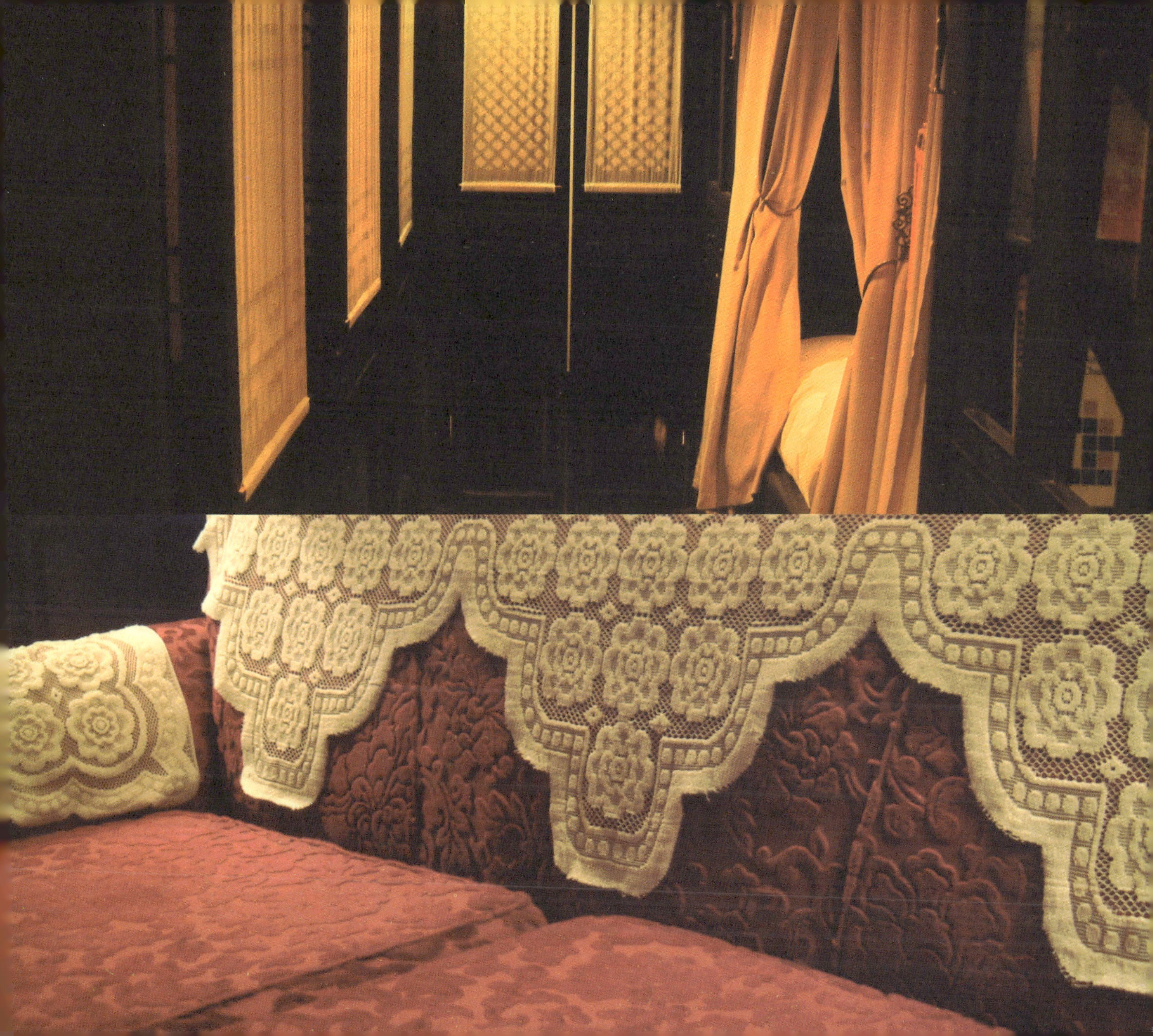

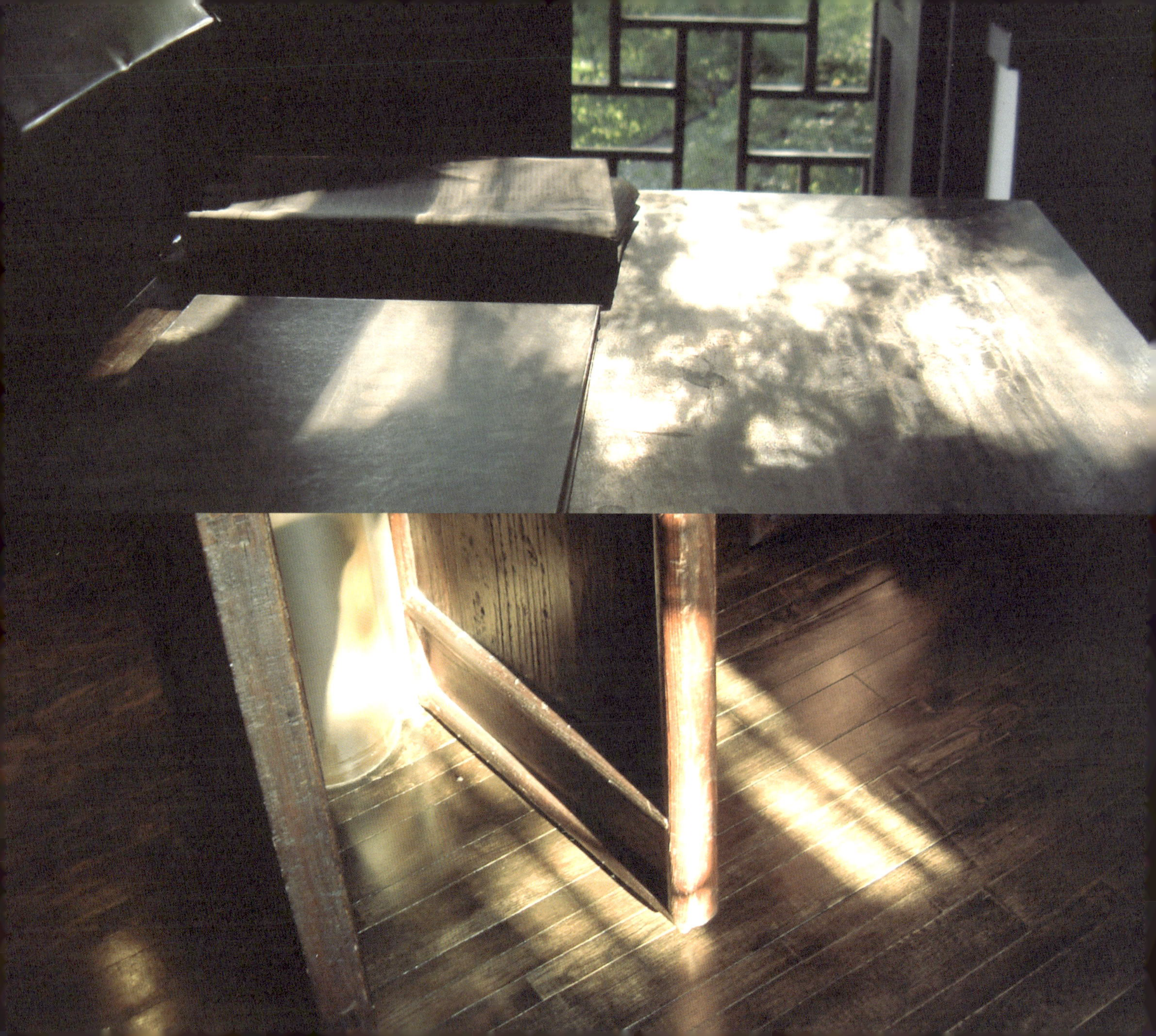

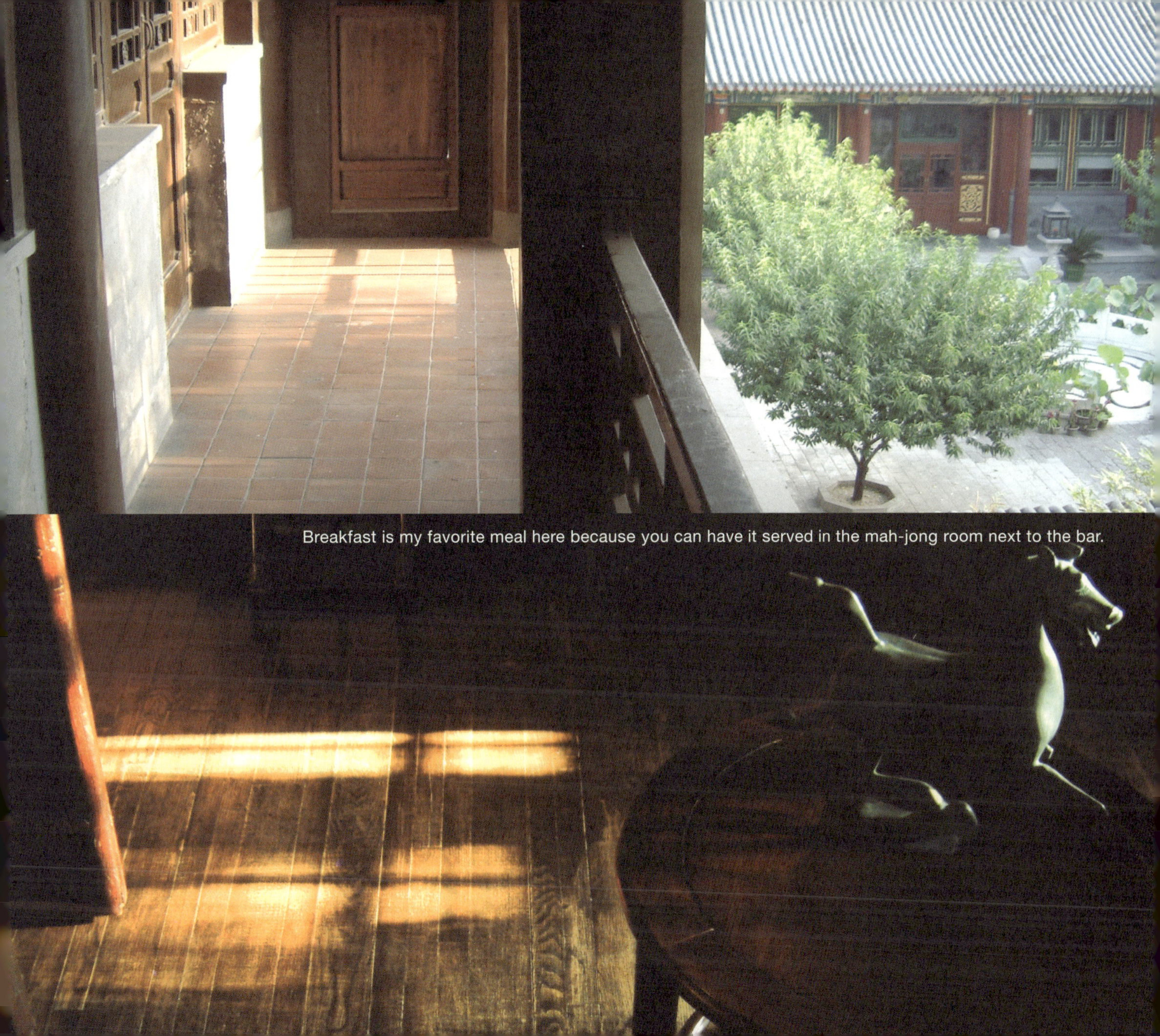

Breakfast is my favorite meal here because you can have it served in the mah-jong room next to the bar.

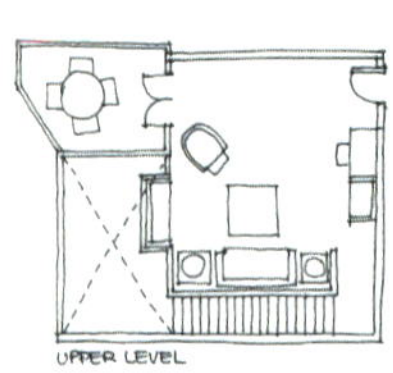

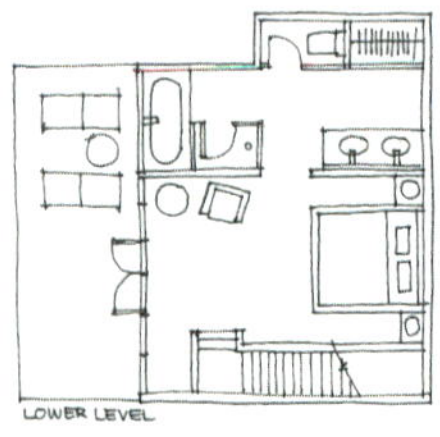

03 FEB 2002 DUPLEX SUITE ?? $282

Four Seasons Hotel at Sayan

OF PALMS AND CYCADS

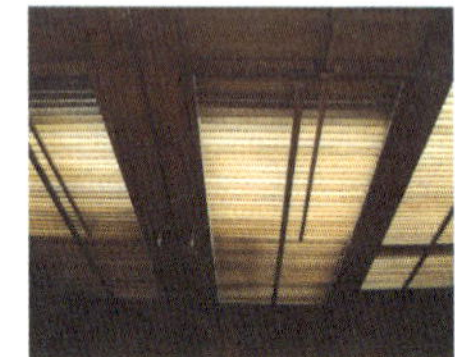

The Four Seasons at Sayan stands above all other hotels of its kind. The beautiful bar looks out onto an expansive misty palm forest, as lush, captivating, and memorable as the one in the opening sequence of Wong Kar-wai's film *Days of Being Wild*, which blew me away when I first saw it in 1990. Placed in harmony with the contours of the slopes on which it is located, the hotel is tucked away in a valley, removed from the busy traffic of the highway. At the top of the complex is a round lotus pond accessed by a wooden walkway. Below that, as you descend the slope, are the hotel lobby, the restaurant, the gym, the spa, the rooms, and finally, the swimming pool. A babbling brook runs just below the pool. I was disappointed by the Four Seasons in Istanbul because it did not preserve any sense of the history associated with the old prison from which it is remodeled. What distinguishes this one from others is the designer's astute sensibility of marrying structure to topography.

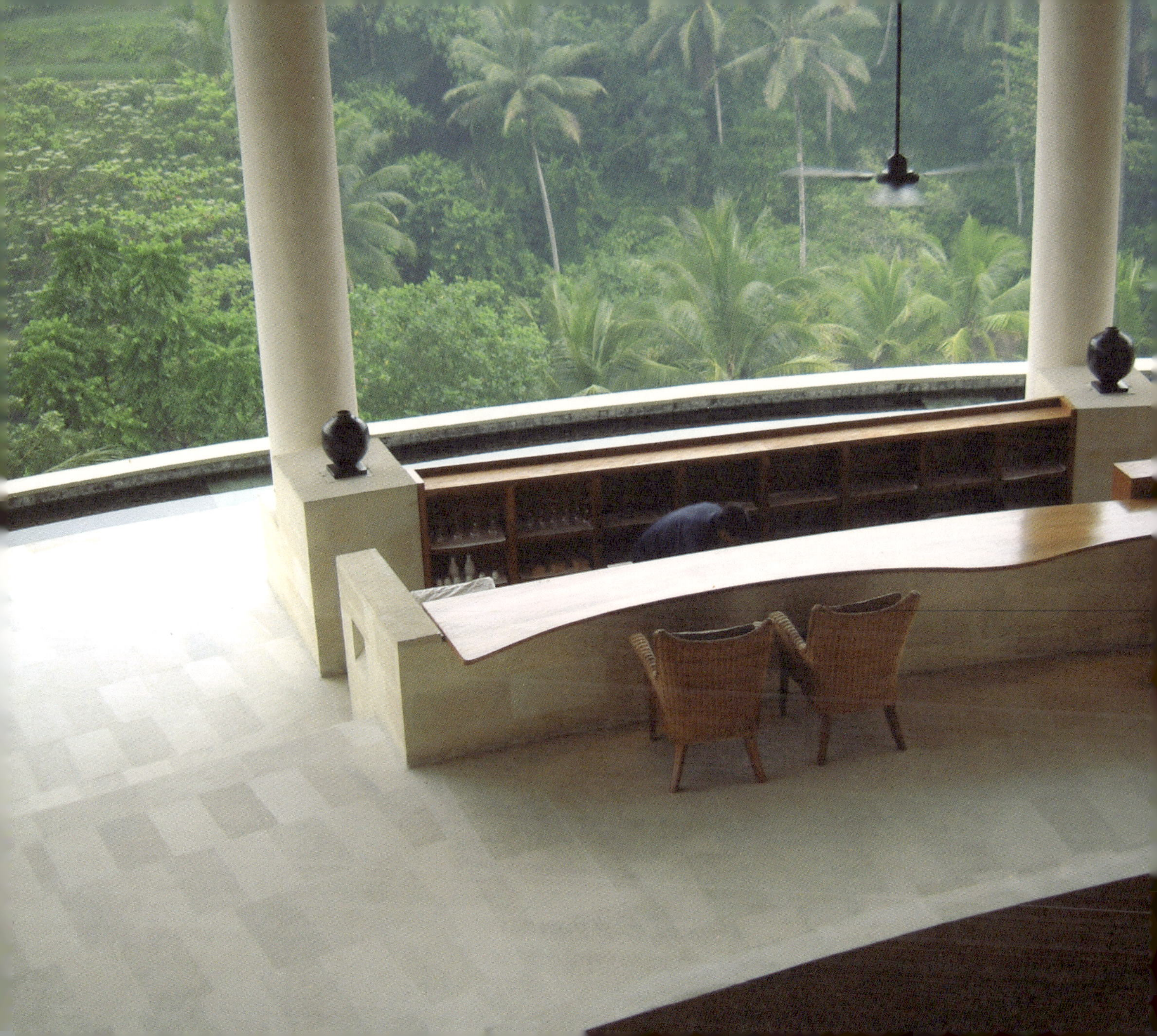

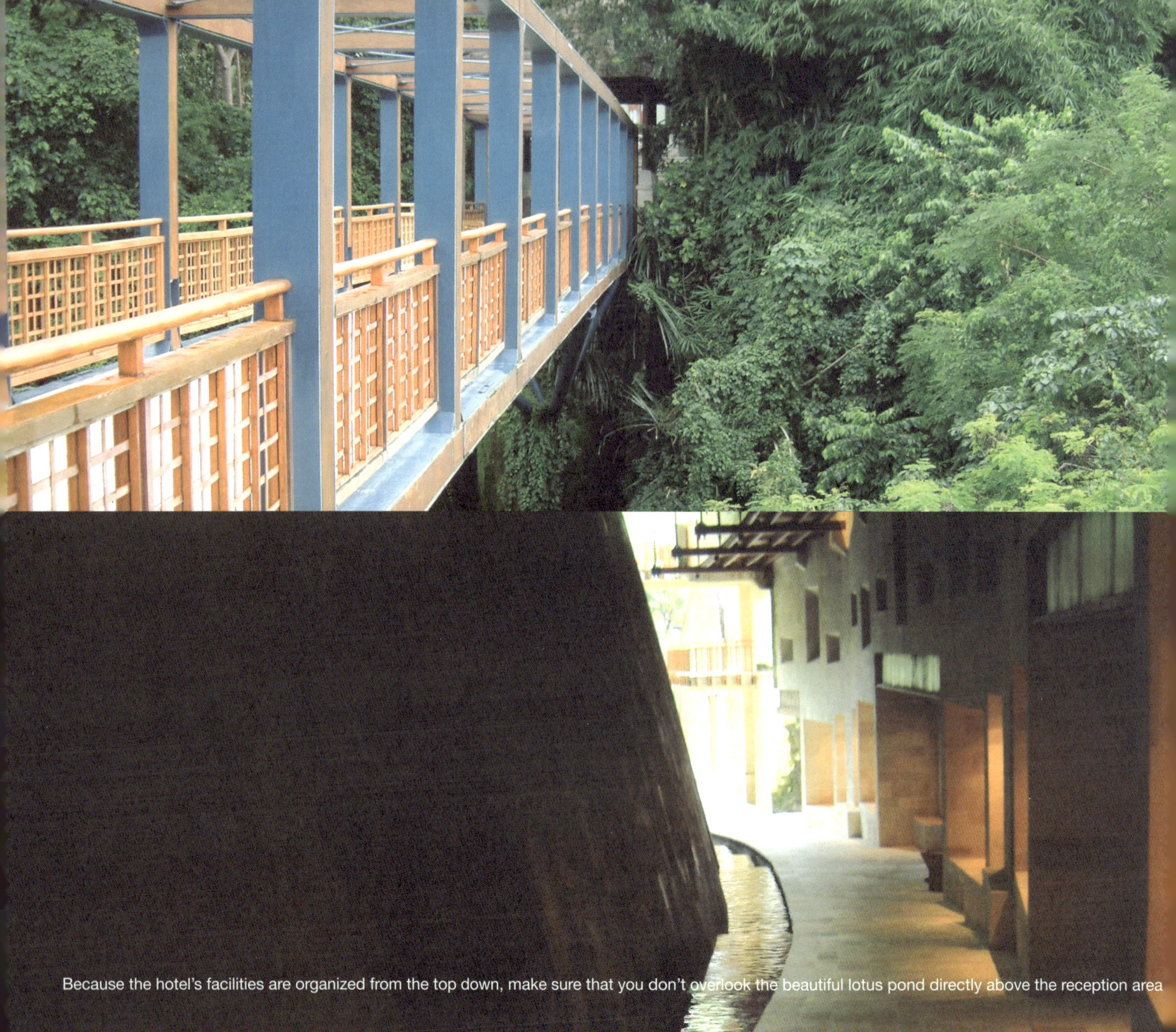

Because the hotel's facilities are organized from the top down, make sure that you don't overlook the beautiful lotus pond directly above the reception area

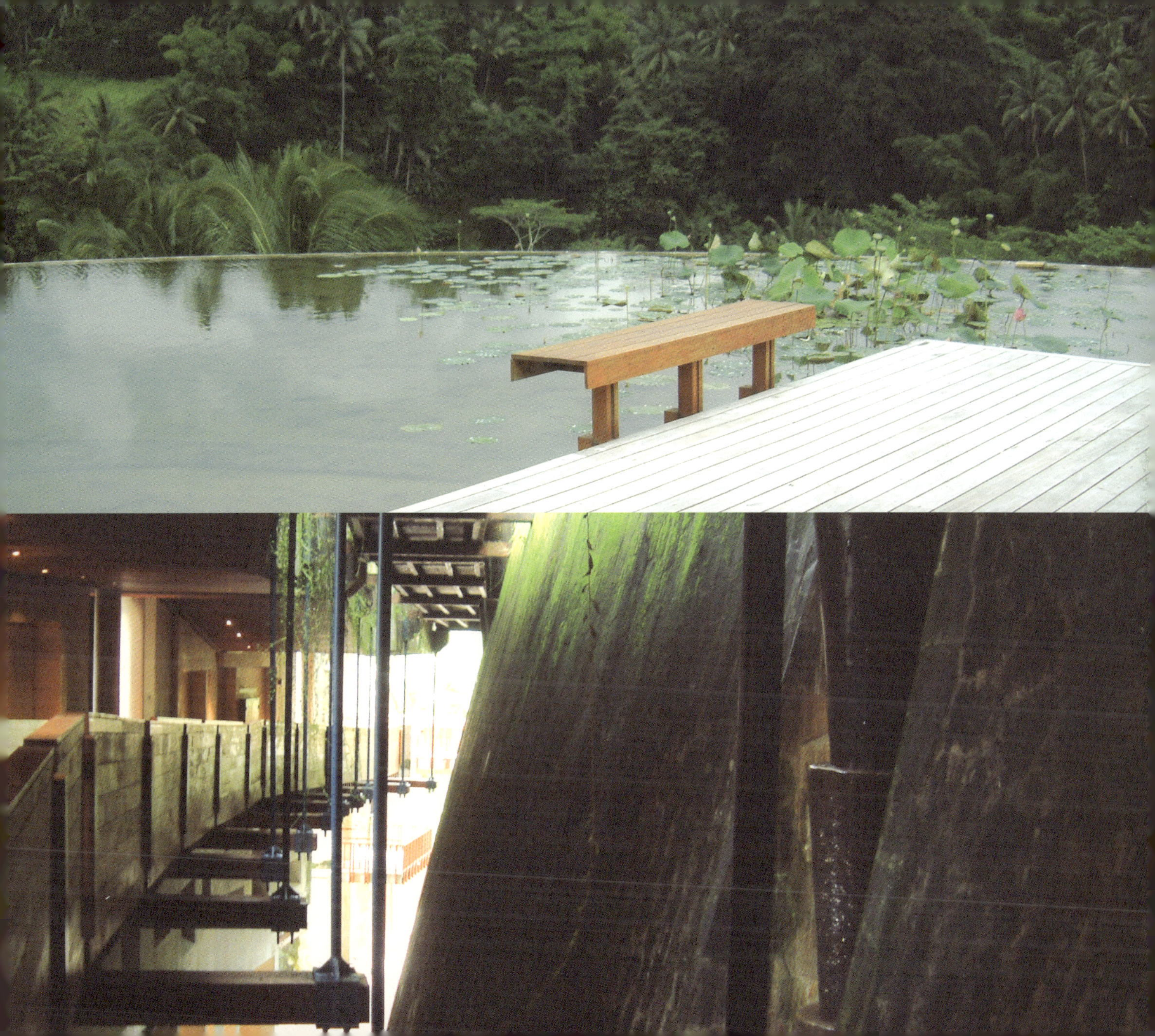

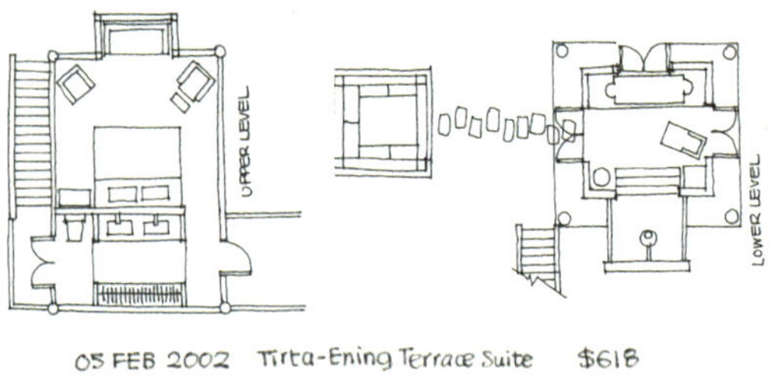

Hotel Begawan Giri

NURTURING NATURE

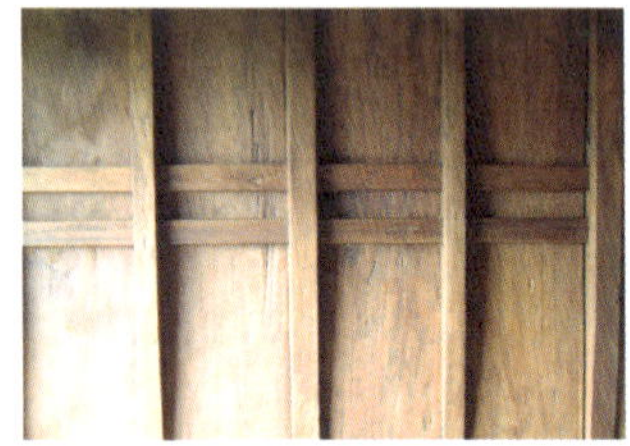

I've come to the central part of Bali to escape the cities. The resort hotel *Begawan Giri* is located in a secluded spot deep in the forest and is accessed via a small road that cuts through the valley. Here, you are immediately struck by the absence of noise, except for the nightly croaking of frogs coming from the nearby river and rice paddies. The hotel doesn't have rooms *per se*. Instead guests stay in fully equipped bungalows or suites: twenty-two in total, grouped together in units of four to five and sharing the common facilities. A butler tends to each small complex.

On my stay, a ten-minute stroll along a mossy path took me to a spa (one of several on the premises), and I spent an entire afternoon luxuriating in it, having the place all to myself. The hotel's secluded, naturalistic location has its unique advantage and charm. There is no need for privacy and enclosure so that the bathrooms, featuring bathtubs that are carved from a single slab of granite, can be located *al fresco*, while the forest is just a few paces away. Paths are illuminated with candles rather than electric lights, and there is even a century-old house built from Java timber, which was painstakingly transported here from Java and now houses an authentic Balinese restaurant. At the Hotel Begawan Giri nature is nurtured in a most un-intrusive way.

It was also a pleasant surprise to learn that a retired husband-and-wife team from Hong Kong once owned the hotel, which is now a member of Singapore's COMO Group.

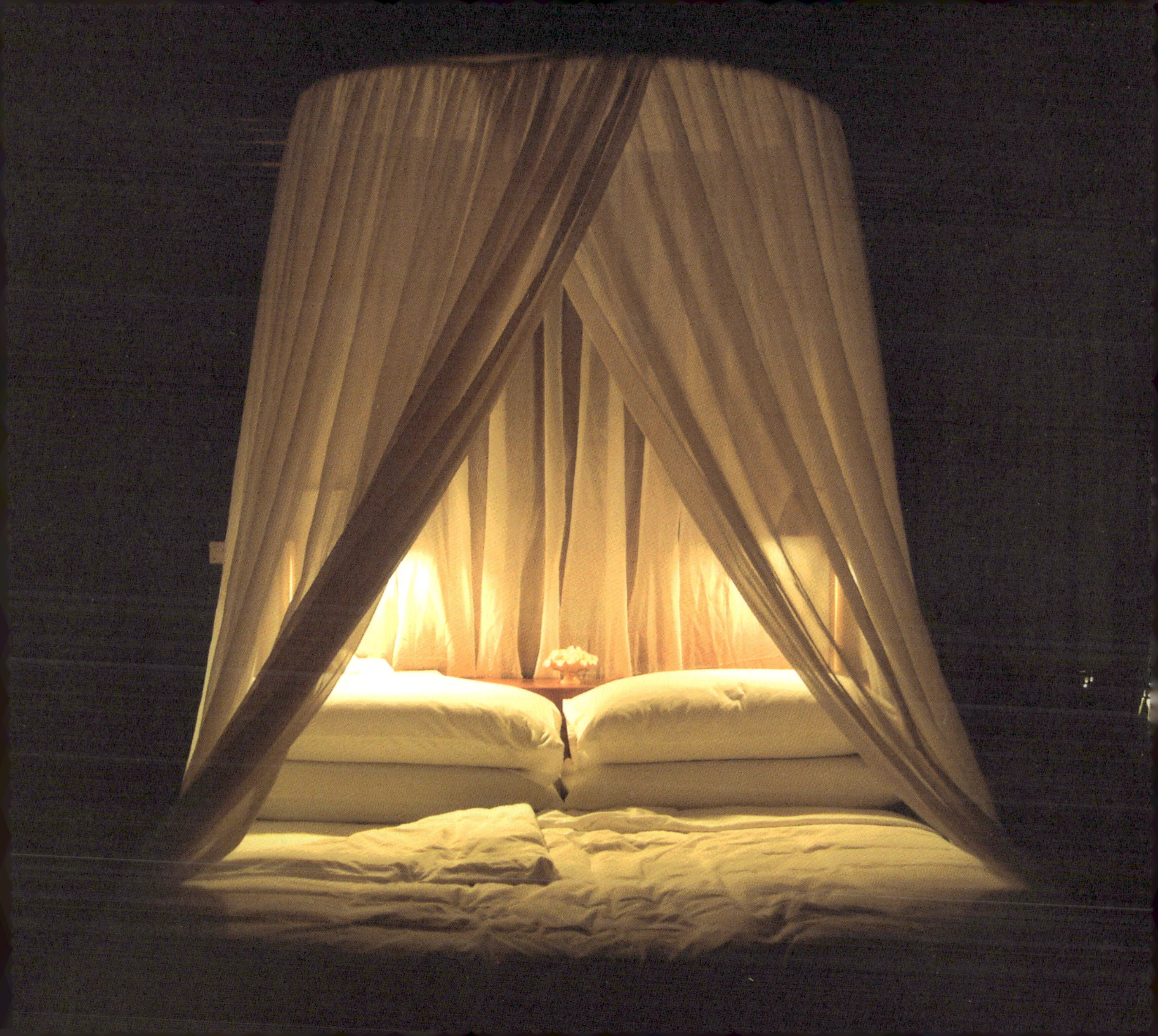

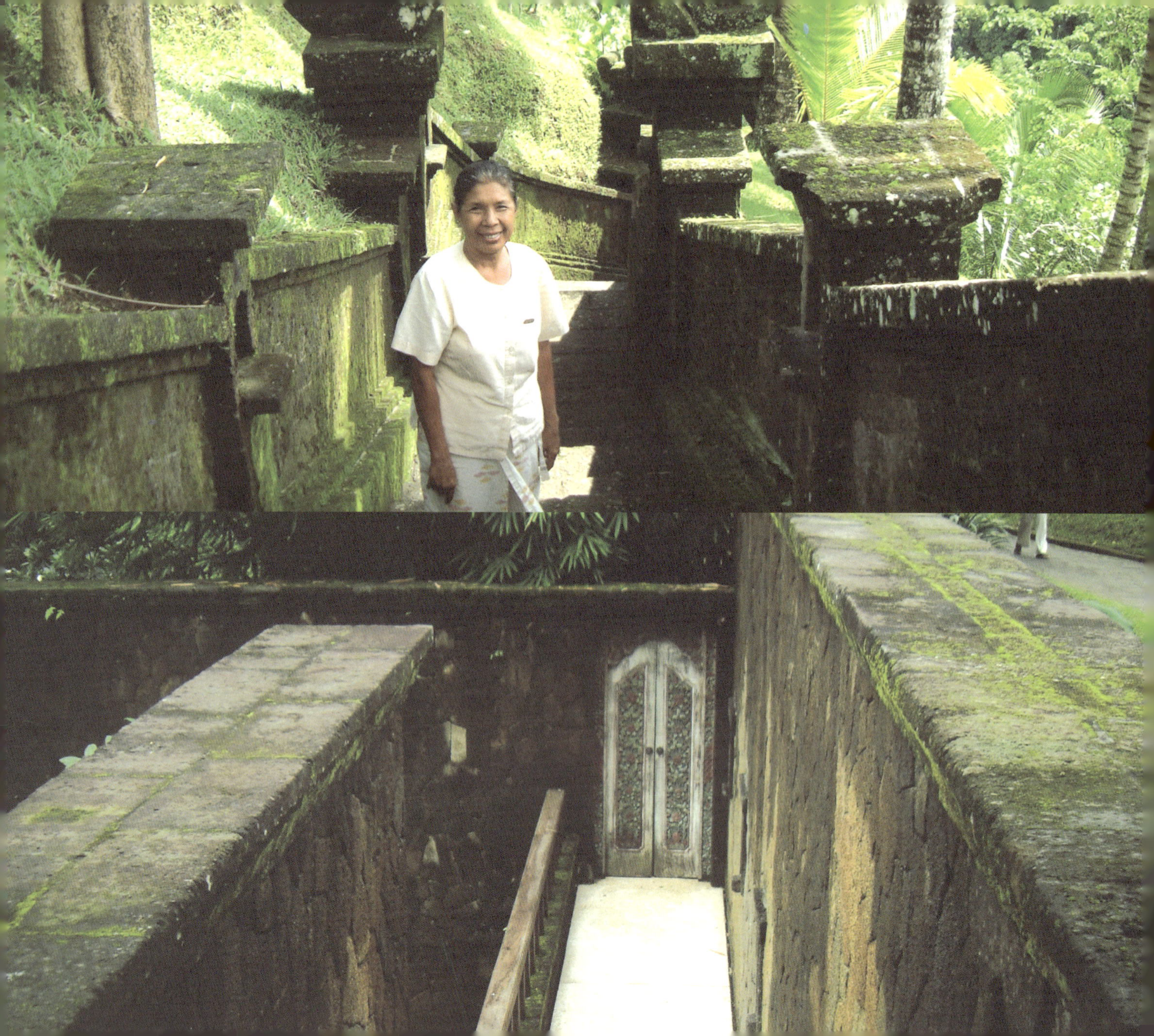

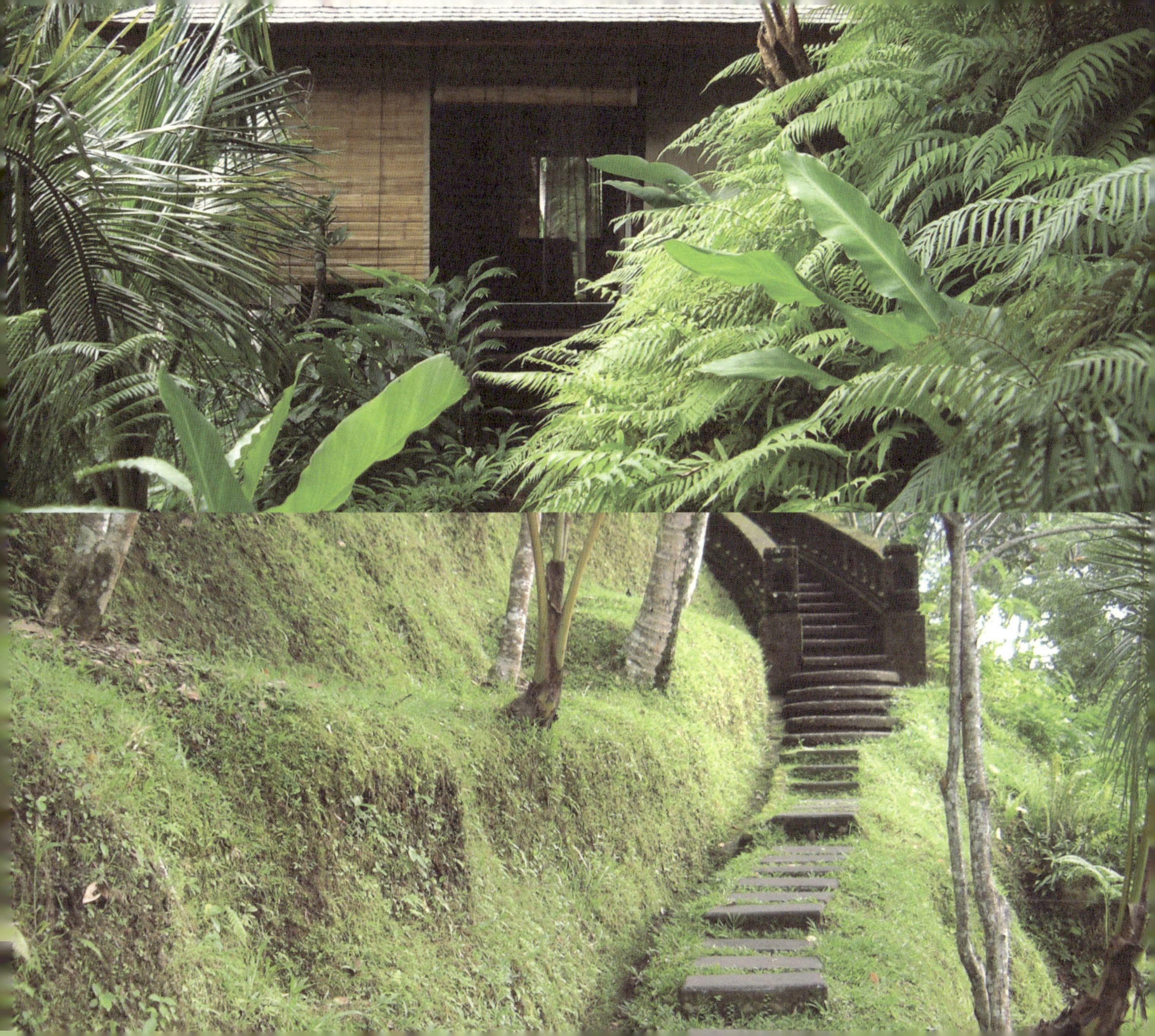

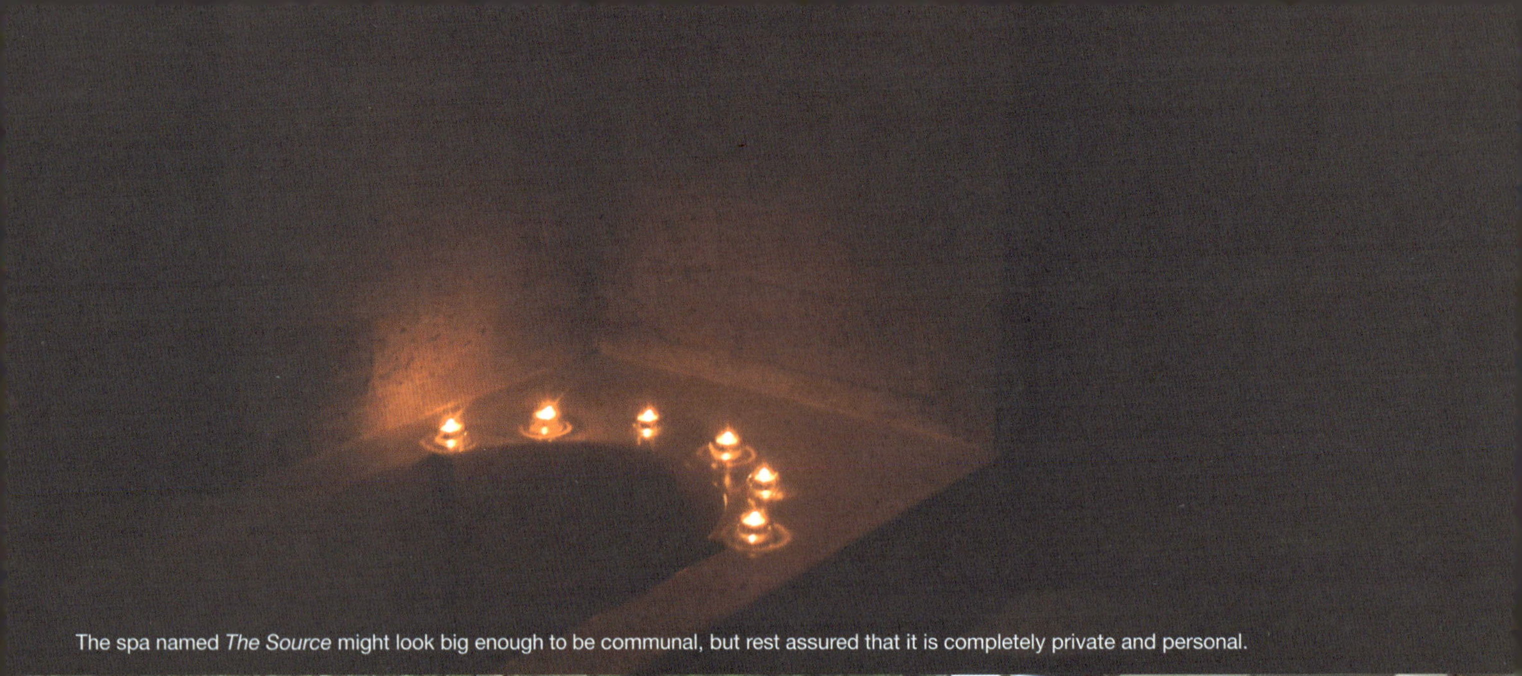

The spa named *The Source* might look big enough to be communal, but rest assured that it is completely private and personal.

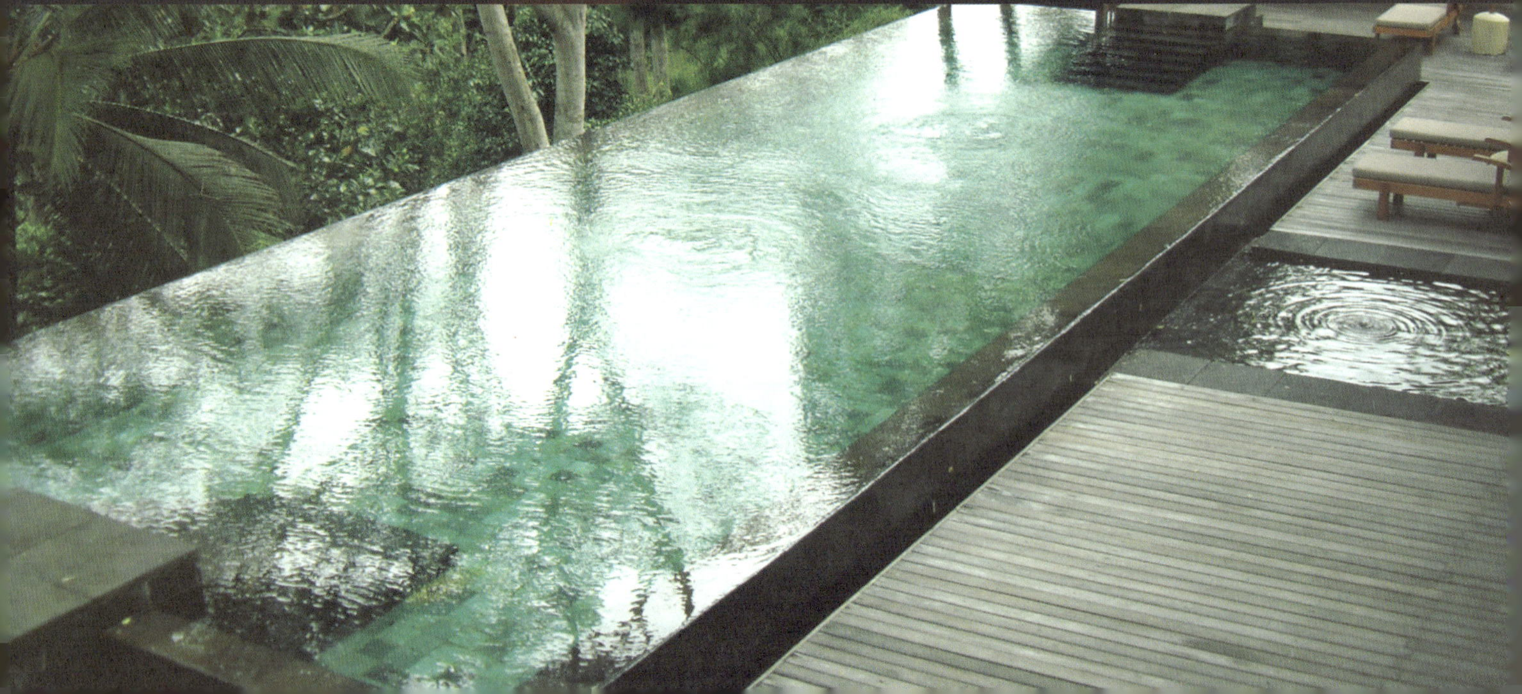

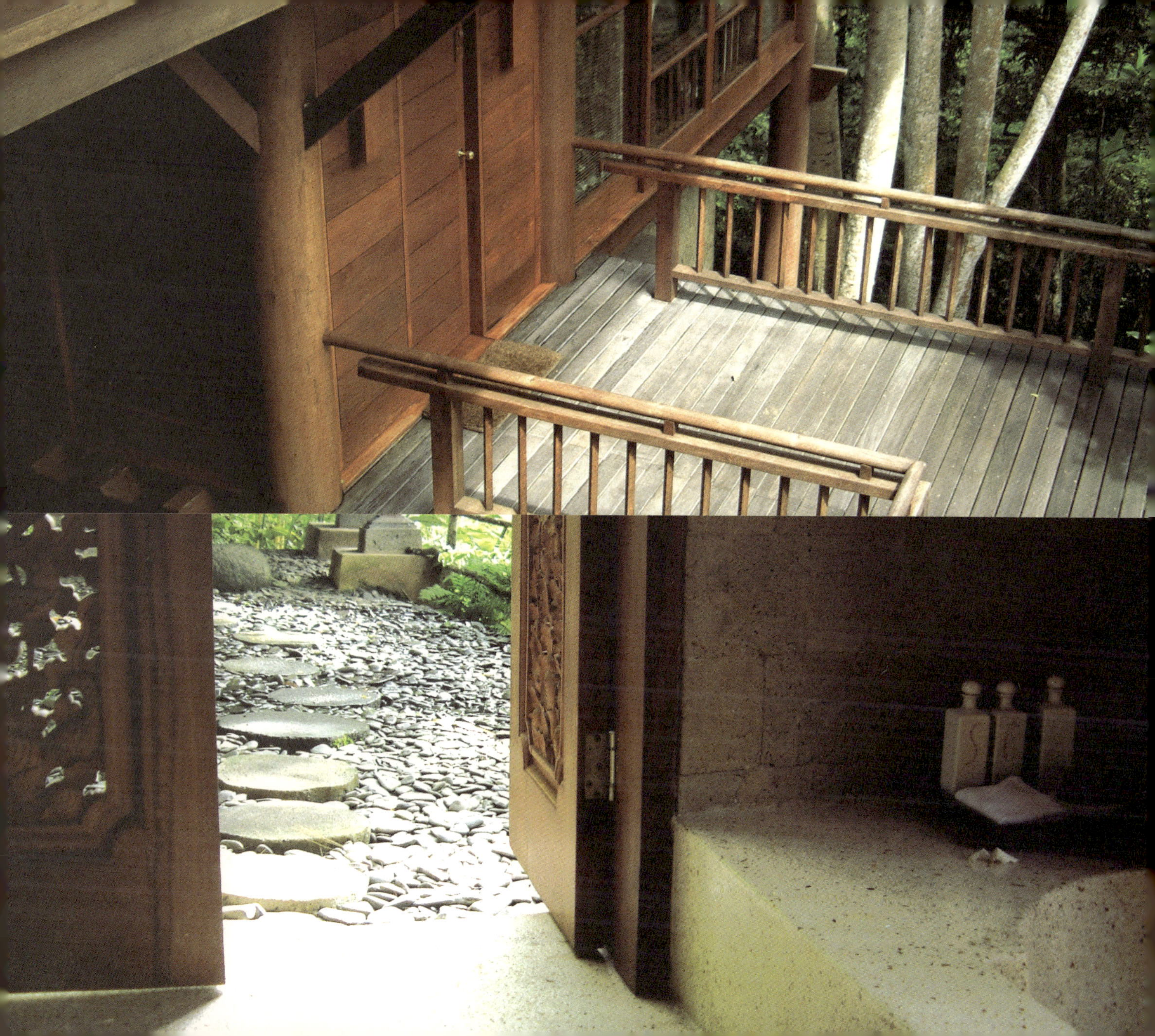

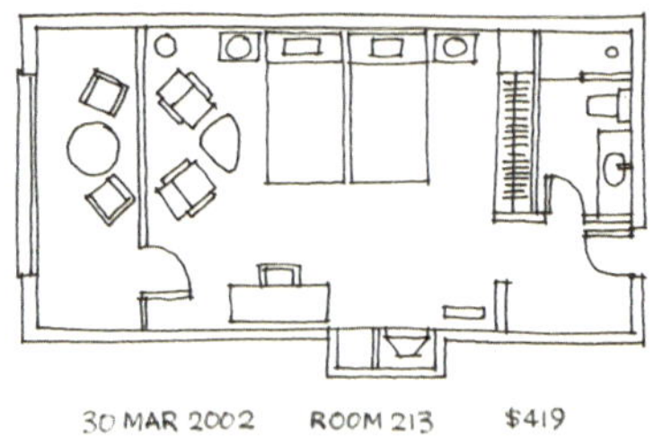

Hotel Parco dei Principi

FOREVER YOUNG

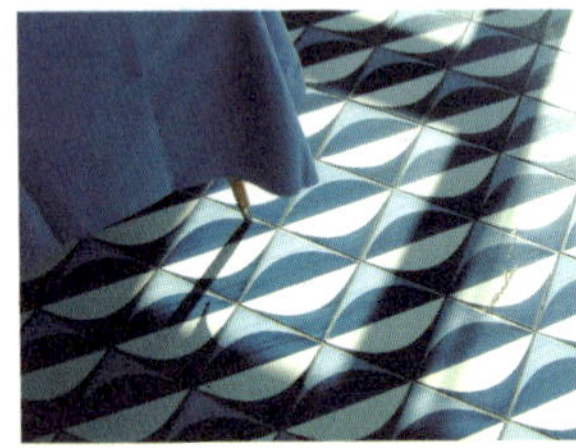

The forty-odd-year-old Hotel Parco dei Principi perches high atop a precipitous cliff. As our bus zigzags its way up the narrow road, I can see the cliff falling vertically down to the azure blue sea far below. I fancy myself a tern soaring freely and effortlessly out to sea. This must have been how Gio Ponti felt when he first thought of designing a hotel at such a breathtaking location. He saw his idea come to fruition late in life in 1962, and what a time it must have been! The eternally youthful master designed over a hundred different tiles for the rooms of his hotel, all based on the simple color schemes of white-and-blue and white-and-green, punctuated by some cleverly placed pebbles. The rooms may look a little like hostel rooms today, but they are by no means dated. Outside, beyond the balcony, lie the seemingly boundless Mediterranean and Italy's only active volcano, Mount Etna. Everything at the Hotel Parco is so simple and pared-down that it absorbs and calms you at the same time. Staying here I ask myself: "In my old age, will I manage to stay as young-at-heart as Ponti in *his* old age?"

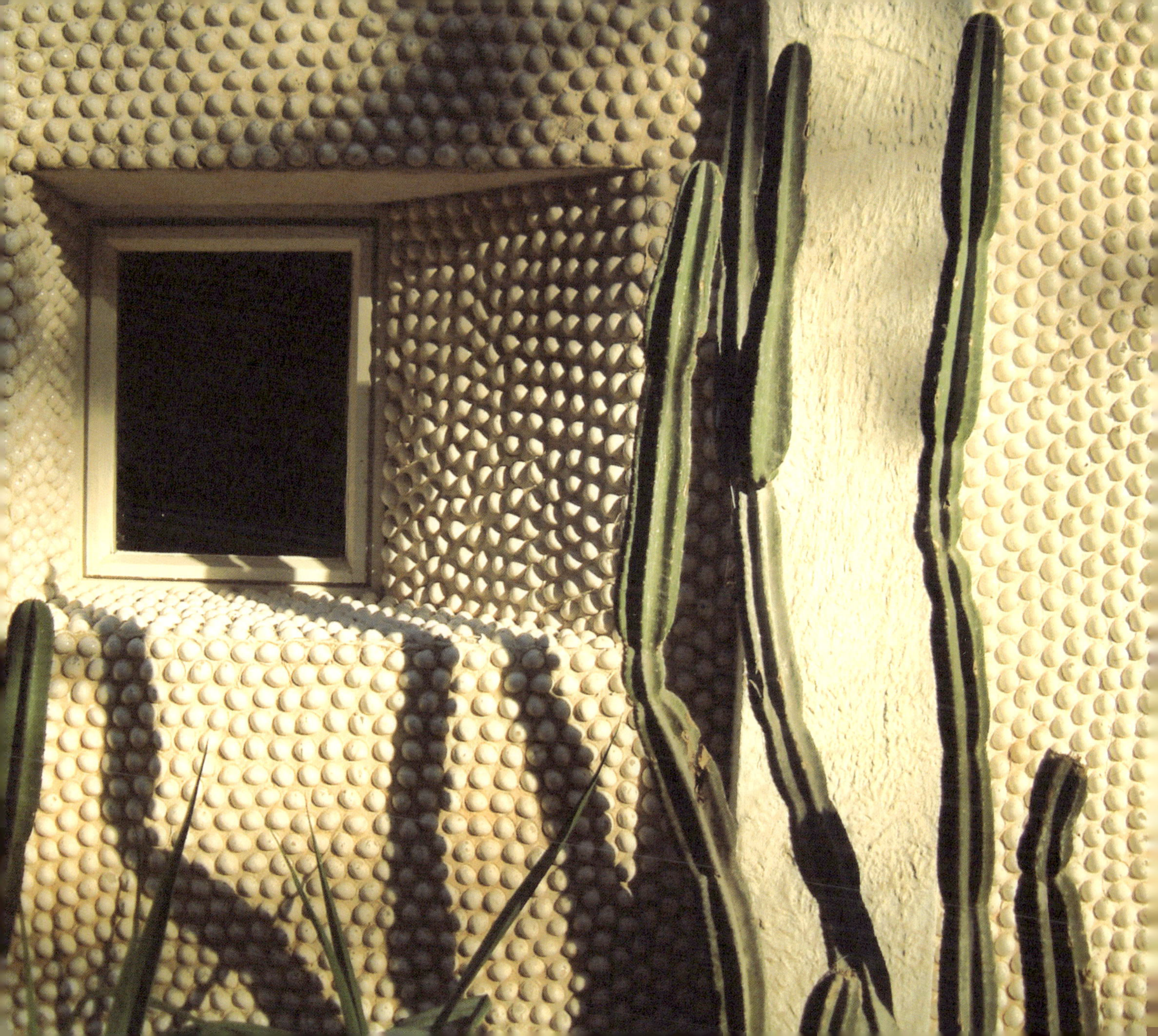

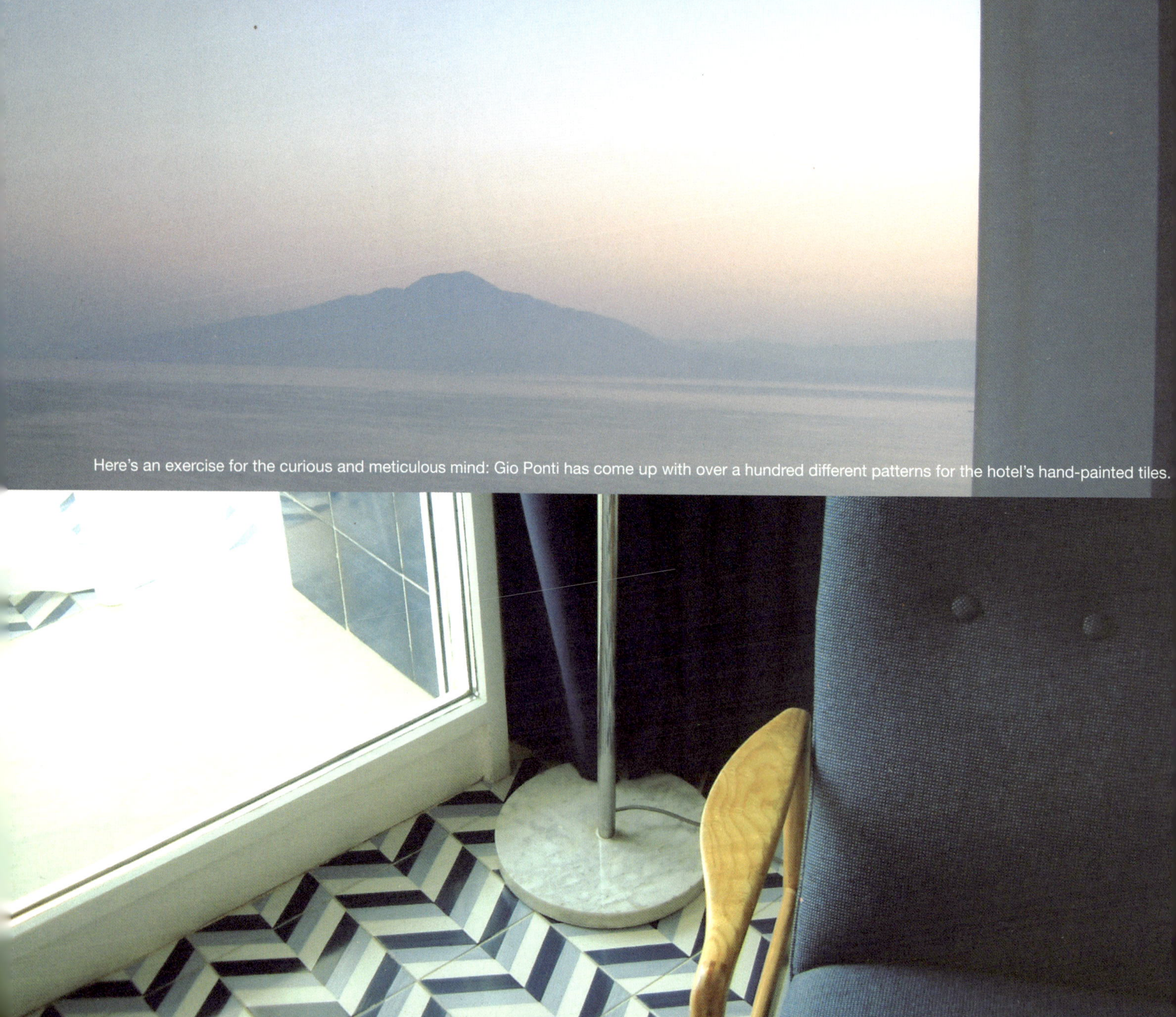

Here's an exercise for the curious and meticulous mind: Gio Ponti has come up with over a hundred different patterns for the hotel's hand-painted tiles.

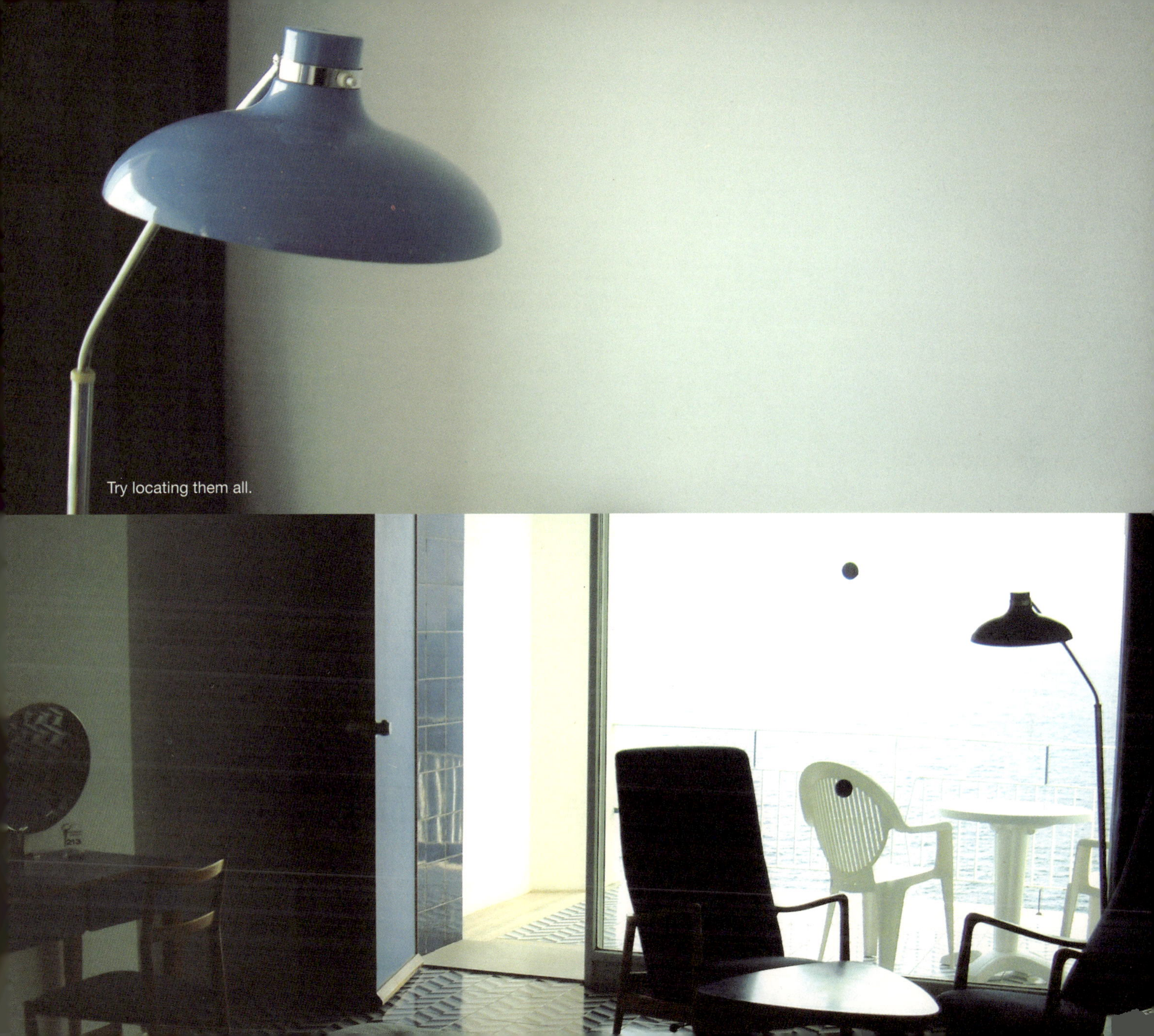

Try locating them all.

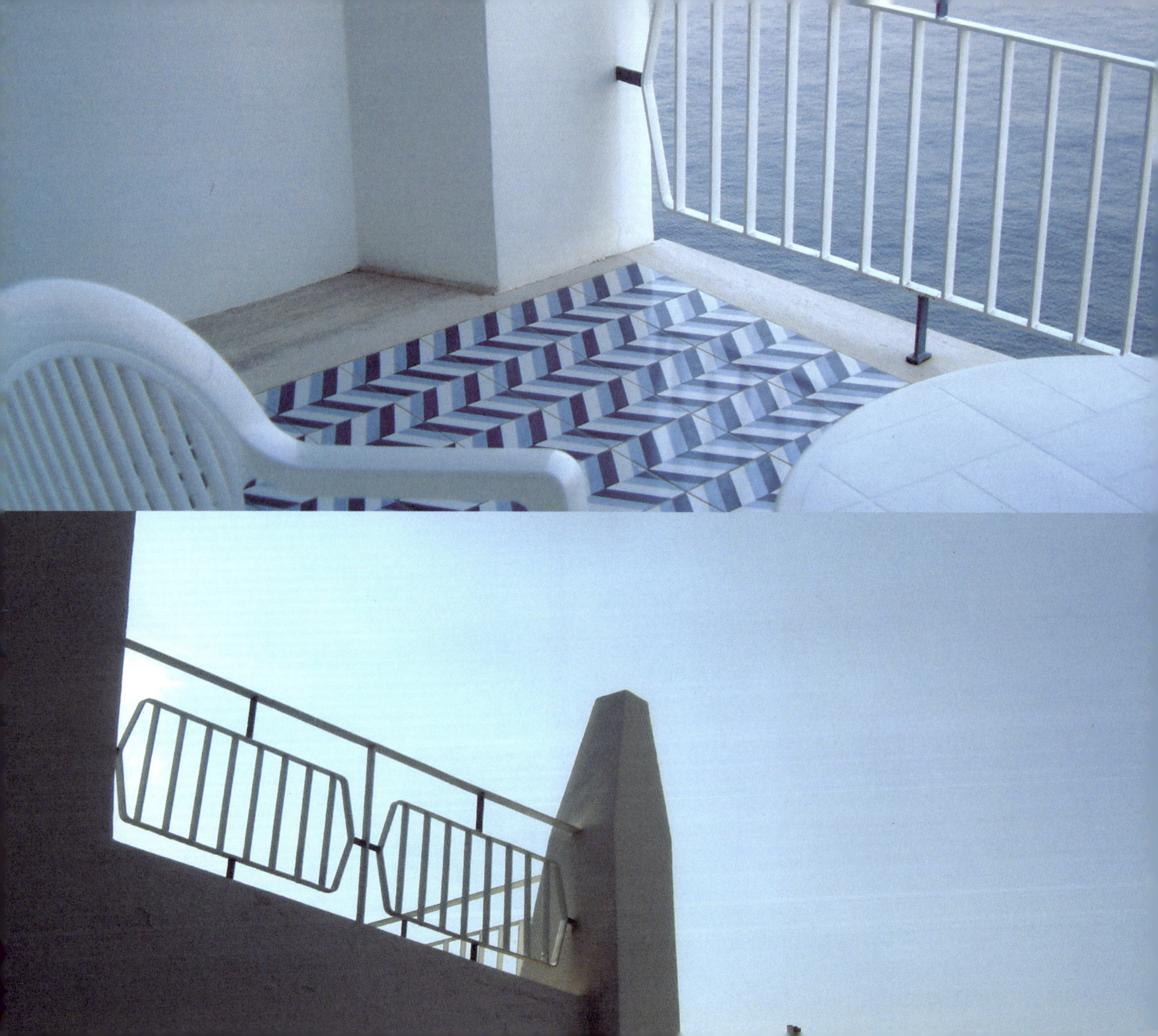

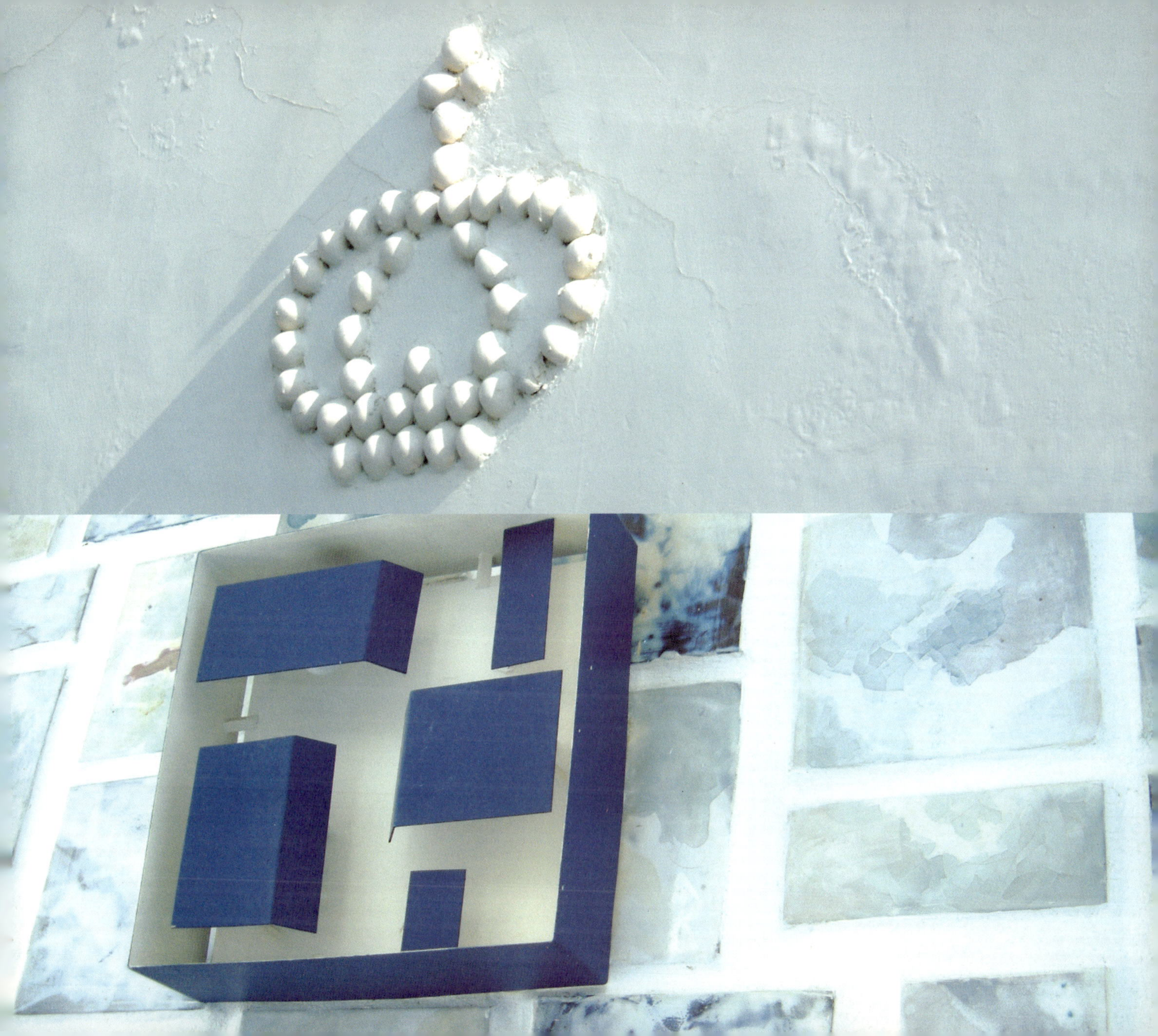

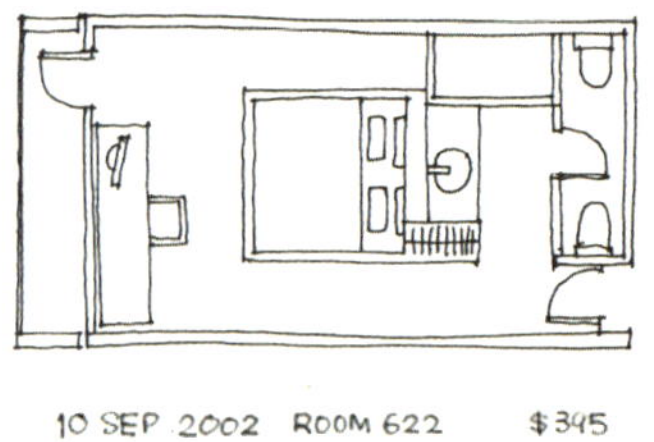

ES Hotel
(now Radisson SAS Hotel)

AN EXPERIMENT IN THE ETERNAL CITY

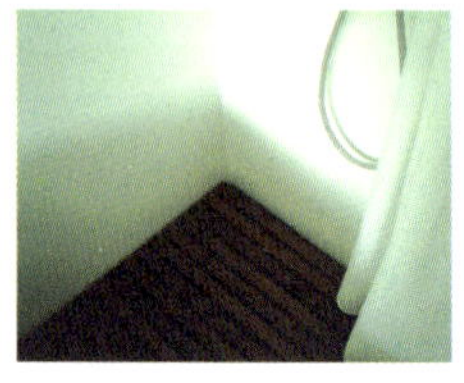

The *ES* is unusual among the new hotels of Rome, as it is not housed in one of the city's myriad antique buildings, but in a brandnew multi-story structure adjacent to the train station. The exterior is not the only thing that gives the hotel its sense of newness and experimentalism—the interior design is remarkable as well. The reception counter is an elliptical structure with changeable shape fashioned out of translucent fabric, and the guest rooms have a unique set of proportions. The rooms' wooden floors curve up to hold the wash basins; the shower is located right behind the bed, shielded by a shower curtain and separated from the bedroom by the bed's undulating headboard; a glass pane, a reflective round panel that also serves as a mirror, defines the bedroom and bathroom areas. Through a huge glass window, the room looks out onto the hotel's other wing, lit by iridescent lighting, which distinguishes the modern hotel from historical Rome.

Still, even as you marvel at all that is new about the ES Hotel, archaeological work goes on in the ground just beneath it—which is probably why the hotel's logo, with its archaic touch, is such an apt symbol of its symbiosis of the very old and the very new.

The hotel was still called ES when I stayed there and wrote this piece. At the time of publication, it had changed hands and is now part of the Radisson SAS chain.

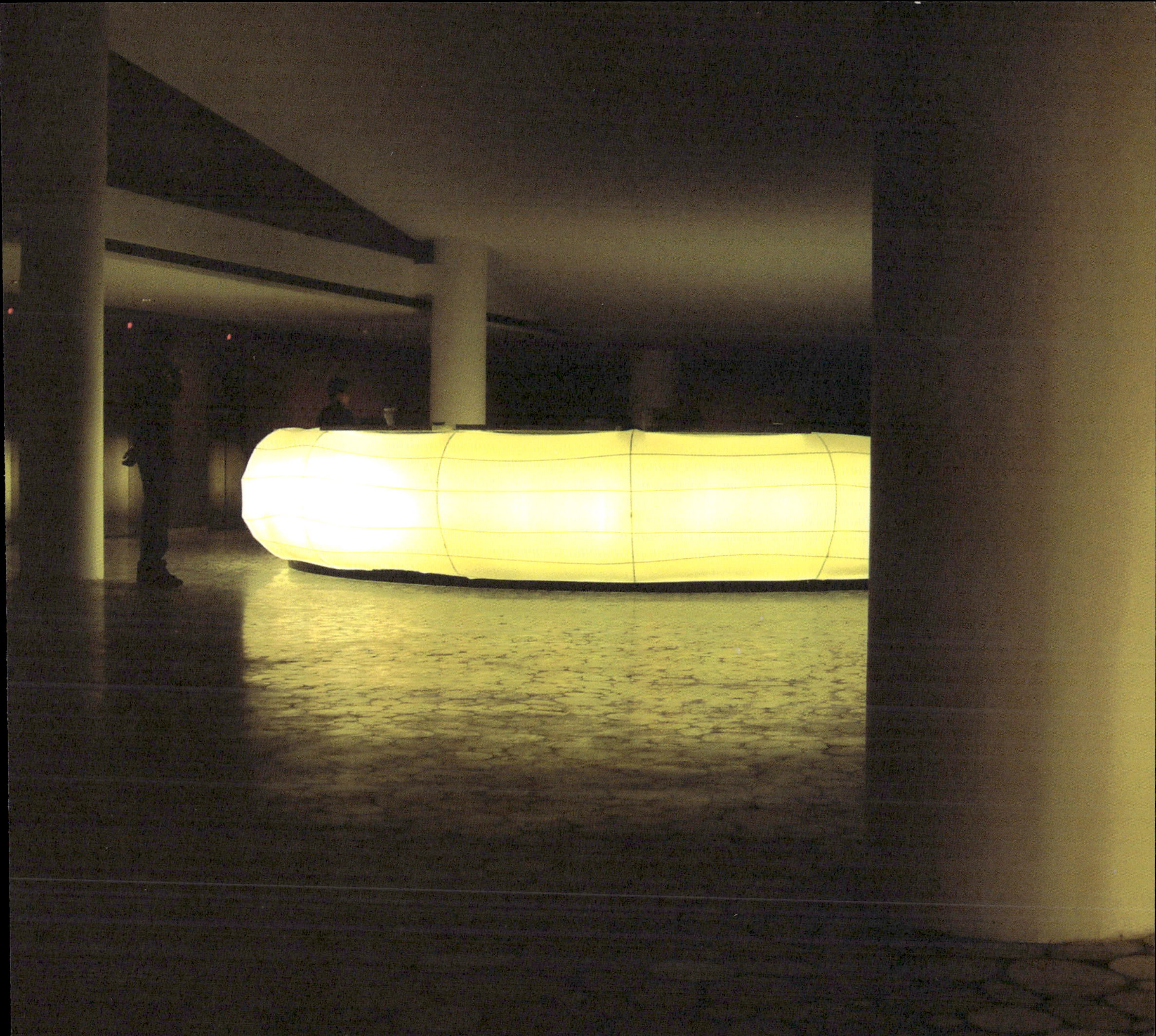

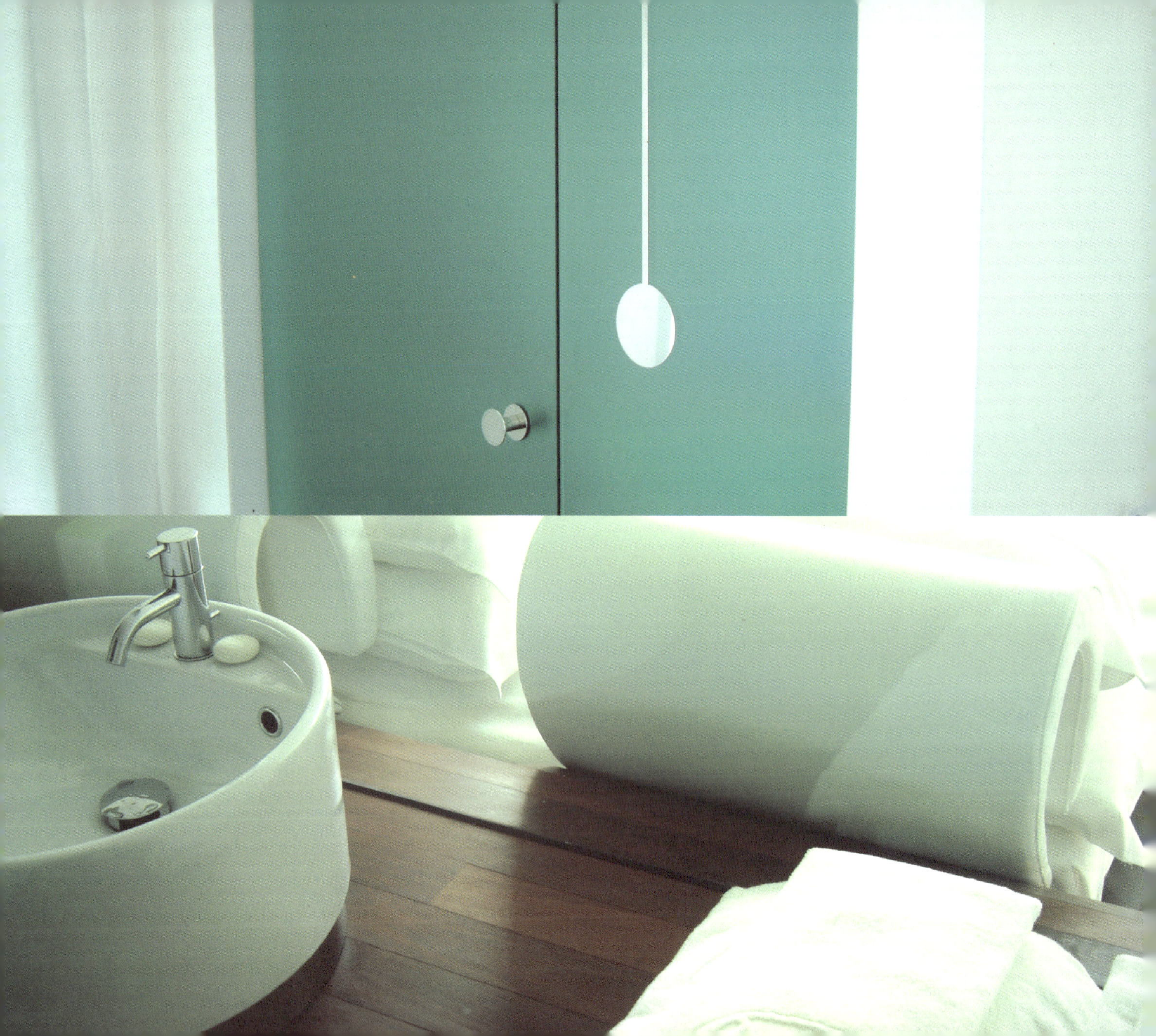

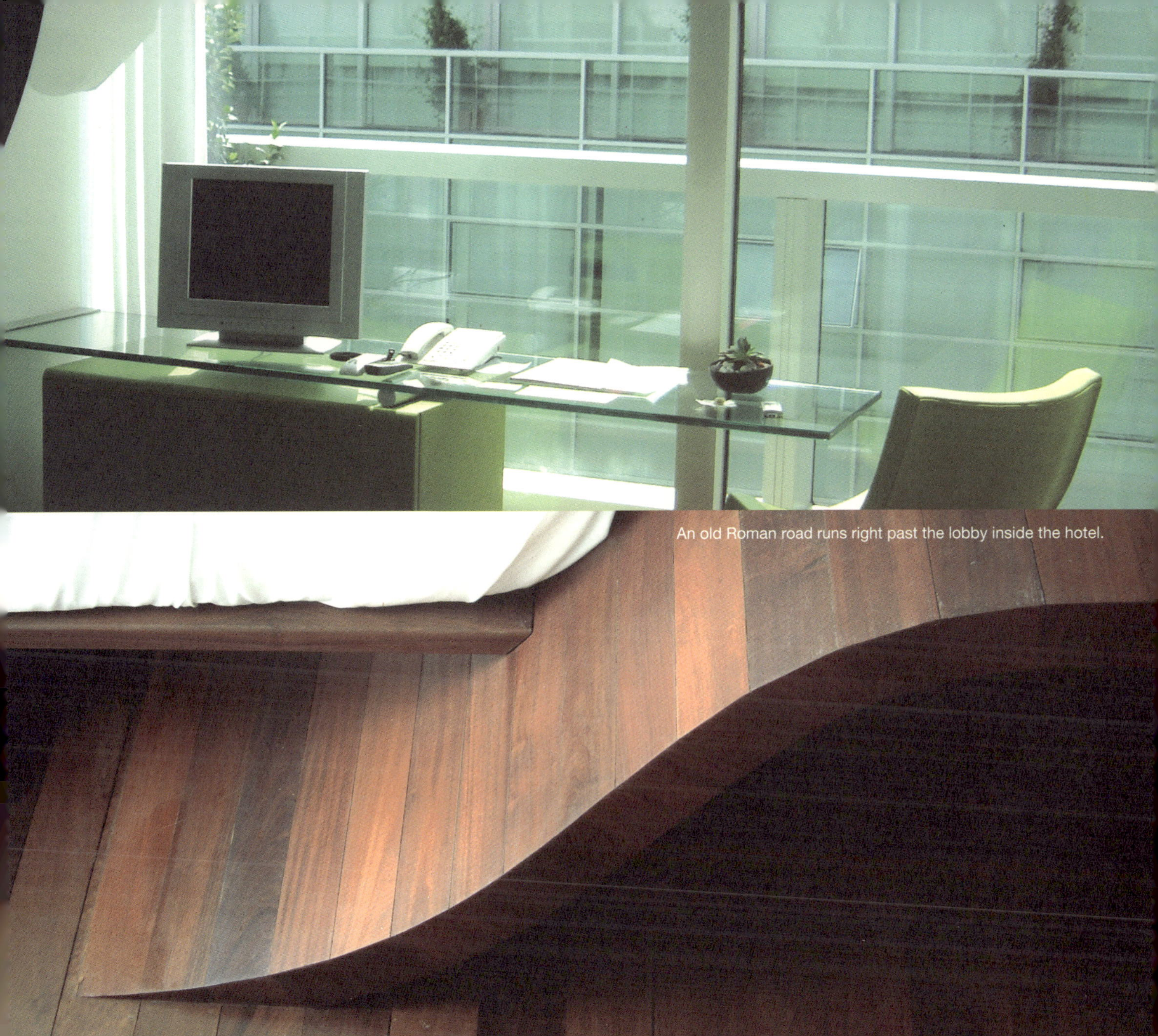

An old Roman road runs right past the lobby inside the hotel.

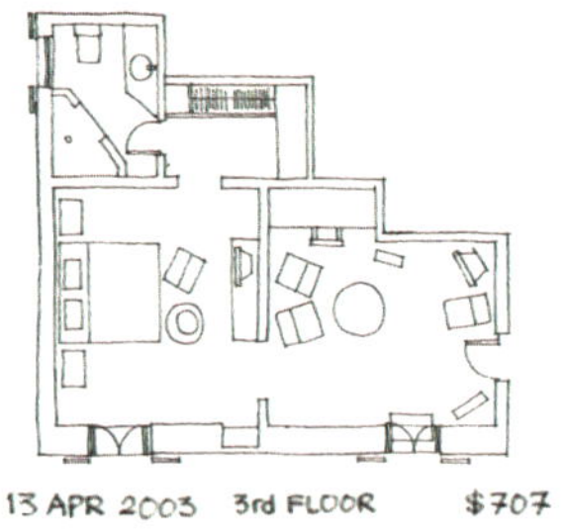

Hotel 3 Rooms

A NEW LEAF IN AN OLD BOOK

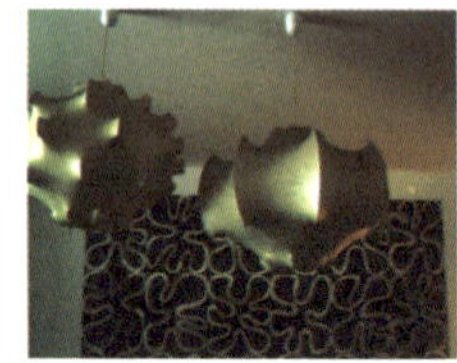

Every aficionado of Milan knows about 10 Corso Como. The concept store founded by Carla Sozzani, former editor-in-chief of the Italian *Vogue*, is even older than Paris's Colette. But unlike Colette, it is not located in the fashionable part of town, but in the city's rather desolate outskirts. Instead of being disadvantaged by this, however, the shop and its surroundings have engaged in a mutually vitalizing relationship. The store has breathed life back into the old proletarian neighborhood and is in turn given a unique identity by the history and character of the area. 10 Corso Como, together with the Hotel 3 Rooms located inside it, is a prime example of urban renewal and has become a center of one of Milan's key redevelopment areas. The hotel literally has only three rooms on three stories, each measuring around 1,000 square feet. Due to their huge size the rooms are more like individual apartments than hotel rooms, and the neighborhood is still inhabited by its original residents. As its brochure states, the hotel is a true "home away from home." Artist Kris Ruths furnished the rooms in an un-self-conscious and user-oriented way. Consideration for the hotel guests is seen in the tiniest detail. After guests check in, they are served with piping hot towels that are reminiscent of fresh-baked bread, and the "slow breakfast" served in the morning isn't prepared by chefs but by food designers. All this contributes to making 10 Corso Como my favorite part of Milan.

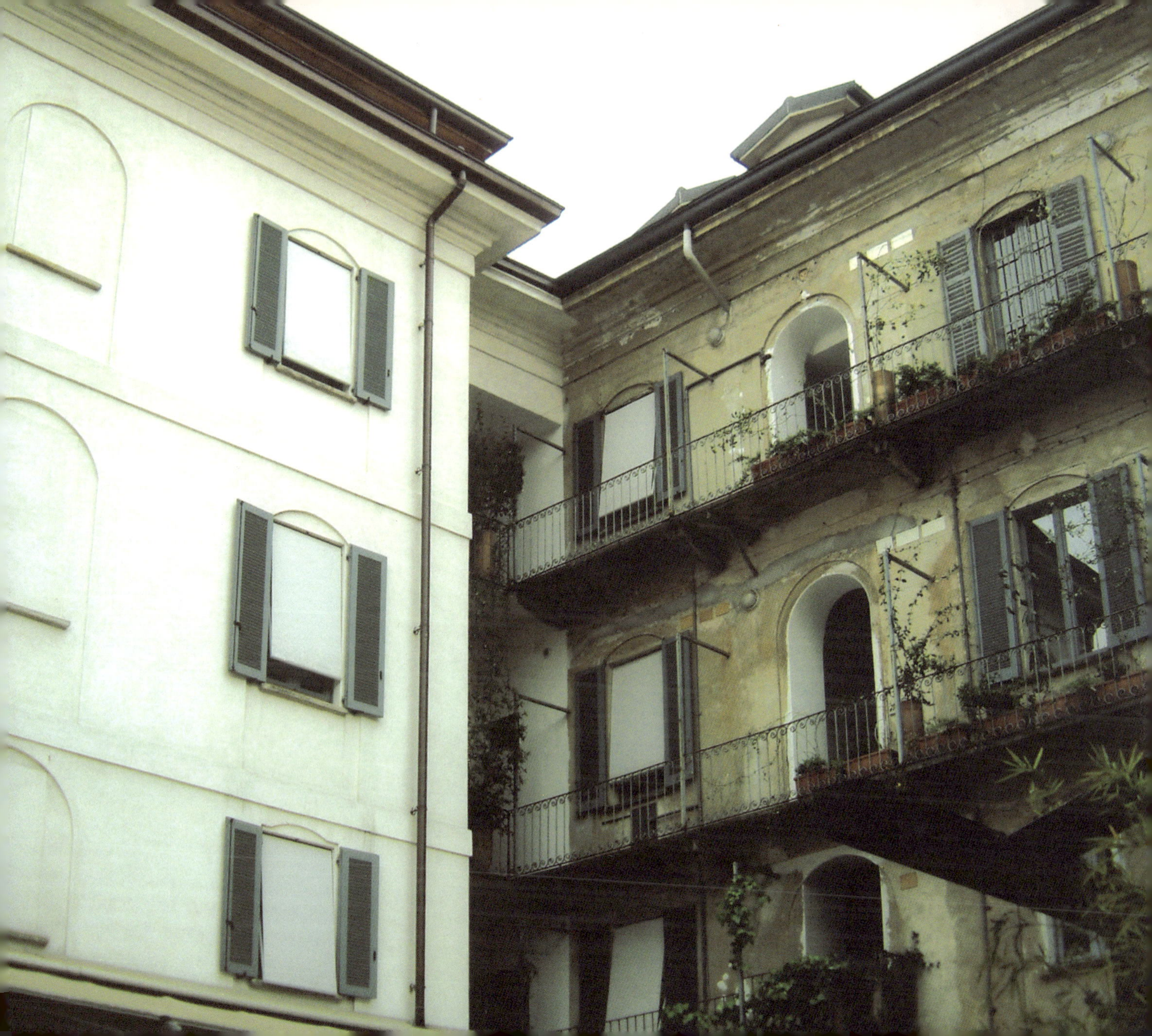

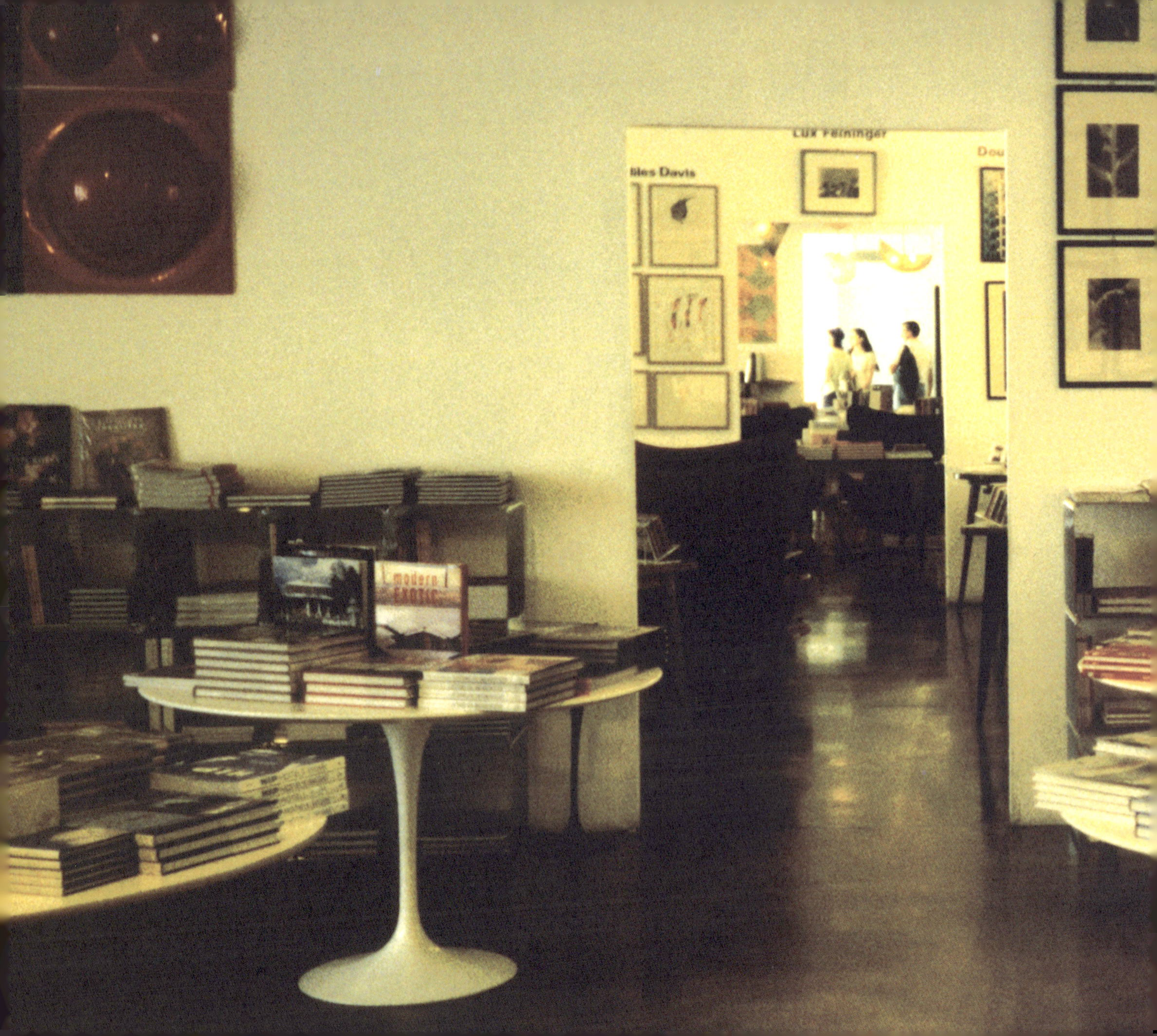
Lux Feininger
iles Davis
modern EXOTIC

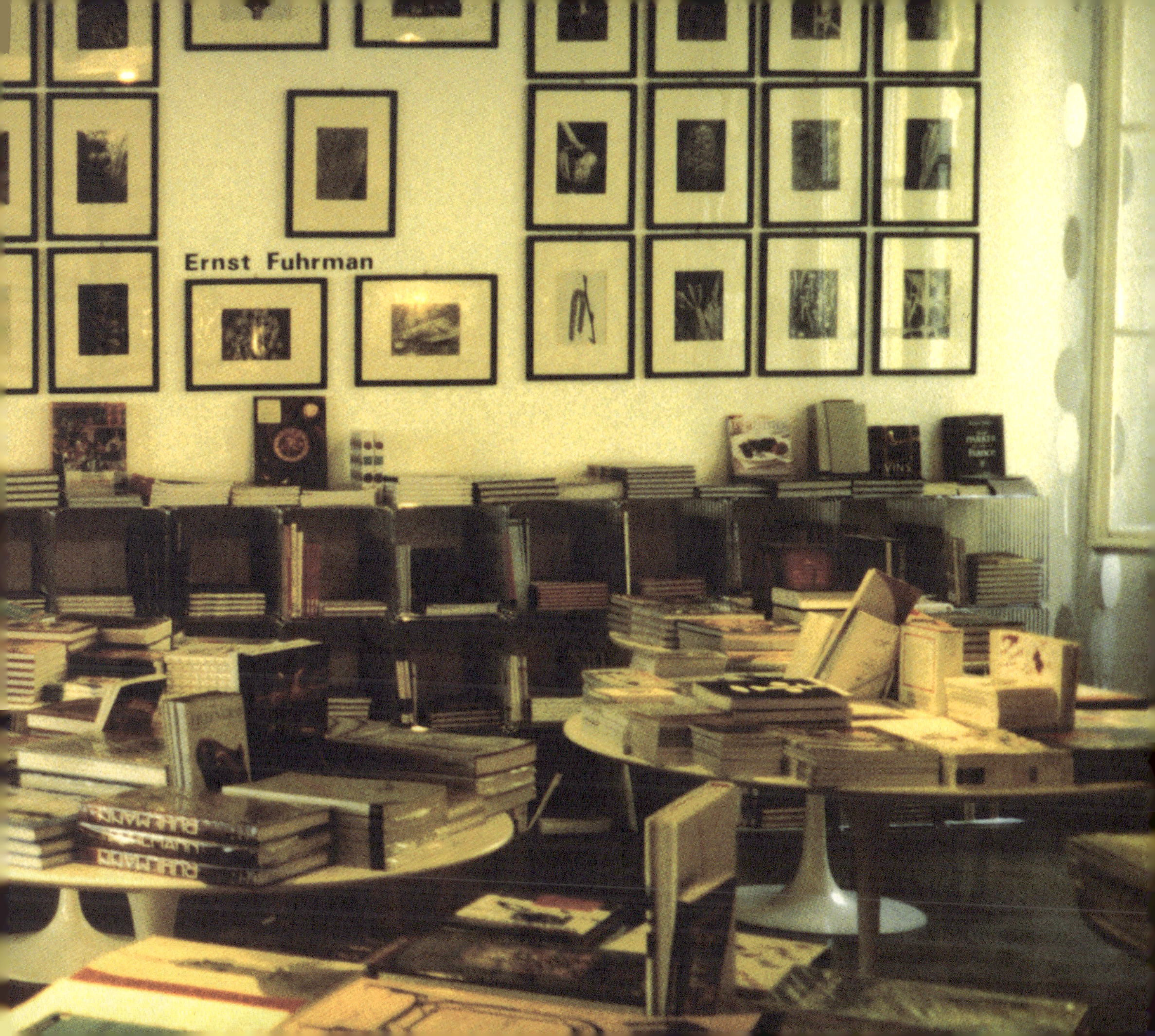
Ernst Fuhrman

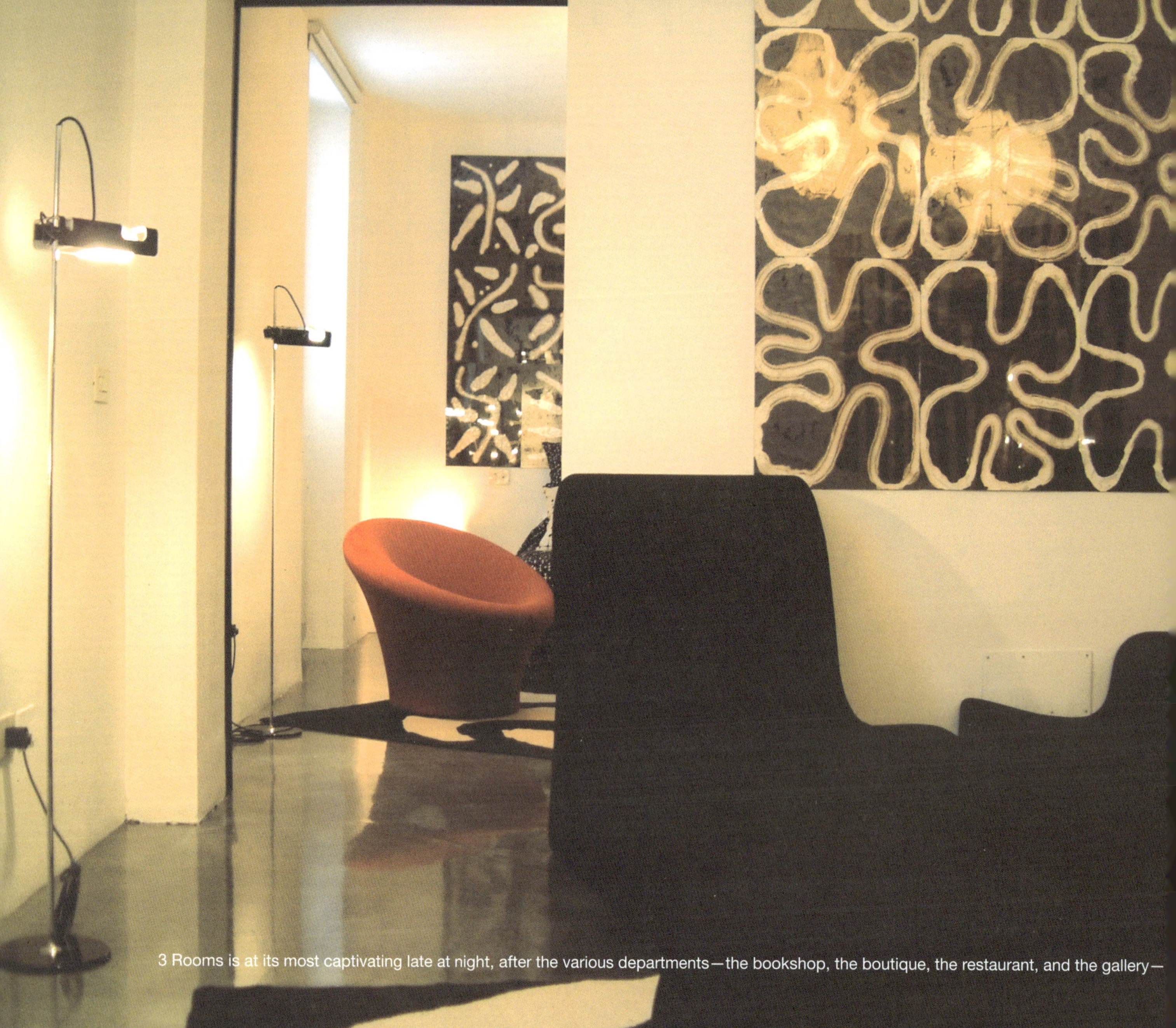

3 Rooms is at its most captivating late at night, after the various departments—the bookshop, the boutique, the restaurant, and the gallery—

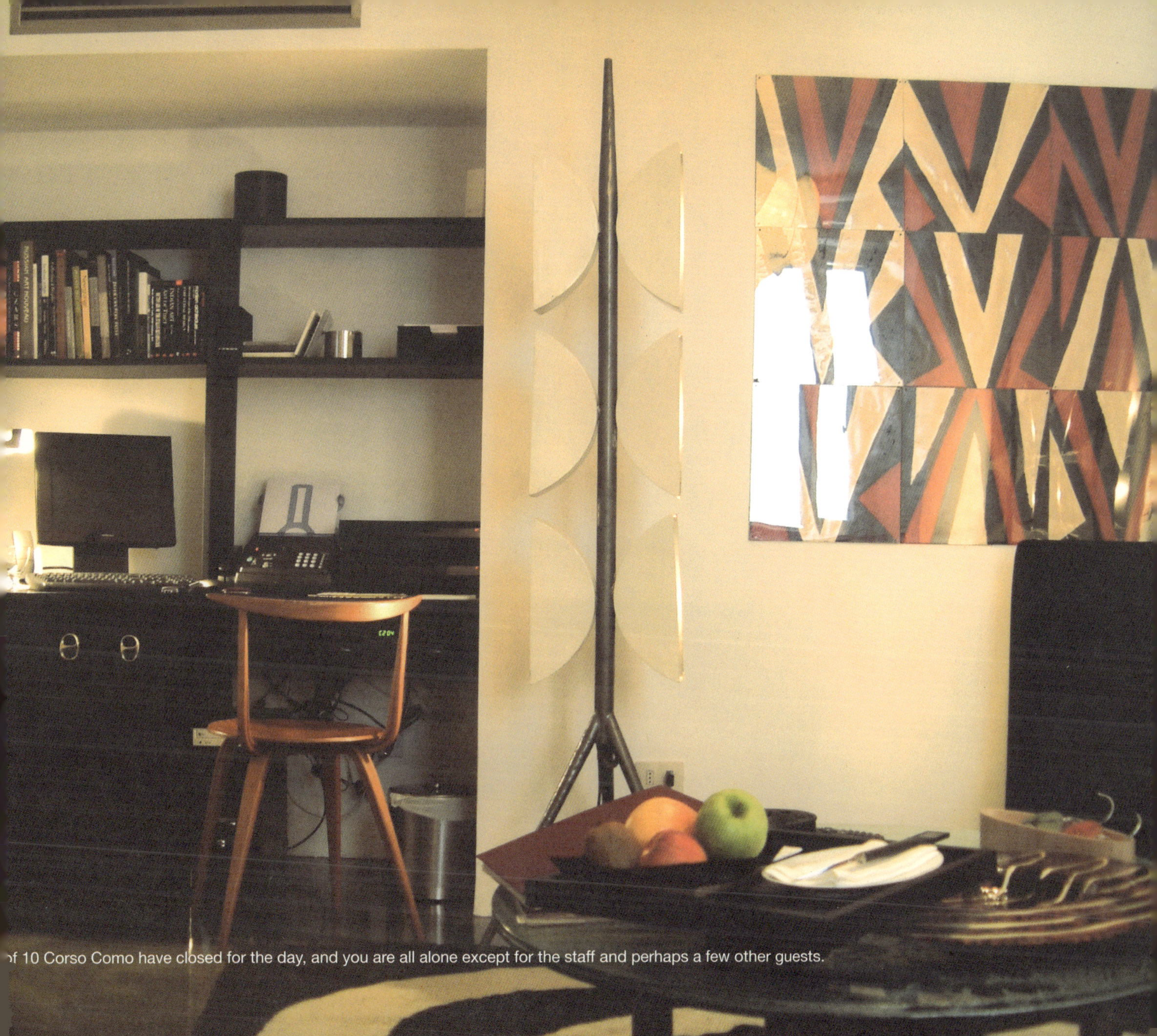

of 10 Corso Como have closed for the day, and you are all alone except for the staff and perhaps a few other guests.

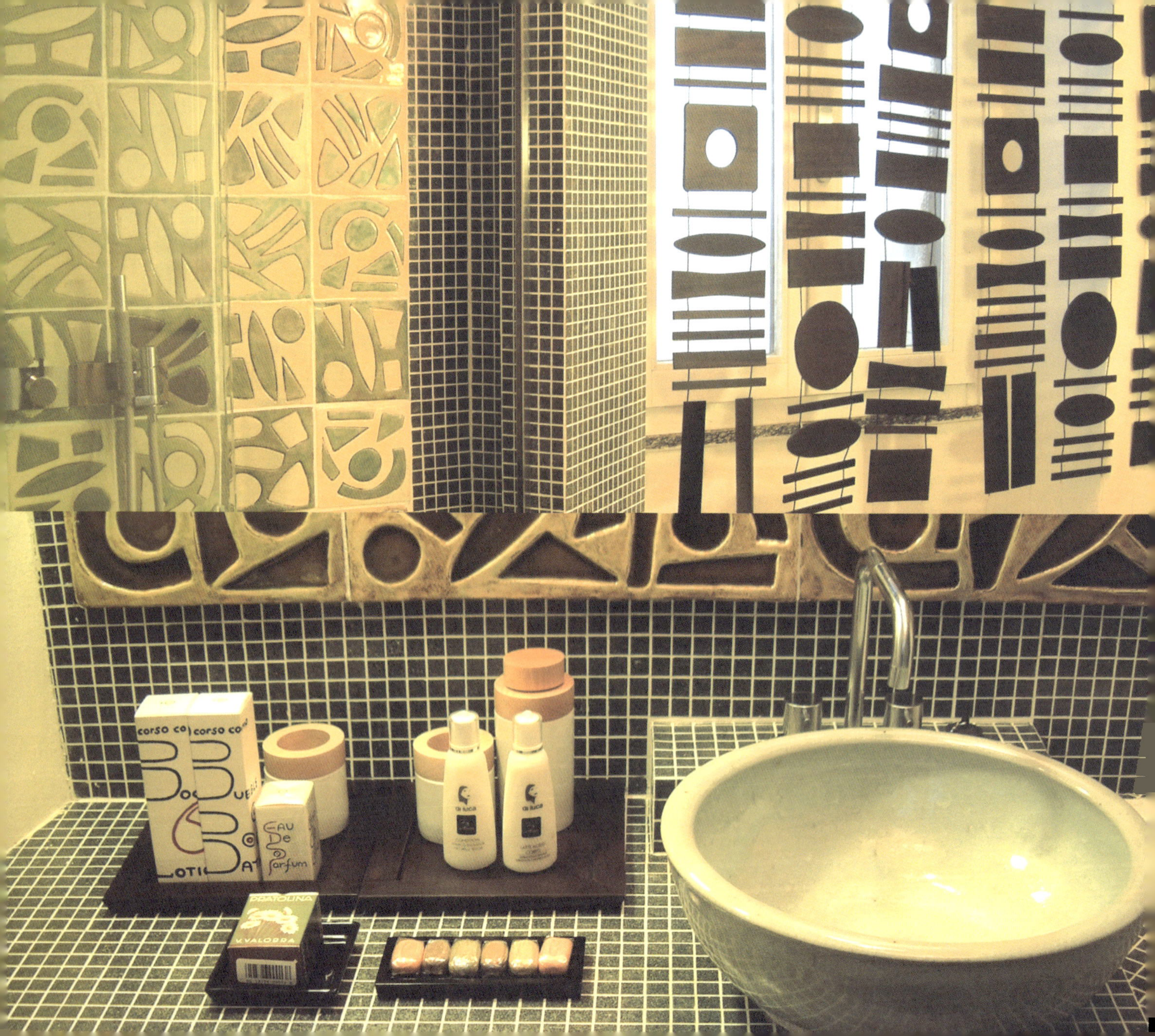
corso co
corso co
Eau De Parfum
PRATOLINA
V. VALODDA

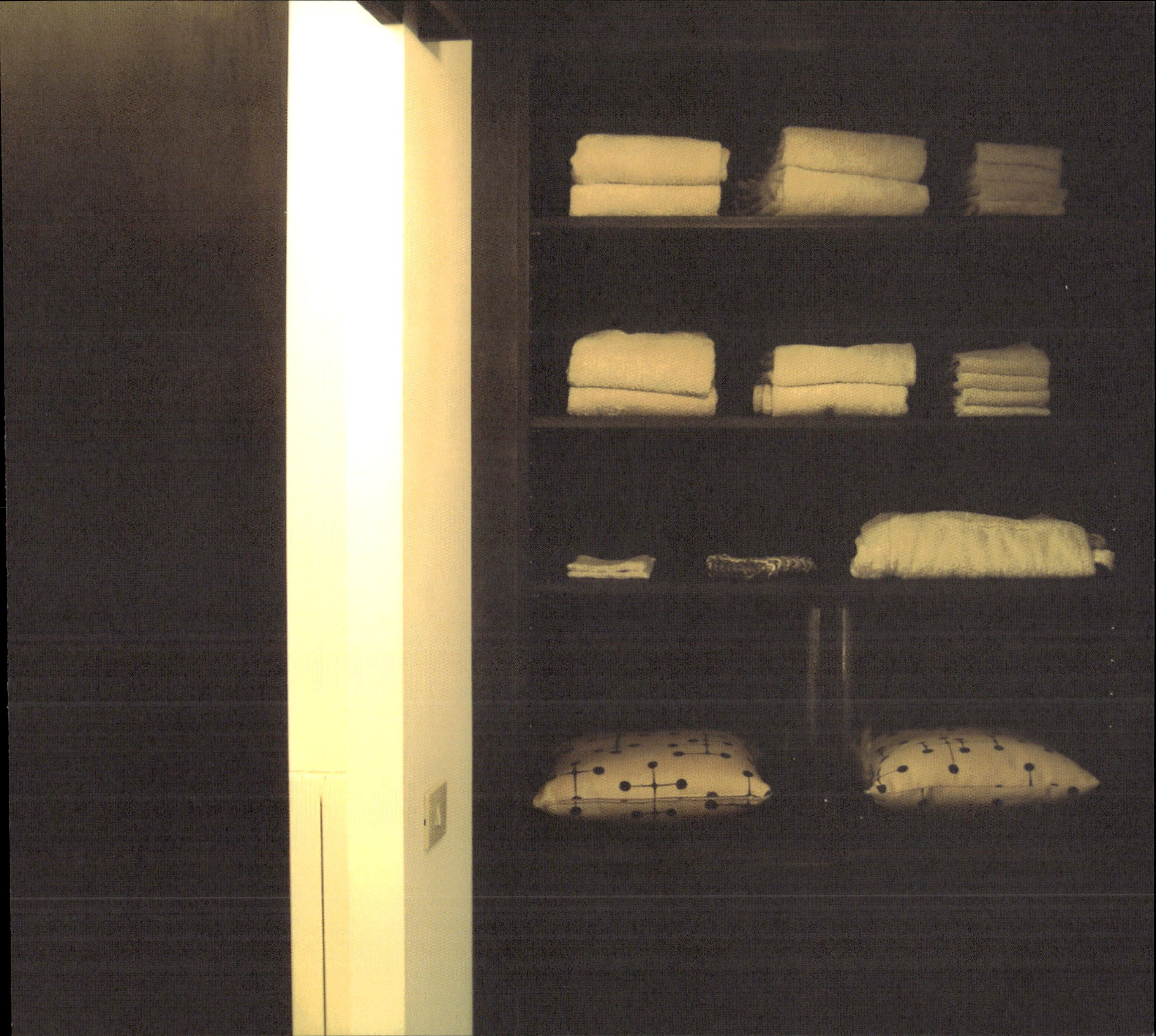

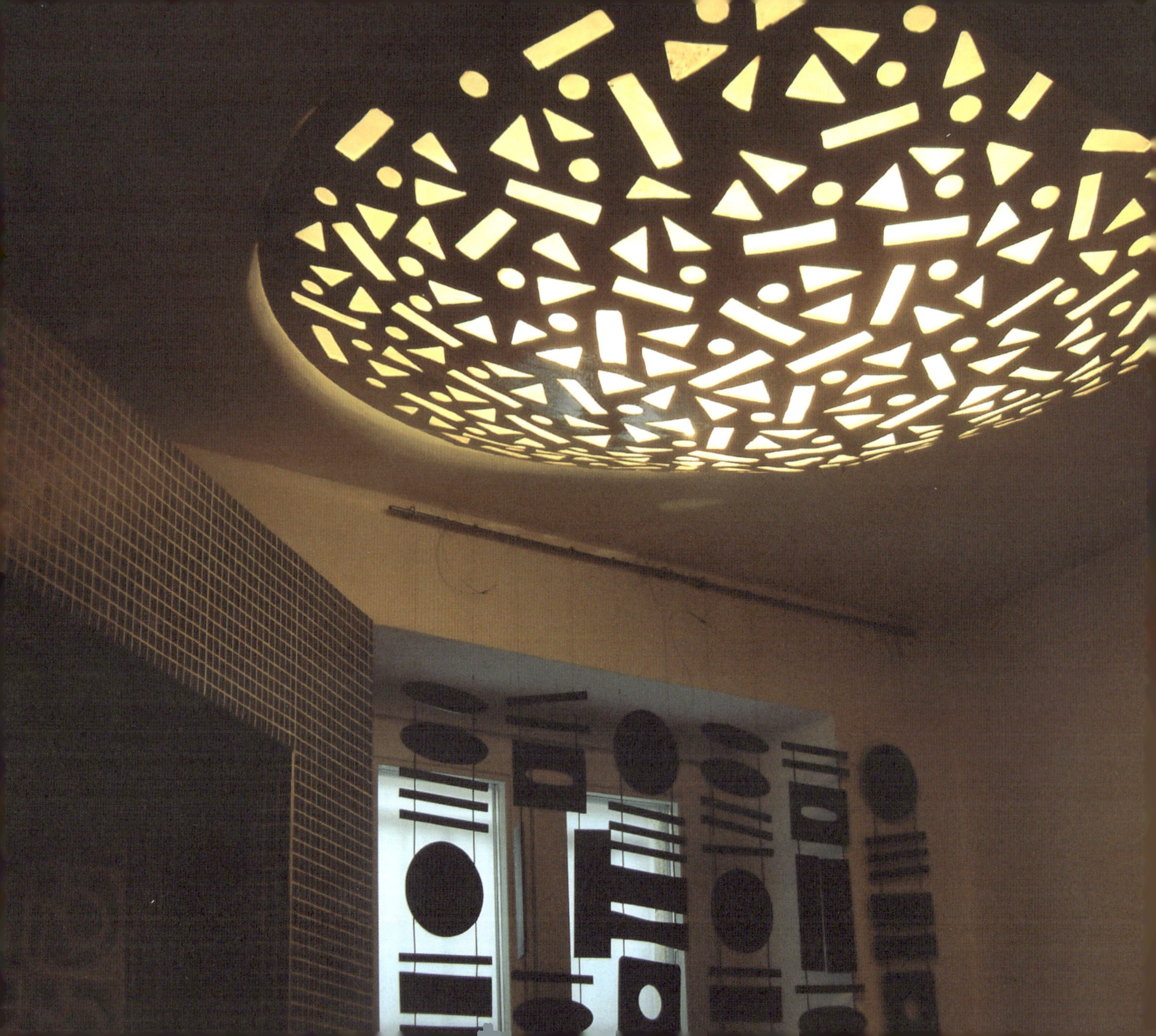

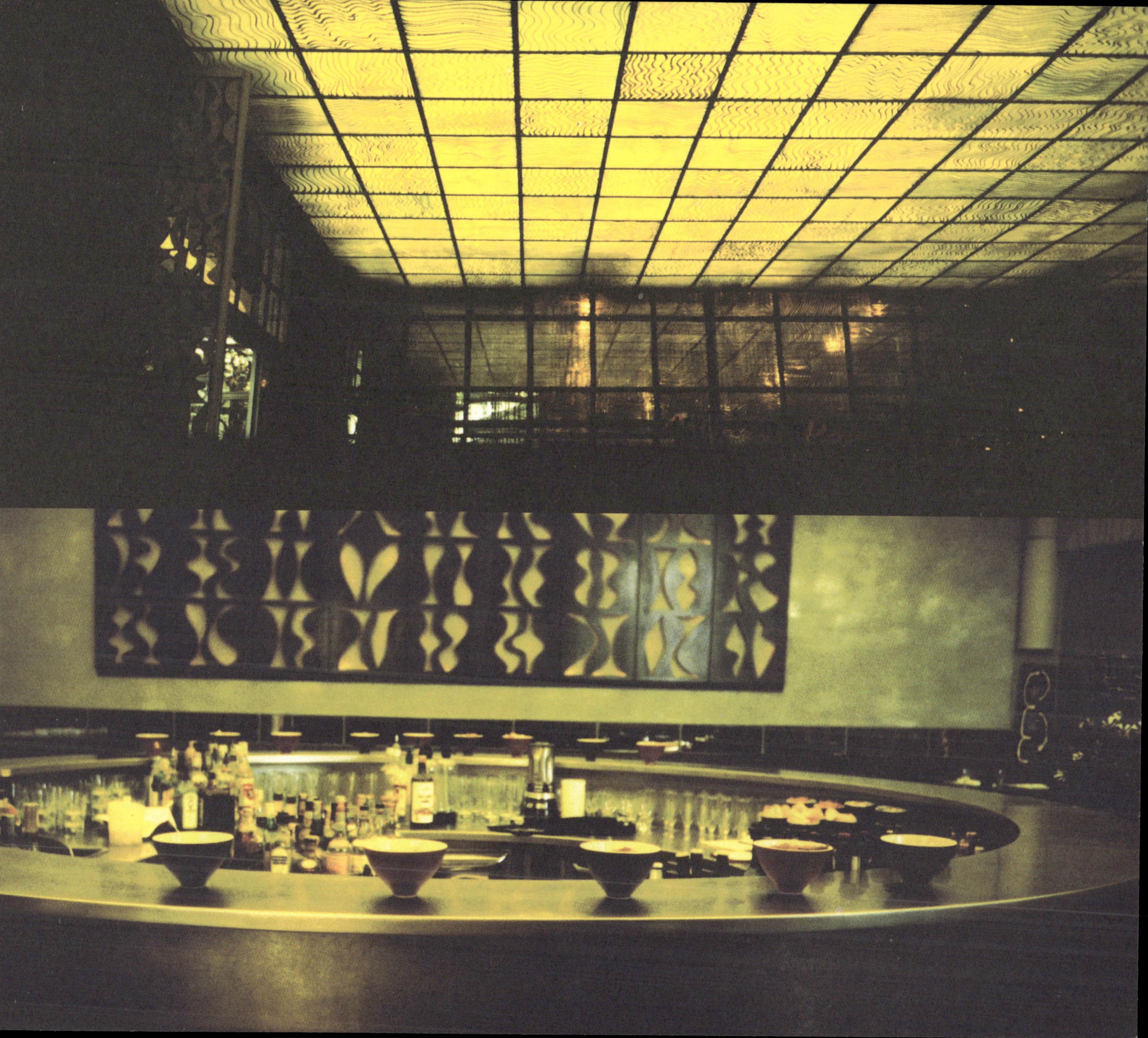

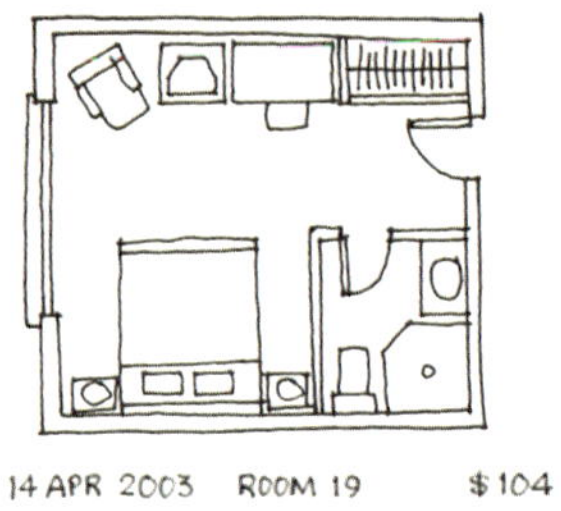

Northern Light Inn

FLY ME TO THE MOON

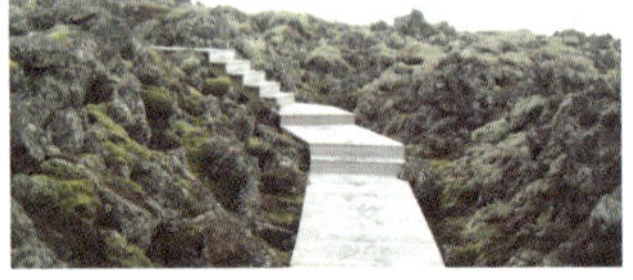

Inspired by the Icelandic-Japanese road movie *Cold Fever*, I found myself in Iceland, supposedly the place on Earth most resembling the moon, at least according to travel guides. It is also the Earth's "youngest" stretch of land, complete with volcanoes, glaciers, and geysers: a veritable compendium of geology.

The Northern Light Inn is set in the midst of a moss- and lichen-covered, umber-colored landscape. The terrain is rugged, splashed with swathes of verdigris and sepia. Even the red roof on the hotel is no match for nature's surrealism. The hotel is located right next to a working power station—a fact that nobody seems to mind, for without it, the hot spring resort wouldn't exist. Pipelines emanating from the station are spreading and sprawling in all directions across the tundra. The pipes bring the thermal water, a by-product of the power plant, into the surrounding lava-filled lakes, and the chemical reaction results in pools of mineral-rich water of azure blue and milky white, whose temperature can go up to 104° Fahrenheit. Like me, many of the hotel guests, have come for the stunning landscape and the reputedly therapeutic water. My favorite days here are those when the sky is overcast and the grey horizon and blue water seem to merge into each other.

GRINDAVIK

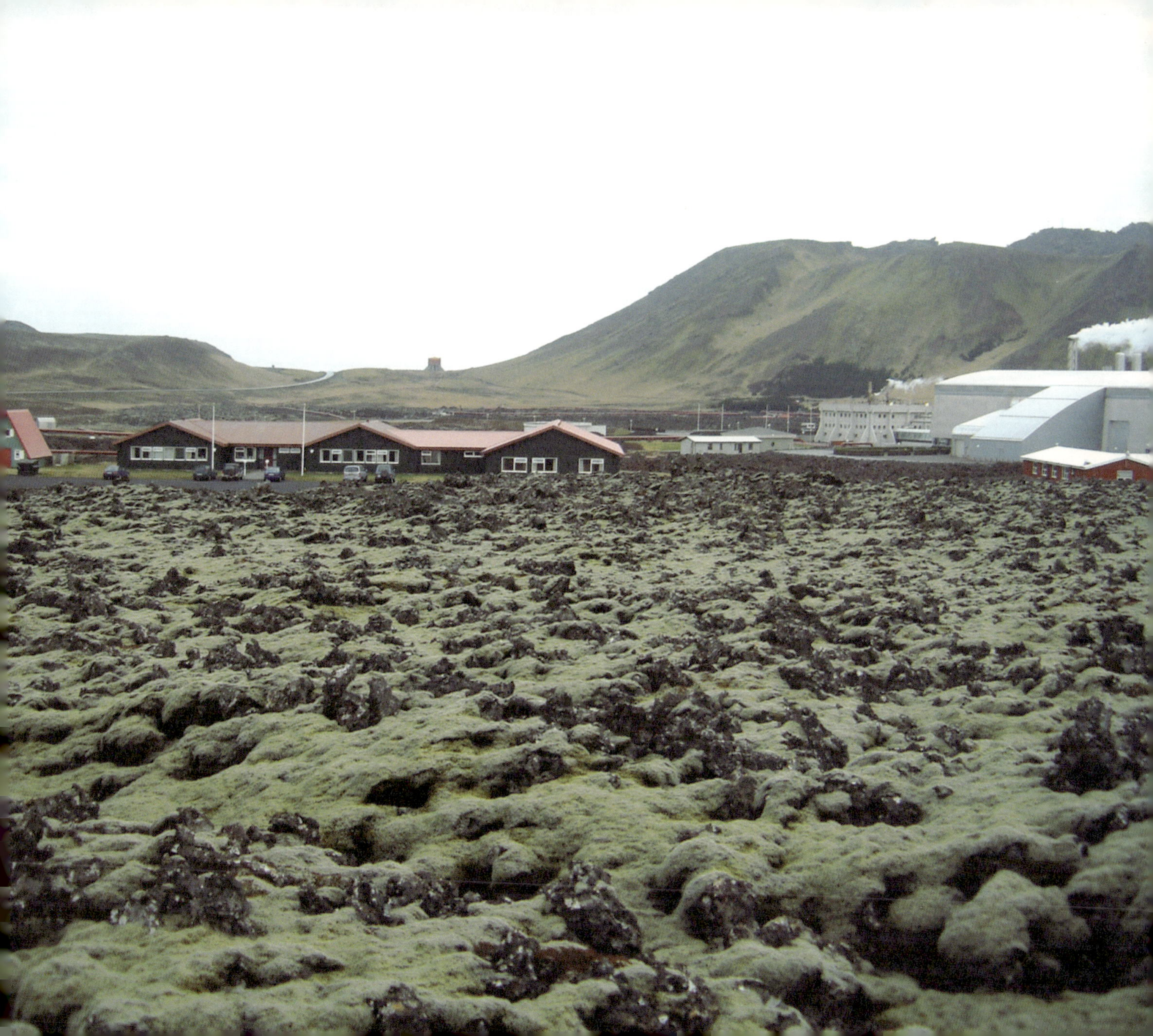

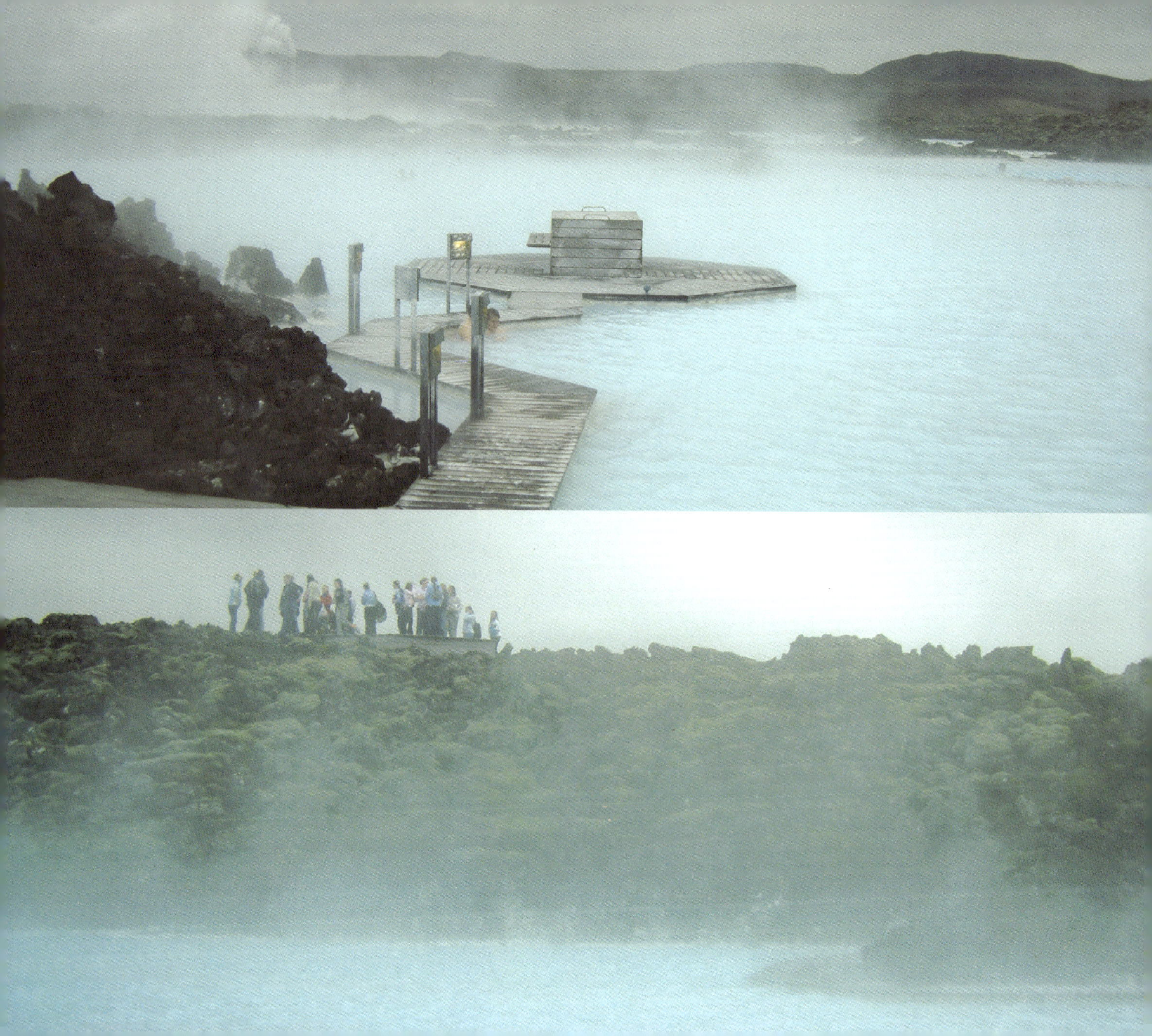

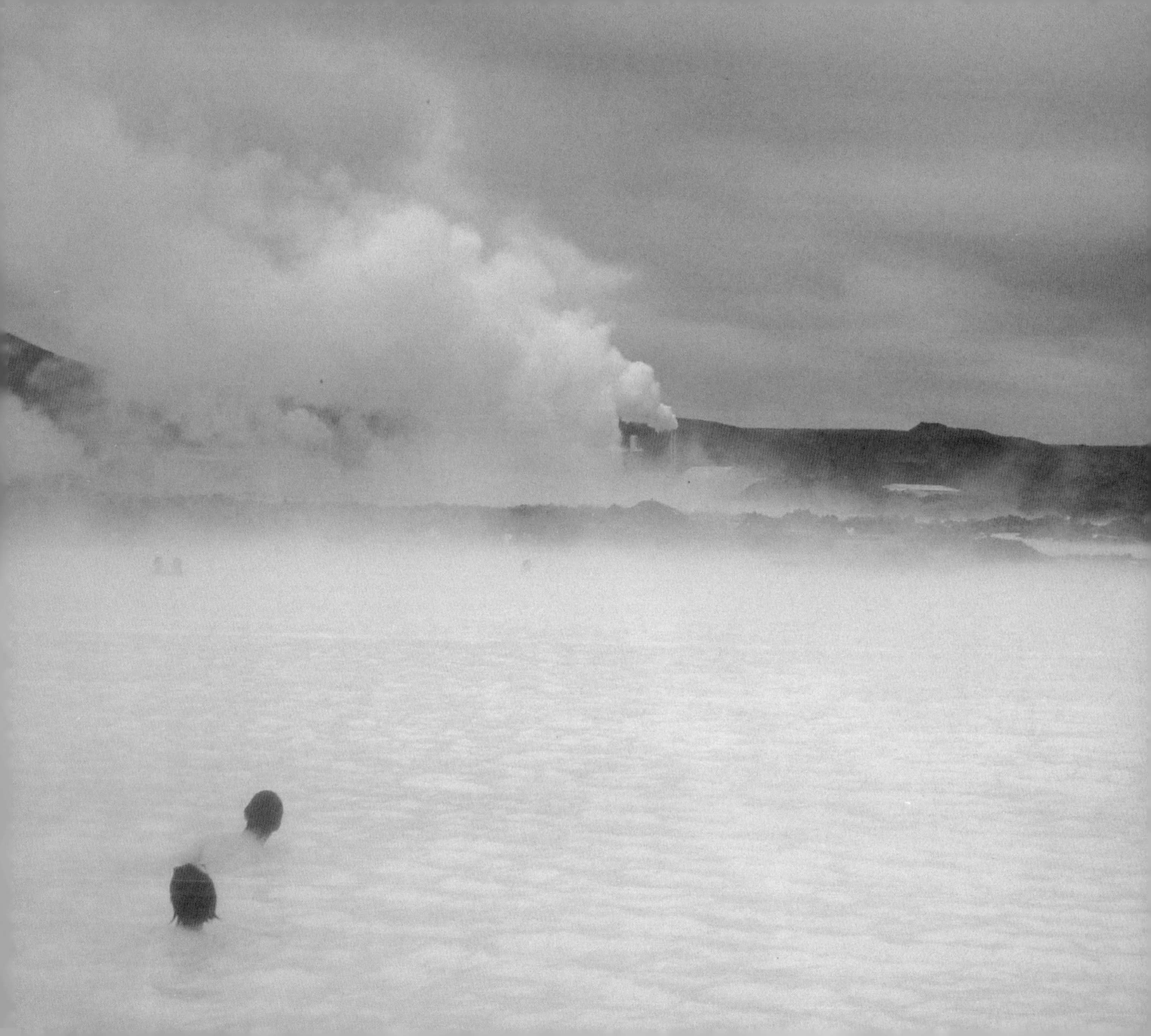

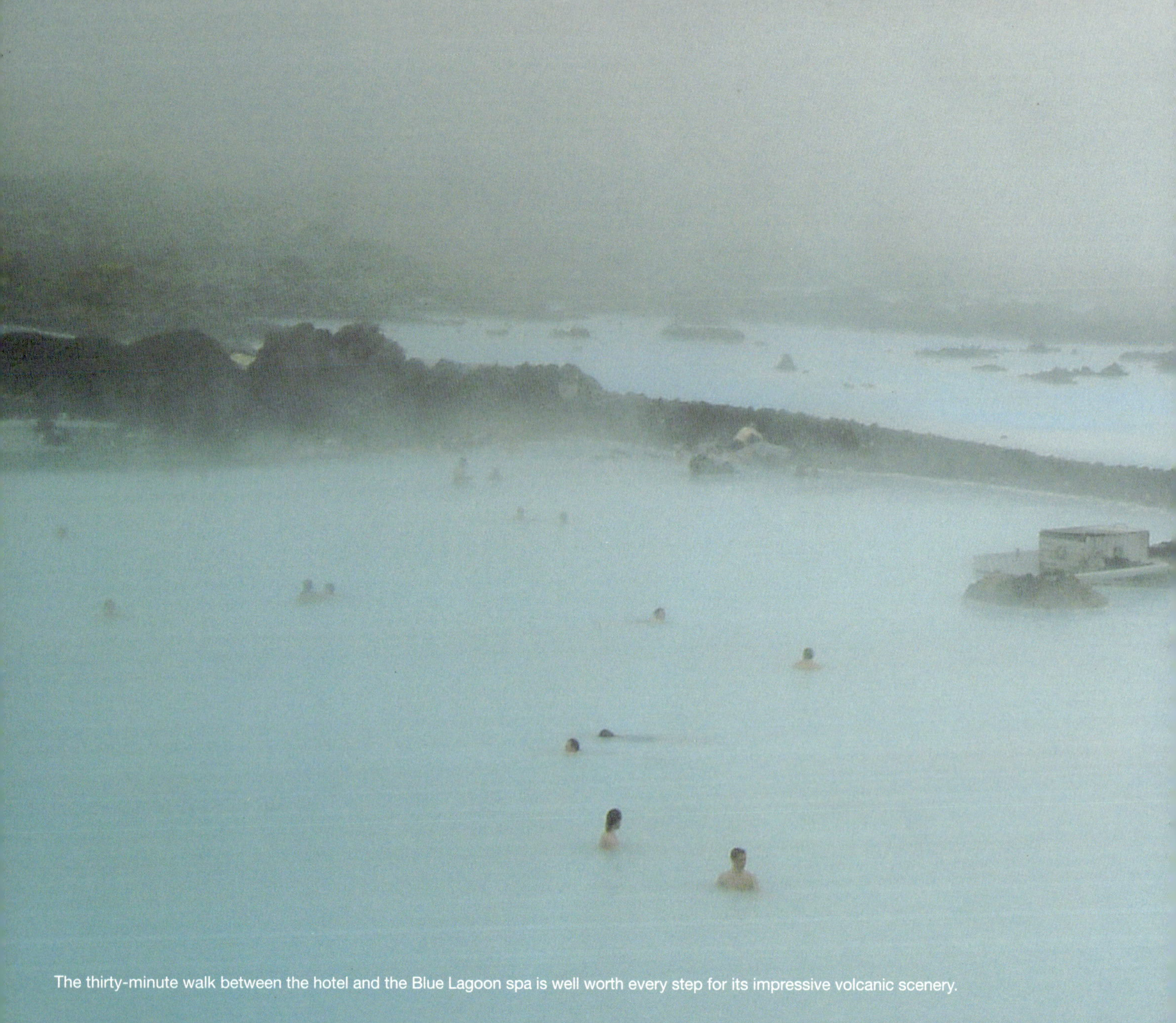

The thirty-minute walk between the hotel and the Blue Lagoon spa is well worth every step for its impressive volcanic scenery.

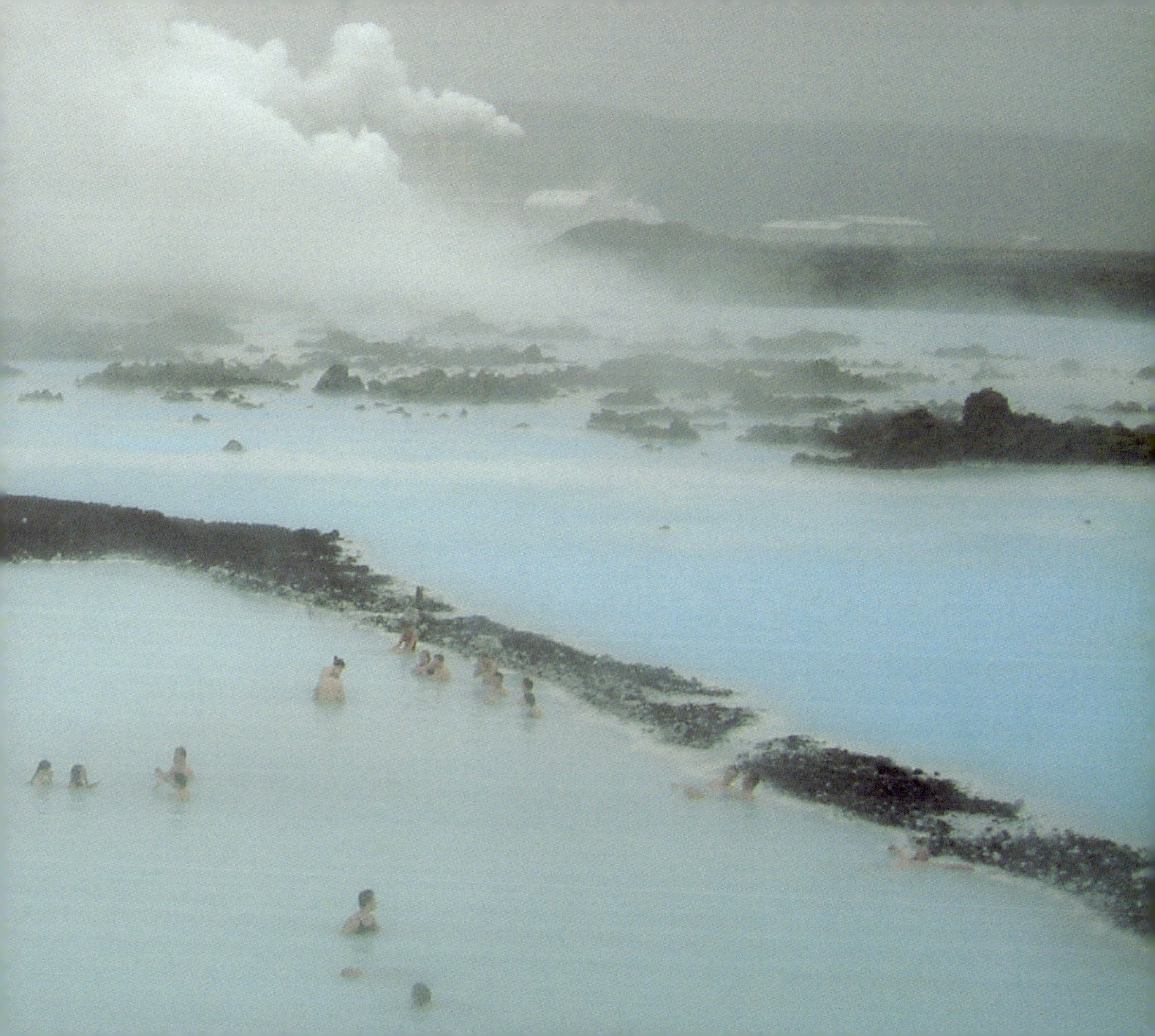

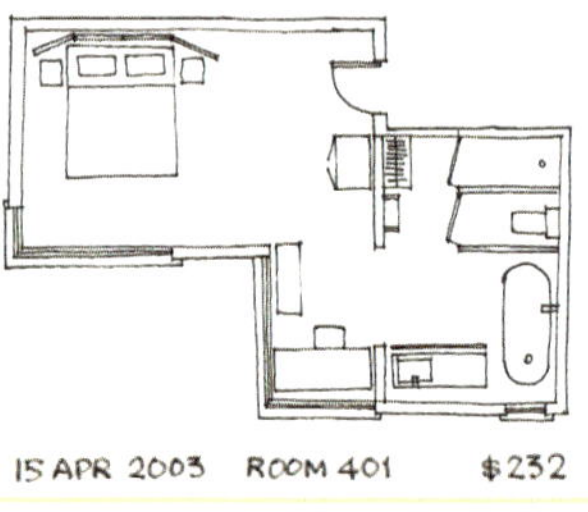

Hotel 101

A PRECIOUS BREATH OF UNSULLIED AIR

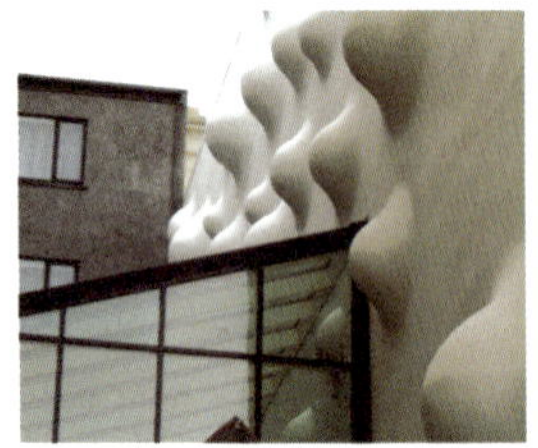

The SARS outbreak of 2003 made people from Hong Kong something of a pariah to everybody else. During my flight from Milan, where I had just attended the (in)famous Furniture Fair, to Iceland, I did not have so much as a sip of water because I didn't want to take my 3M-N95 clinical mask off. So the first thing I did when we landed in Reykjavik was to take a big breath of Iceland's memorably fresh air. Hotel 101 was so spotlessly clean and the air so pure that I was quite prepared to spend my entire five days in it. Reykjavik, albeit the country's capital, seemed as calm and quiet as a sleepy small town. The April weather was perfect. Even as late as eleven o'clock at night, the sky was so bright that it seemed as if you should be able to see the hotel's past and present spread out in front of you. Built in 1935 to serve as the headquarters of the Social Democrats, Hotel 101 is located in the oldest part of town. After the 1980s, it became an office building housing small firms. Now a hotel, the building still retains its 1930s characteristics. Like the city itself, it is unremarkable and serene on the surface, but full of calming colors and glamour on the inside.

The room I stayed in was furnished primarily in black and white metallic materials, but the warm and soft black lacquer finish on the white walls saved it from appearing cold and forbidding. The bed was incredibly comfortable, and the designer's consideration for the guests was apparent in the smallest of details. The curtains, when drawn, left a tiny border of light, for example, so that the room wouldn't feel claustrophobic. From the five windows in my corner suite, I could see everything from Reykjavik's National Opera House, its government offices, and the Supreme Court to the humble old granny in the apartment block next door. Out in the distance the sea and the snow-capped mountains were visible, both looking as still and solid as permanence itself. Closer to home, I was fascinated by the wall connecting the hotel with the opera house next door, created by the designer's then-pregnant artist sister. Bumps and bubbles rise from its surface to add a sense of playfulness and humor to the otherwise orderly architecture of the building.

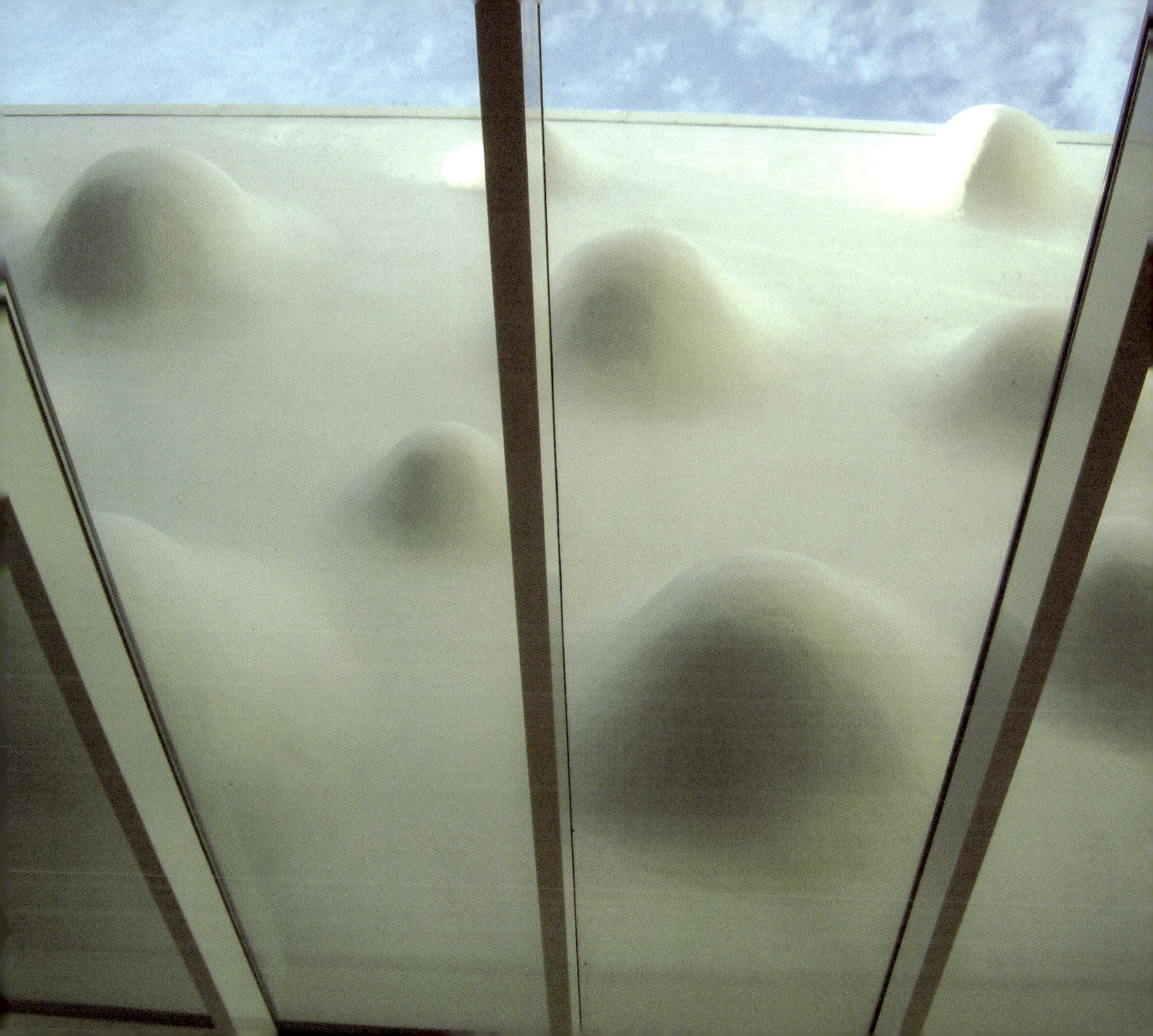

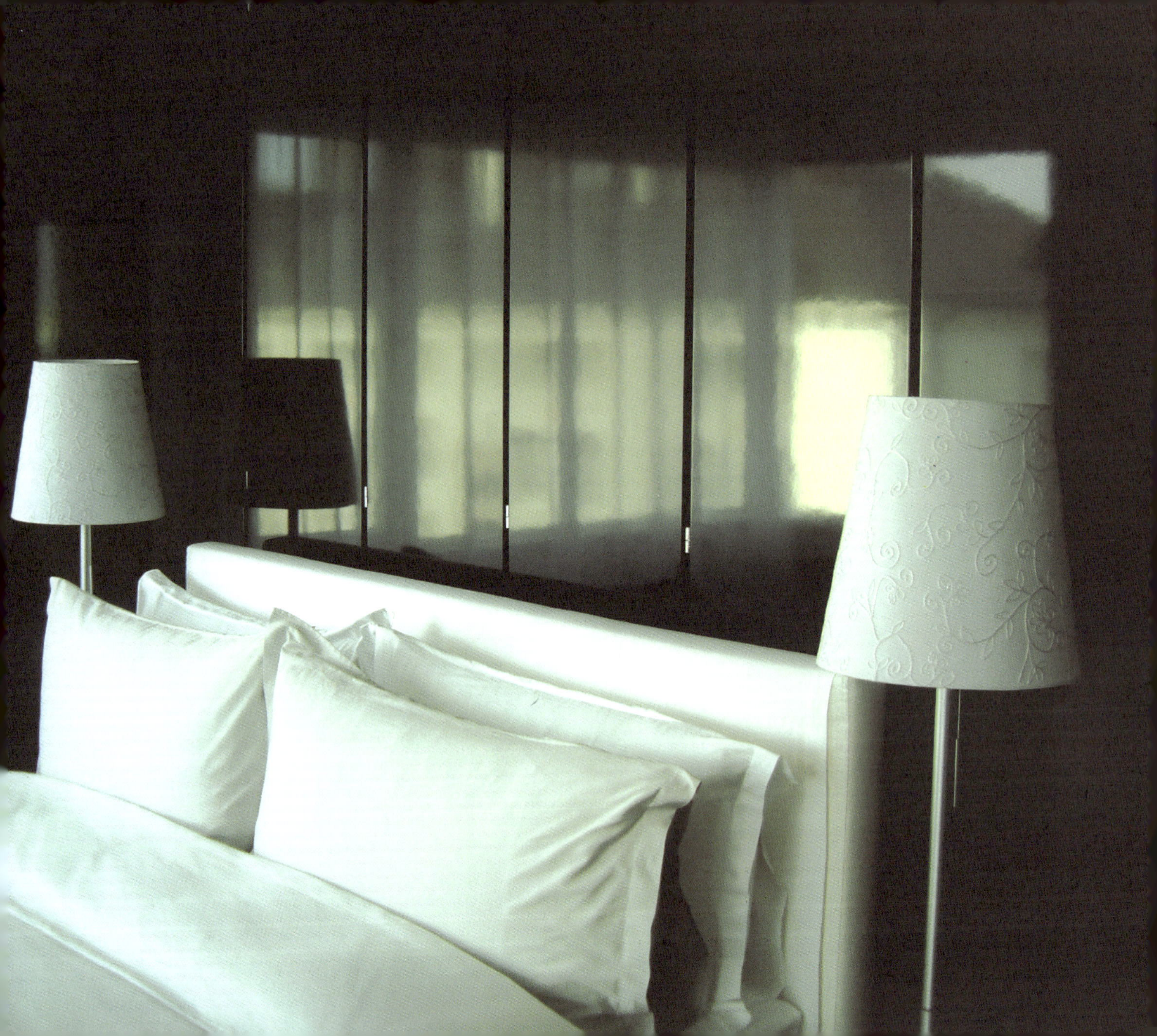

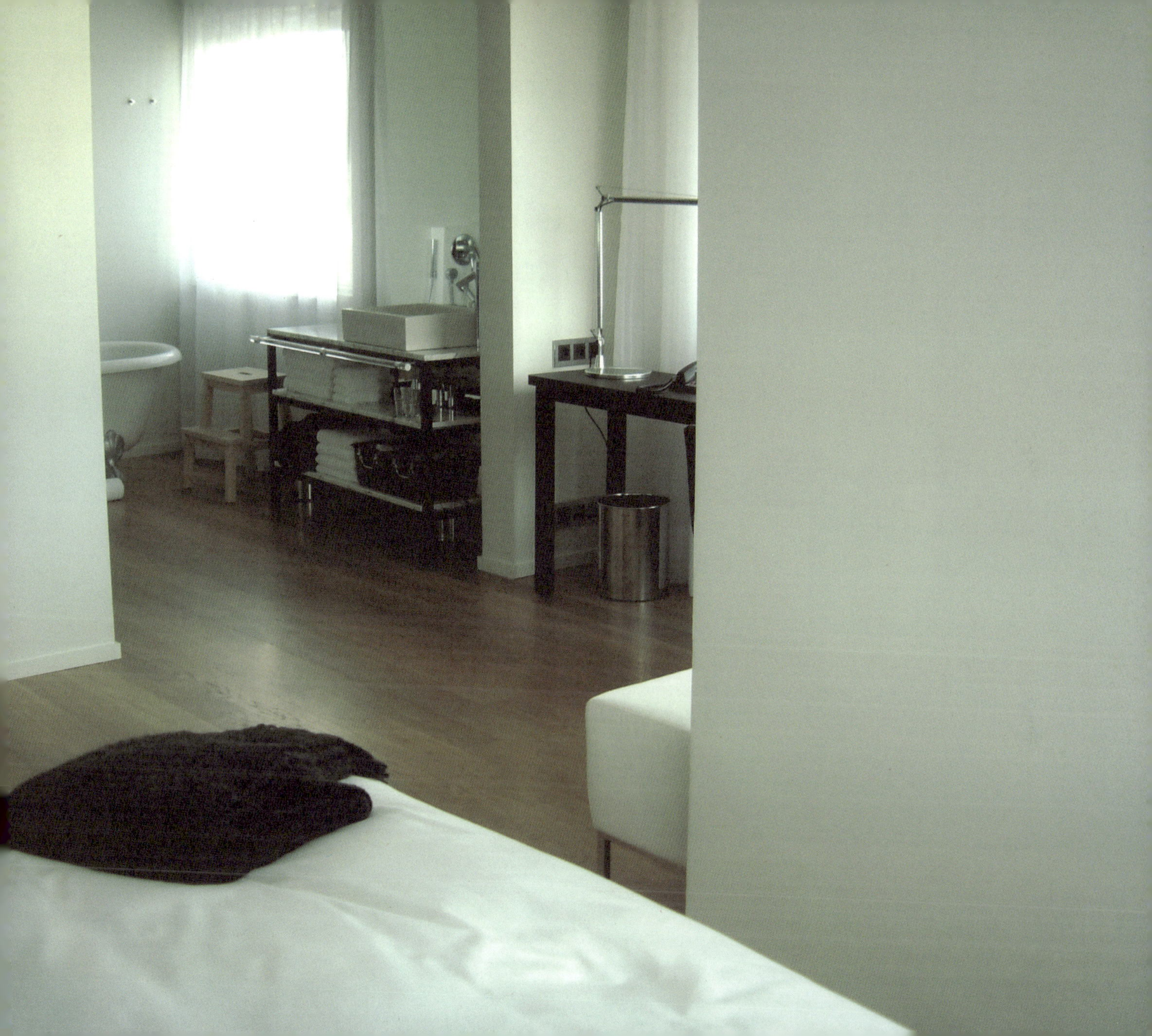

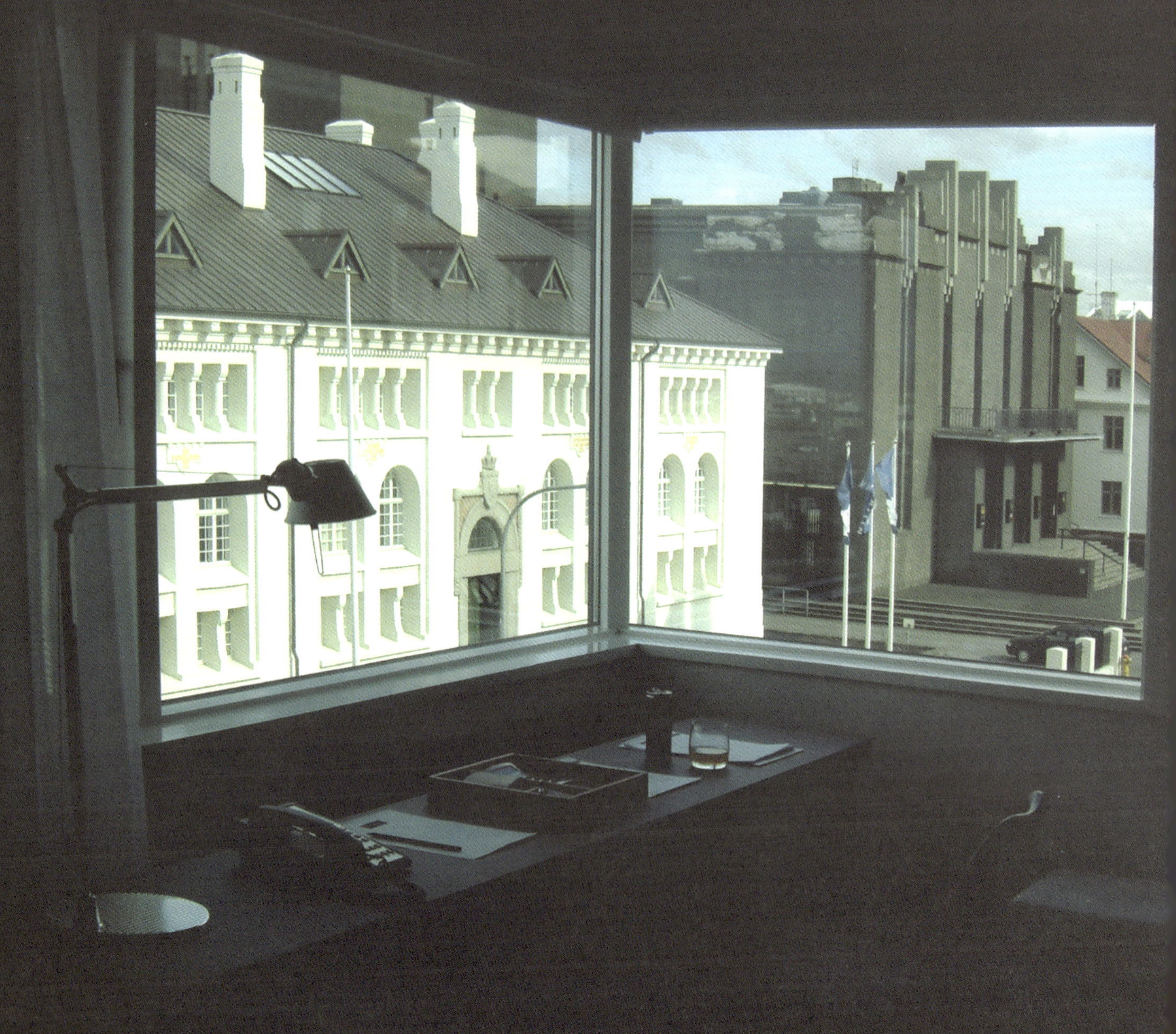

Although the hotel's playful bubble wall is visible from inside its restaurant, don't settle for just that

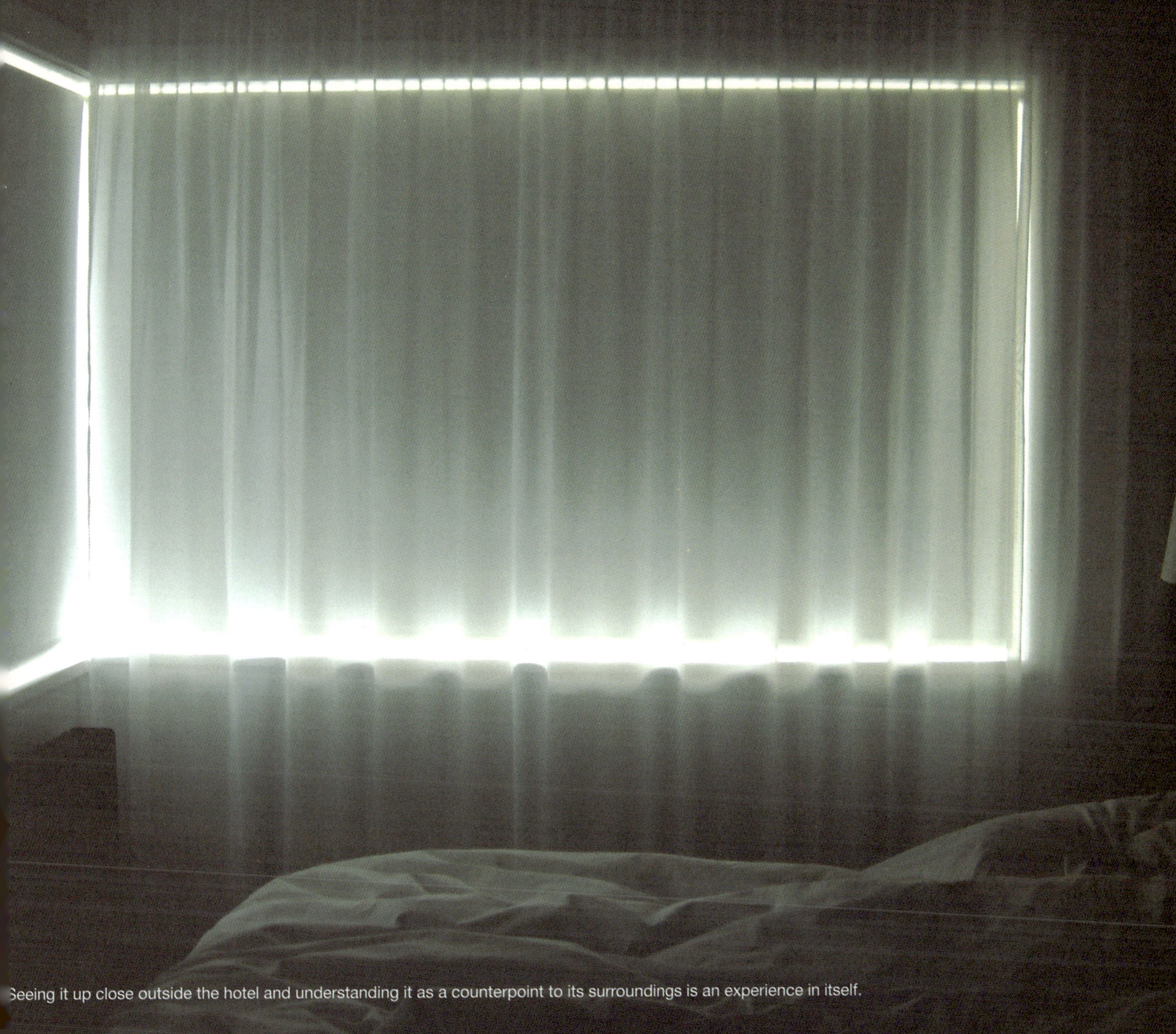

Seeing it up close outside the hotel and understanding it as a counterpoint to its surroundings is an experience in itself.

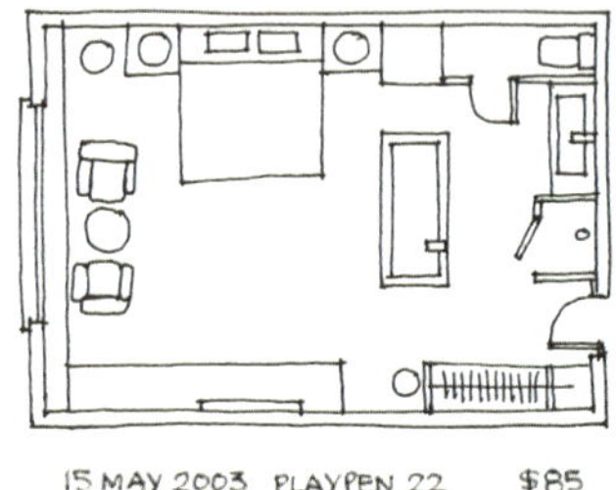

Soho House New York

PRIVATE SCREENING

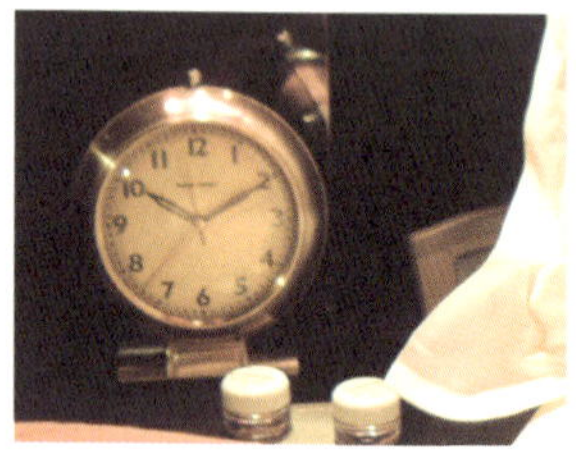

I knew that a hotel whose design was coordinated by the editor-in-chief of *Elle* was always going to be a hotspot for the media crowd. What took me by surprise was that, besides the fifty-six-inch plasma TV I found in my room, Soho House Hotel also boasts a very respectable movie theater, which screens both old and new films, complete with a fully functional bar. Its glossy black leather sofas reminded me of the plush velvet seats of an opera house. On weekends, adults can watch films here while their children are tended to by professionals at the Children's Club. The hotel has only twenty-four rooms, which are ranked as "playpen," "playroom," "playhouse," and "playground," according to respective sizes, as opposed to the usual unfathomable "superior" or "deluxe." The attention to detail in the rooms goes down to the bottle of sleep-enhancing massage oil on the bedside table. But what I found most exciting was the large "mini-bar" made up of numerous smaller drawers. Each opening of a drawer was an adventure in itself. I never knew what to expect inside: perhaps a magazine, toiletry products, a tourist guide, or maybe even some mouth-watering ice cream. What more could a novelty-obsessed media person wish for?

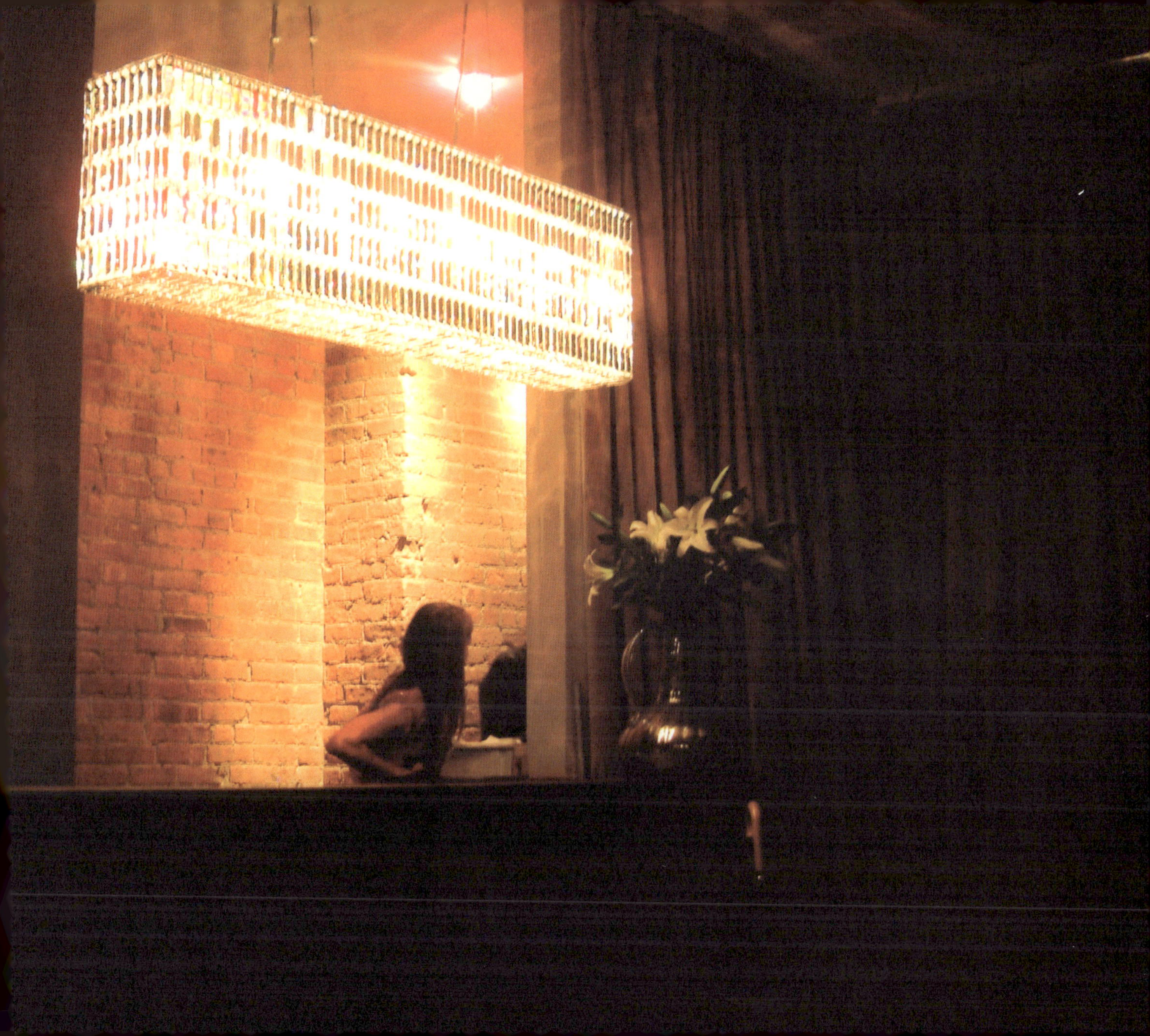

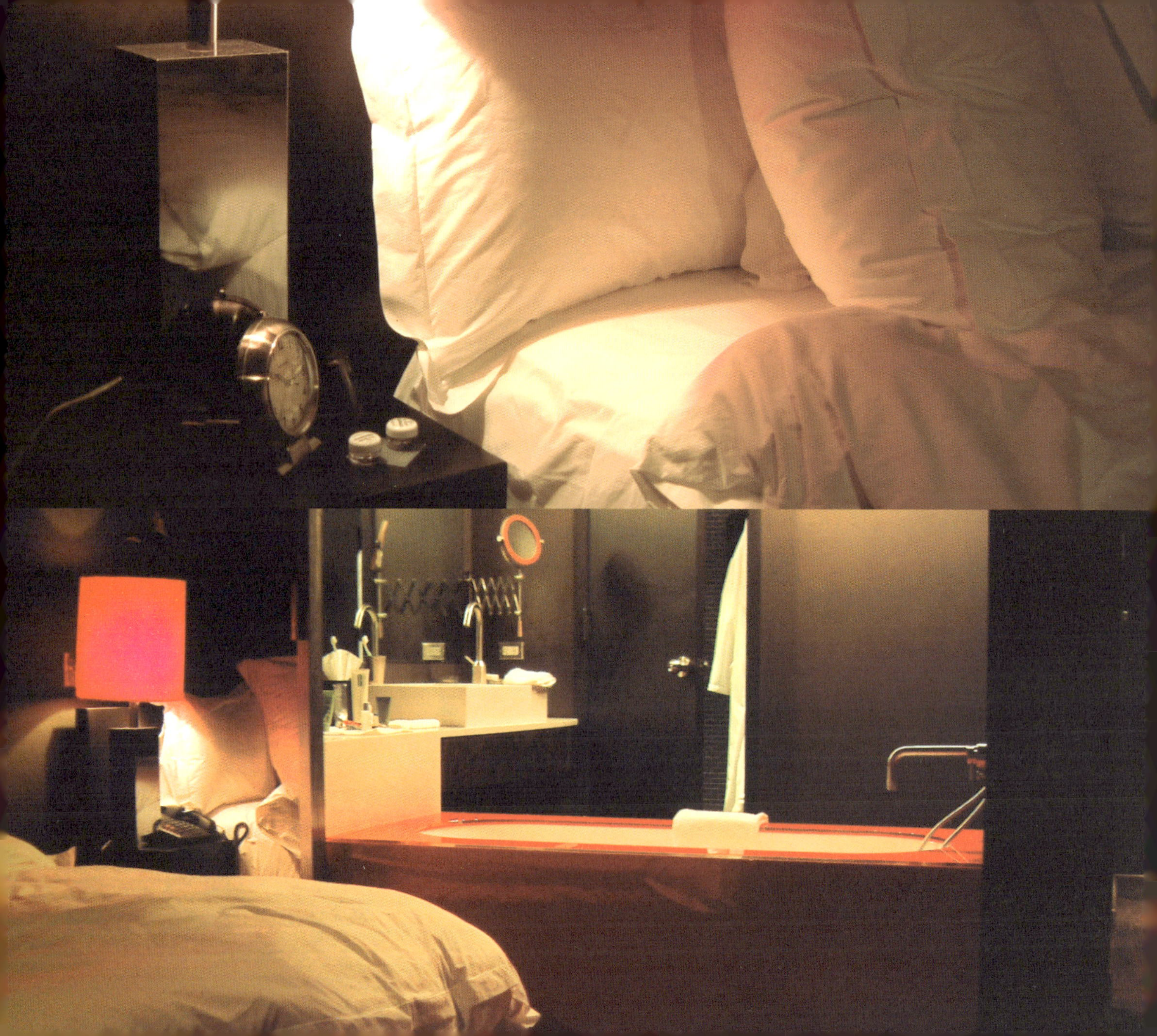

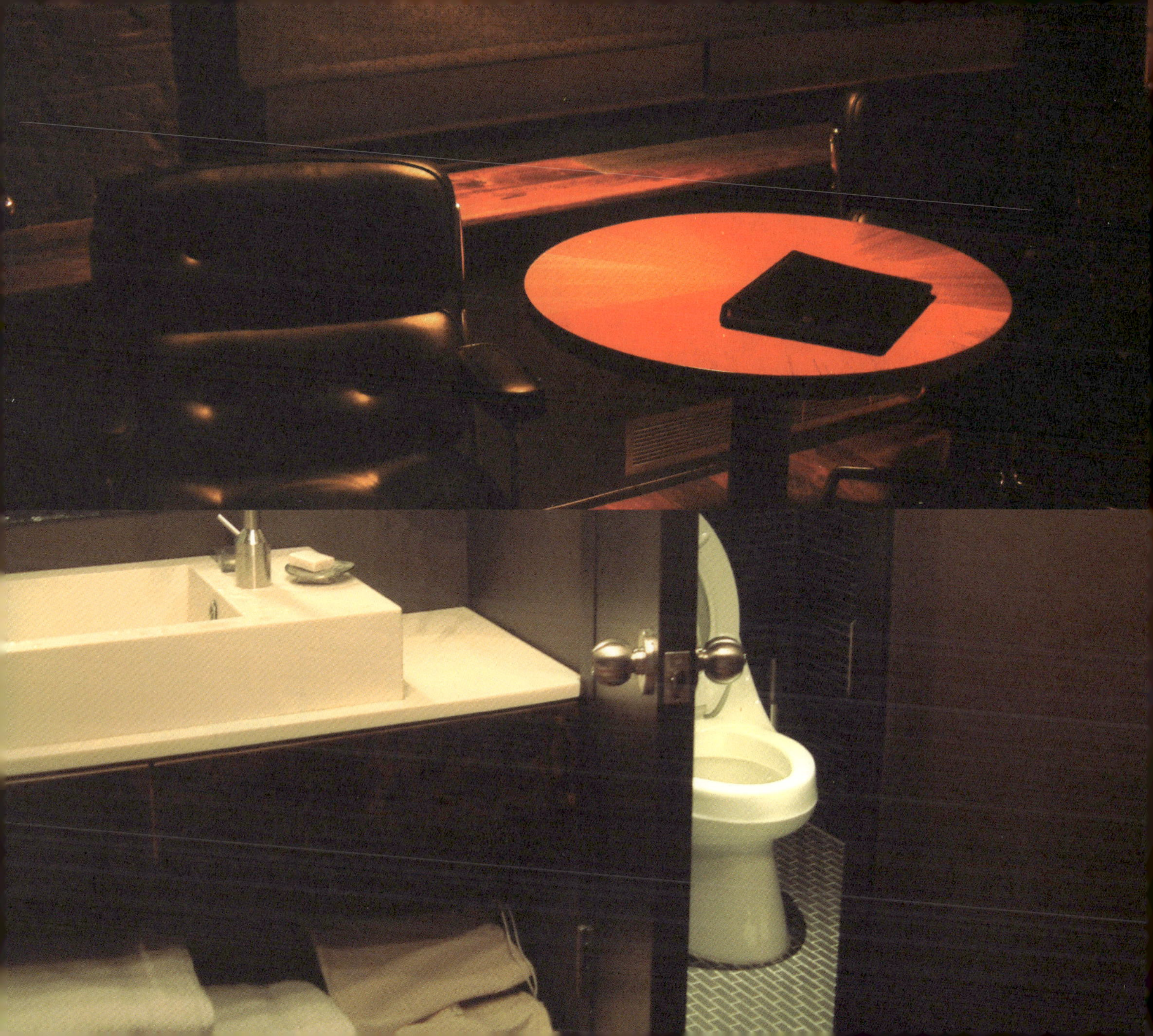

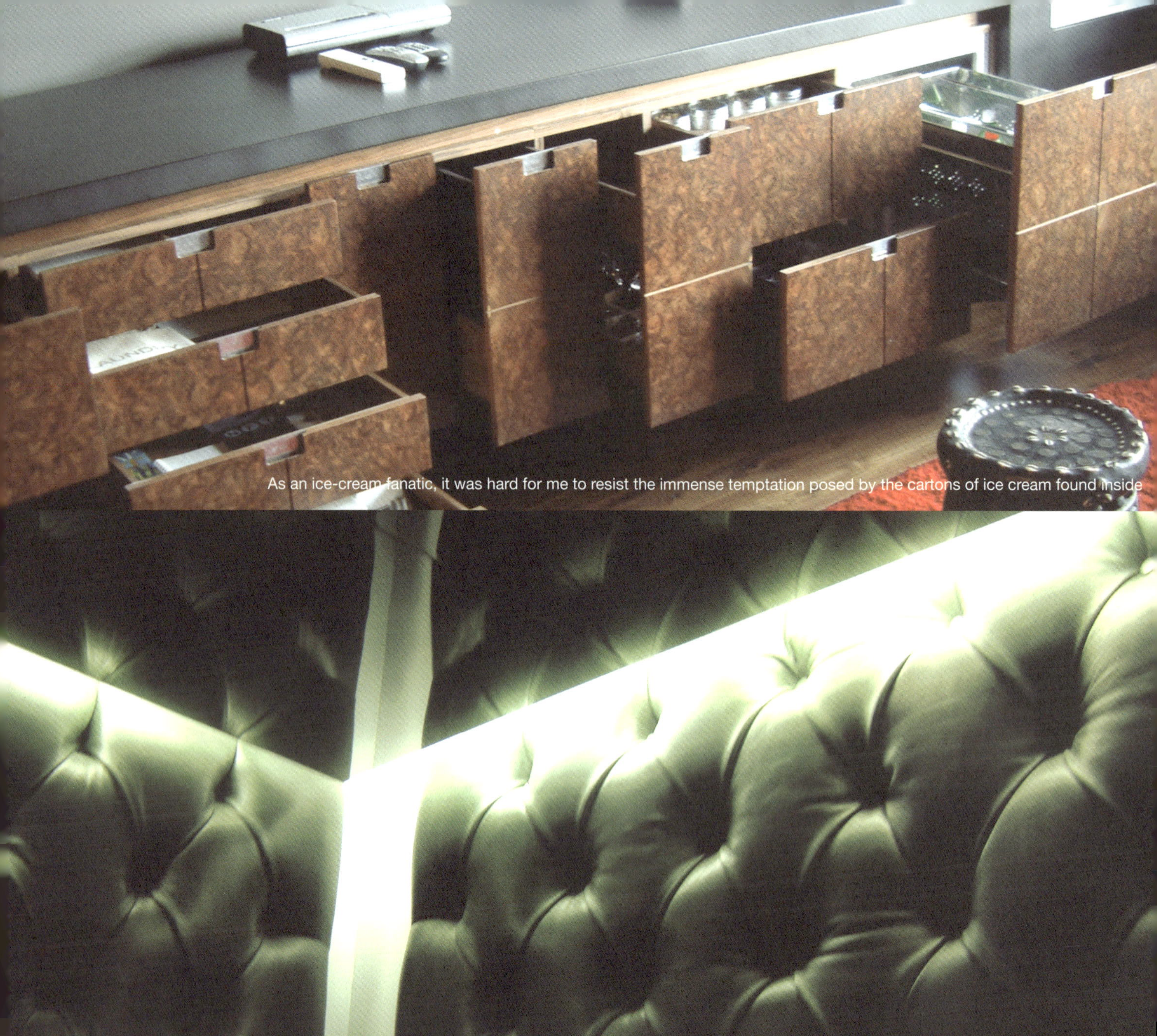

As an ice-cream fanatic, it was hard for me to resist the immense temptation posed by the cartons of ice cream found inside

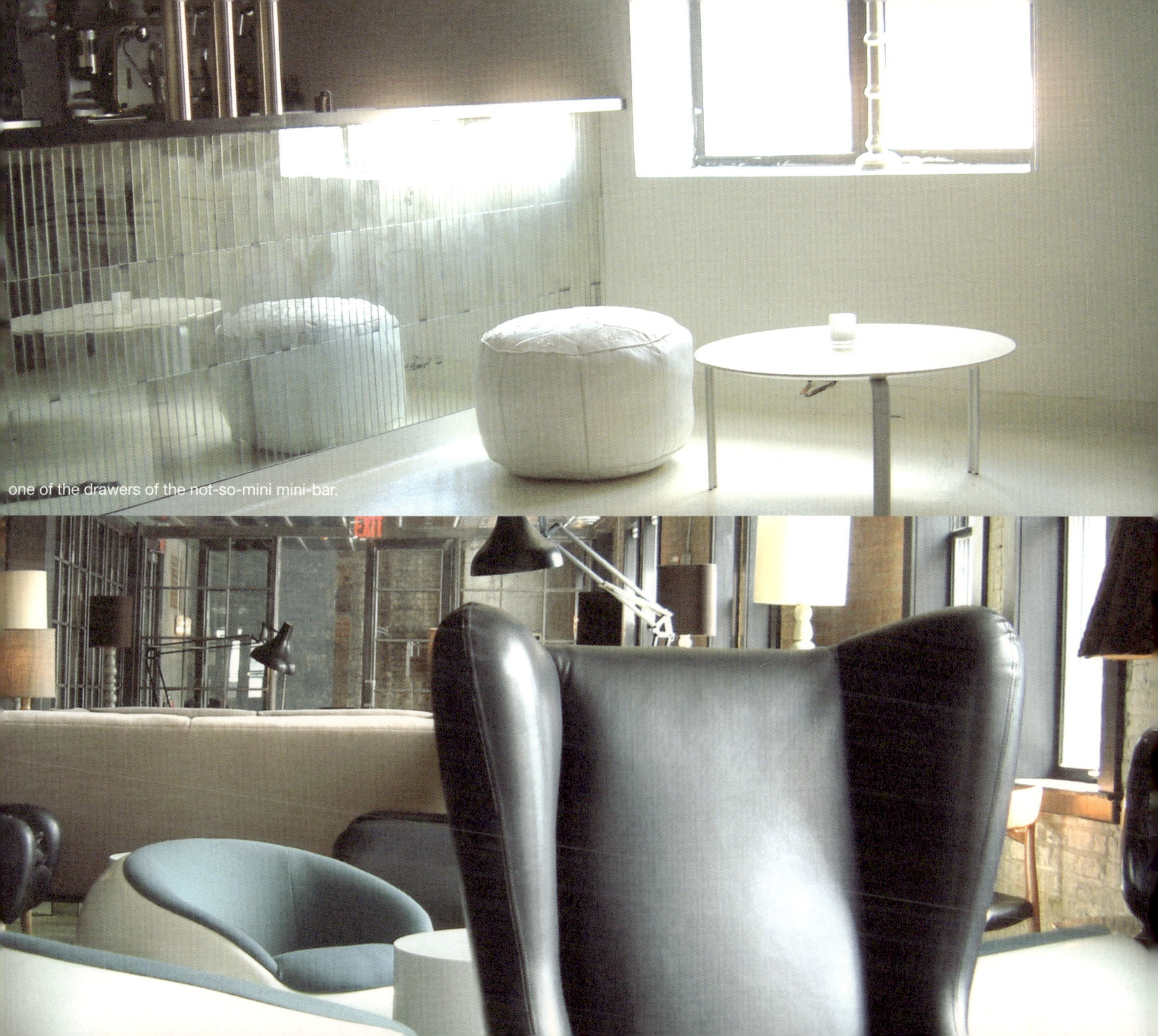

one of the drawers of the not-so-mini mini-bar.

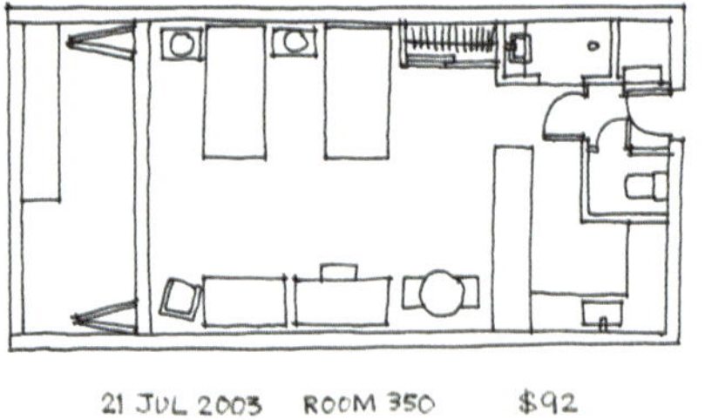

Hotel Le Corbusier

A MASTER'S VISION

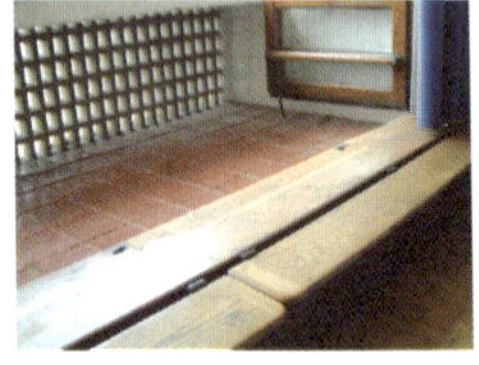

Located in the port city of Marseilles, France's second largest city, Hotel Le Corbusier is an age-transcending monument by the master architect. Built in the 1950s, it is a testimony and exemplar of his urban holism, apparent in his search for the perfect city and community from as early as the 1920s. If the building looks familiar, it is because its influences are far and wide, extending even to the 1960s public housing estates in Hong Kong. The hotel, bought last year by the Albans, a husband-and-wife team, is just a part of a larger complex. Le Corbusier himself compared the building to an ocean-liner: not only does each room afford a view of the surrounding scenery, but all the fixtures are maritime in style, complete with handrails everywhere. The bathroom has an unusually high threshold, just like on a ship, and the rooftop with its crèche, gym, and pool, resembles a ship deck soaked in the Mediterranean sun. There is a supermarket, a bakery, and a community center on the mid-level floors, equally easy to access by guests above and below. Such holistic and all-inclusive planning seems all the more prescient in light of what we are used to today. Not everything stylish survives the unrelenting march of time, but Le Corbusier's vision and the international style he inspired most certainly have.

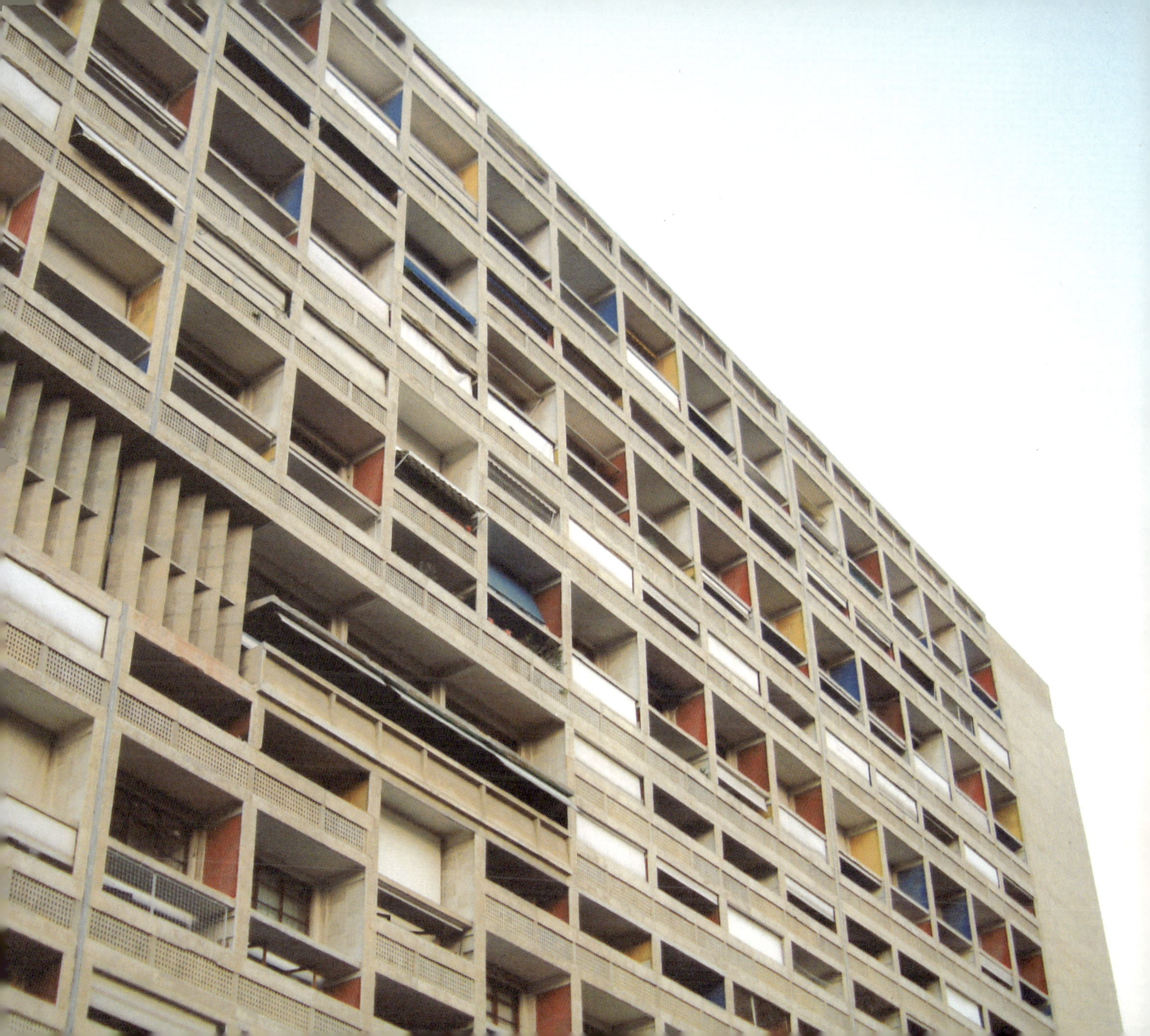

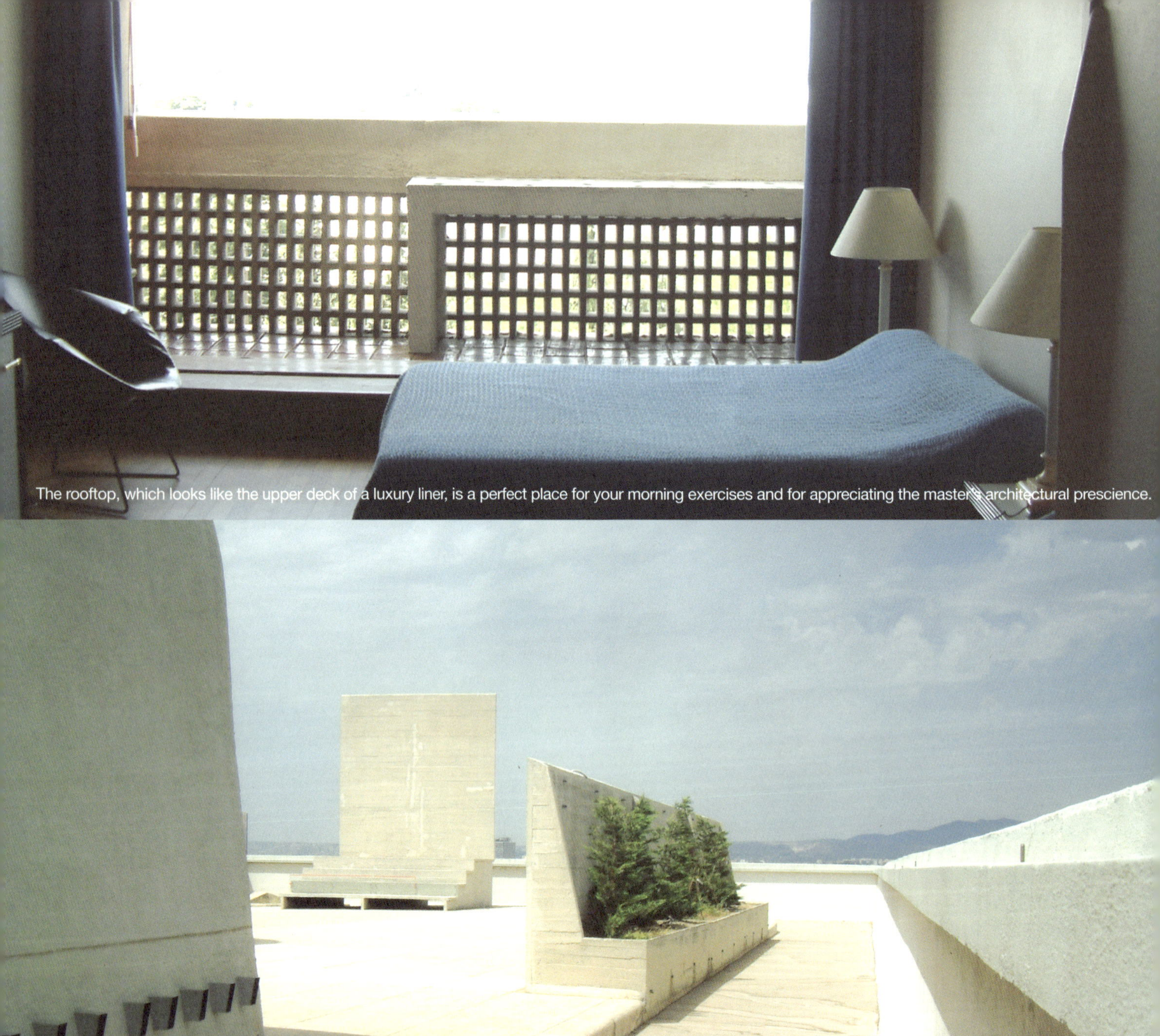

The rooftop, which looks like the upper deck of a luxury liner, is a perfect place for your morning exercises and for appreciating the master's architectural prescience.

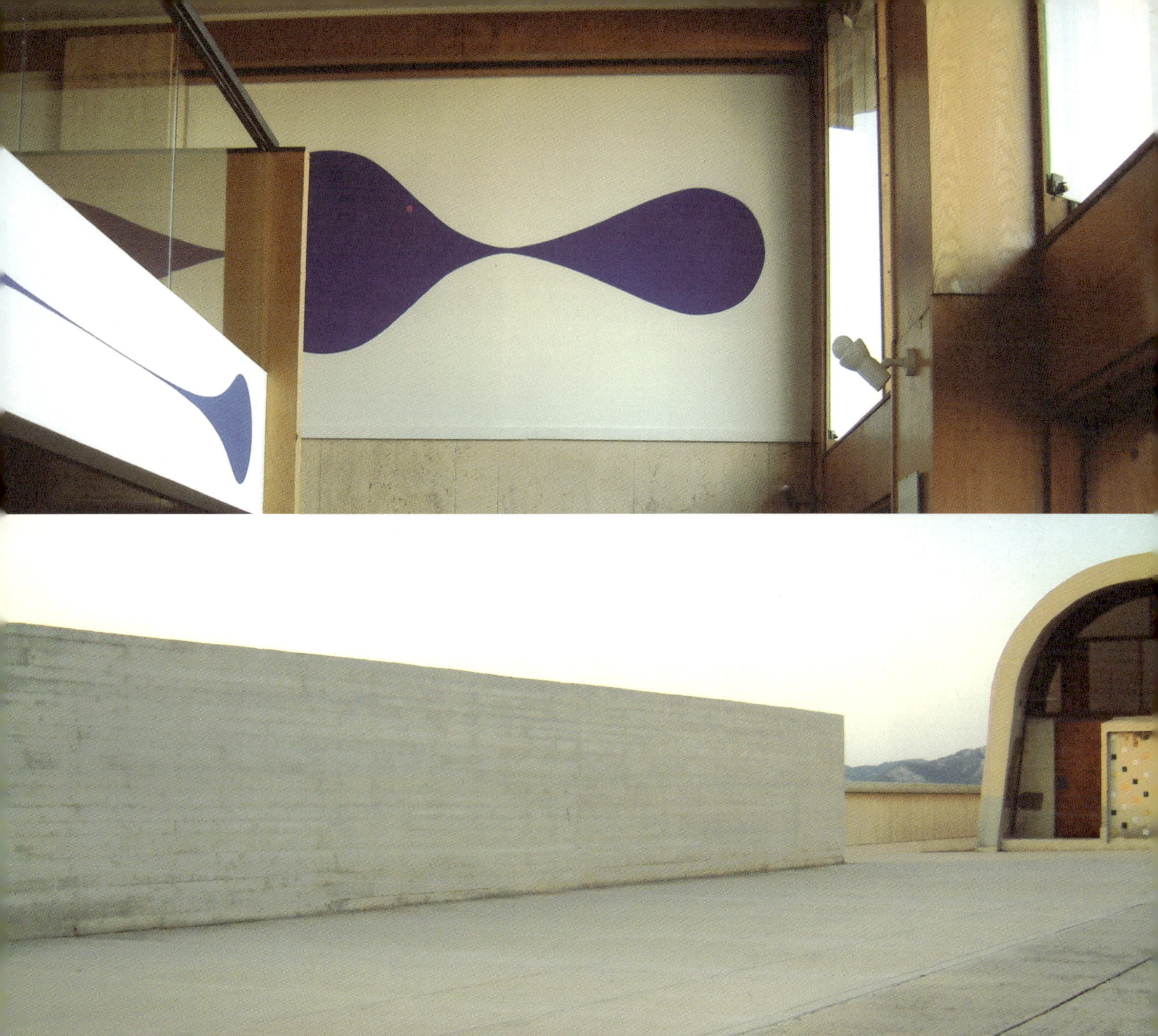

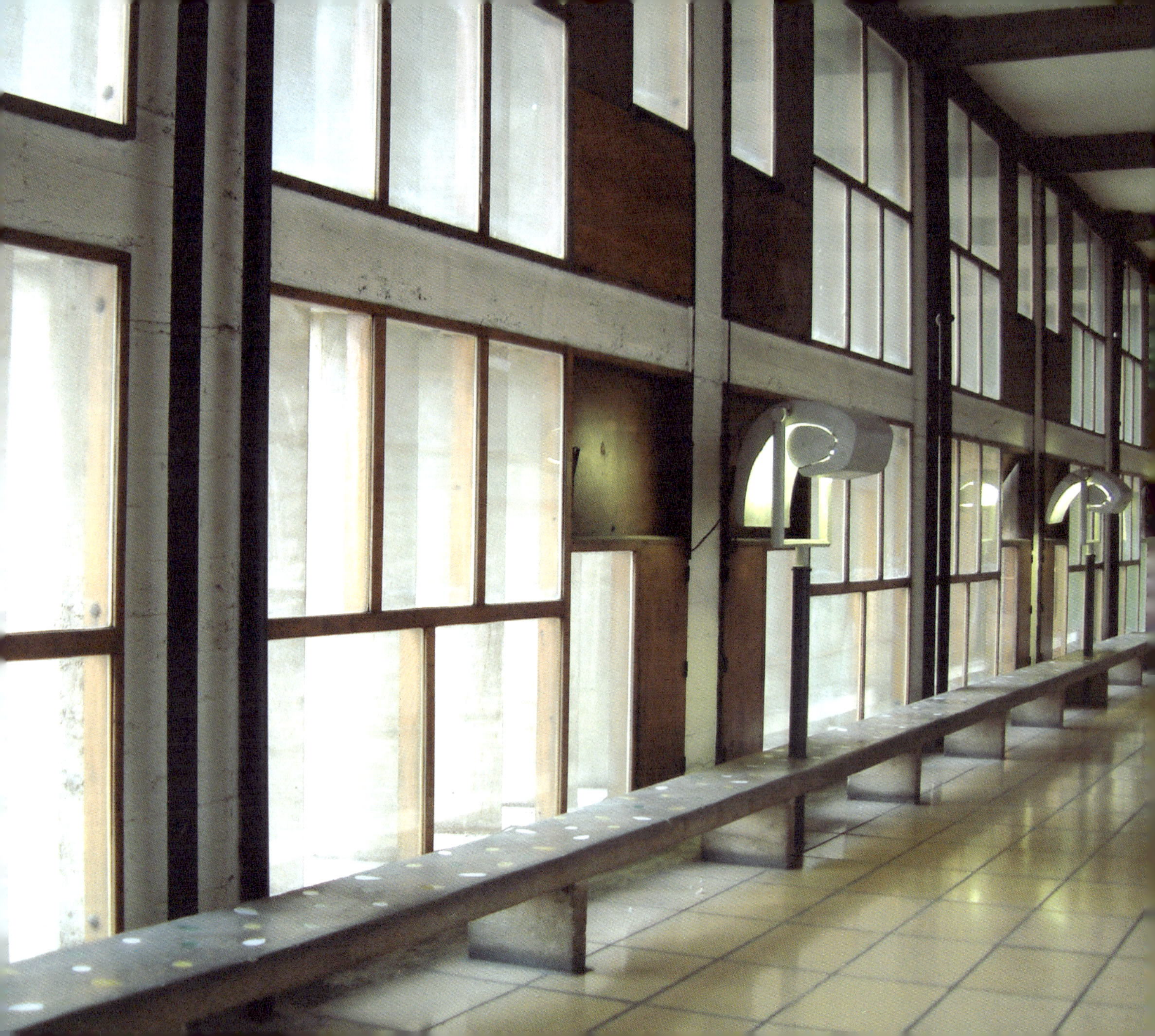

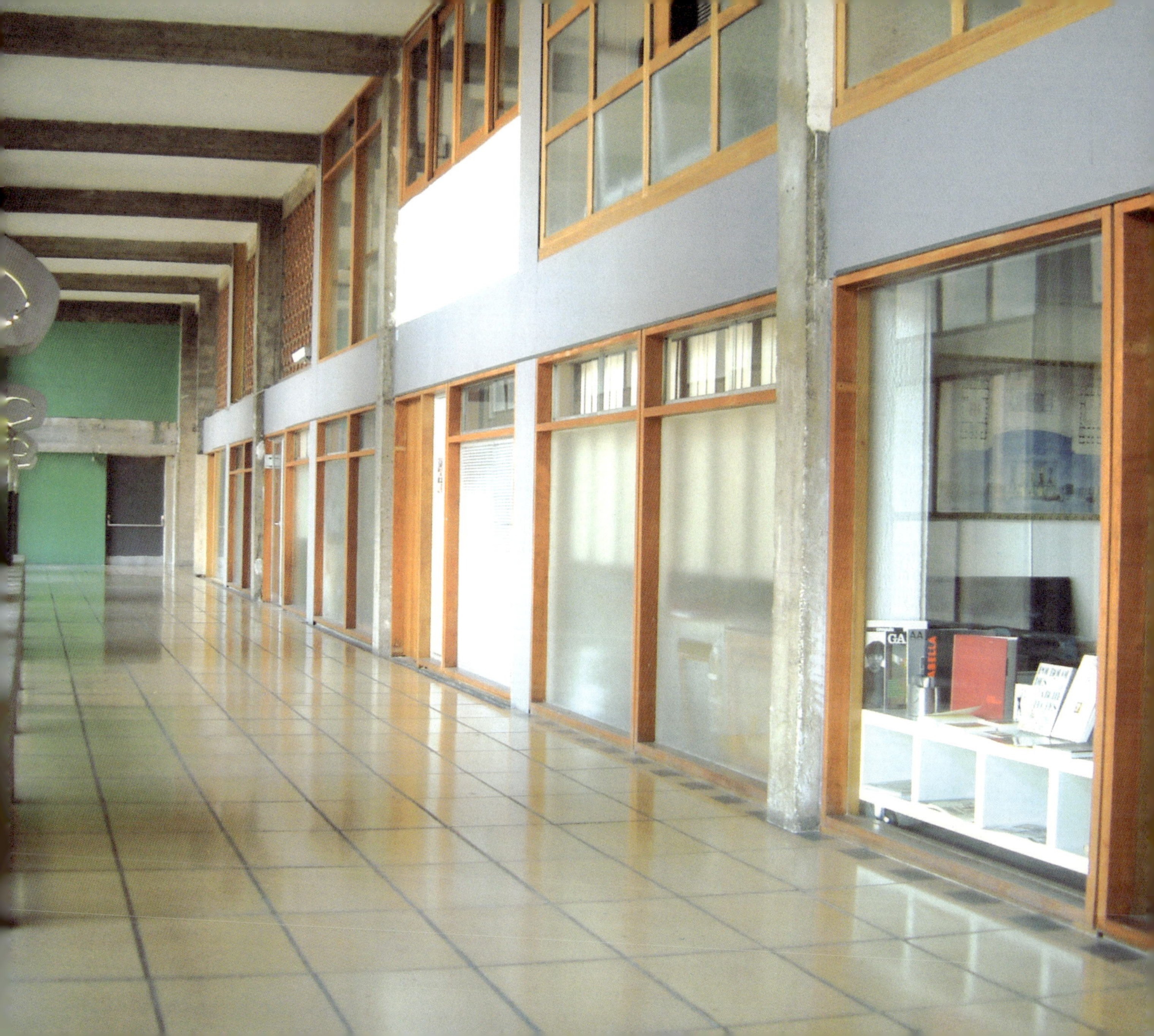
GA
AA

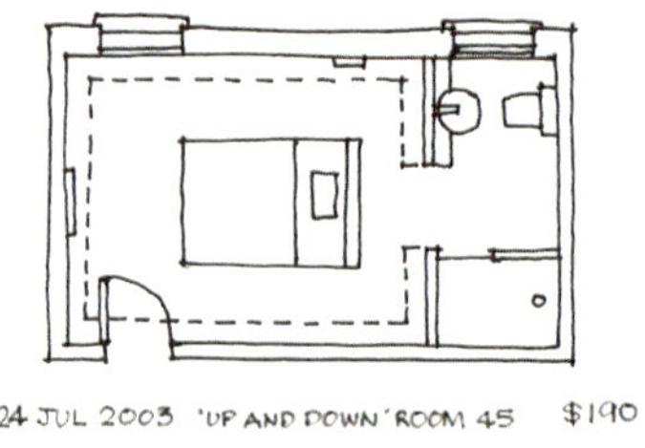

Hi Hotel

ENDLESS SURPRISES

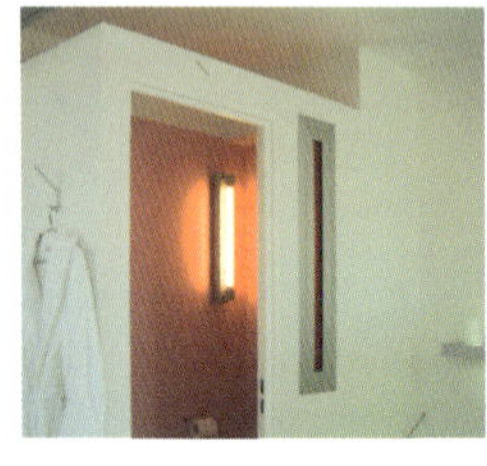

Hi Hotel sets a new standard for what a hotel can be. Its thirty-eight rooms are divided into nine different themes—nine different ways of using space—all conceptually linked by the motif of reinterpretation. Designed by the industrial designer Matali Crasset (whose hairstyle somehow reminds me of Joan of Arc), it is full of surprising yet highly practical innovations. The building itself is a simple 1930s structure, but in the deft hands of Crasset, the explorer-at-play, the hotel invites its guests to become explorers themselves. I stayed in two rooms, a "white-and-white" and an "up-and-down." As the label suggests, the "white-and-white" is complete, unadulterated whiteness. Inside, what looks like a desk is actually the bed, while a bed frame serves as the bath. The chairs look like suitcases with arms that fold down to become coffee tables. The one-hundred-odd-square-foot "up-and-down" has shelves wrought from cherry branches, which run along the walls and divide the room into an upper and lower space. The hotel's spa is an inviting space for relaxation and includes a chill-out room that is lit only by three lights. Outside, the bright "Hi" sign on the roof extends a friendly greeting before it quickly changes color.

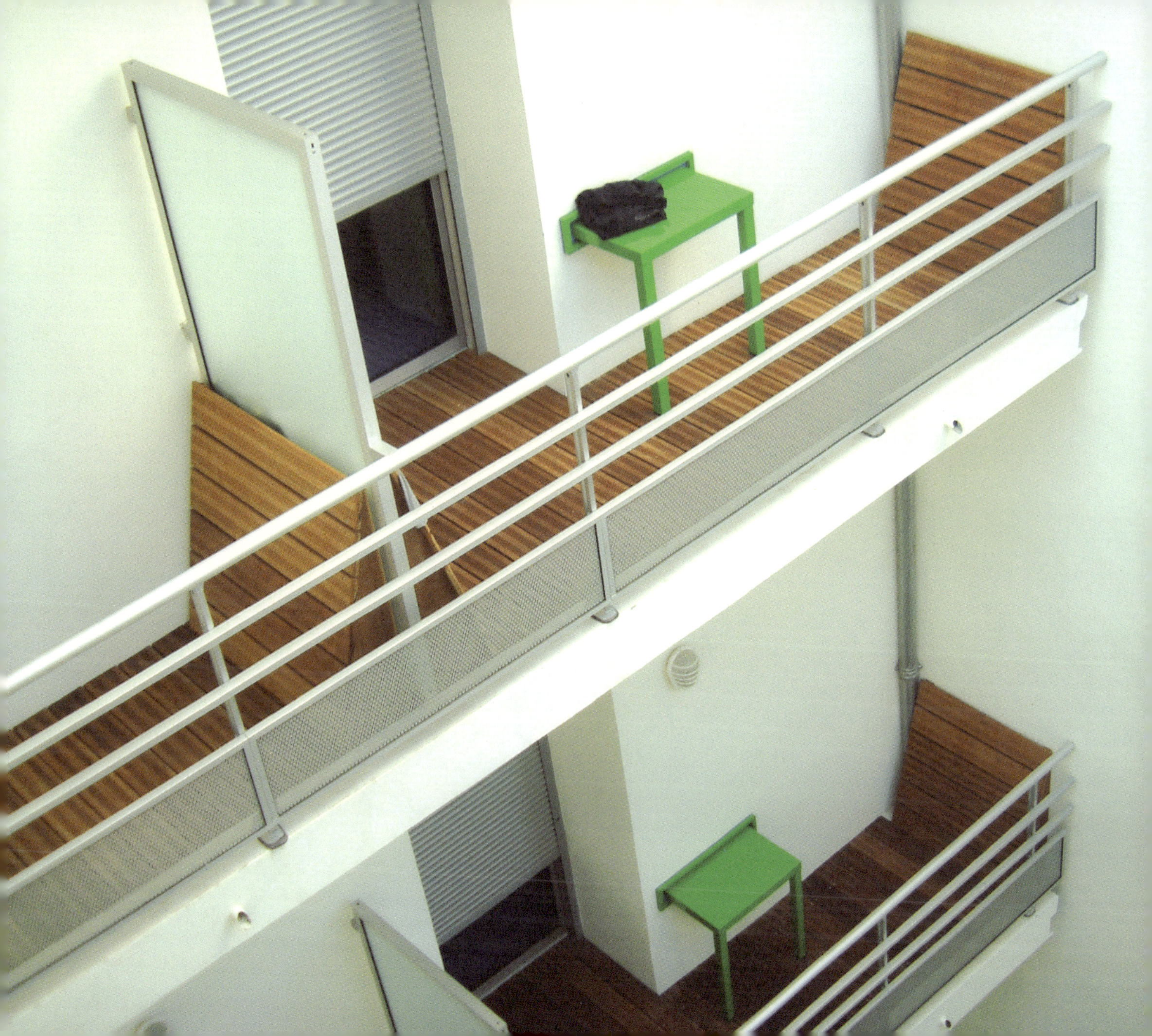

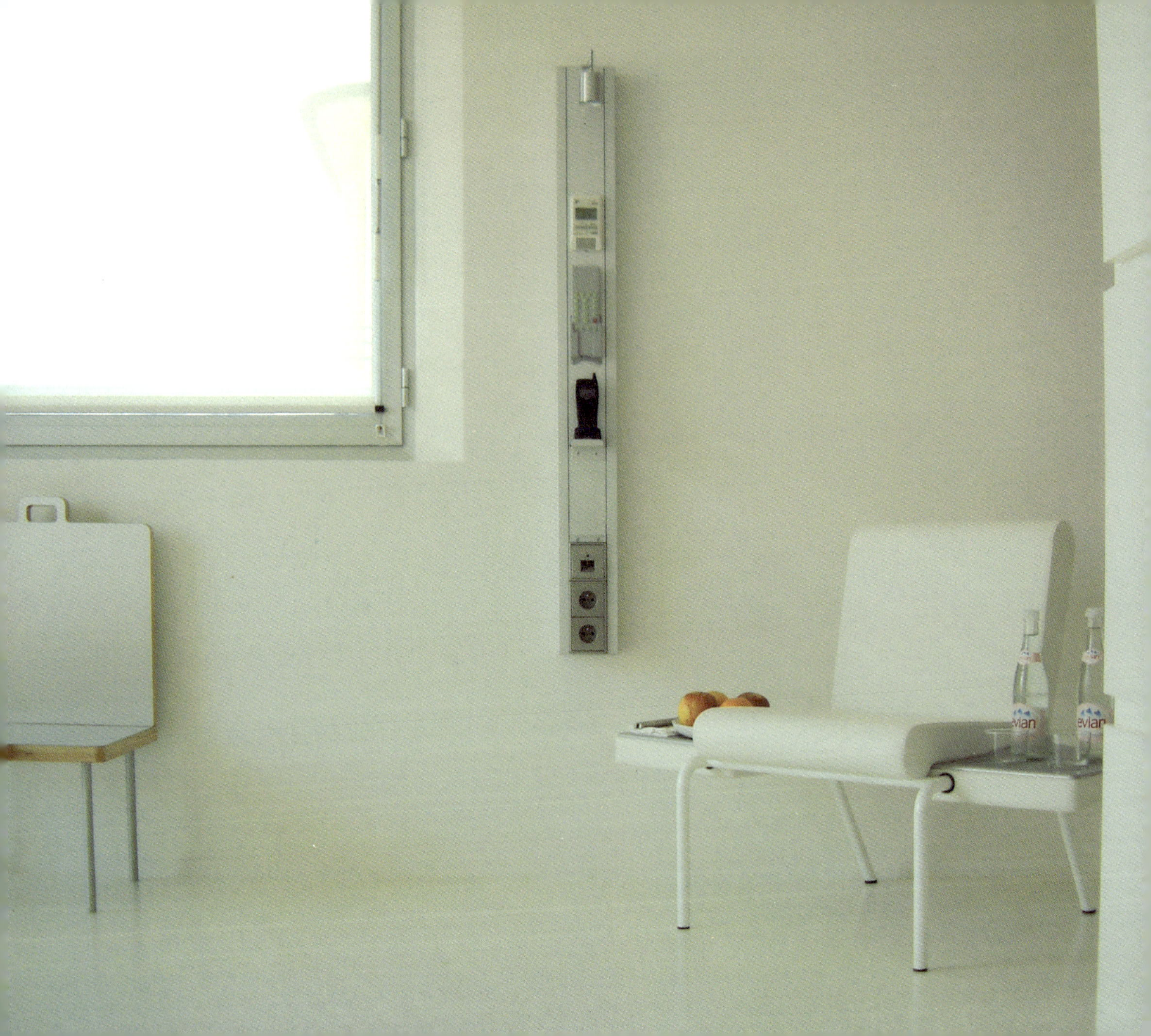
evian

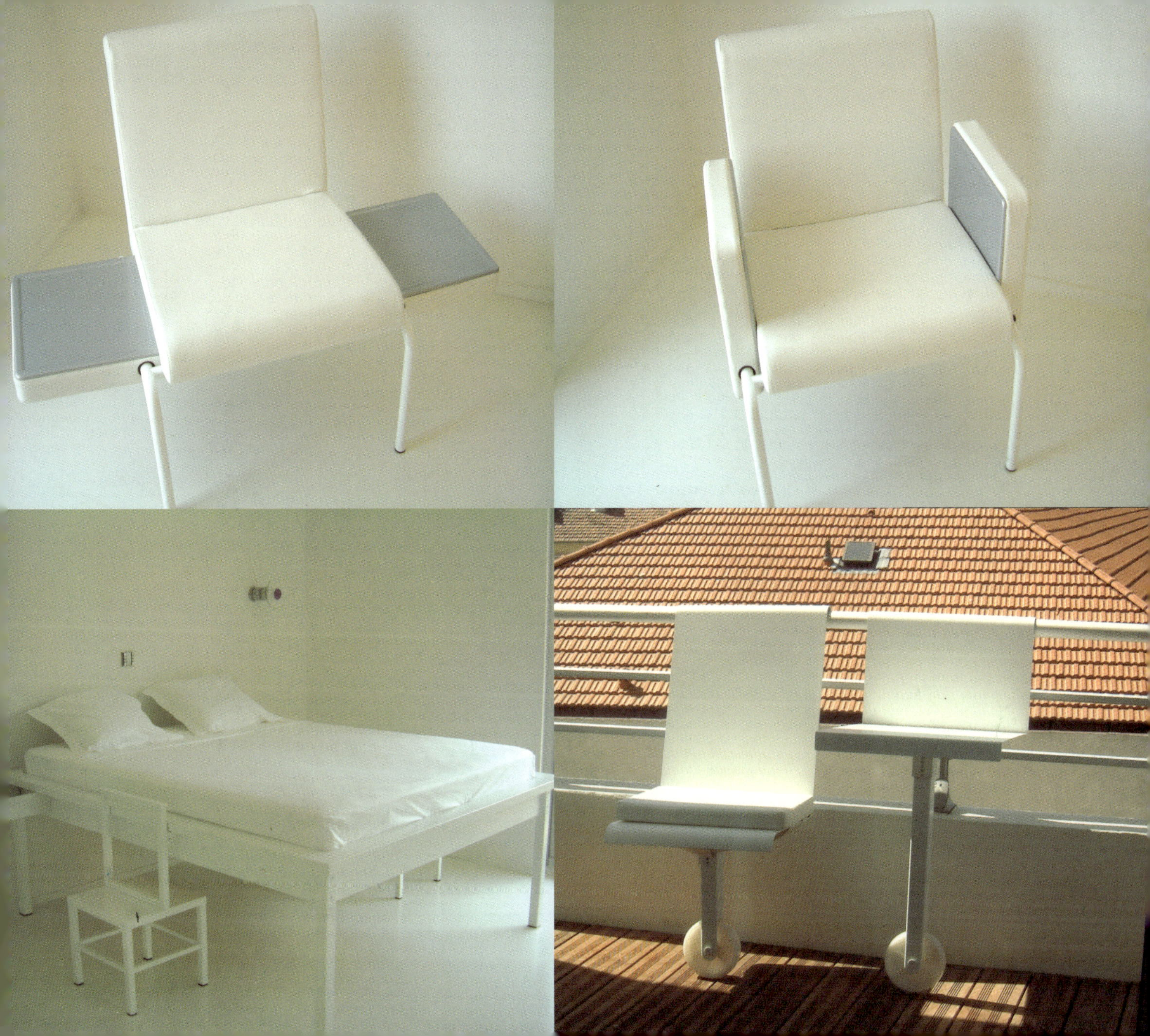

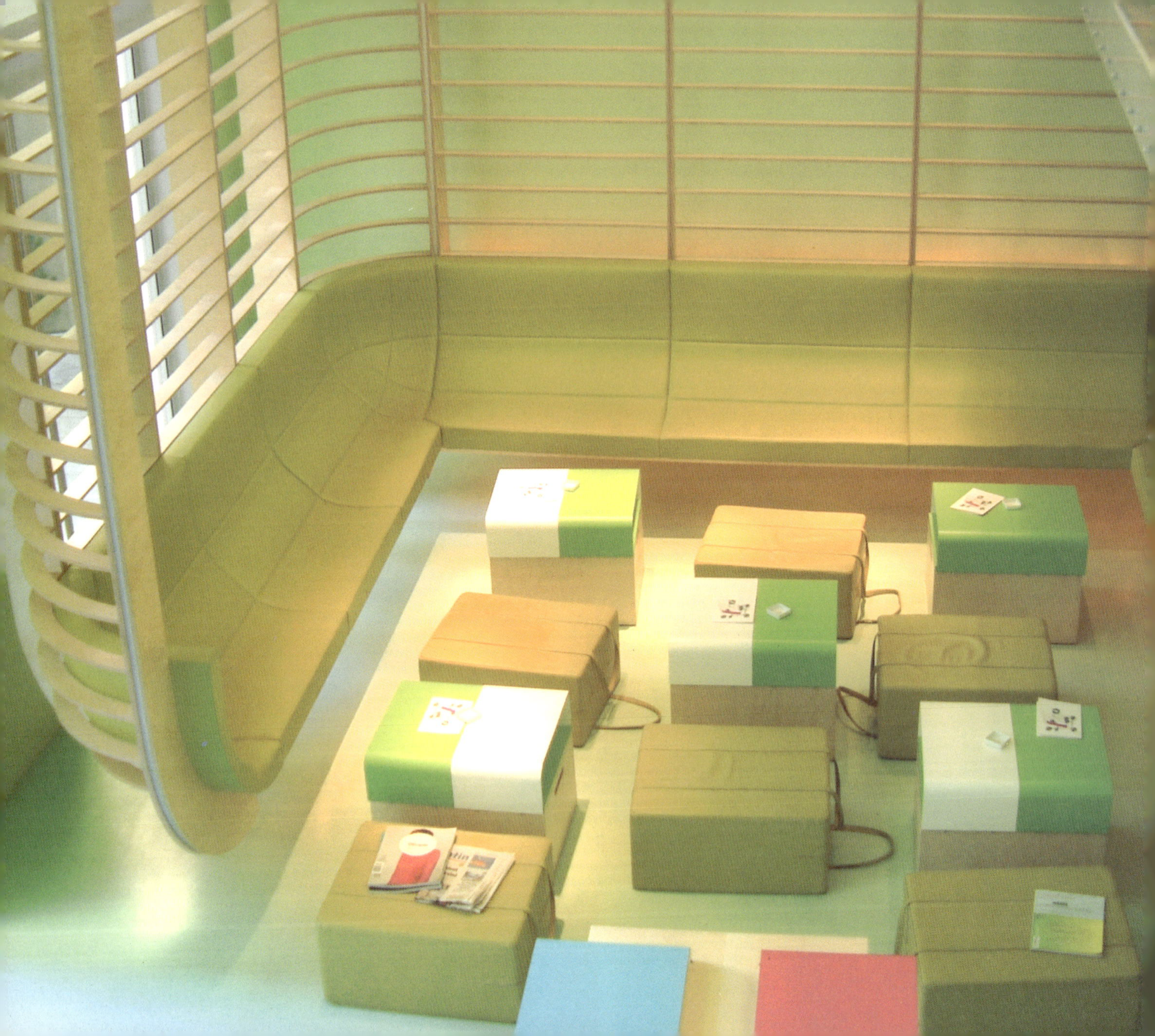

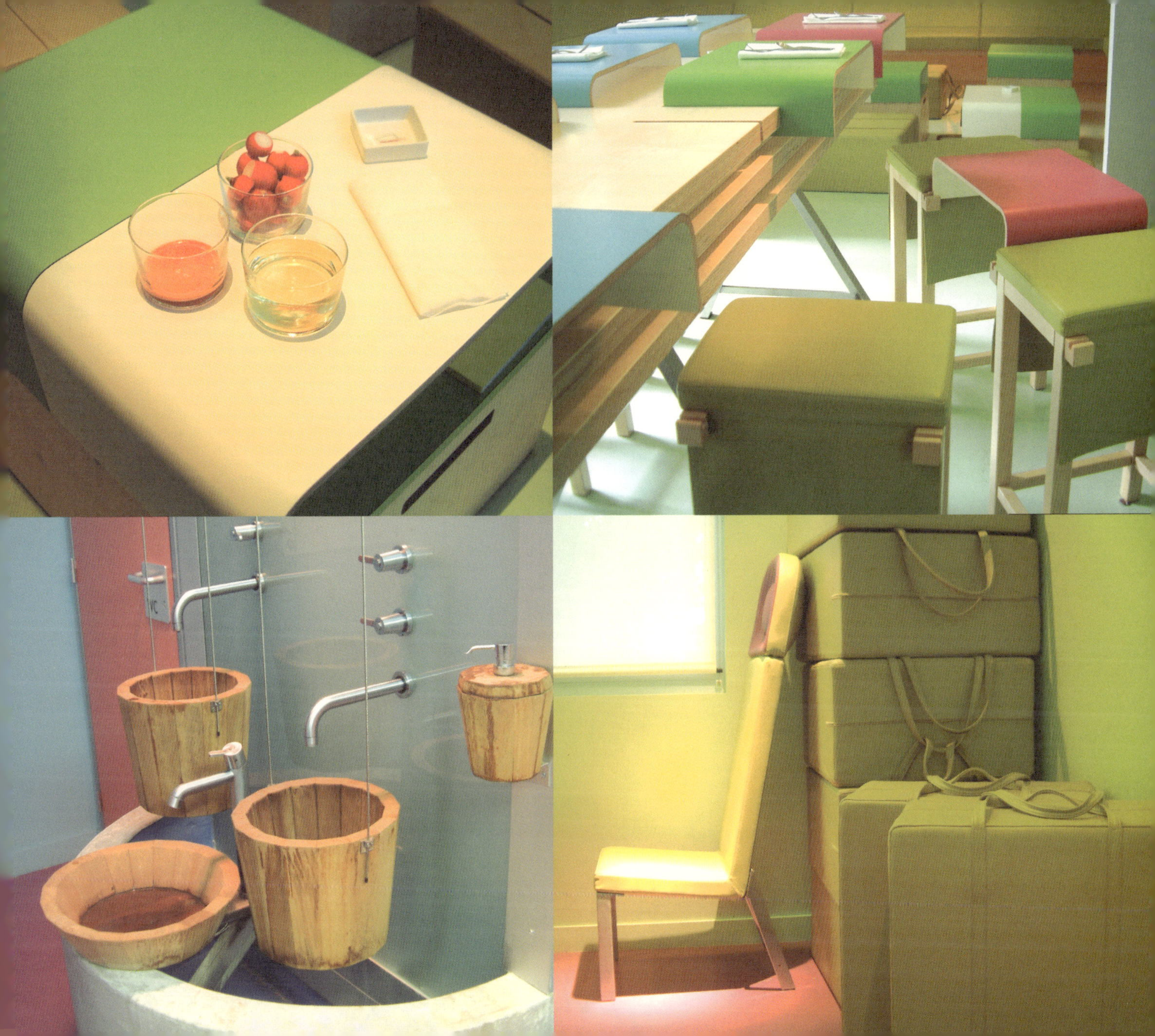

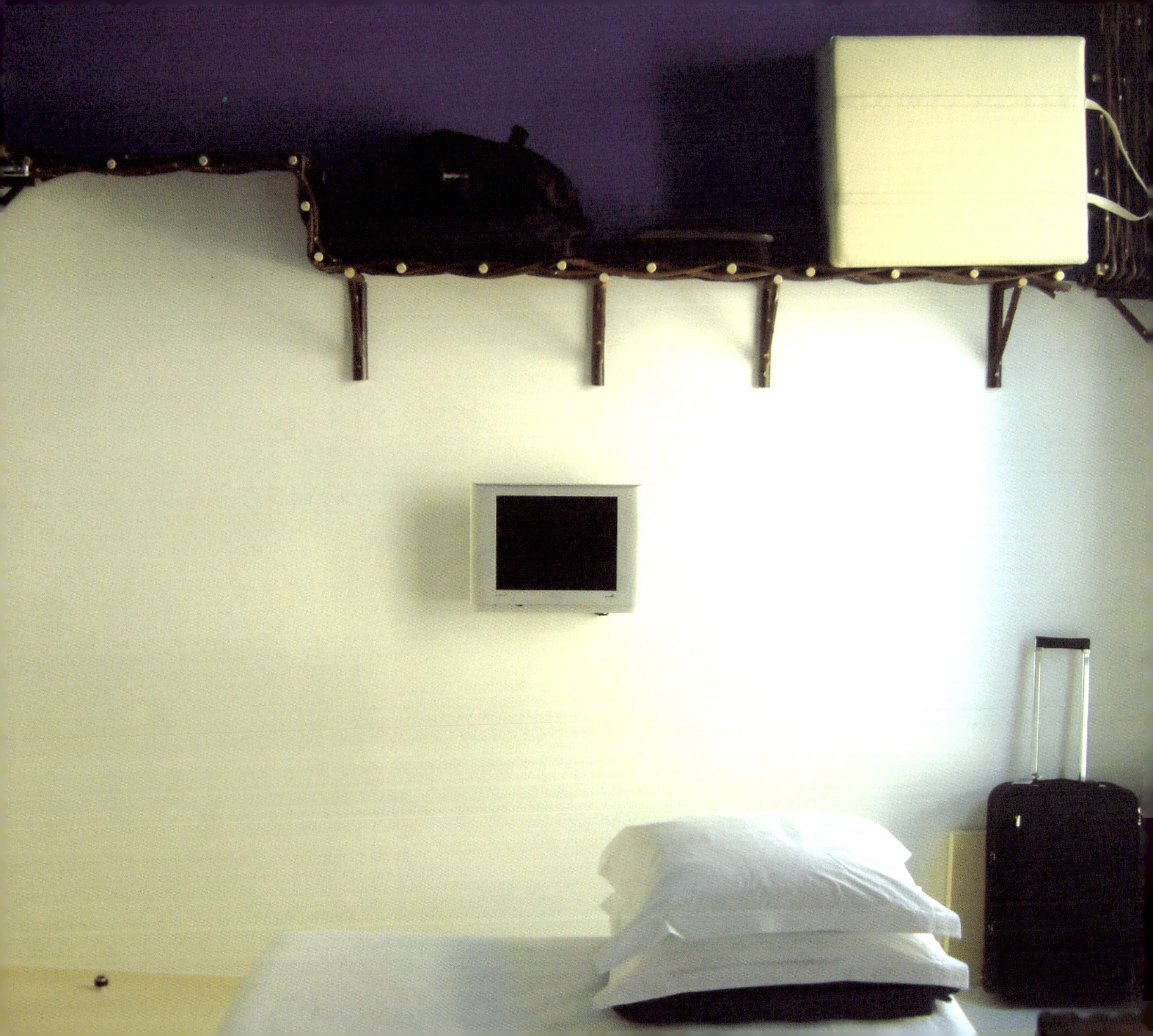

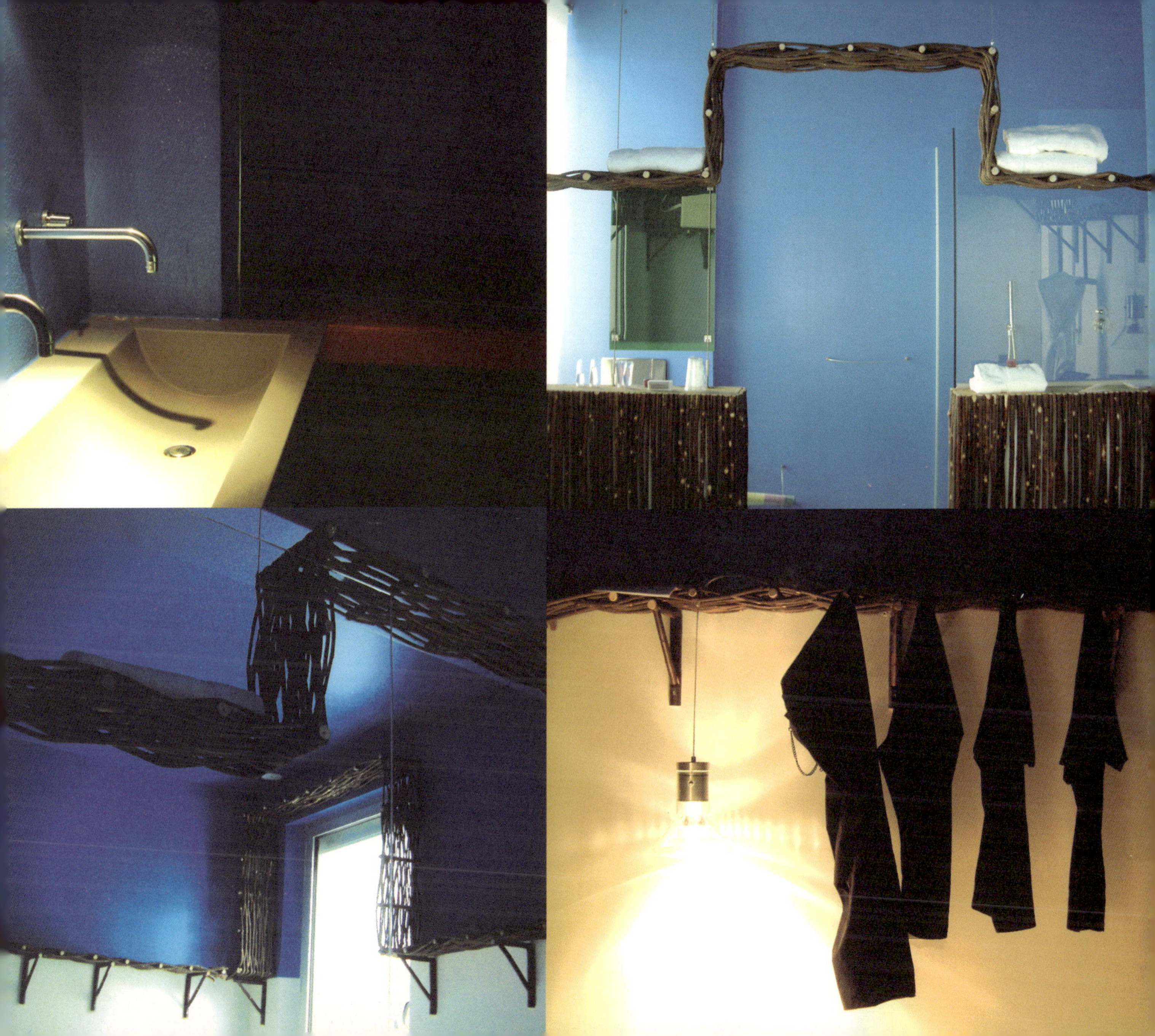

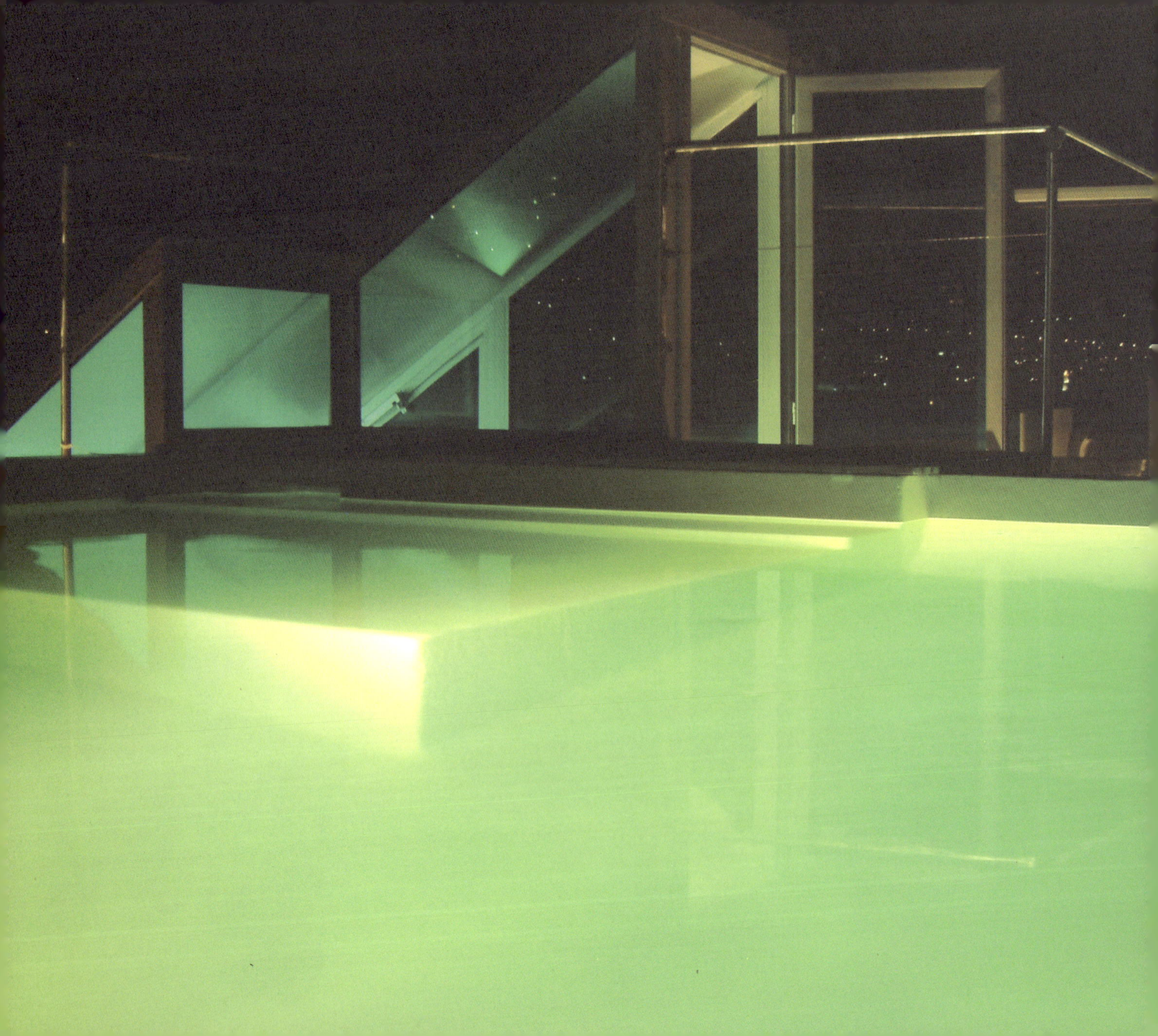

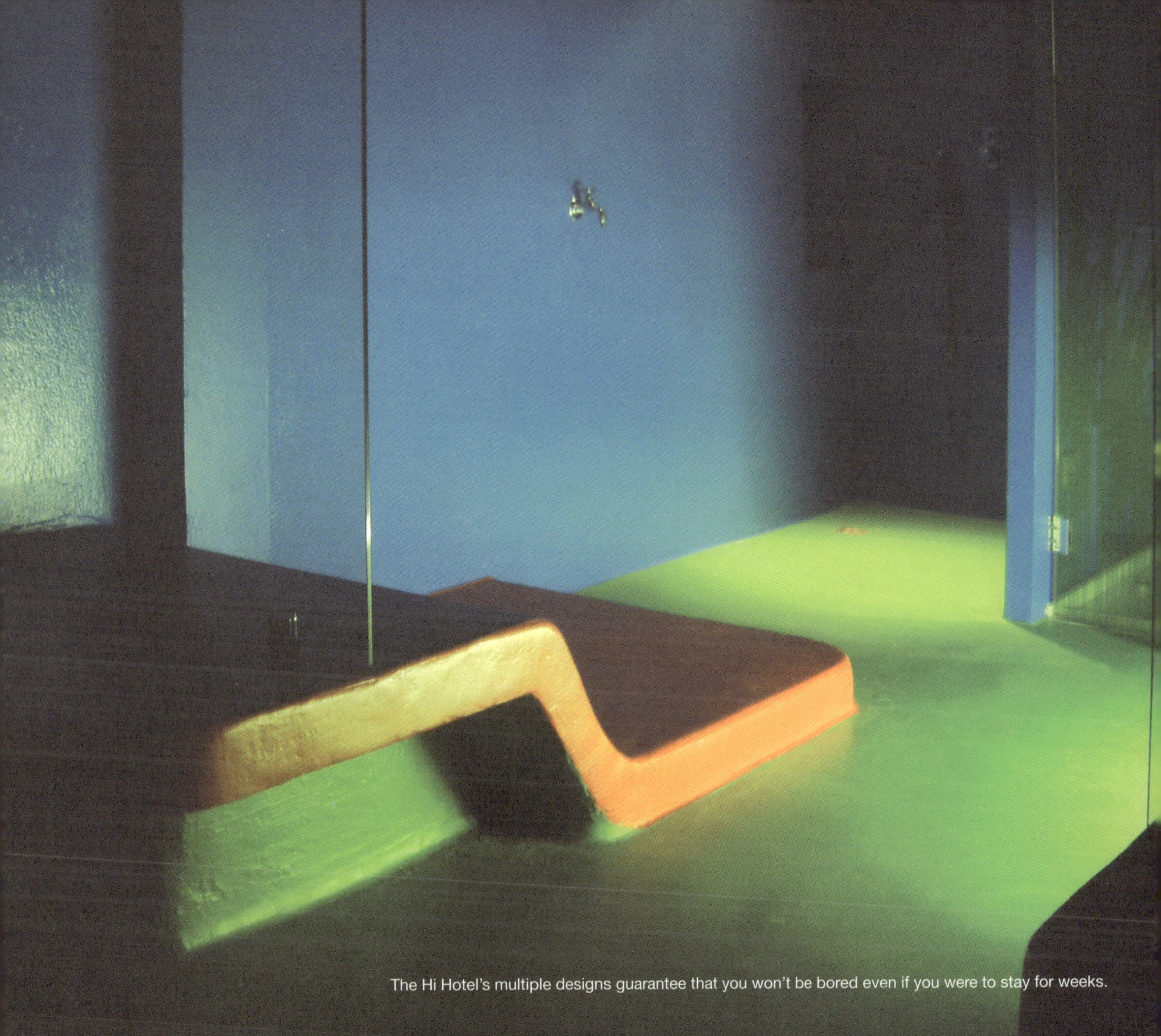

The Hi Hotel's multiple designs guarantee that you won't be bored even if you were to stay for weeks.

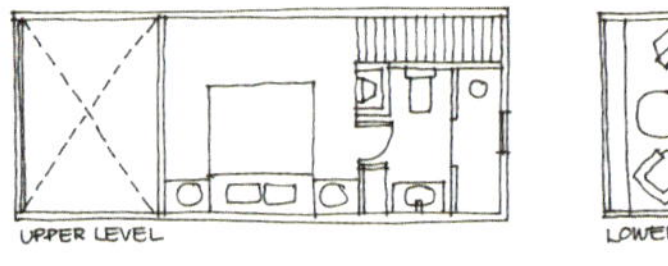

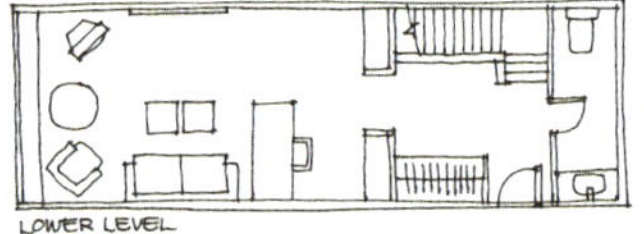

15 AUG 2003 DUPLEX LOFT 532 $328

W Hotels

(now Blue Wolloomooloo Bay)

STYLE AND INDIVIDUALITY

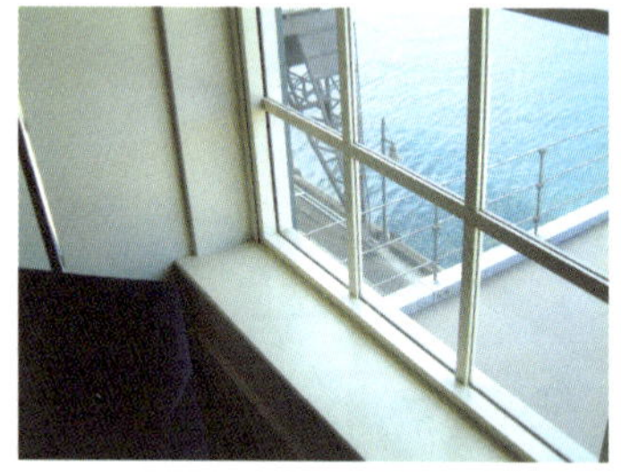

When individuality and character are all the rage, even big hotel chains realize that standardization might not be everyone's cup of tea. So what gives the Sydney W its character? To begin with, it is housed in an old warehouse on an old wharf. While Wharf Woolloomooloo has long shed its former identity as a working wharf to become the latest addition of private residences and hotels to the waterfront redevelopment of the Sydney Harbor—already graced by numerous parks, galleries, malls, government offices, and the Sydney Opera House—its original 1200-foot-long warehouse building has been retained. One third of its interior has been turned into apartments, while the W takes up the remainder, making its layout rather unusual for a hotel. The lobby sits in the middle of the lengthy structure, flanked by guest rooms on either side. The original system of cargo conveyor belts, which still runs through the hotel interior, is a constant reminder of the building's origin.

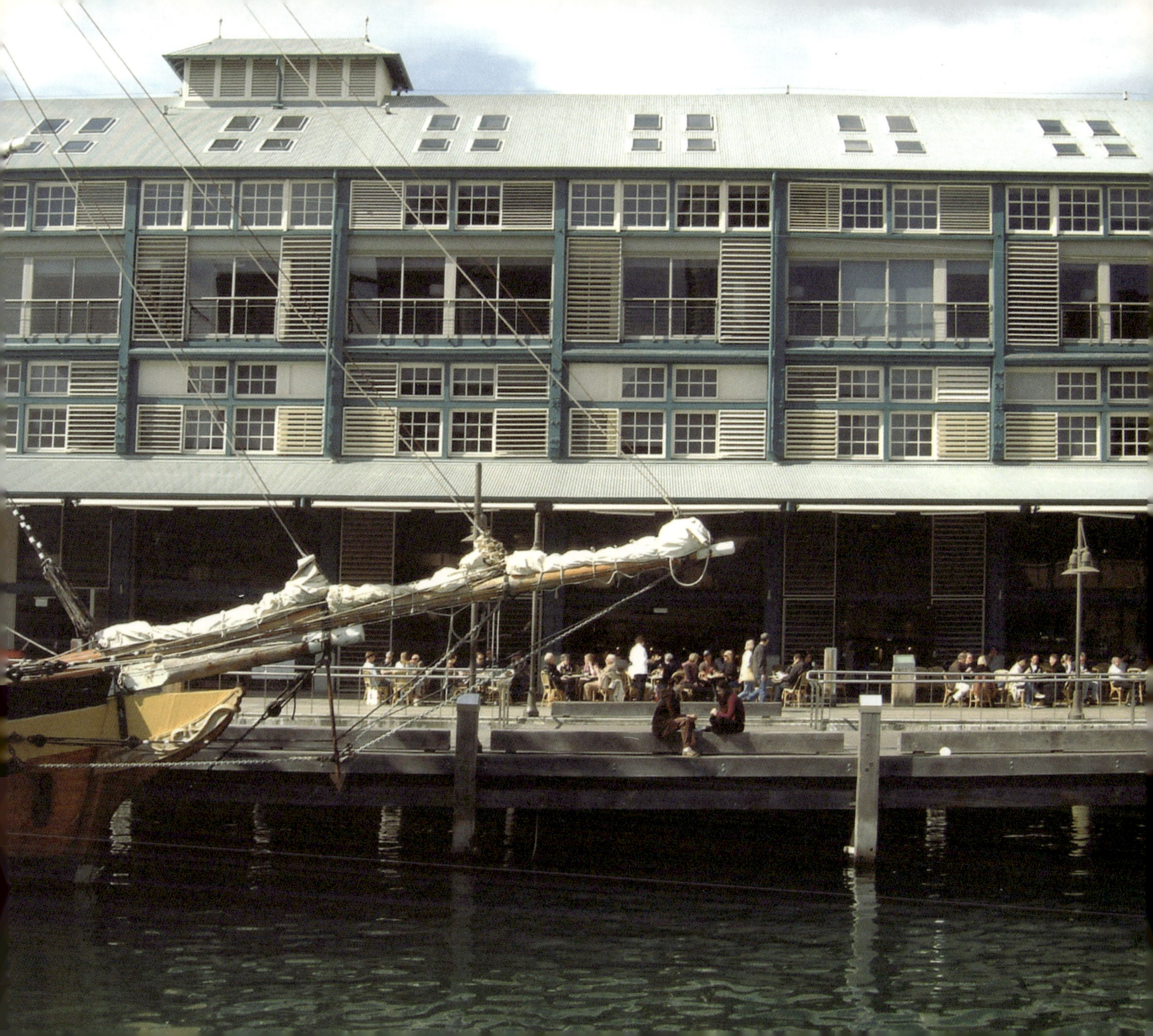

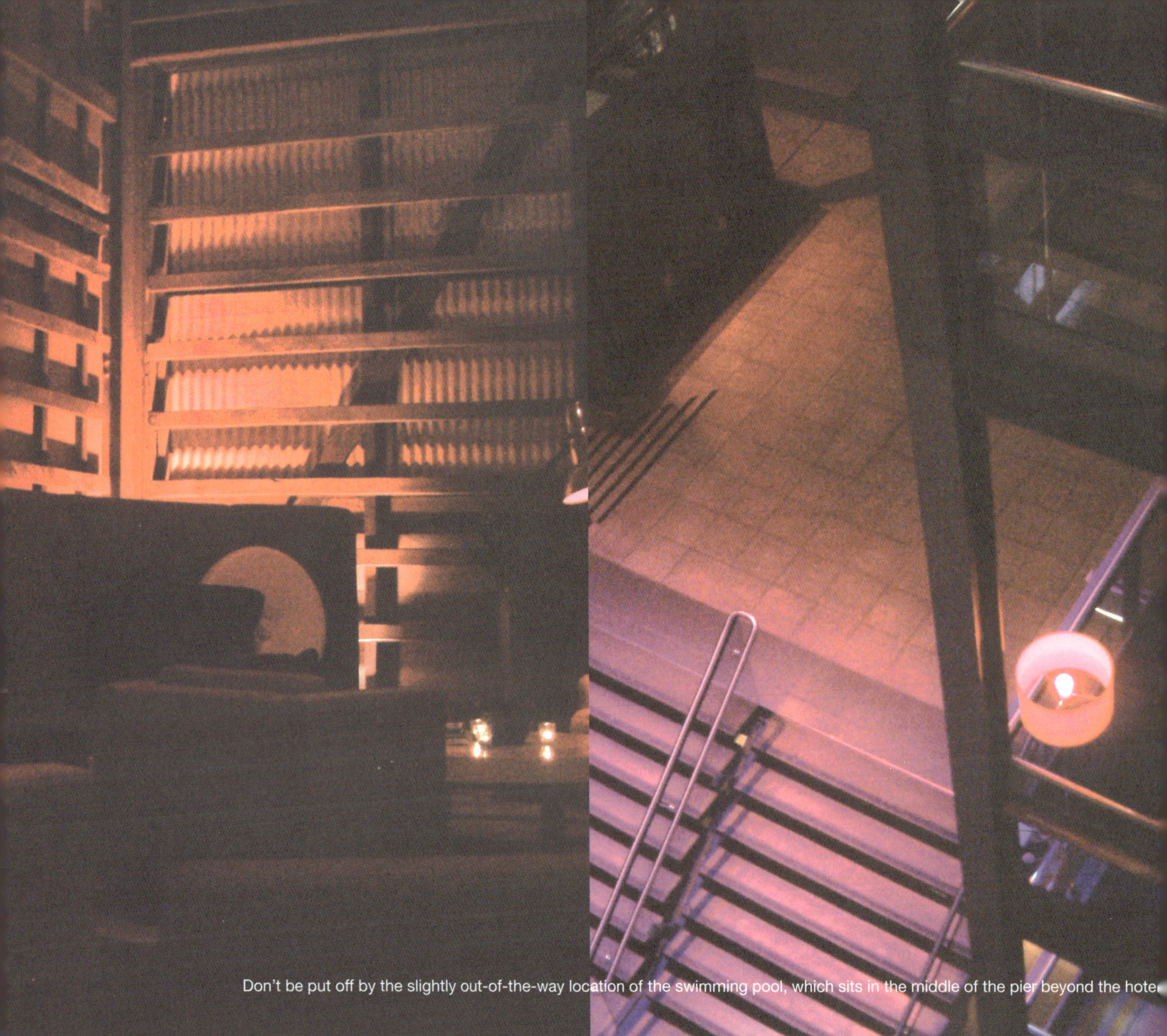

Don't be put off by the slightly out-of-the-way location of the swimming pool, which sits in the middle of the pier beyond the hote

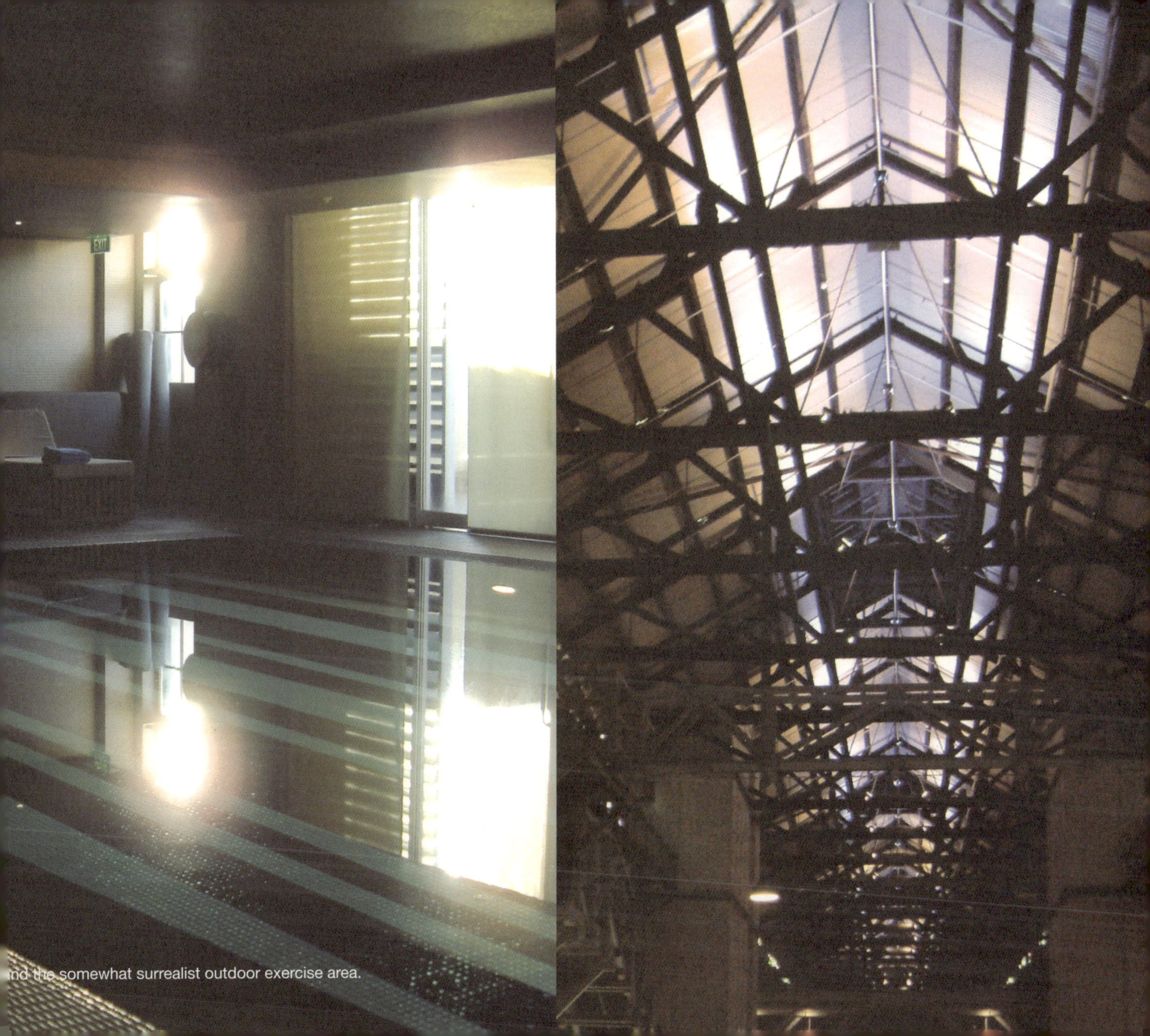

nd the somewhat surrealist outdoor exercise area.

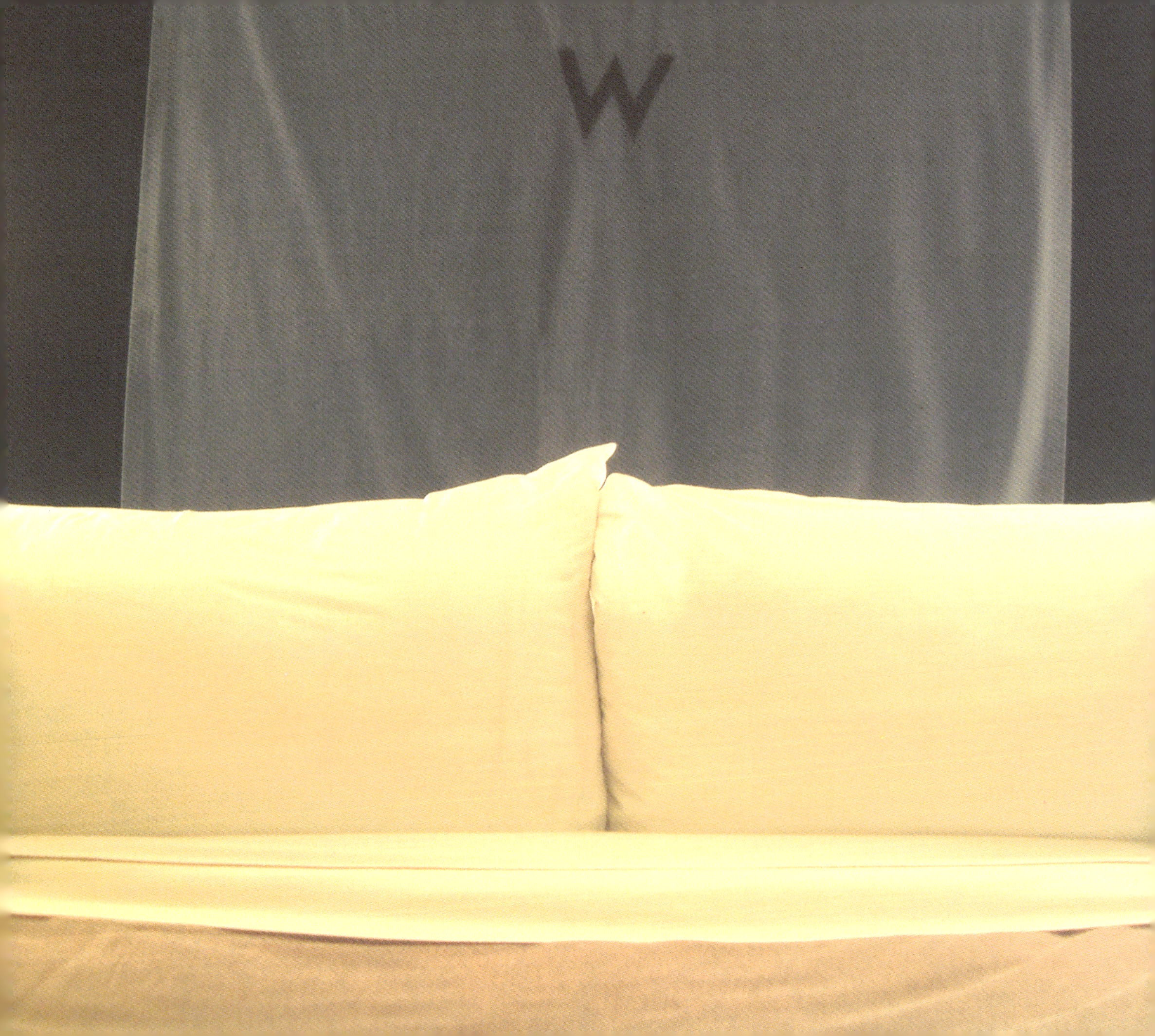
W

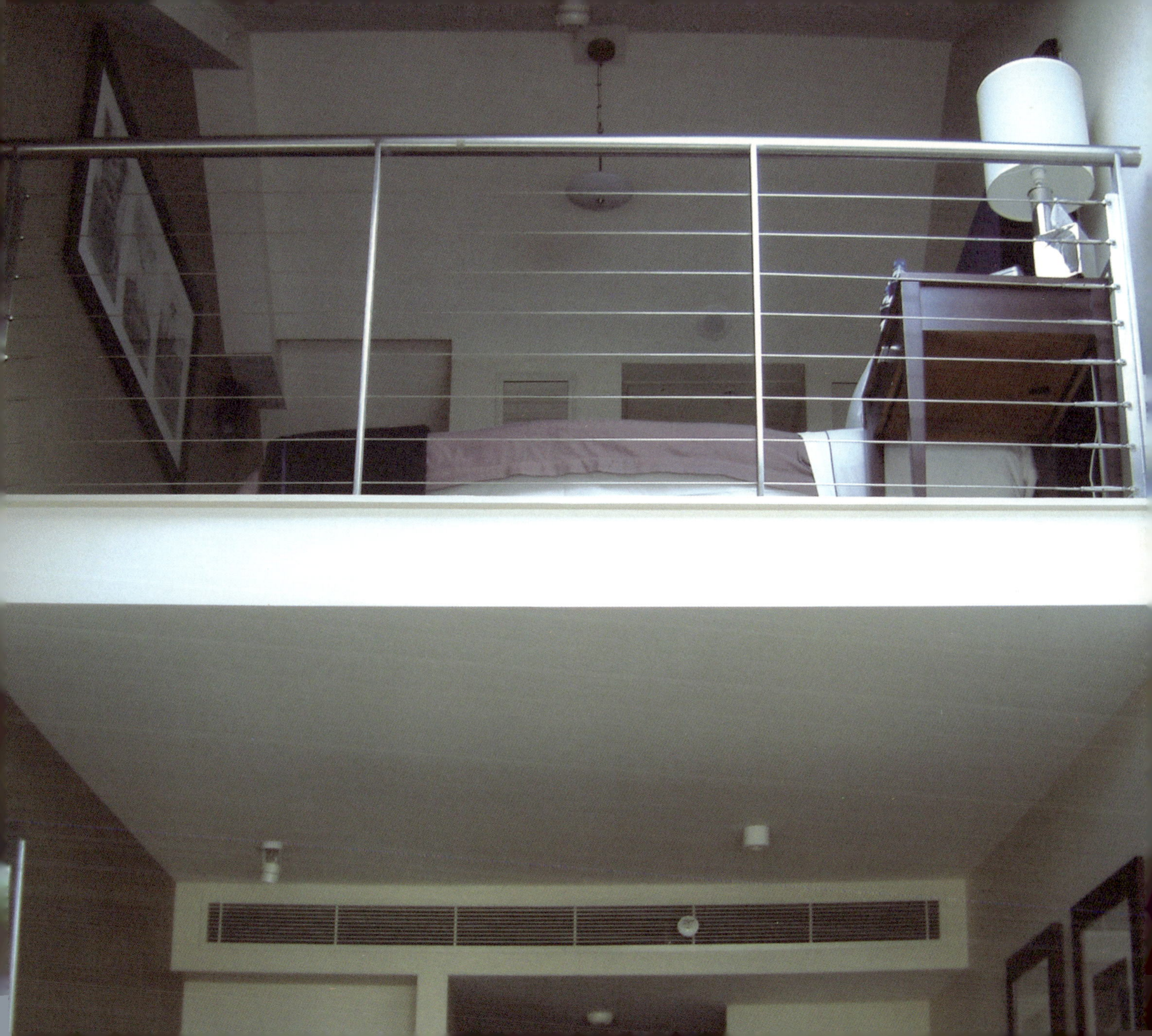

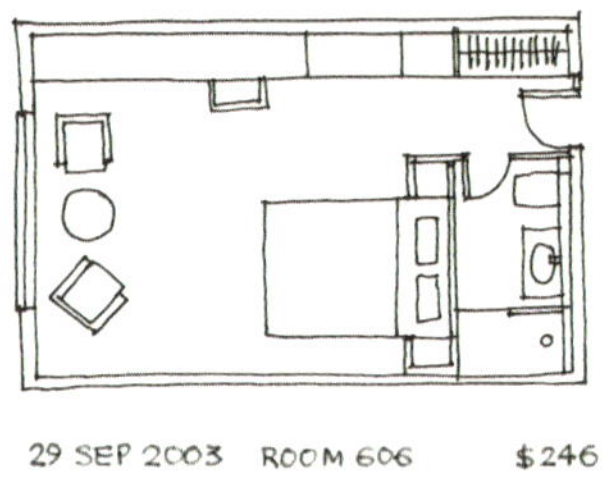

The Maritime Hotel

A PIECE OF HONG KONG IN NEW YORK

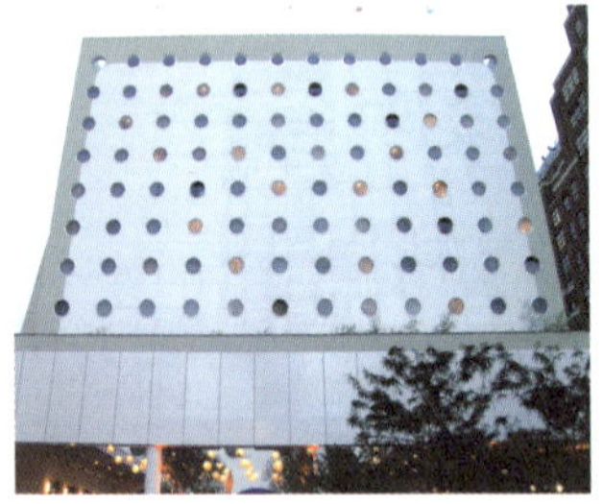

The Jardines House in Hong Kong, which used to be called the Connaught Centre, is one of those landmarked buildings that have left an indelible mark on the city's collective memory. When I first saw the Hotel Maritime in New York, I couldn't help but think of the Connaught Centre because of all its retro, round windows. Built in the 1960s, the building has an exceptionally thin structure, which makes it resemble a flat piece of toy building block. To this day, even after having been turned into a hotel, it cannot shed its former maritime-training-school self; the large round windows still call to mind portholes, and the teak-paneled walls and ceilings still sport the rounded corners found in ship cabins. But the design's nostalgia is saved from degenerating into cliché by the Japanese blue-and-white printed fabric used for the rooms' window drapes. Now, what would a Jardines House-turned-hotel be like, I wonder?

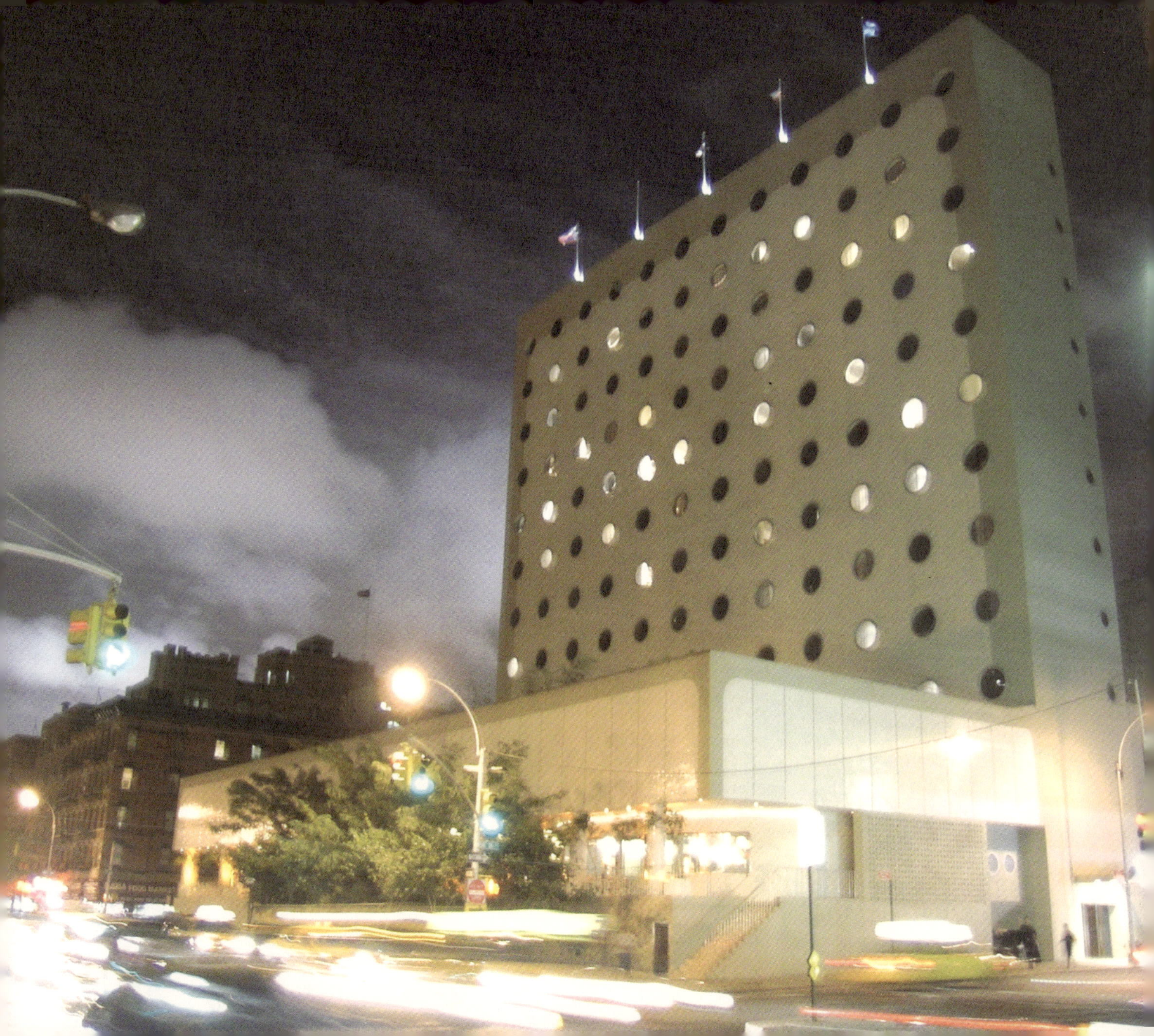

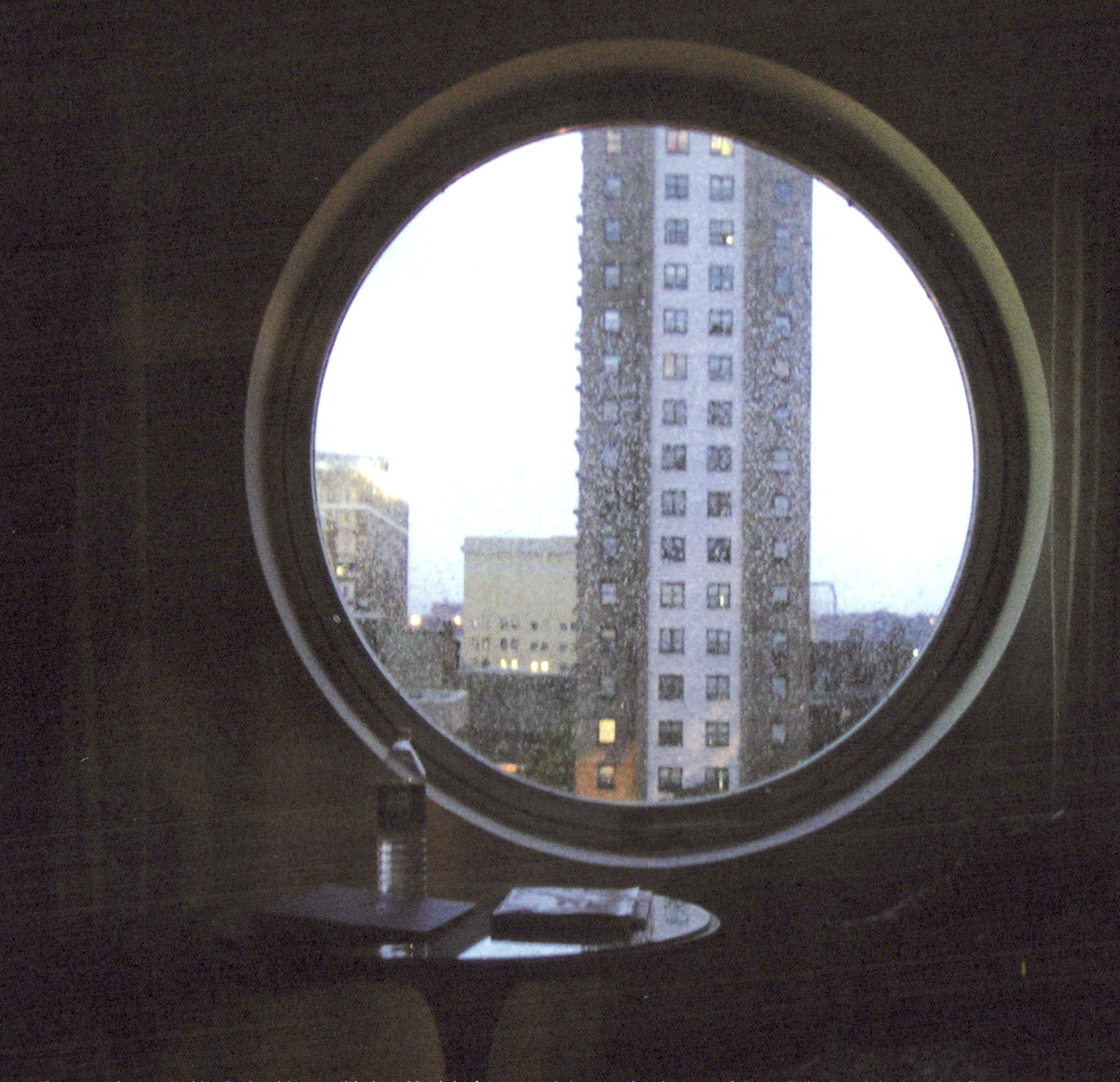

If you are interested in design history, this hotel is right for you as it has retained many of the building's original period fixtures.

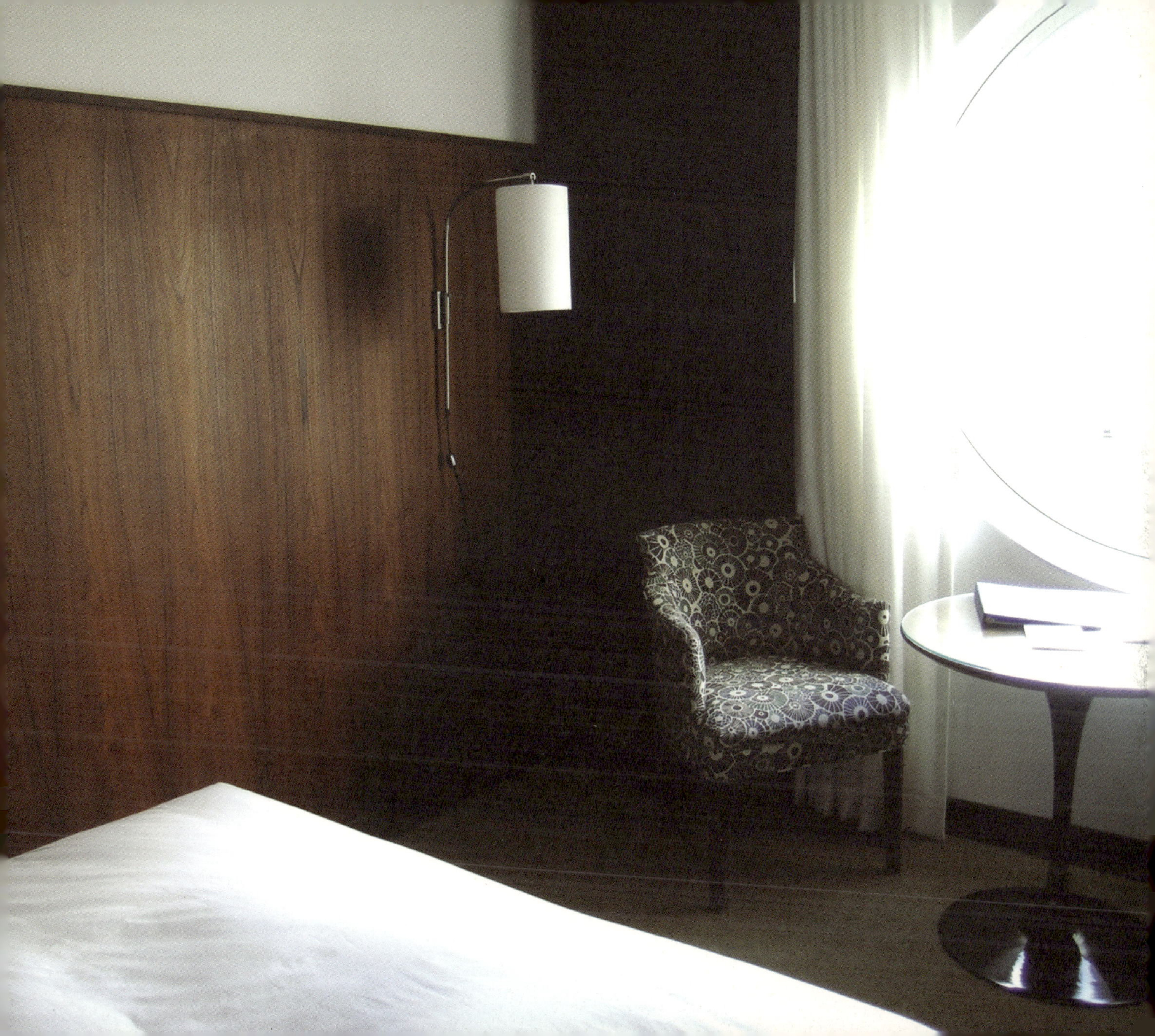

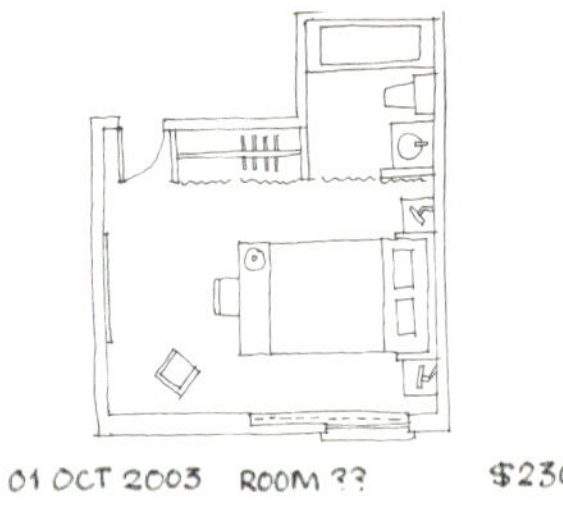

Hudson Hotel

STARCK'S *TROMPE L'OEIL*

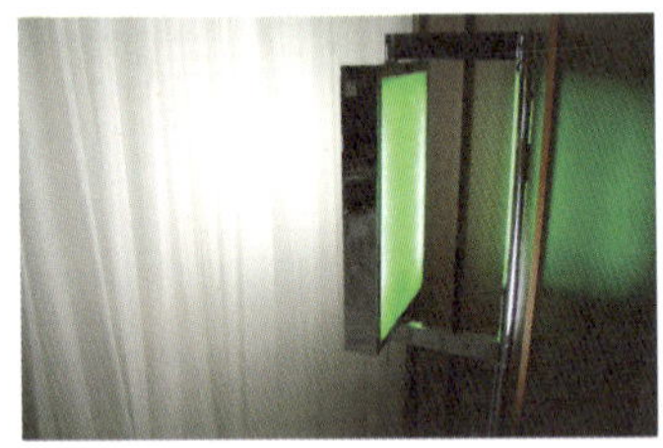

I've always been a fan of everything Starck, from the Café Costes near the Centre de Pompidou in Paris to the Felix in the Peninsula Hotel in Hong Kong. What I find so captivating about Starck is that he never fails to surprise—not even with his design of the Hudson Hotel's one thousand or so rooms, for which he had to stick to a small budget. For New York, the Hudson is a relatively inexpensive hotel. (Its air-conditioning uses window units rather than a central system.) Just entering the building is a journey in itself. A green-and-yellow escalator ensconced between two walls takes you to level three, where the lobby—chandelier-bedecked and decorated *à la* true-to-form Starck—is located. What distinguishes the rooms at the Hudson from other Starck designs is their small size, which has inspired him to make imaginative use of contrast and unusual proportions to turn the potentially trite into the most magical of illusions. A small bar and vending machine are placed in the hallway, turning a usually uneventful functional space into a rather entertaining one. The scarcity in space necessitated a rigorous selectivity, and Starck has risen triumphantly to the occasion. The building's only fault is the Formica ceiling in the business center. I keep wondering whether it is a deliberate, deconstructive comment by the designer on himself.

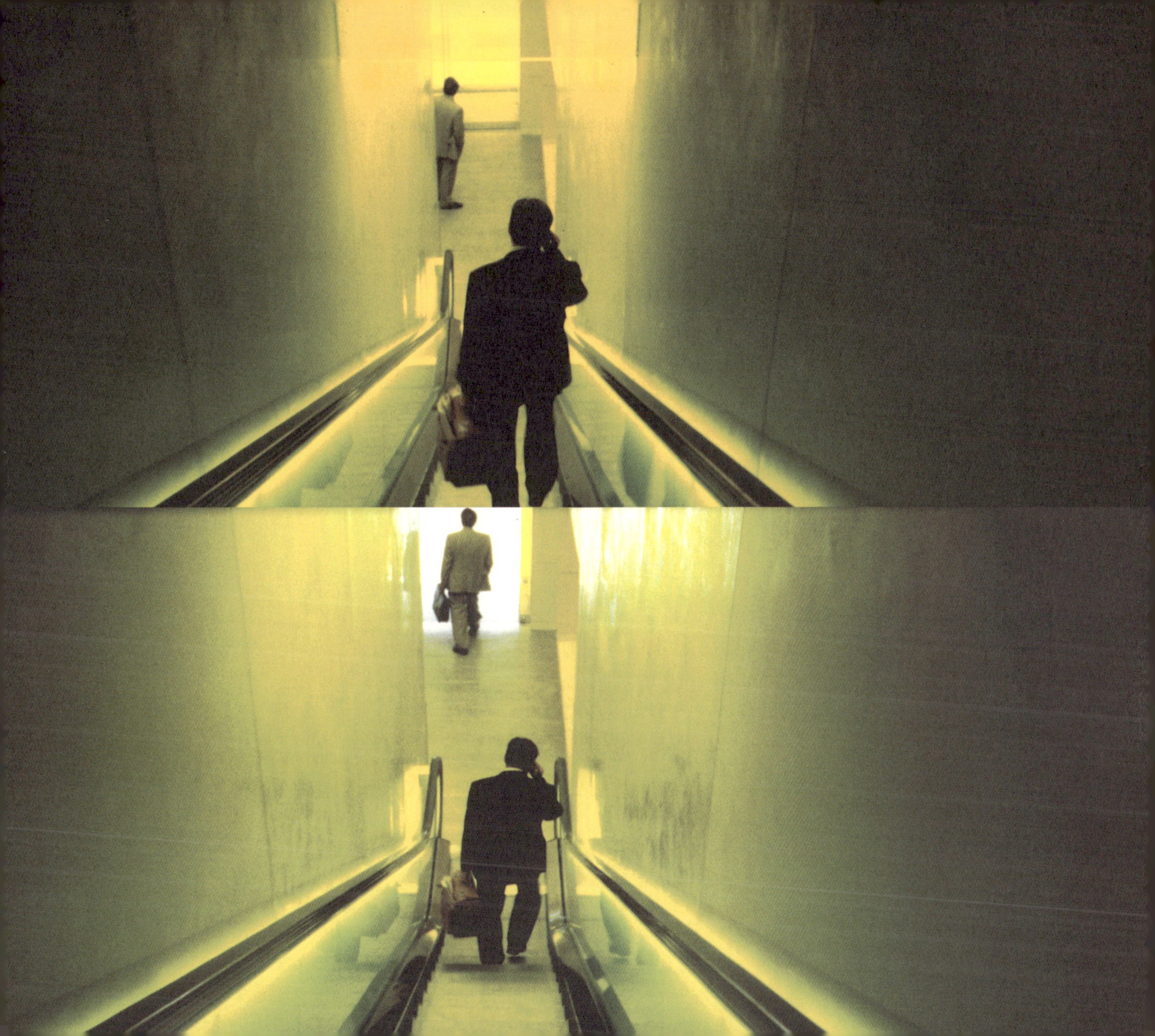

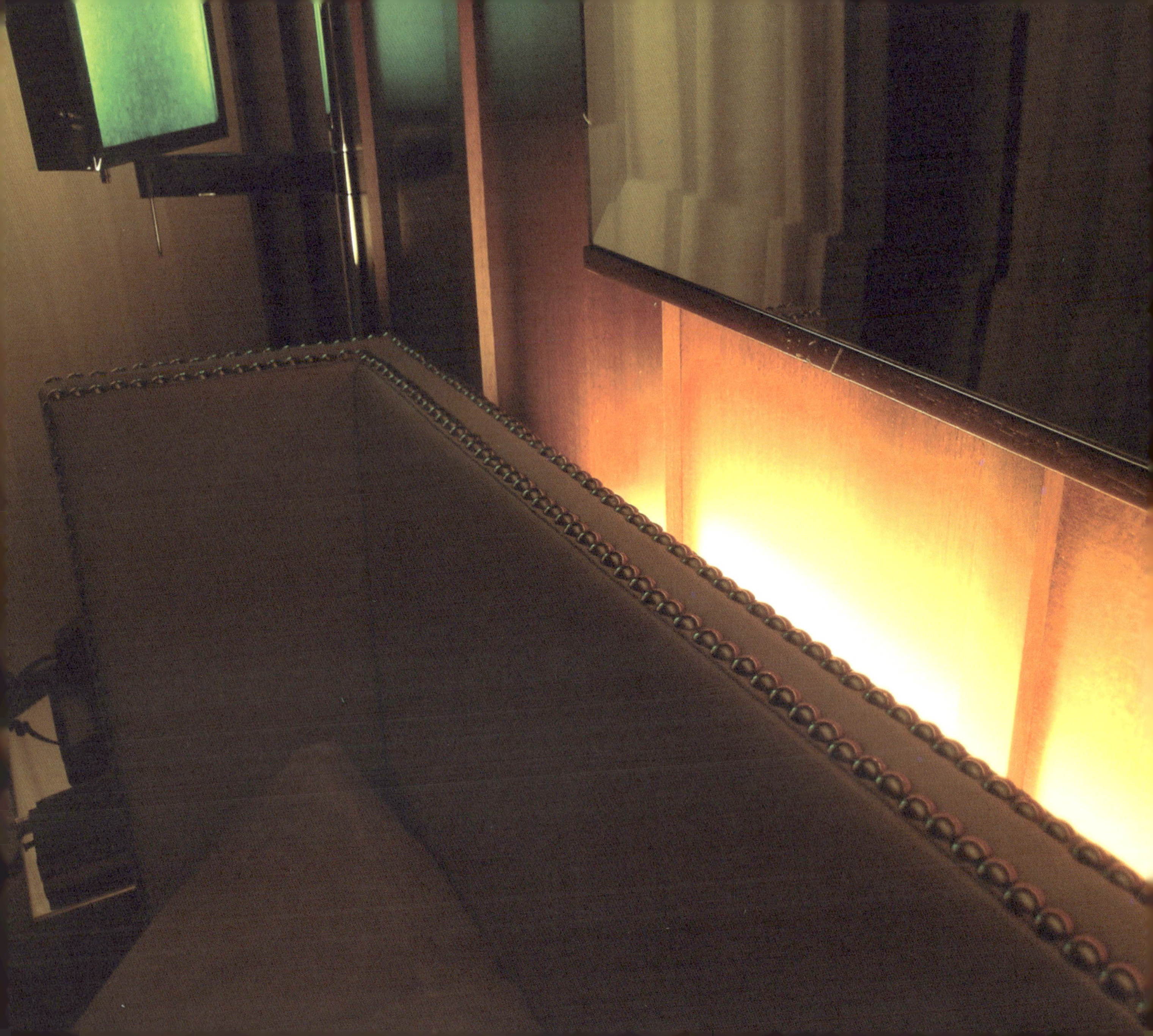

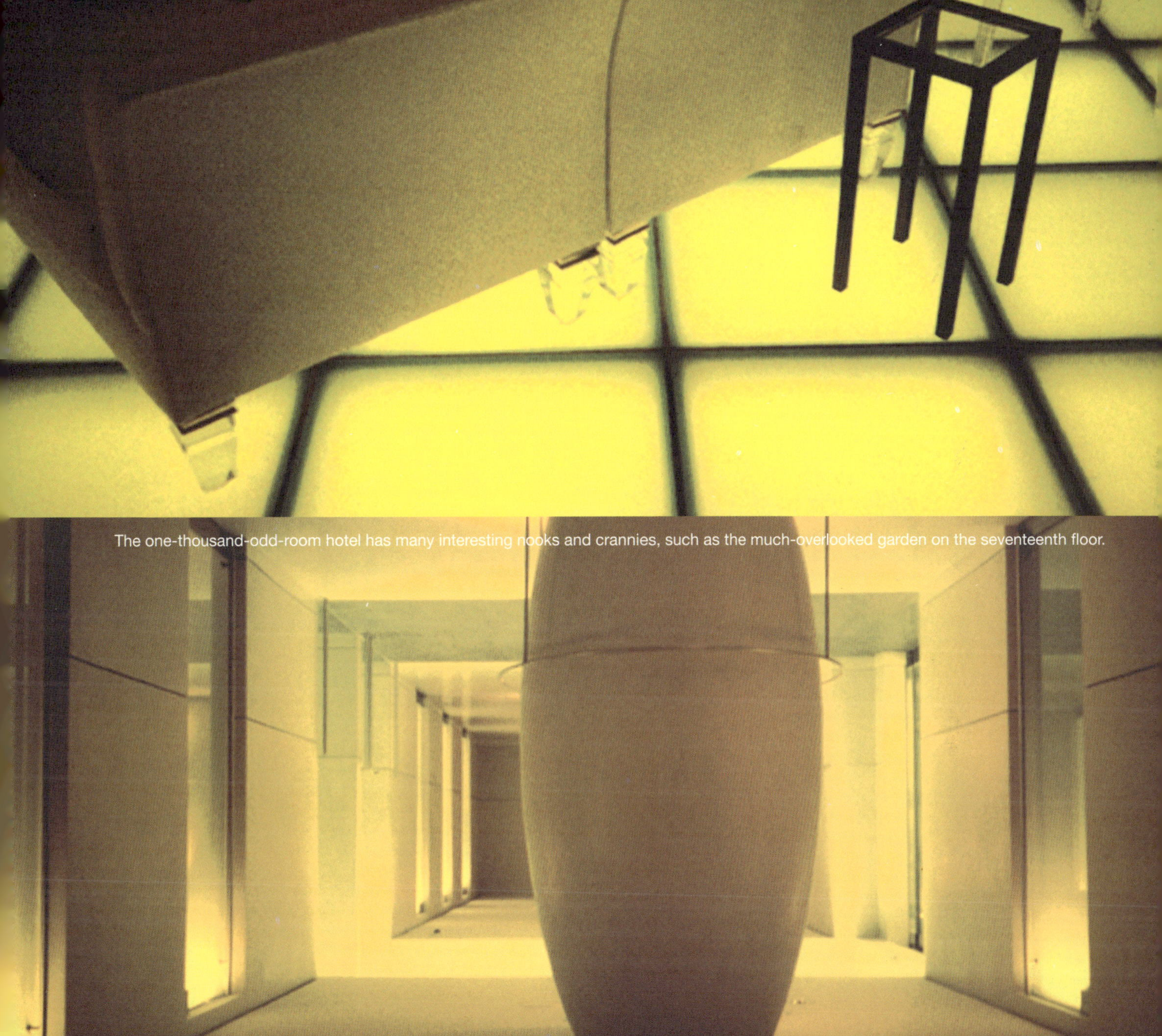

The one-thousand-odd-room hotel has many interesting nooks and crannies, such as the much-overlooked garden on the seventeenth floor.

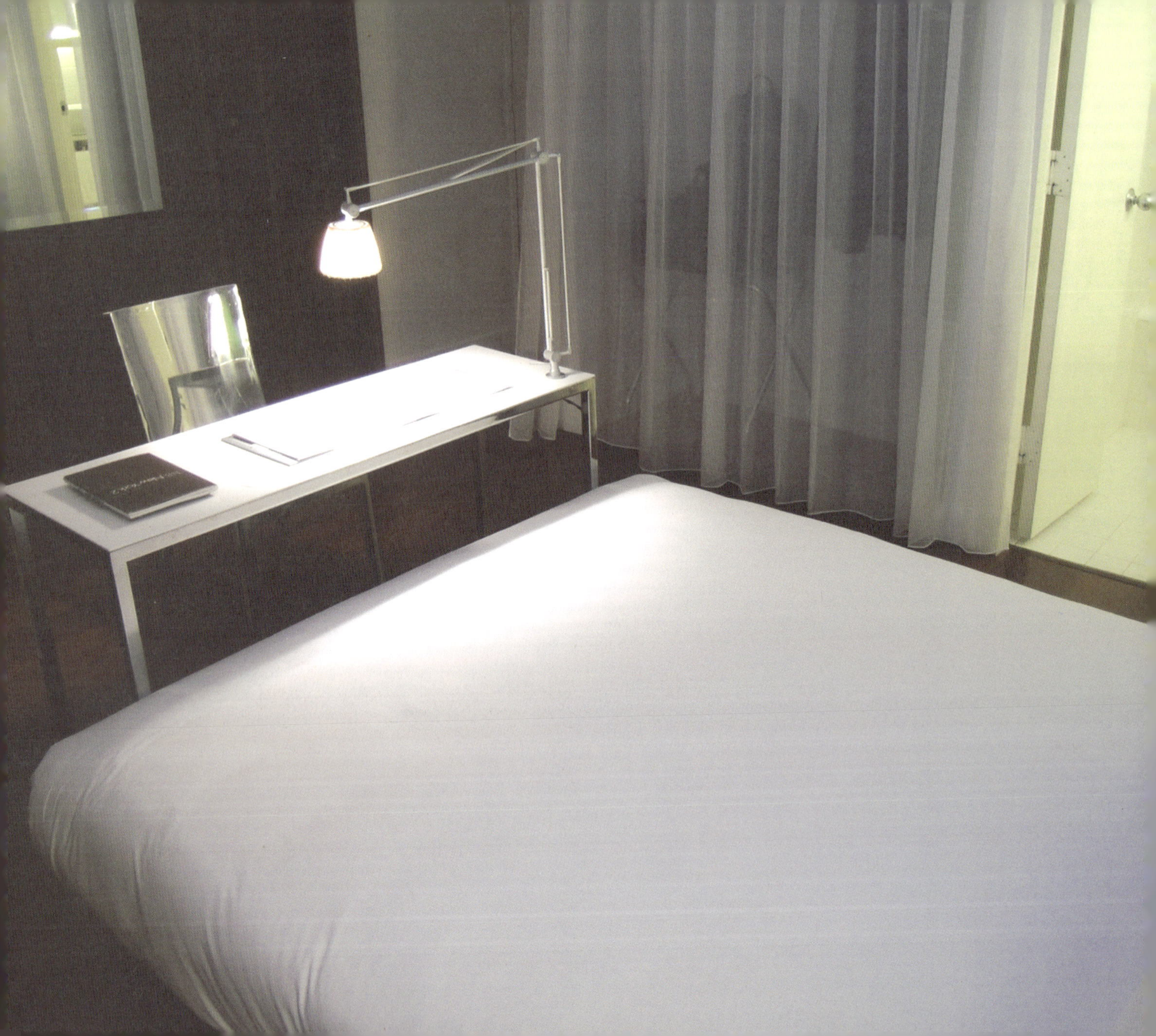

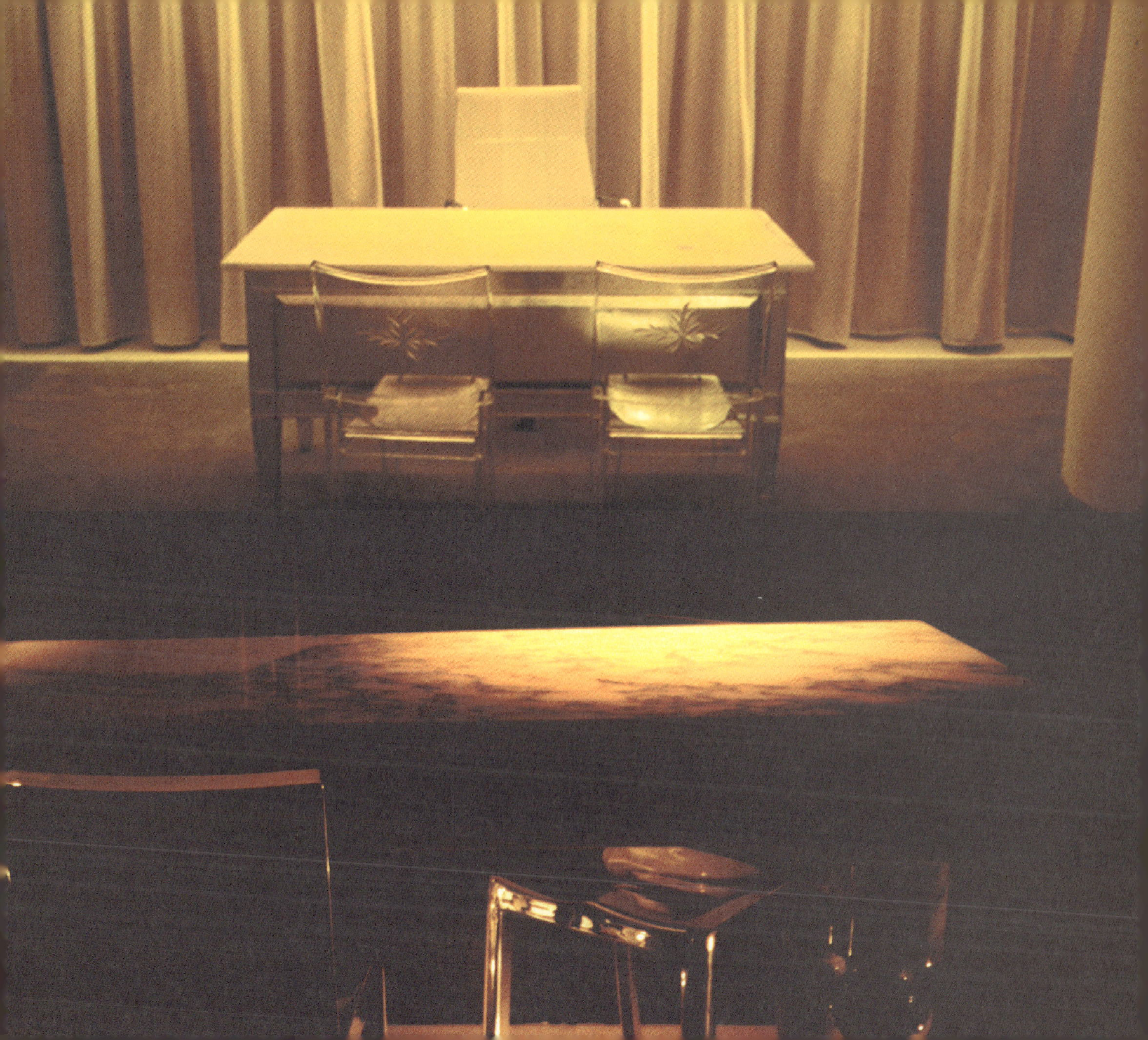

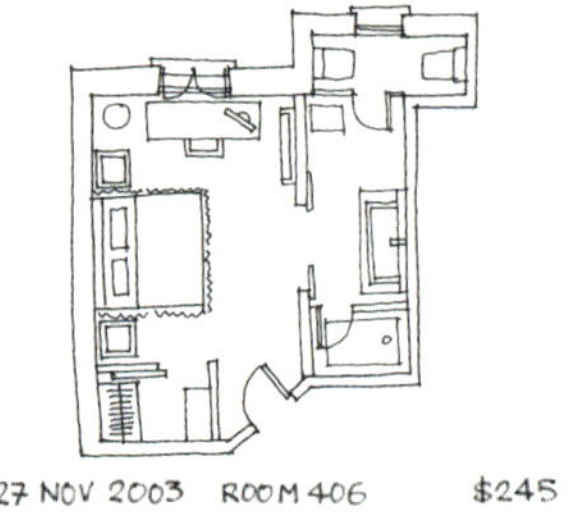

Hotel Continentale

A MATERIAL GAME

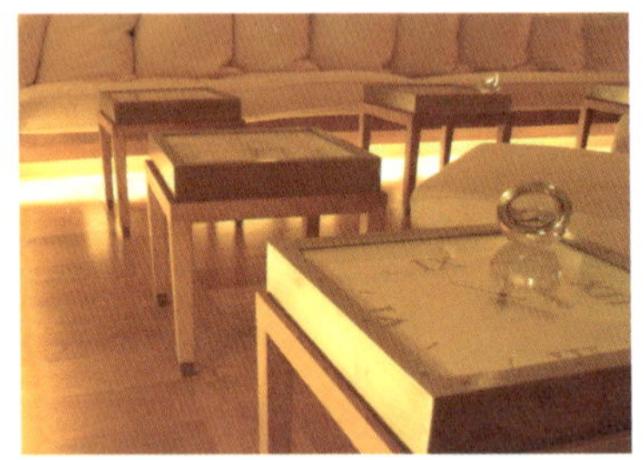

Hotels developed by fashion houses have become something of a trend these days: Versace on the Australian Gold Coast, Bvlgari in Milan and Bali, Armani in the Middle East, and of course, the Hotel Continentale in Florence run by Florence-based Ferragamo. Sitting right opposite the Ponte Vecchio, the hotel ingeniously brings Florence's enchanting scenery into its 1960s-themed lobby with the use of a big screen that plays images of the outside captured by a closed-circuit TV: a road movie without an ending. The rooms are a world of materials. The cozy bed encircled by pure-white drapes gives you a sense of security. The suitcase-shaped desk is completely made of leather, and when opened, turns into a stack of drawers and a chair, while the bathroom floor is a delightful amalgam of marble and wood. But my all-time favorite remains the elevator, which is equipped with a sofa and transforms into a moving bar.

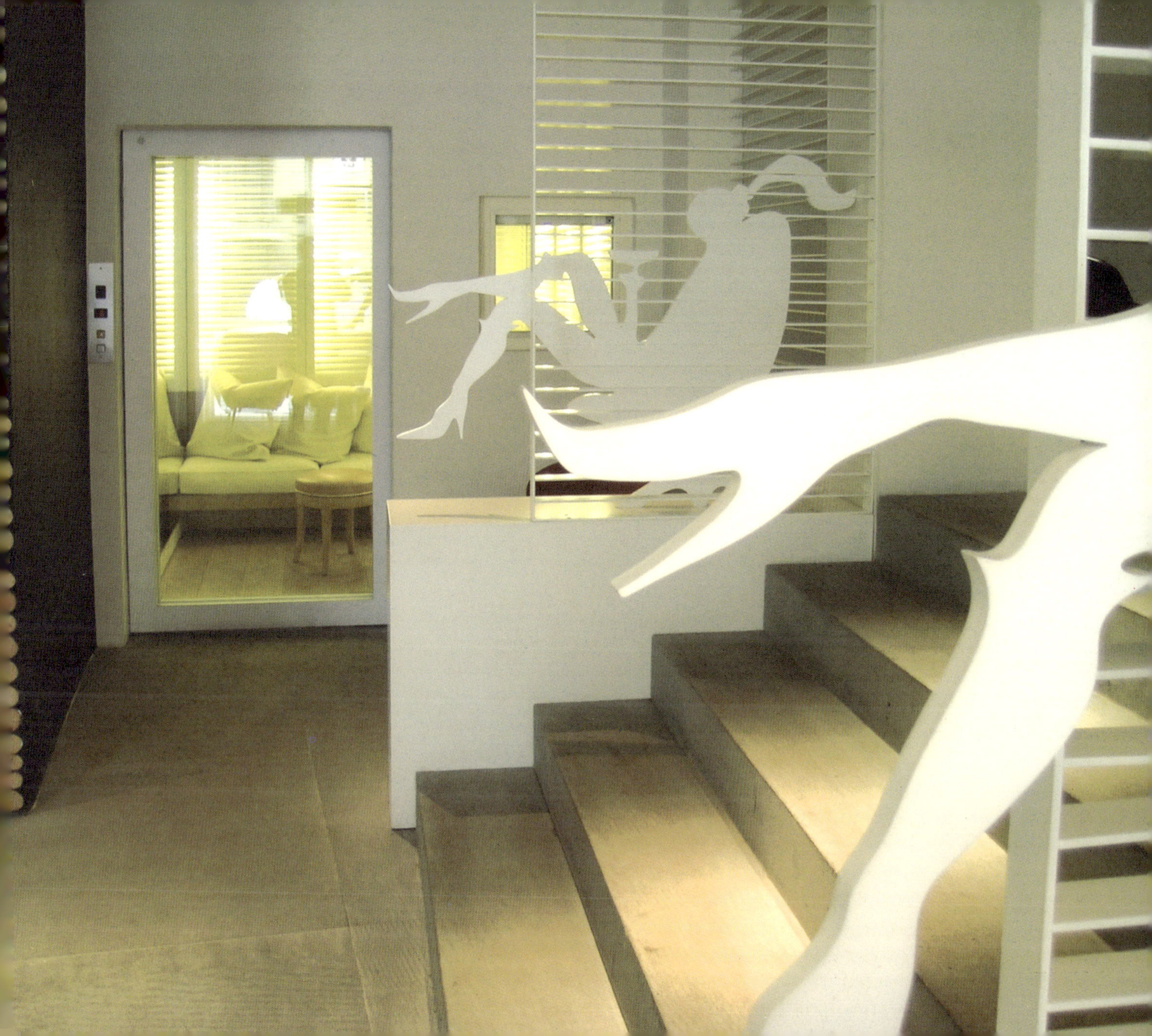

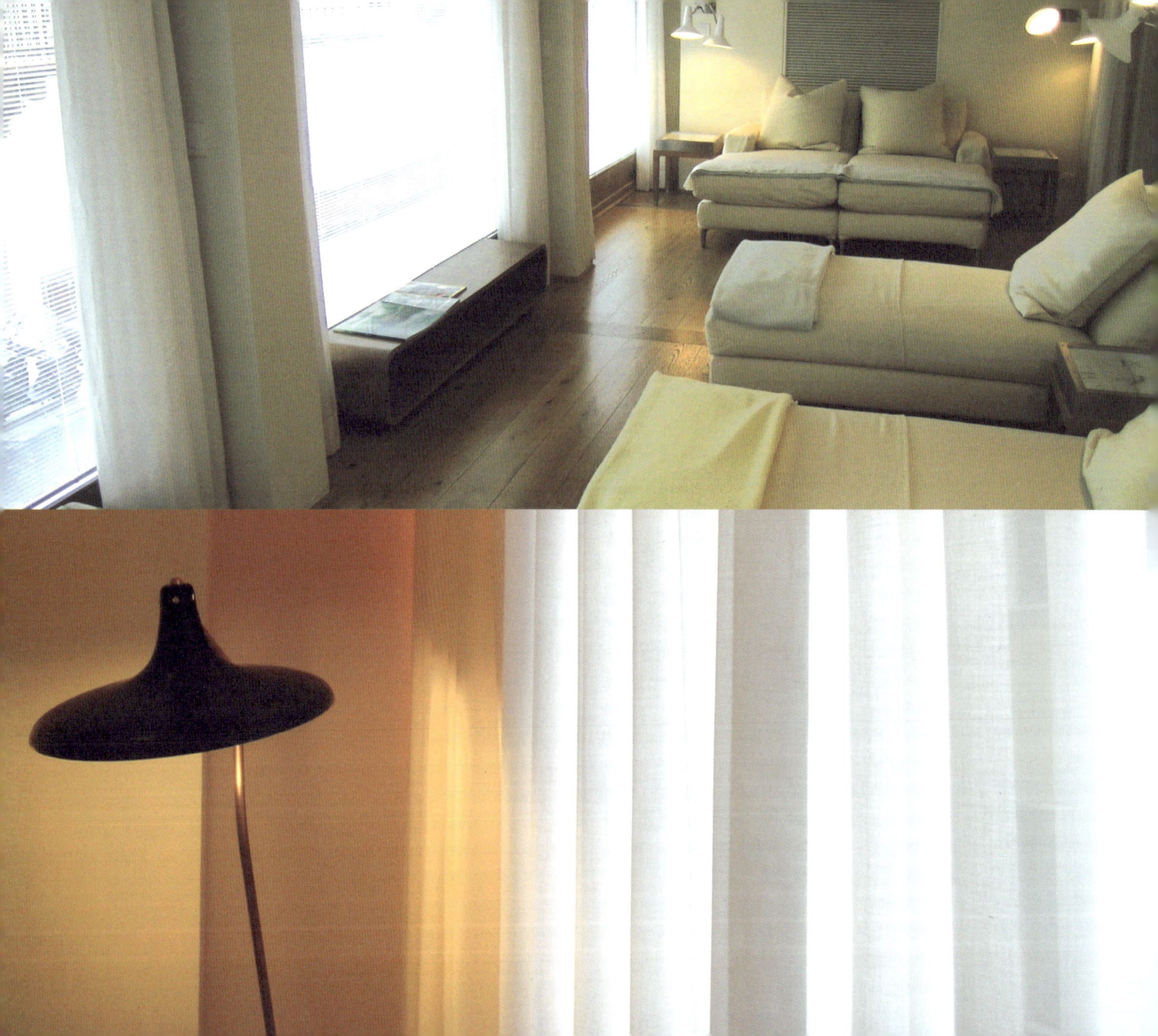

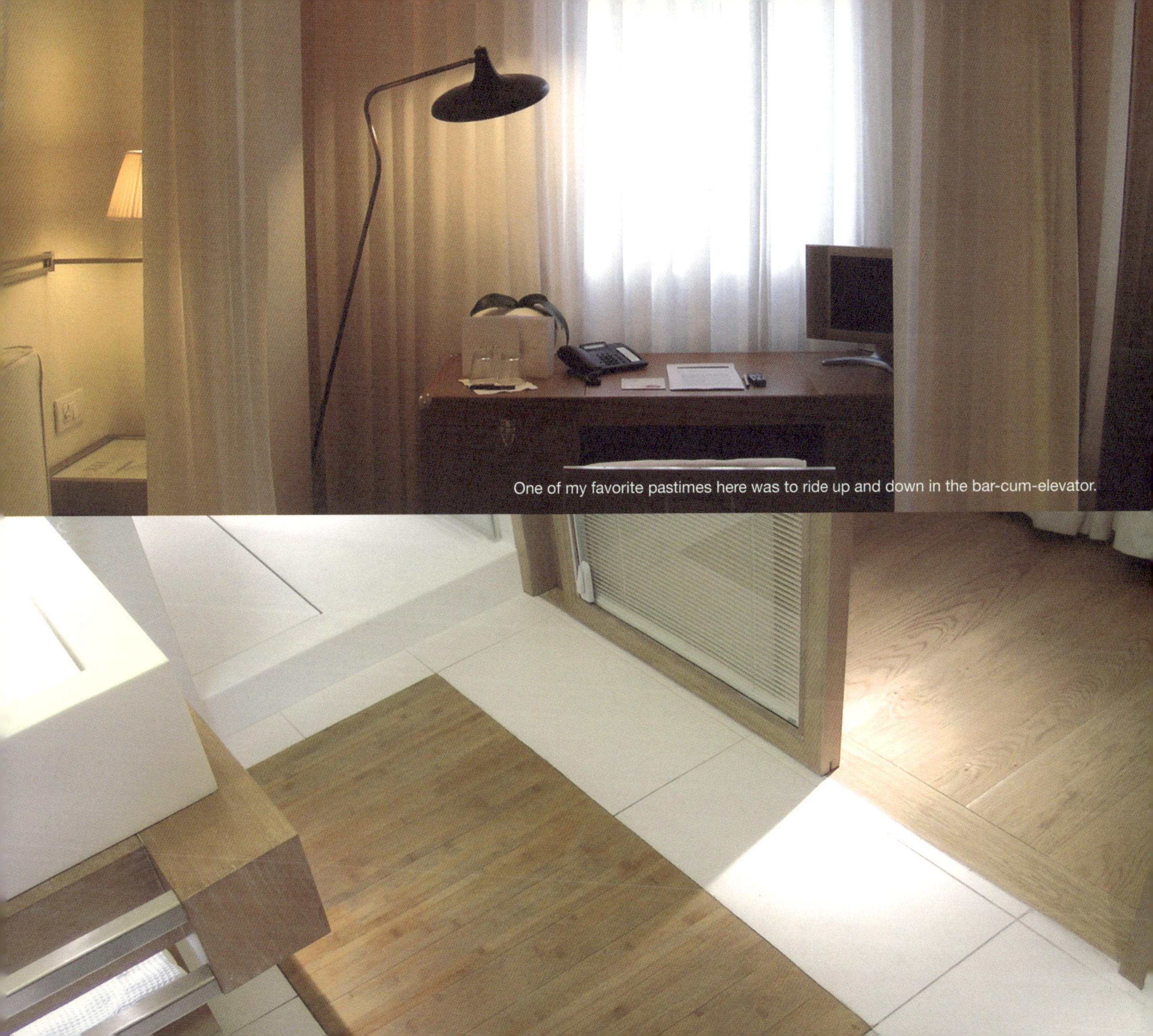

One of my favorite pastimes here was to ride up and down in the bar-cum-elevator.

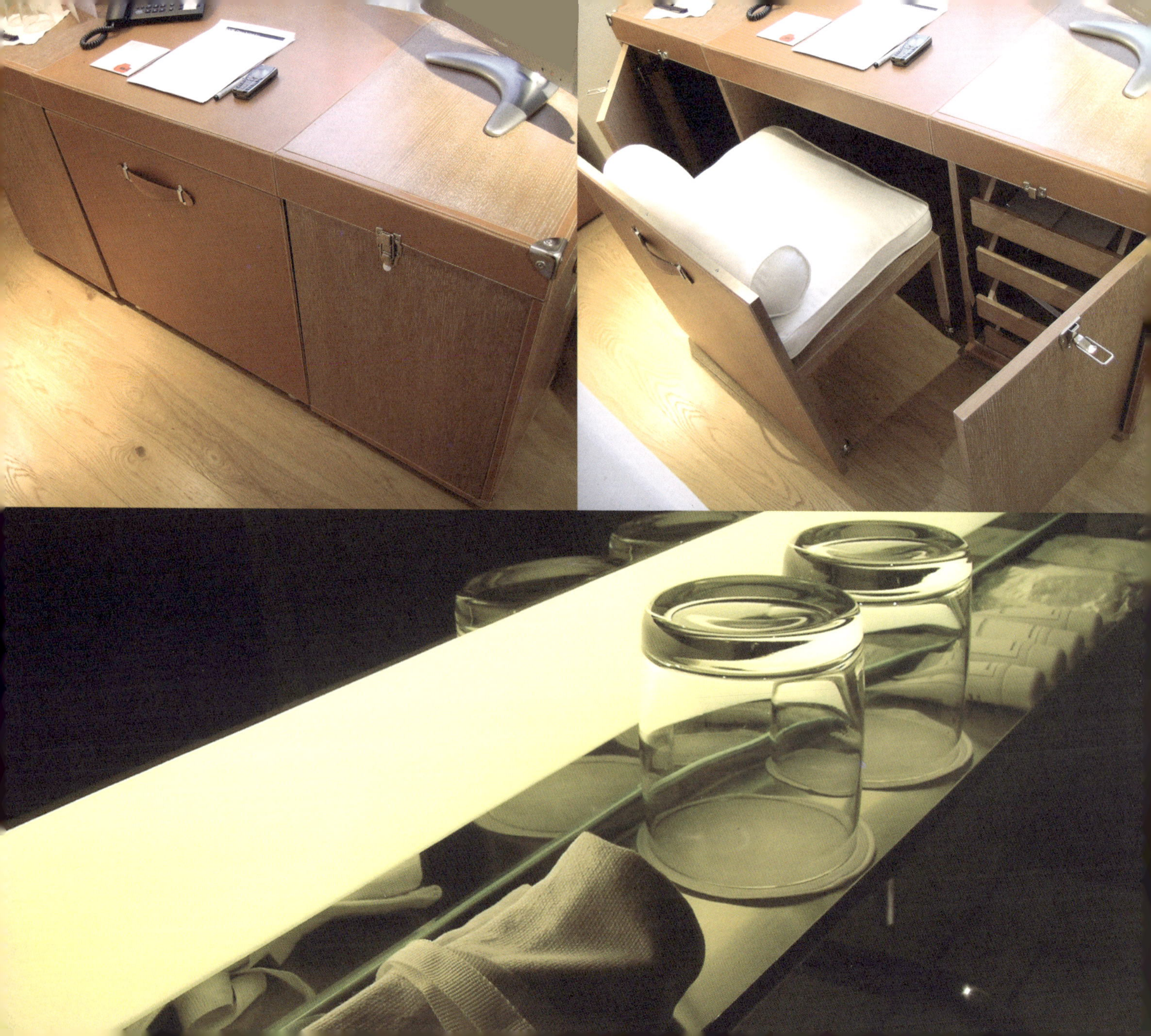

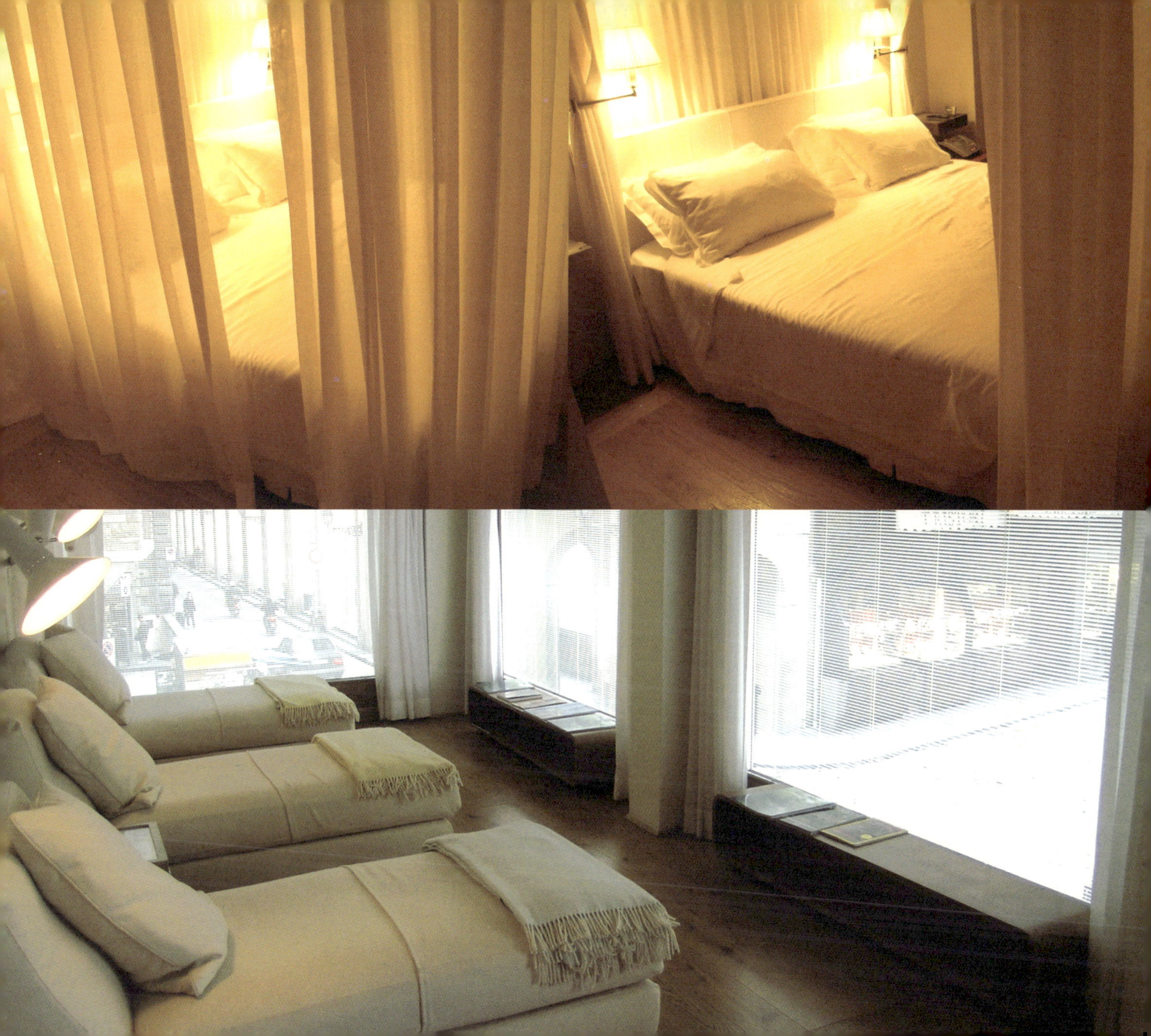

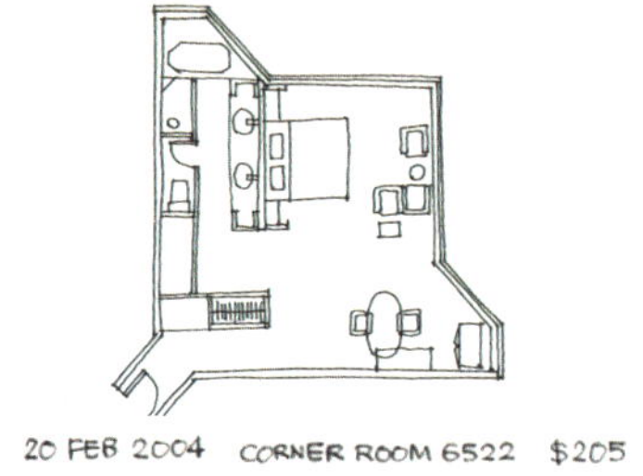

Grand Hyatt Shanghai

A CASTLE IN THE CLOUDS

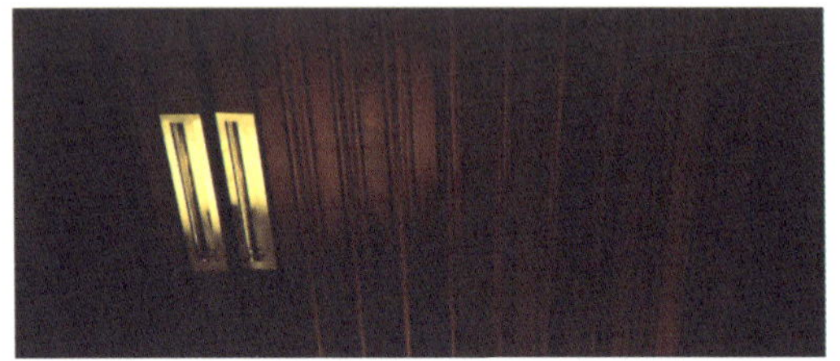

The one hotel that I have stayed in most often has to be the Pudong Grand Hyatt in Shanghai. I know it almost as well as my own home. Although some tend to think that it's over-hyped by the media, others (including myself) still consider it Shanghai's best hotel. Personally, I like it for its surreal height. The lobby is on the fifty-fourth floor, and above it are the guest rooms—staying here is almost like living in an airplane among the clouds. I especially enjoy this on overcast days, when I make a point of getting up extra early to take in the morning mist. While some might say, the higher the better, I prefer the mid-level rooms, halfway between the heavens and the earthly world.

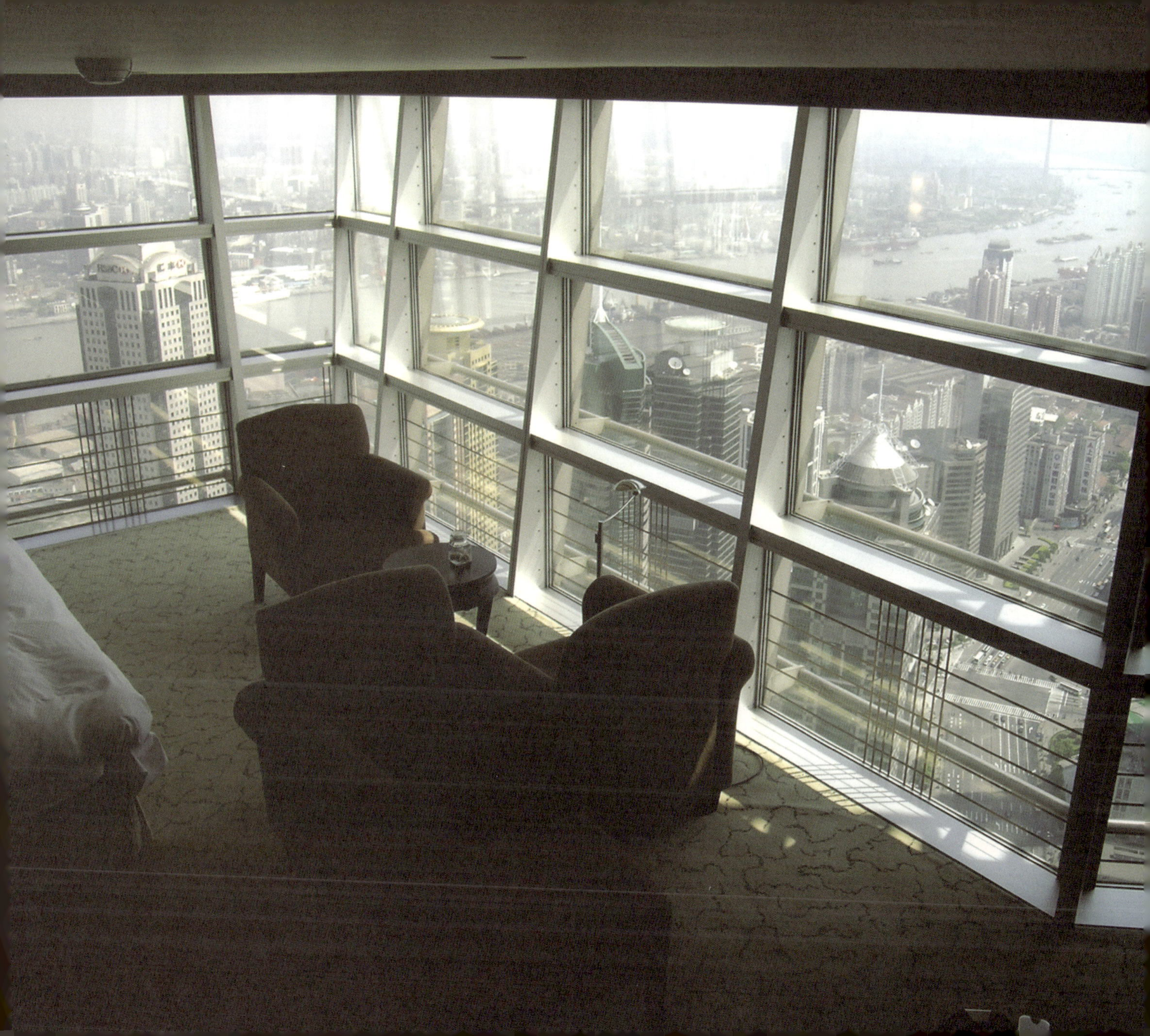

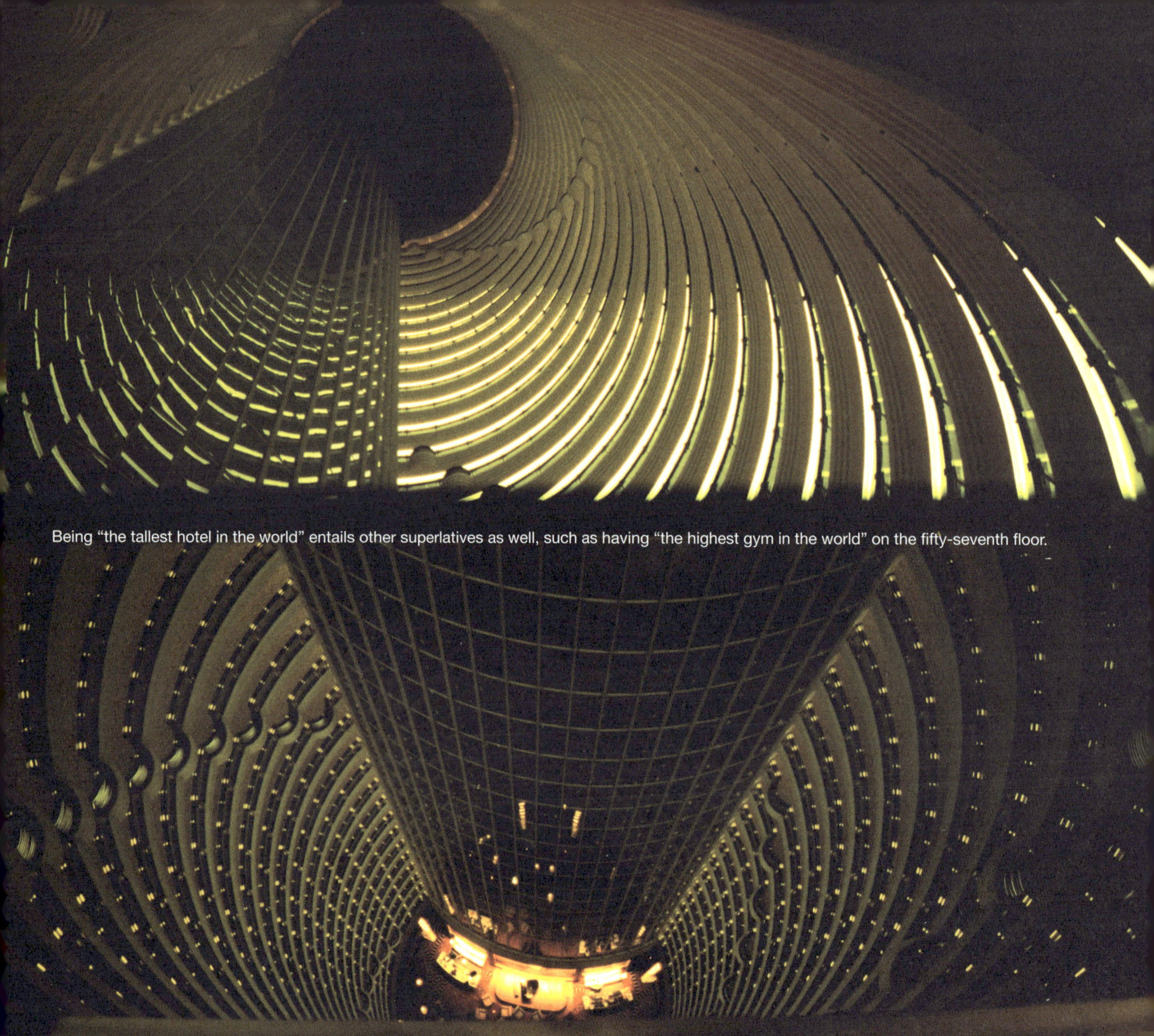

Being "the tallest hotel in the world" entails other superlatives as well, such as having "the highest gym in the world" on the fifty-seventh floor.

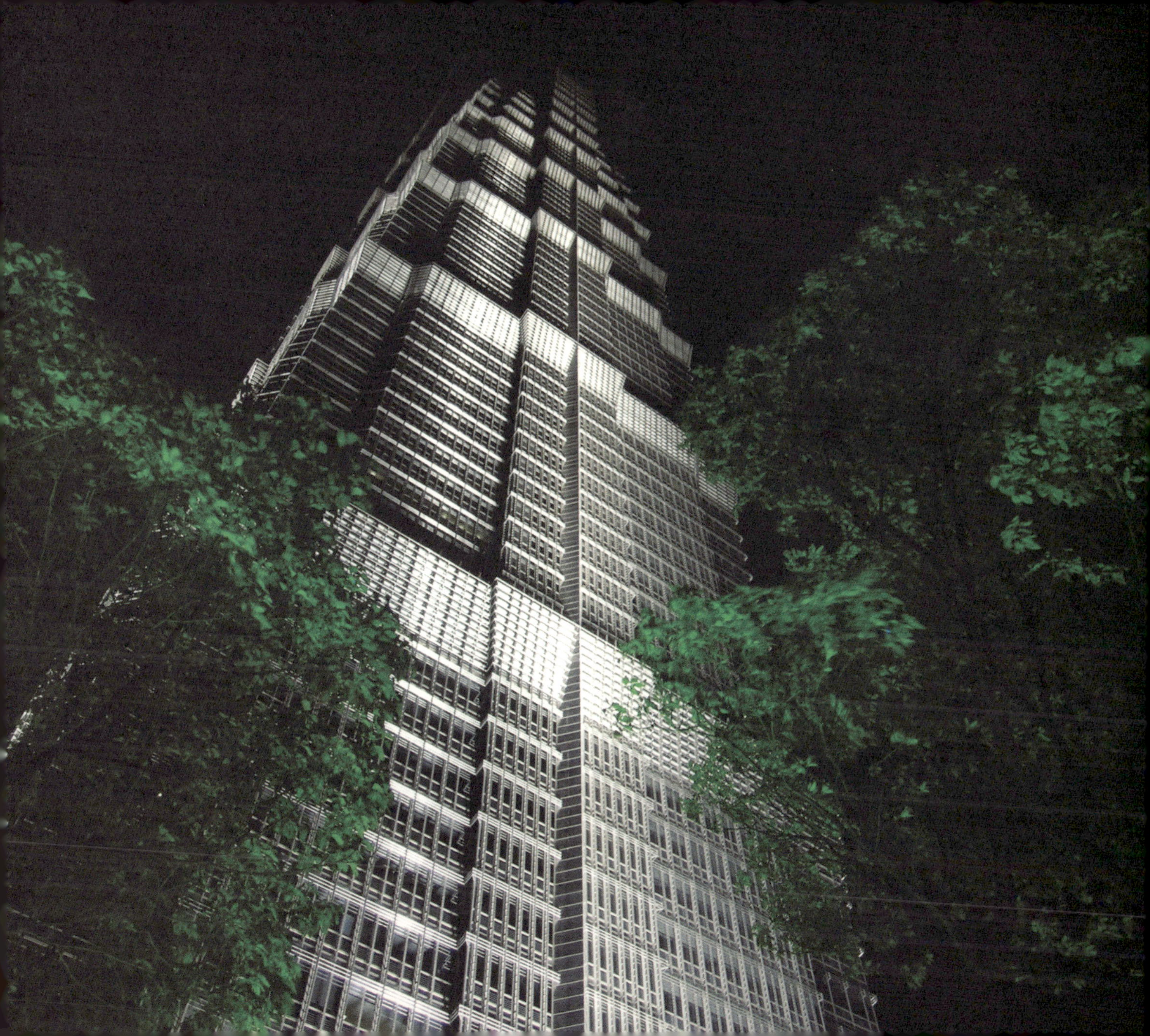

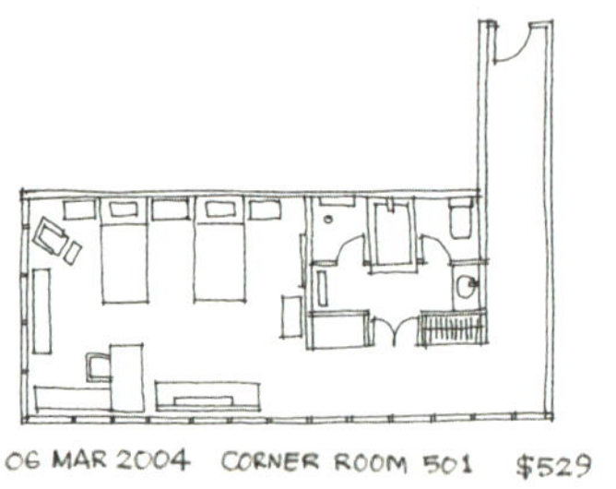

Four Seasons Hotel at Marunouchi

THE SILENT DOCUMENTARY OF A TRAIN STATION

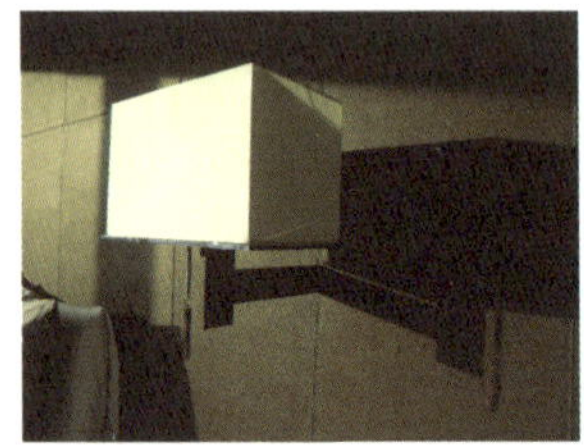

The Four Seasons is located right next to Tokyo's busy train station, so that the hotel itself seems to be part of the frantic transportation hub. Within five minutes, you could be on a train to anywhere in the country. During my stay here I would sometimes invite friends to join me in my room to watch the unending, ever-changing, ever-unfolding silent documentary of people and trains through the room's immense, sound-proof picture window. The curtains almost seem unnecessary.

It is rather rare for top-end hotels to locate themselves in areas of high-density traffic such as this. Tokyo's *Four Seasons at Marunouchi*, however, manages to turn adversity into a boon for itself.

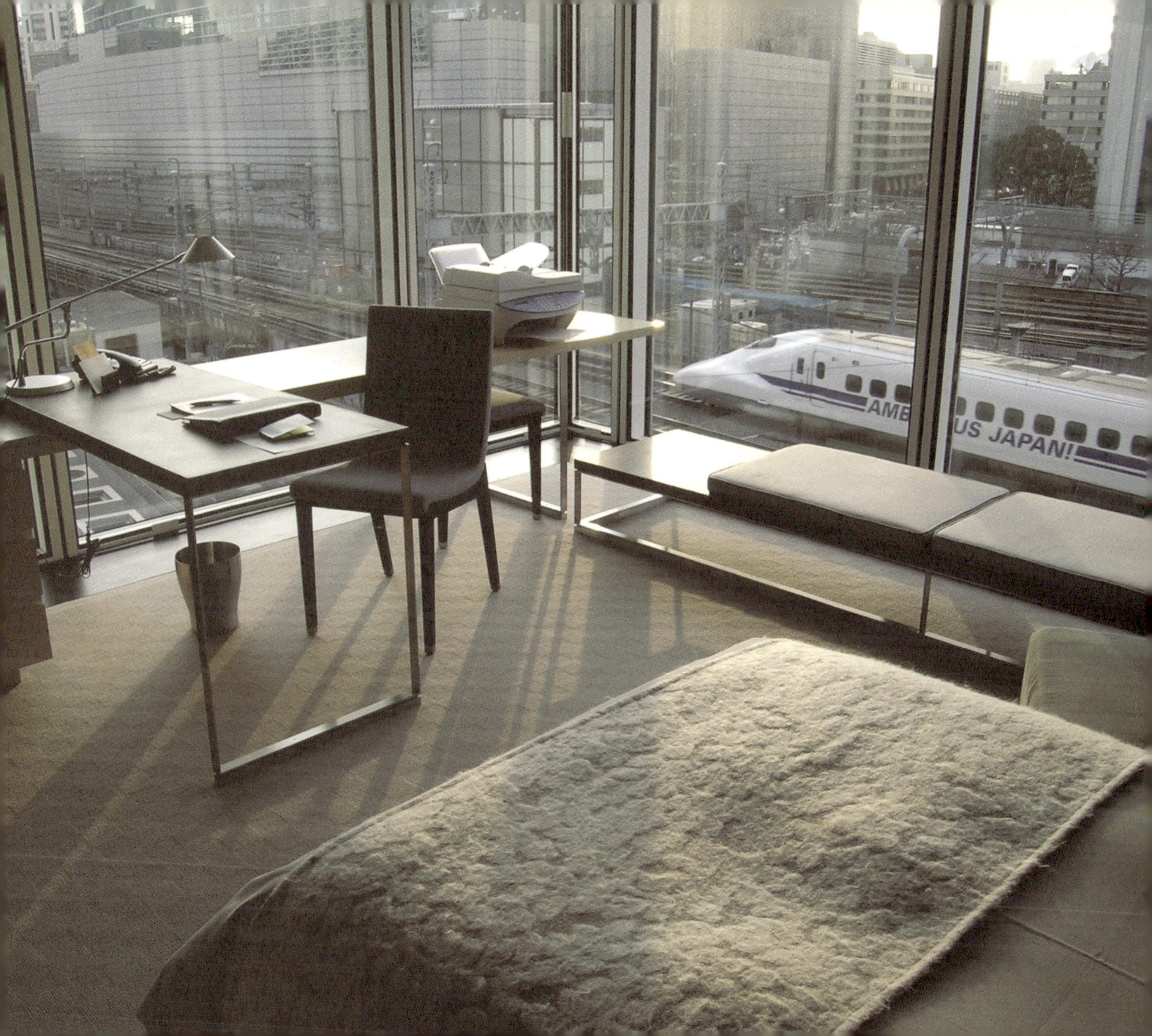
AMB
US JAPAN!

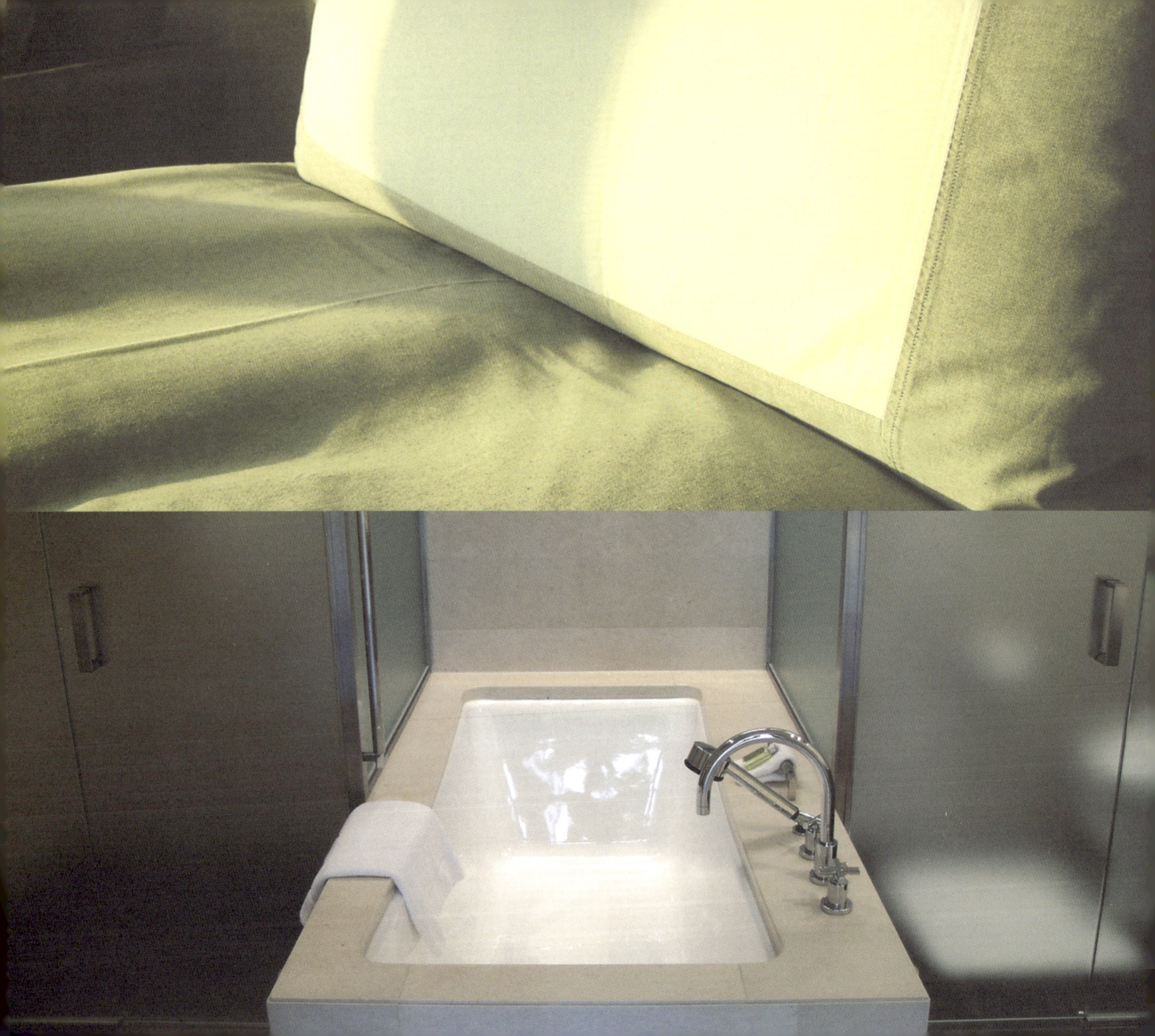

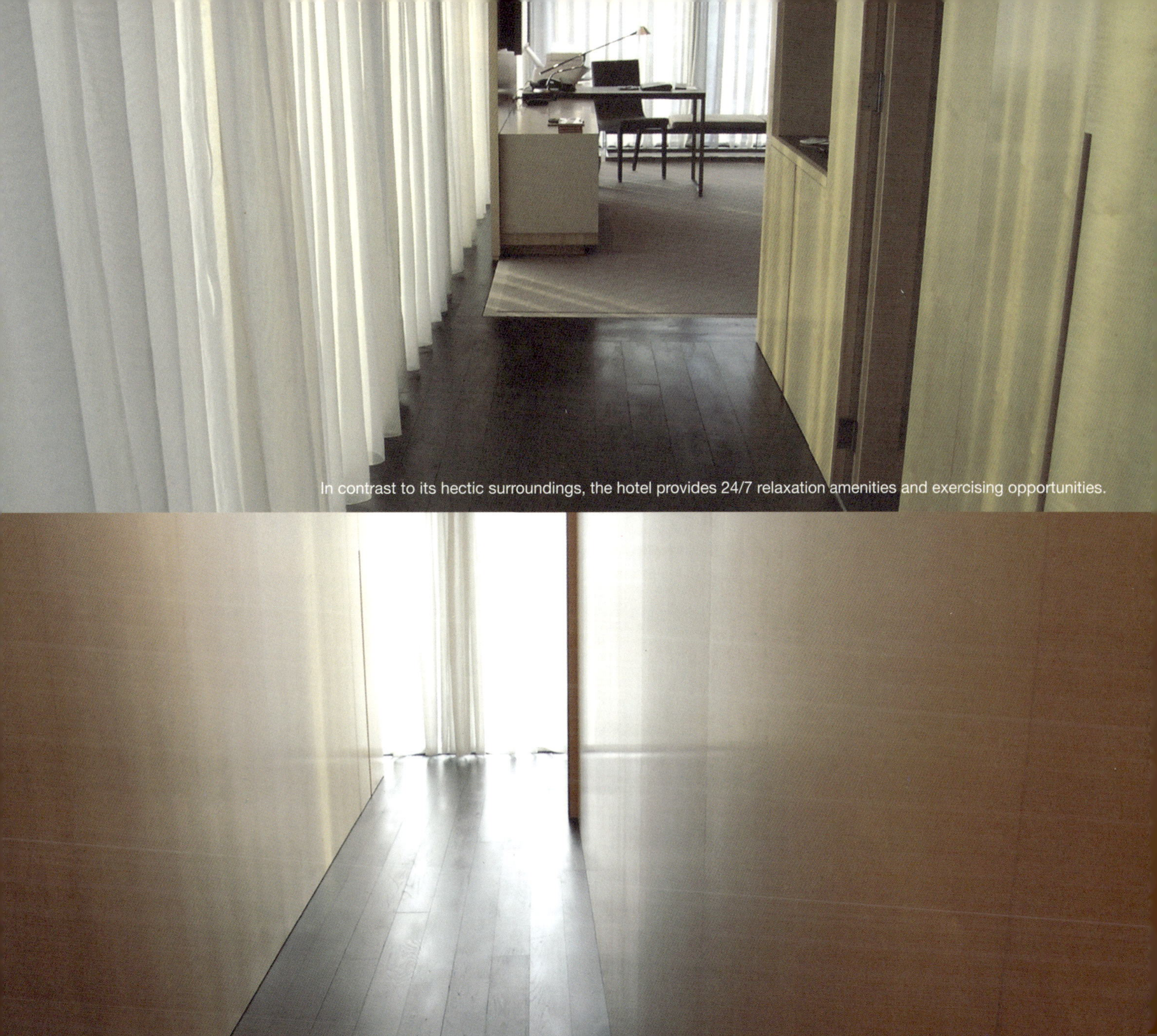

In contrast to its hectic surroundings, the hotel provides 24/7 relaxation amenities and exercising opportunities.

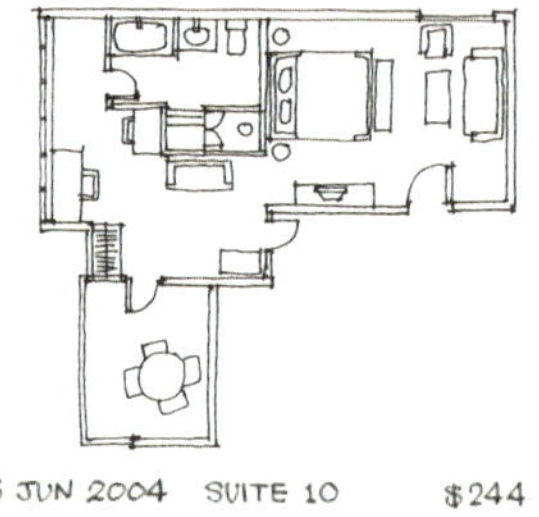

Westover Hall Hotel

A SEA OF SILVER

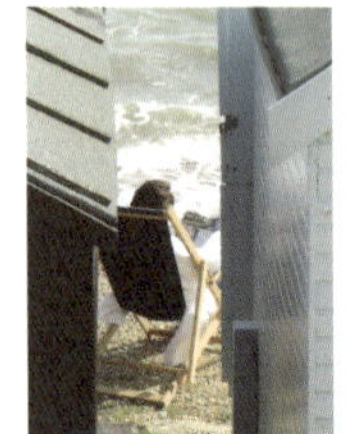

I must admit I came here on a whim (as one should on an ideal trip). What brought me to the Westover Hall in southern England was a picture in a book: an unforgettable image of a silver-white sea. The book stated that Westover was the ultimate destination, which of course made me wonder whether it would be *my* ultimate destination. I have always had a weakness for the English seaside: its quiet desolateness, the overgrown but yet somehow orderly grass, the faded deck chairs whose color starts to resemble the surrounding grass, and, of course, the endless coastline. With no fanfare or any big to-do, the century-old Westover Hall sits on the scenic seaside facing the Isle of Wight, coexisting harmoniously with its neighboring cottages. The sense of harmony continues inside in the hotel's all-oak finishing, including the furniture and the old oak floor rediscovered during renovation. Even the doors seem to just melt into the walls. The design might not be anything particularly new, but its authenticity completely captured the antique fetishist in me. The hotel's perfectly apt decoration is matched by the staff's attention to service details. When I arrived, the hotelier addressed me by name and graciously inquired what newspaper I would like to read the next morning. The young woman behind the reception counter is perhaps a perfect symbol for the old mansion's youth and vitality.

As you sit in the restaurant enjoying the panoramic view, the people outside look like a frolicking crowd in a silent film. Time becomes blurred and so does space: I kept having a hard time calculating how long it would take me to walk from the beach to the nearby castle and back, with the seemingly endless scenery in between.

MILFORD-ON-SEA

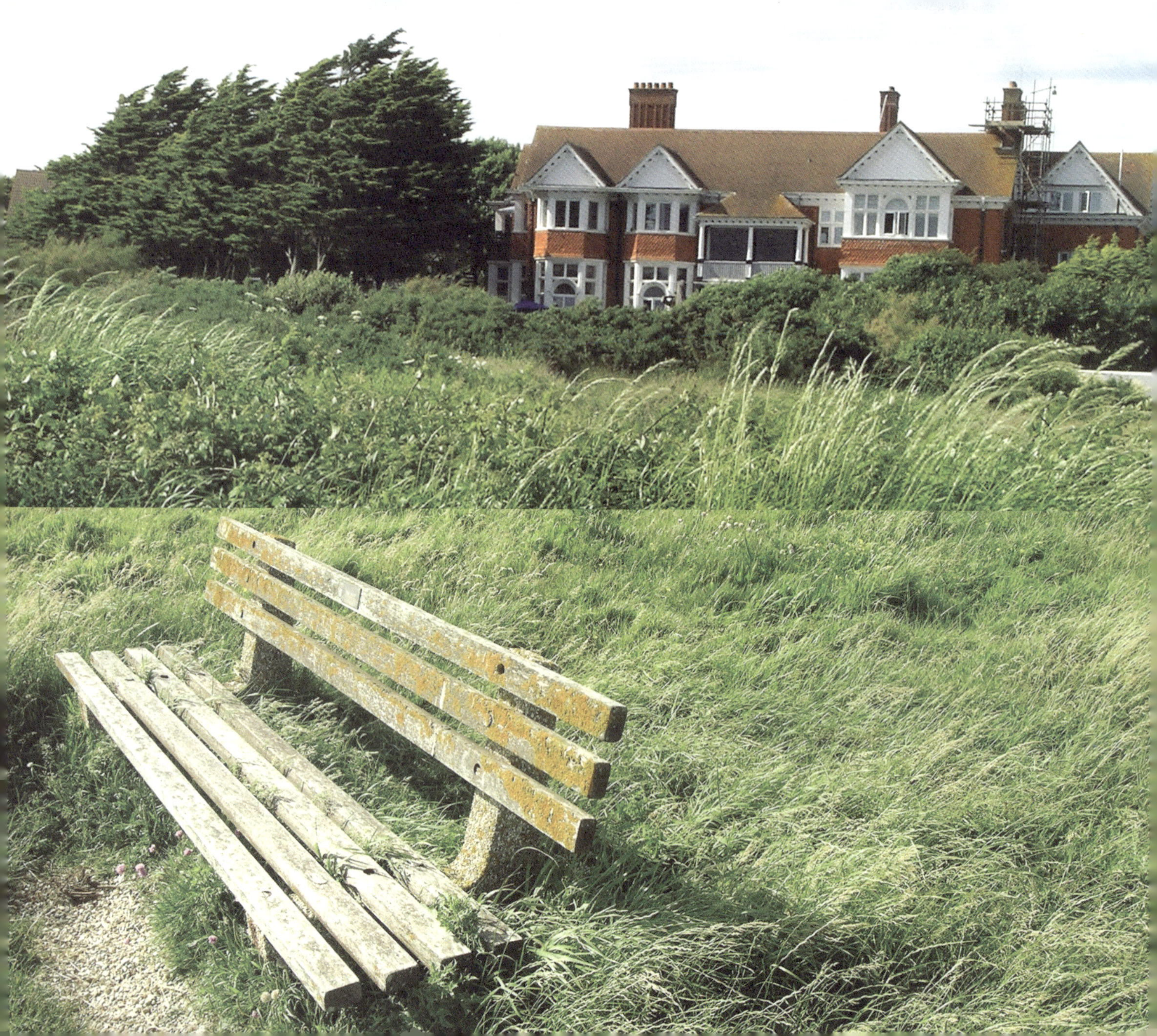

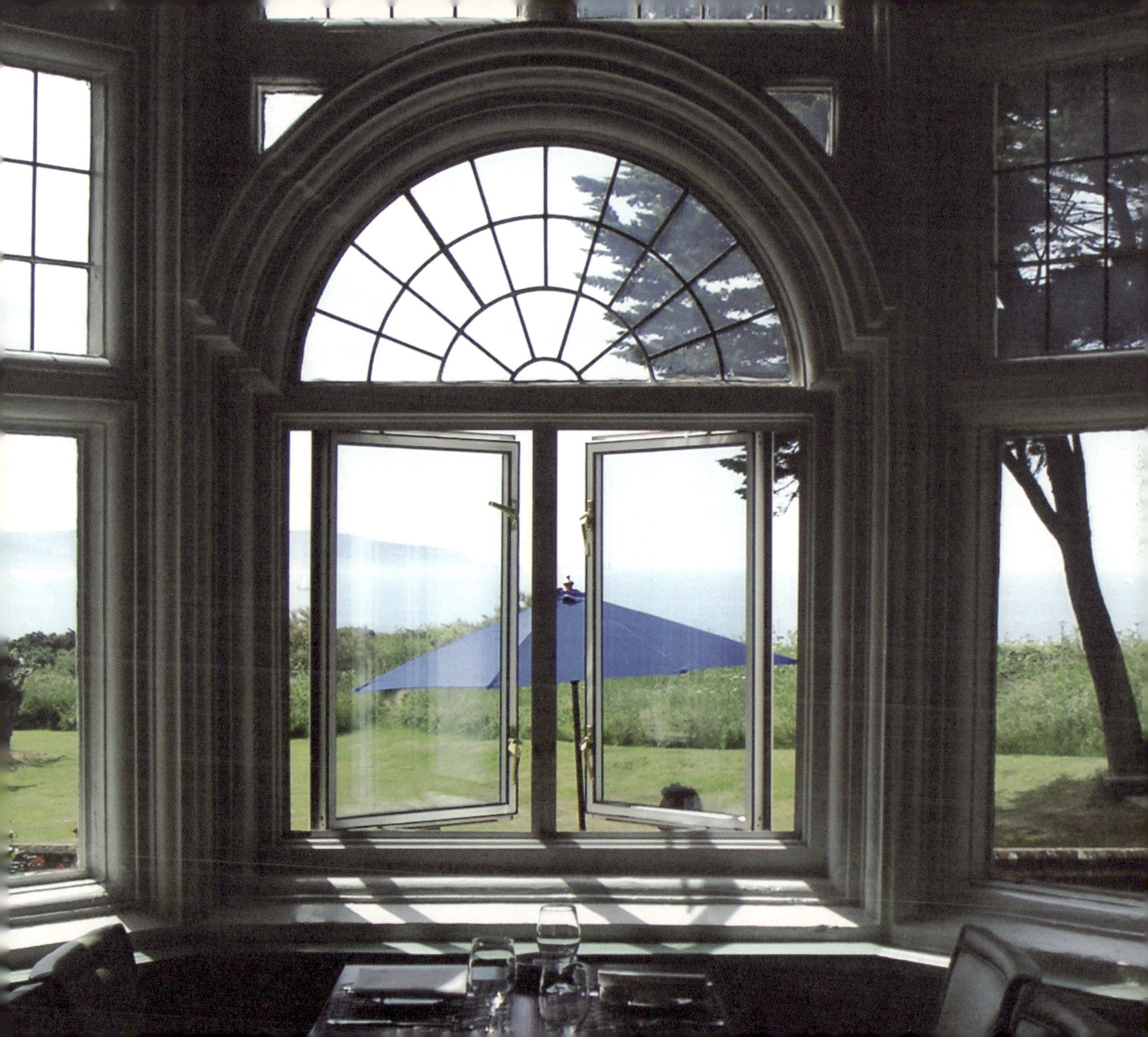

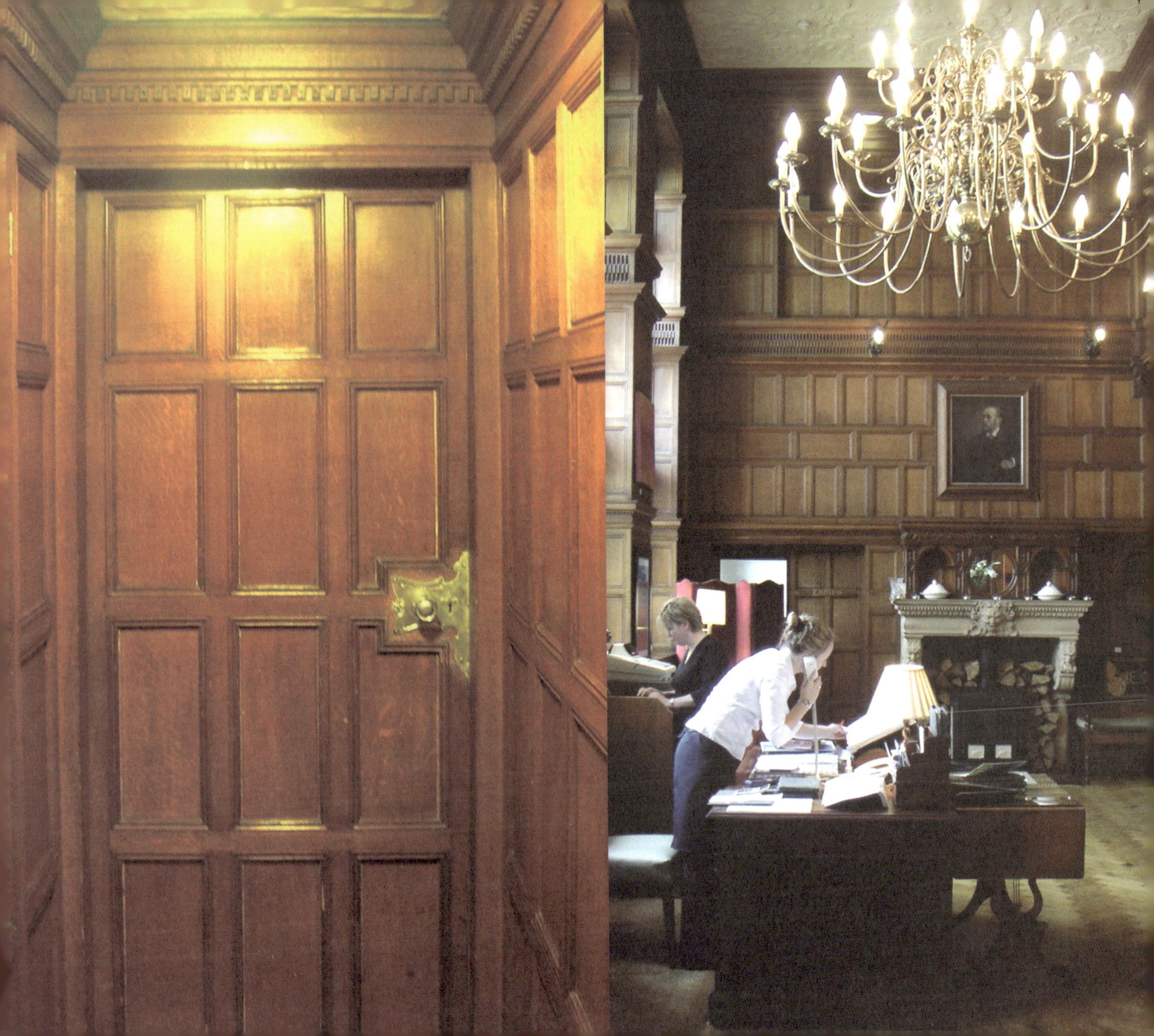

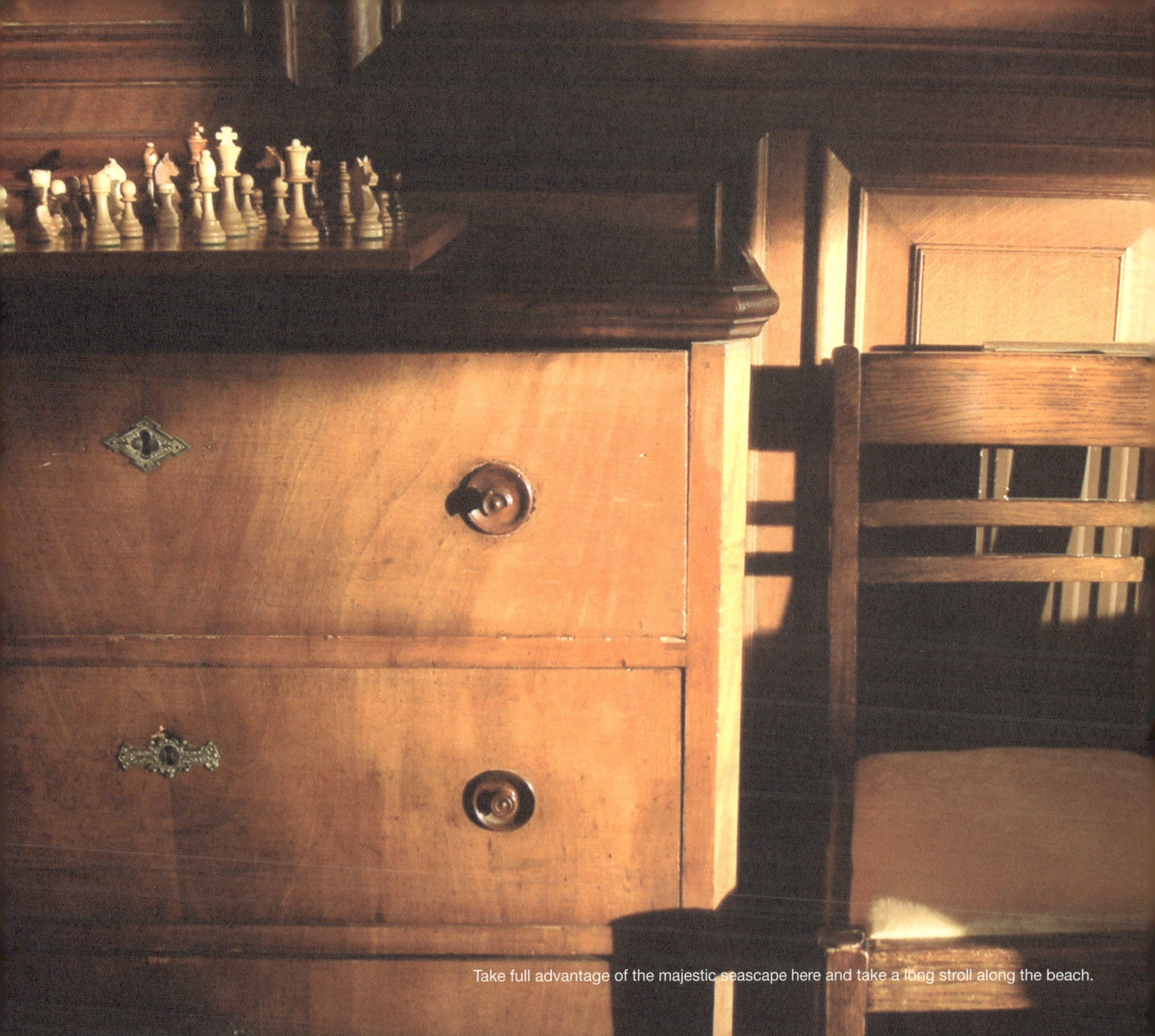

Take full advantage of the majestic seascape here and take a long stroll along the beach.

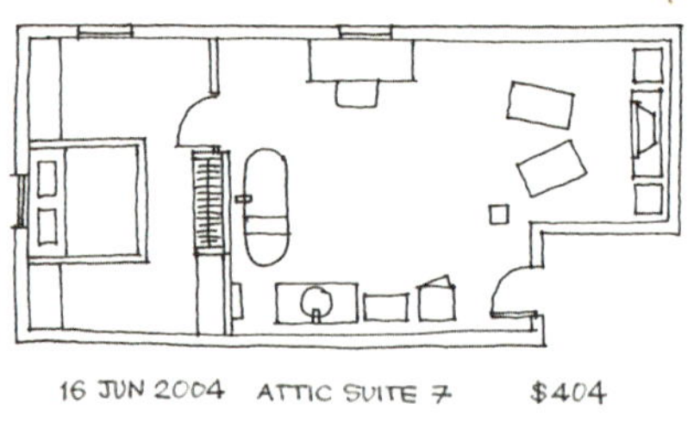

Babington House

LONDON IN SOMERSET

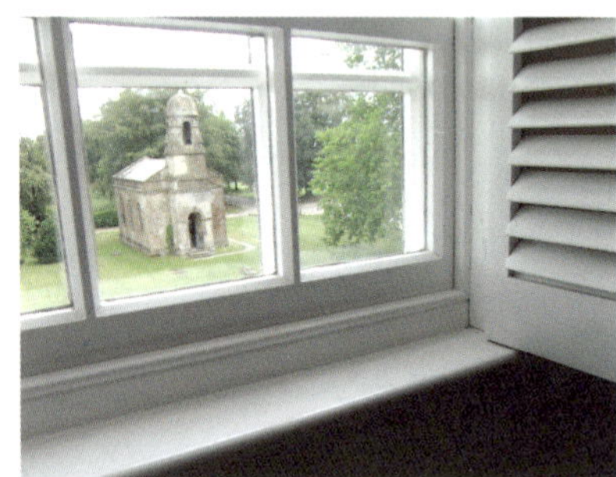

Frankly, the rumor that this hotel, an old stone structure nestled in the Somerset county, is the favorite vacation hideout for London's clubbing crowd really piqued my interest. But when you come to think of it, the hippest has often metamorphosed from the most traditional. Babington House is one of the best examples of the many old English castles and mansions that have been transformed into hotels after various fashions. Whereas Westover Hall excels in its "Jeeves"-styled service steeped in tradition, Babington House prides itself on marrying history with cutting-edge design and management. It is as if London had been relocated here, with its characteristic juxtaposition of the very old and the very new, but without the city's hectic pace. The place is the epitome of England's idyllic peace and leisure. Even London's celebrities lose themselves here, watching children and ducks play. (There's a movie theater, too, for those not quite ready to give up their "mod cons" cold turkey.) The chapel on the estate is a predictably popular site for weddings. The hotel's most expensive rooms have been converted from former stables and provide complete privacy, for which many guests are quite willing to pay the high rates. I stayed in a room in the attic, which had its own cozy charm, with its sunlit desk and a bathtub in the middle of the room. All the toiletries are the hotel's own products, made from ingredients cultivated on the nearby farm.

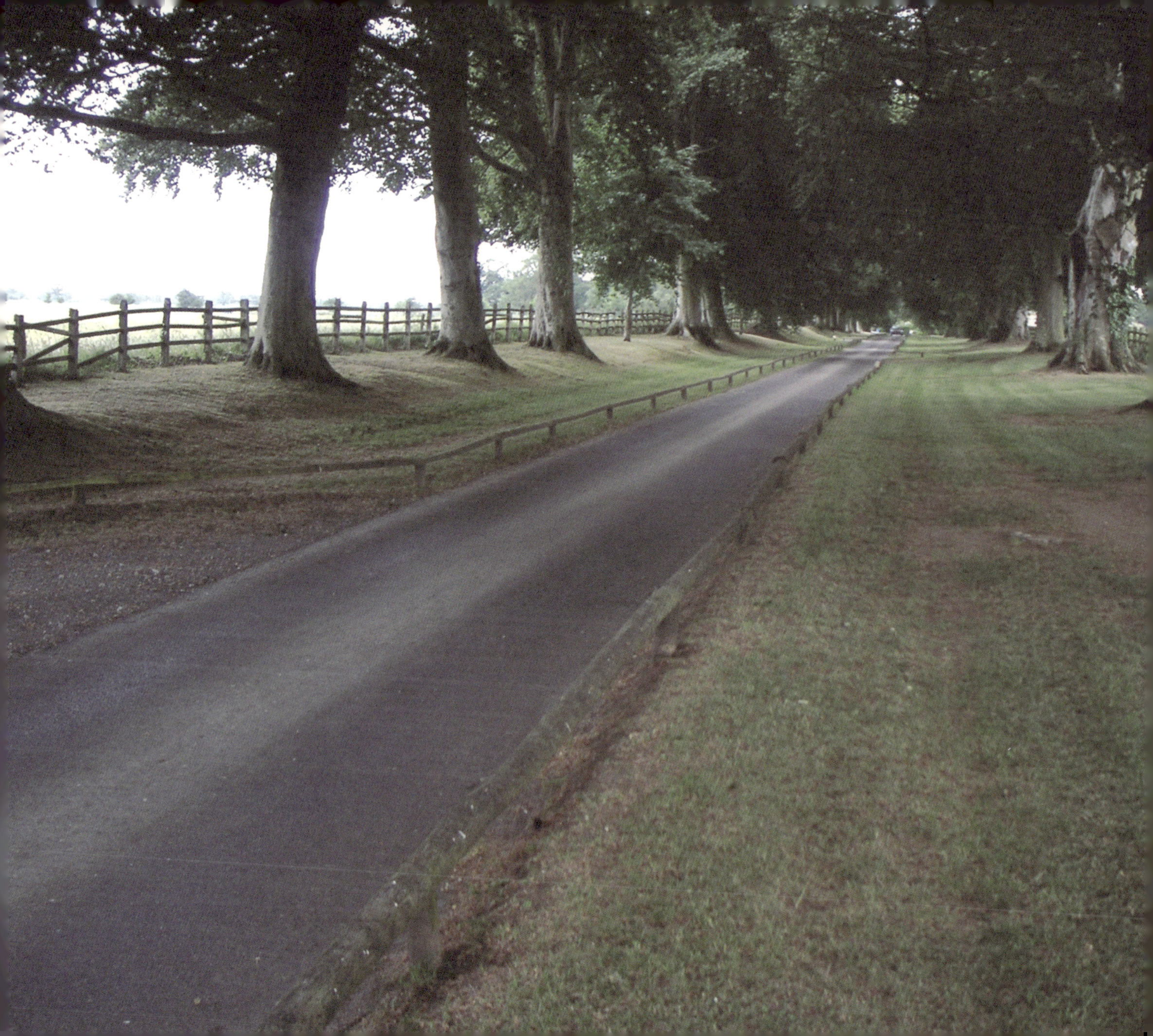

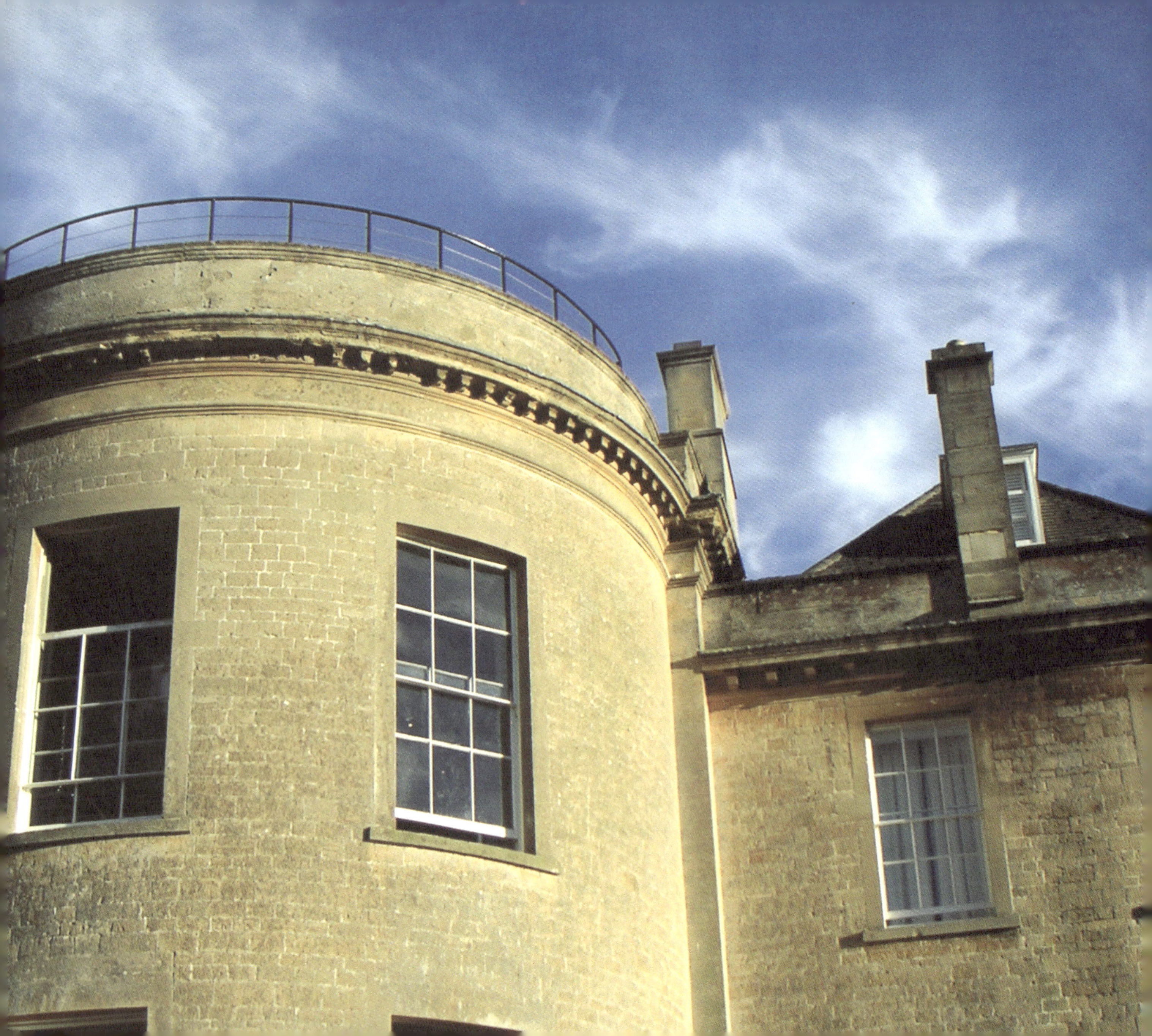

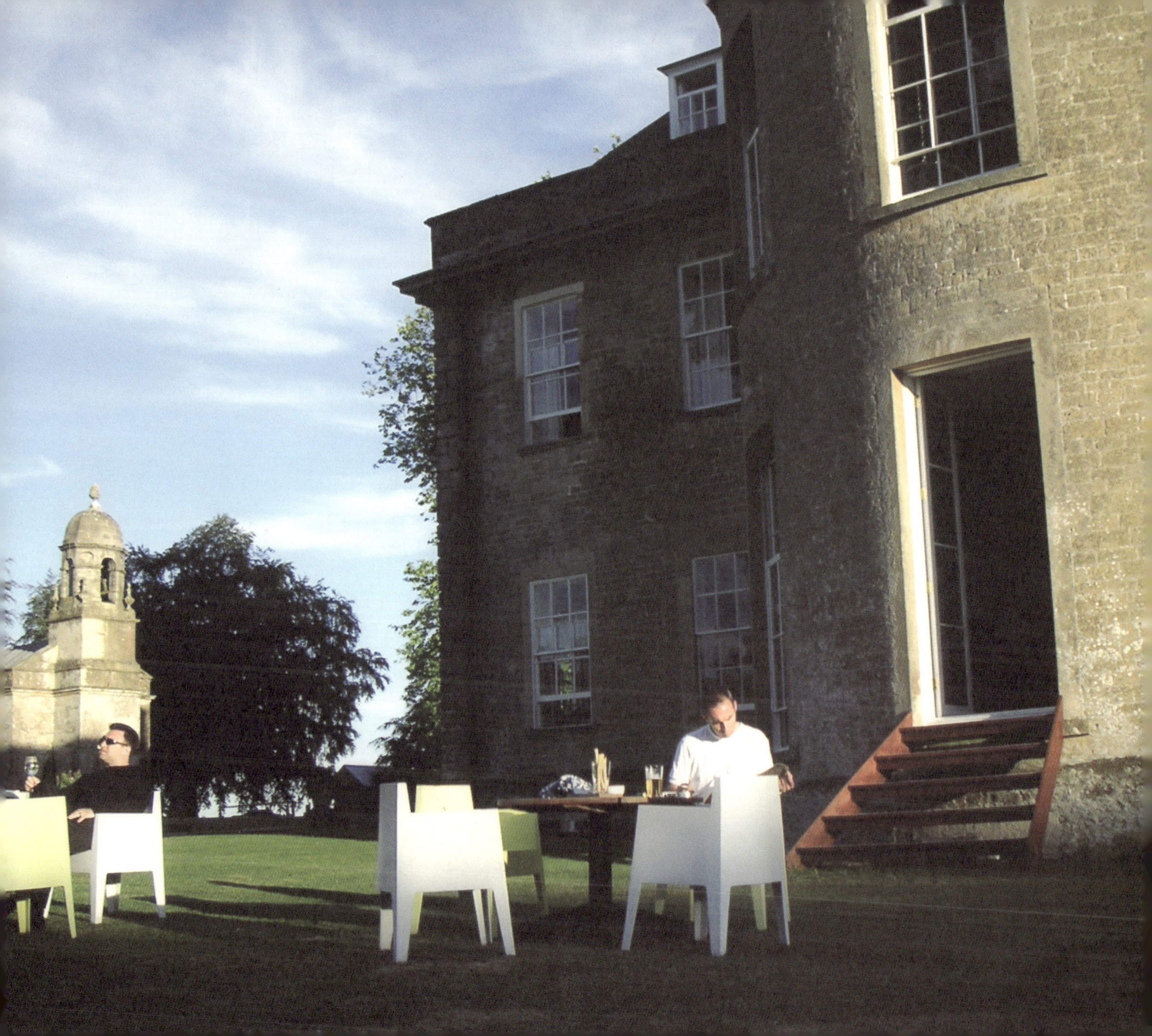

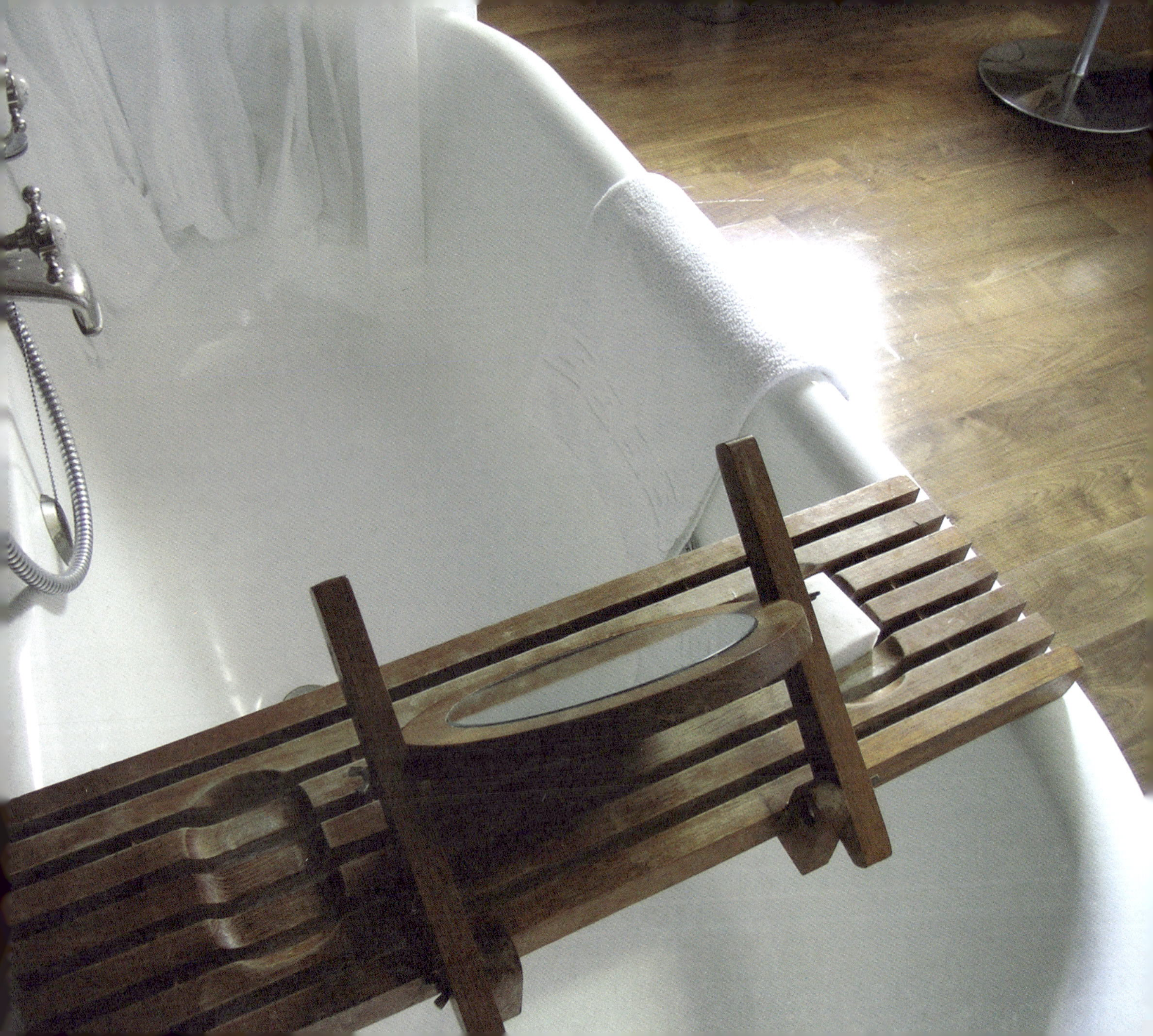

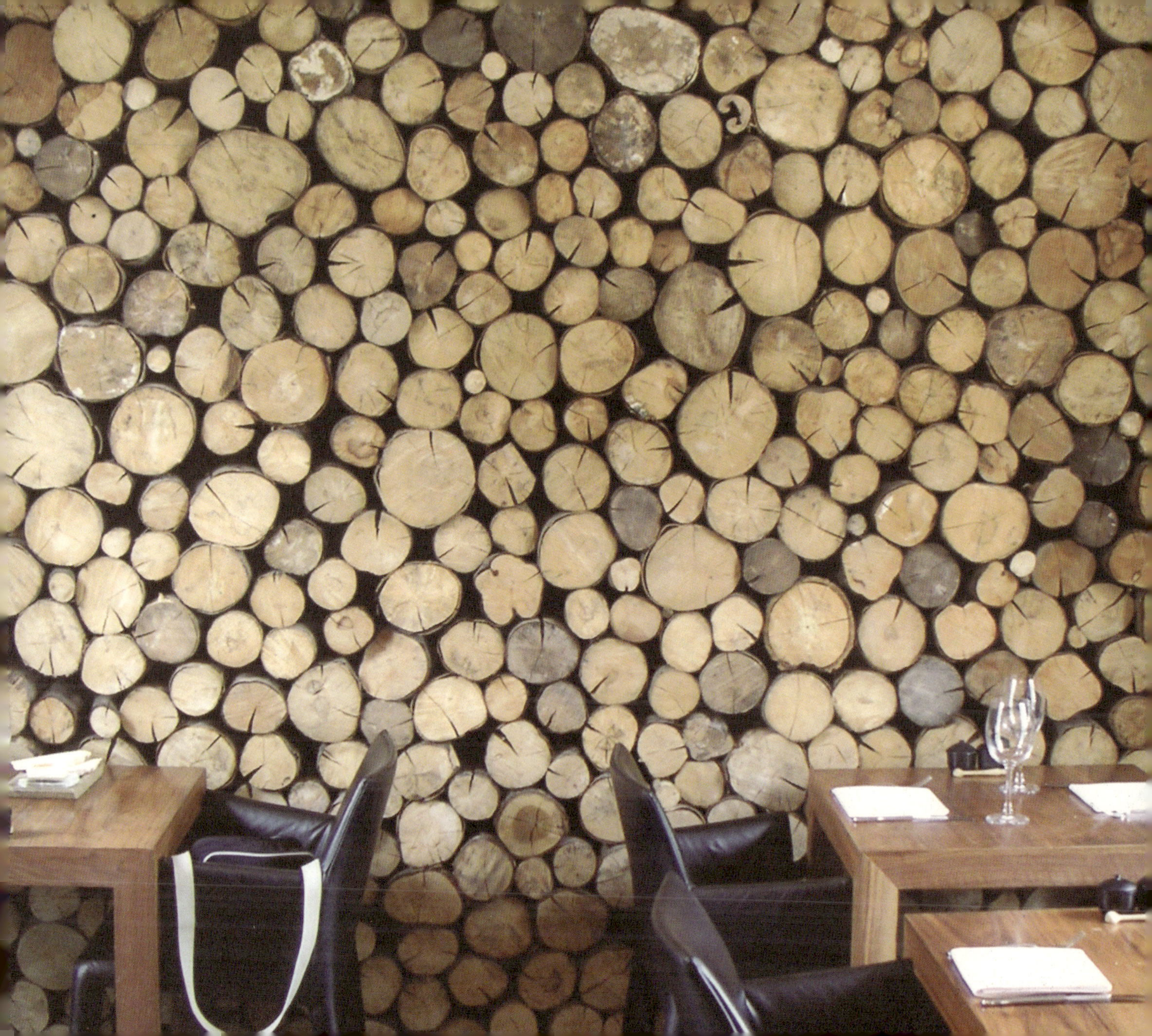

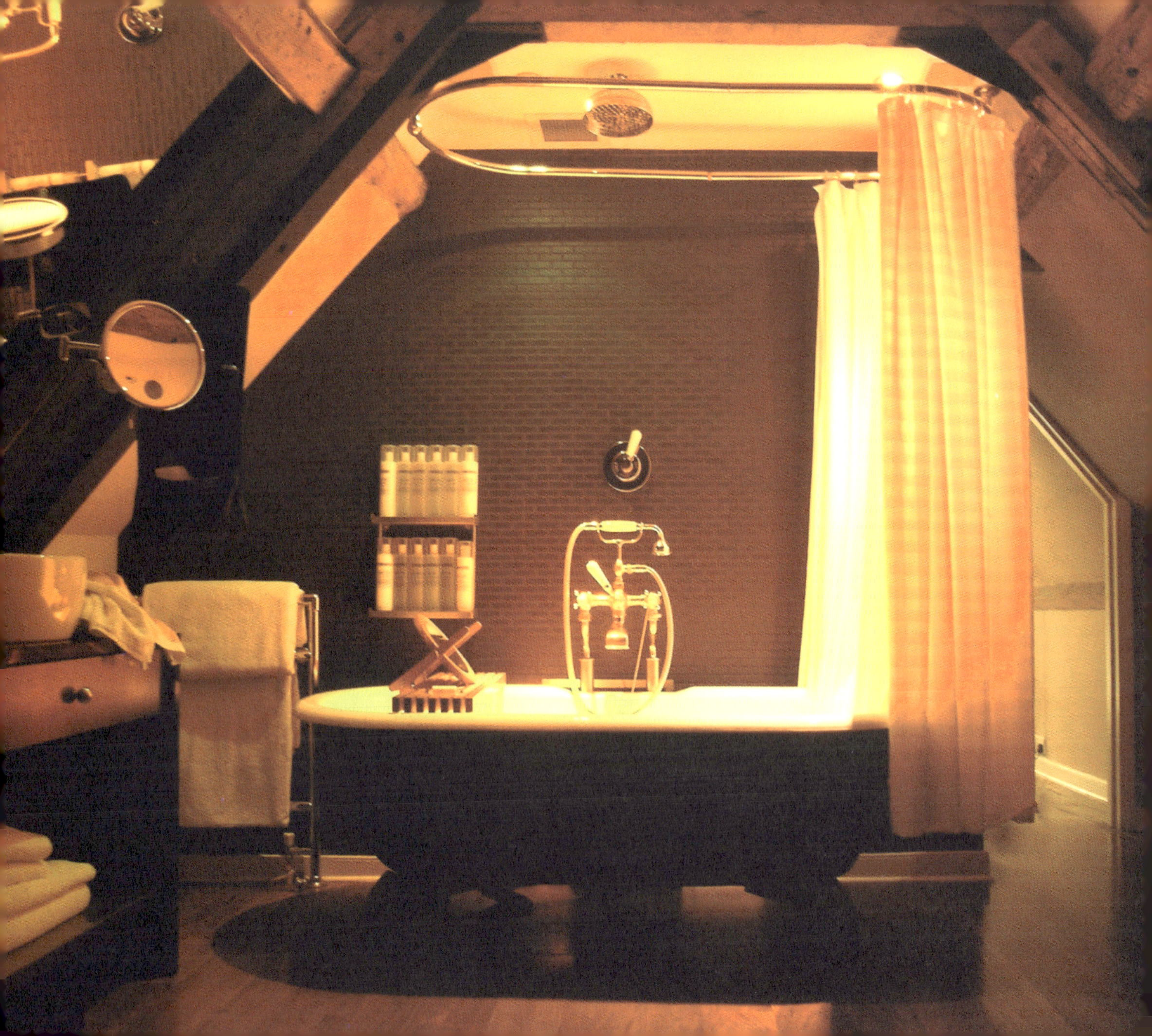

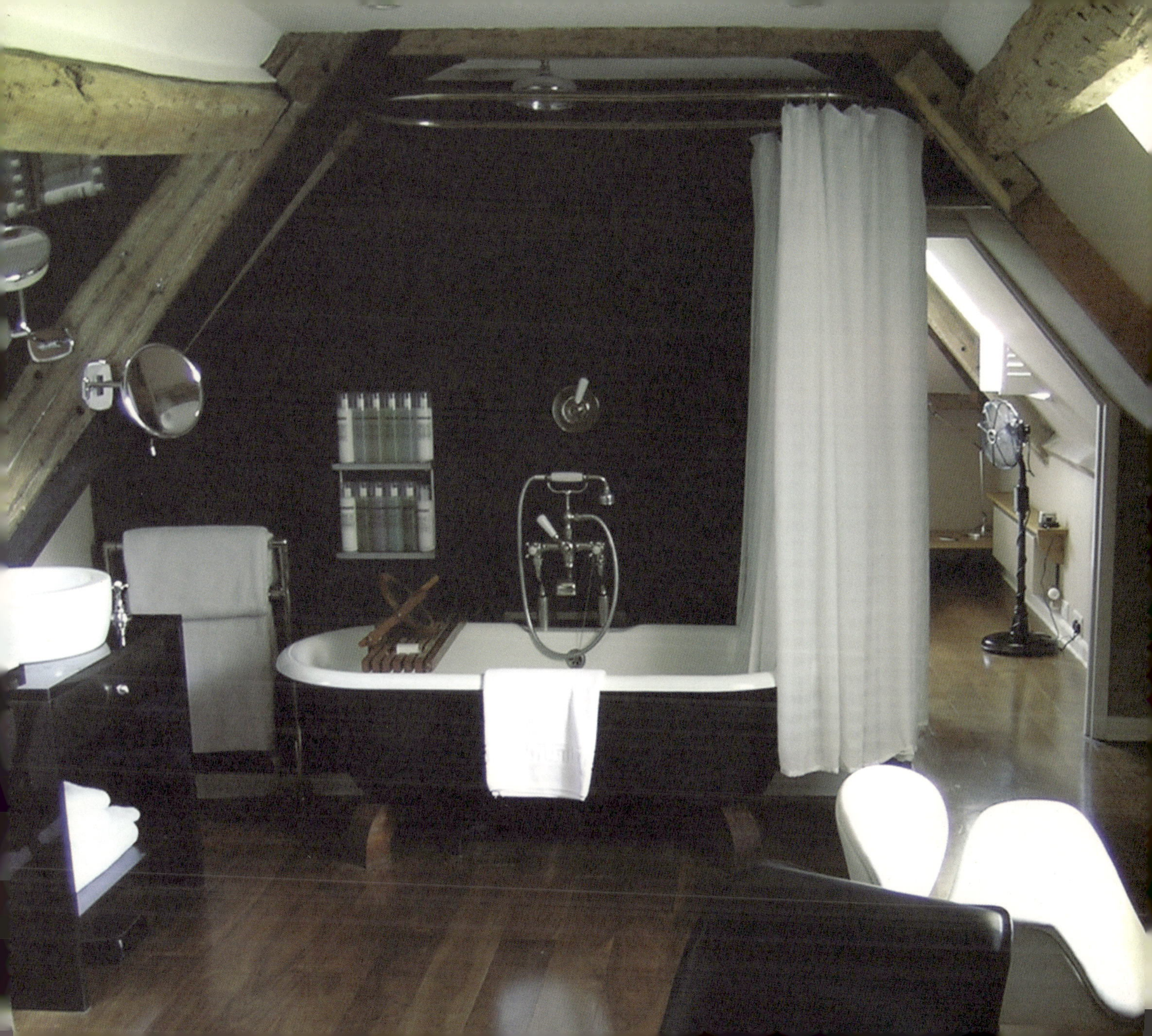

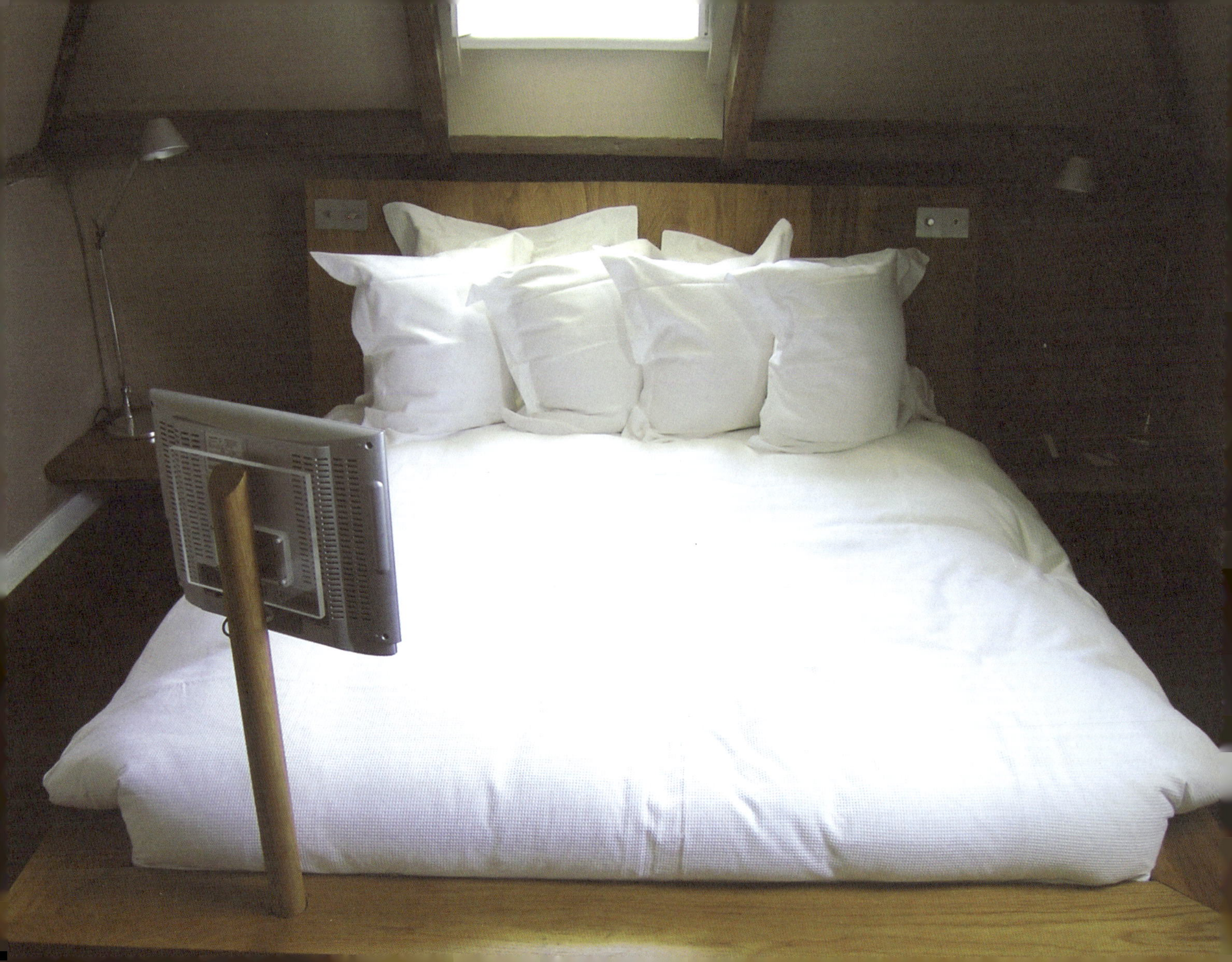

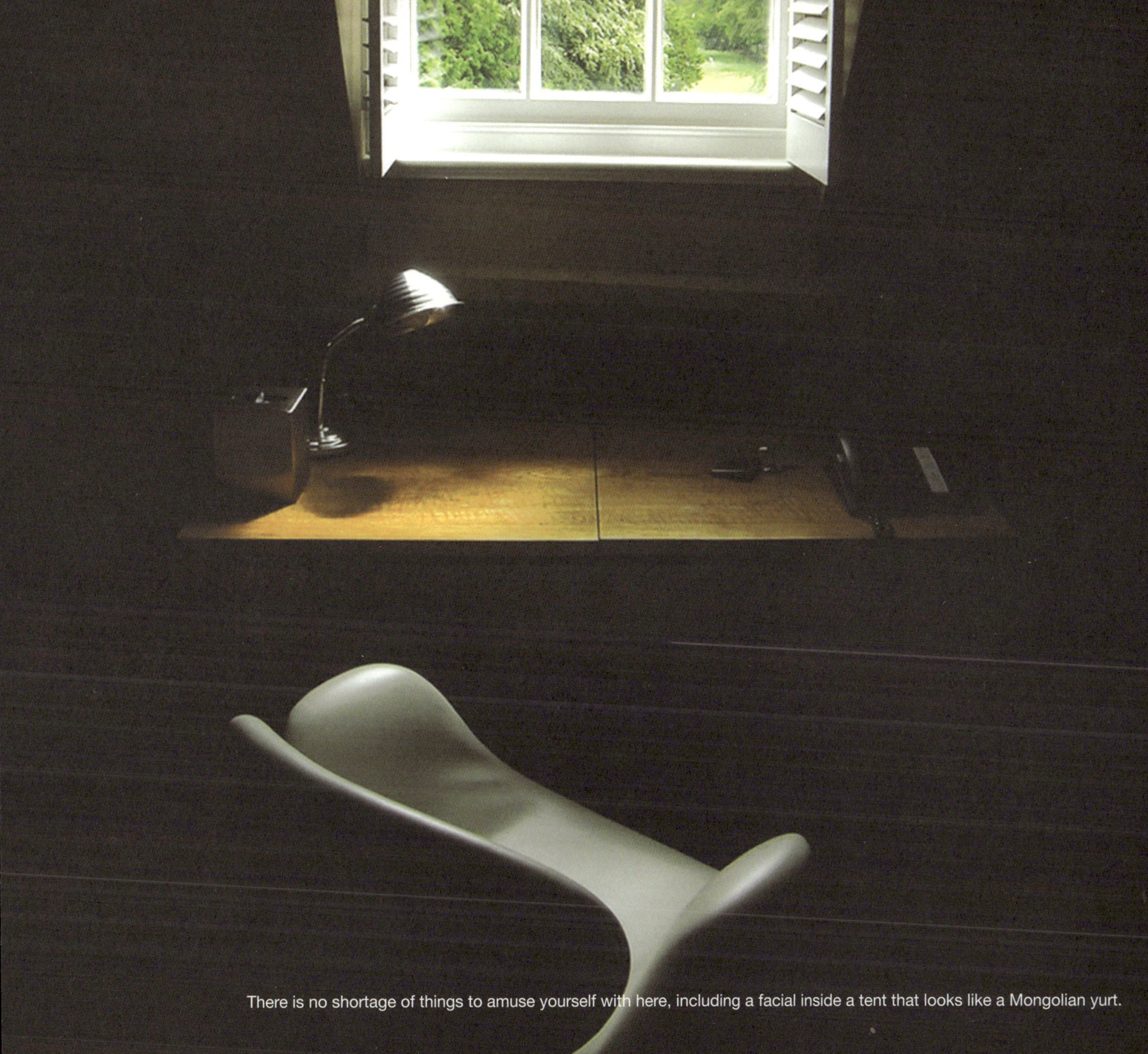

There is no shortage of things to amuse yourself with here, including a facial inside a tent that looks like a Mongolian yurt.

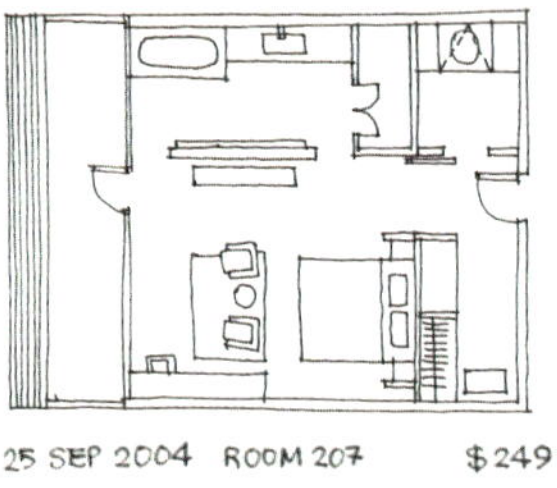

Hotel Vigilius Mountain Resort

BACK TO NATURE

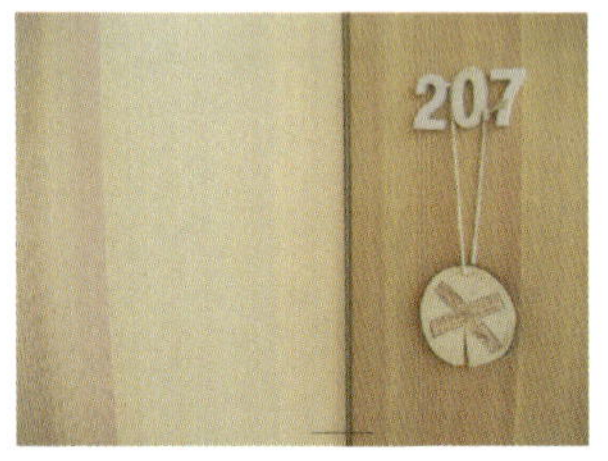

Perched high up on a mountain 4,900 feet above sea level, Hotel Vigilius, a back-to-nature resort surrounded by penetratingly pristine air, can only be accessed by cable car. Some have described this creation by Matteo Thun as “a tree on a mountain,” but I’d rather look at it as a prime example of the designer’s brand of eco-architecture. The hotel is only Thun’s second attempt at hotel design, but it impresses nonetheless with its attention to detail, both in how it blends into its natural environment and in its choice of building materials. Its light and warm color scheme, and wooden floor and wall finishings (strategically punctuated by spirited dashes of red) compliment the native Alpine flora perfectly. The wood used in the restaurant has been recycled from a three-hundred-year-old Austrian granary. Up here on top of the perennially snow-capped mountain, warmth and light are of paramount importance. The rooms are well-heated; even the stonewall separating the bedroom and the bathroom has heating elements embedded in it. If there were paradise on earth, this wouldn’t be far off.

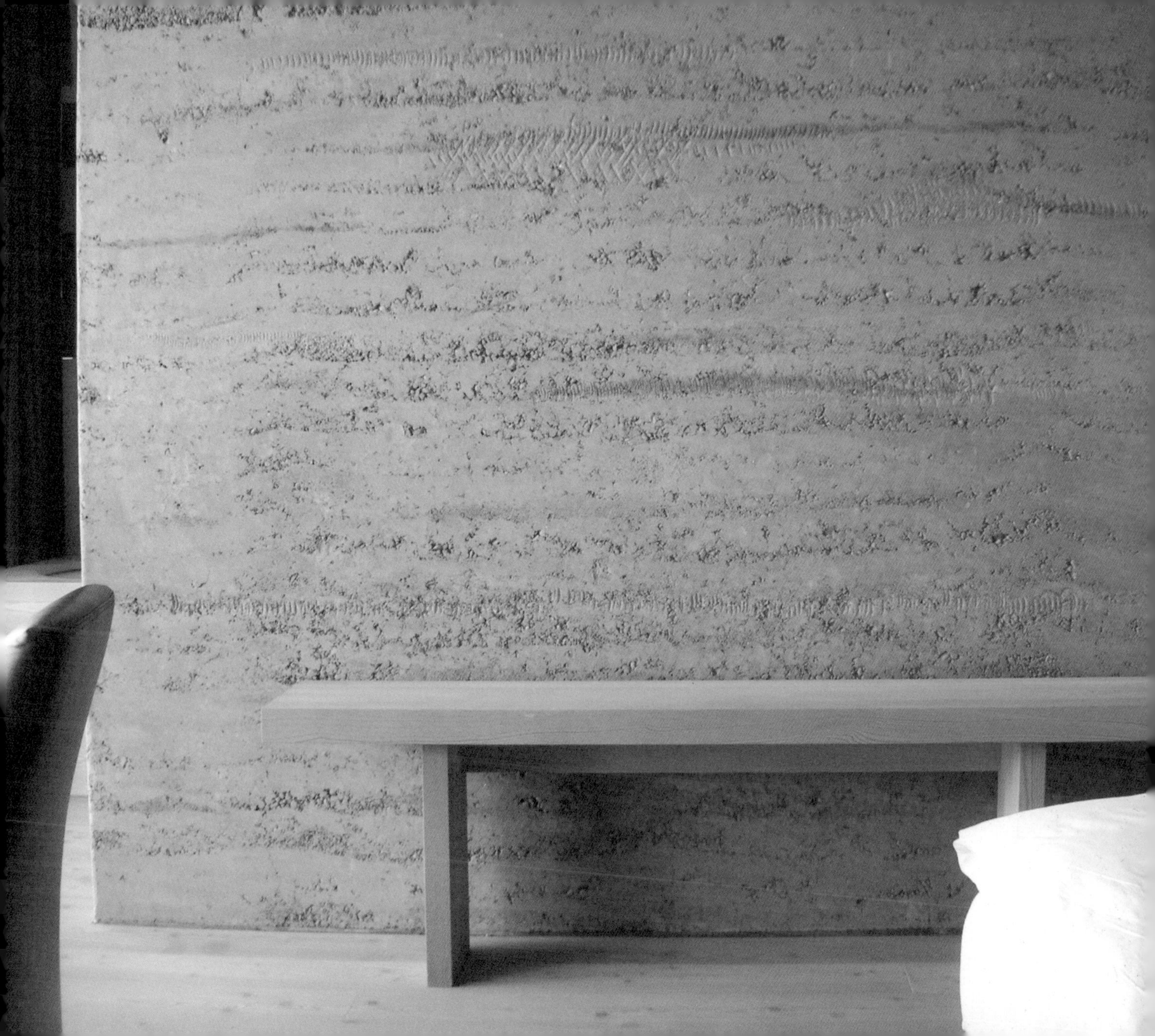

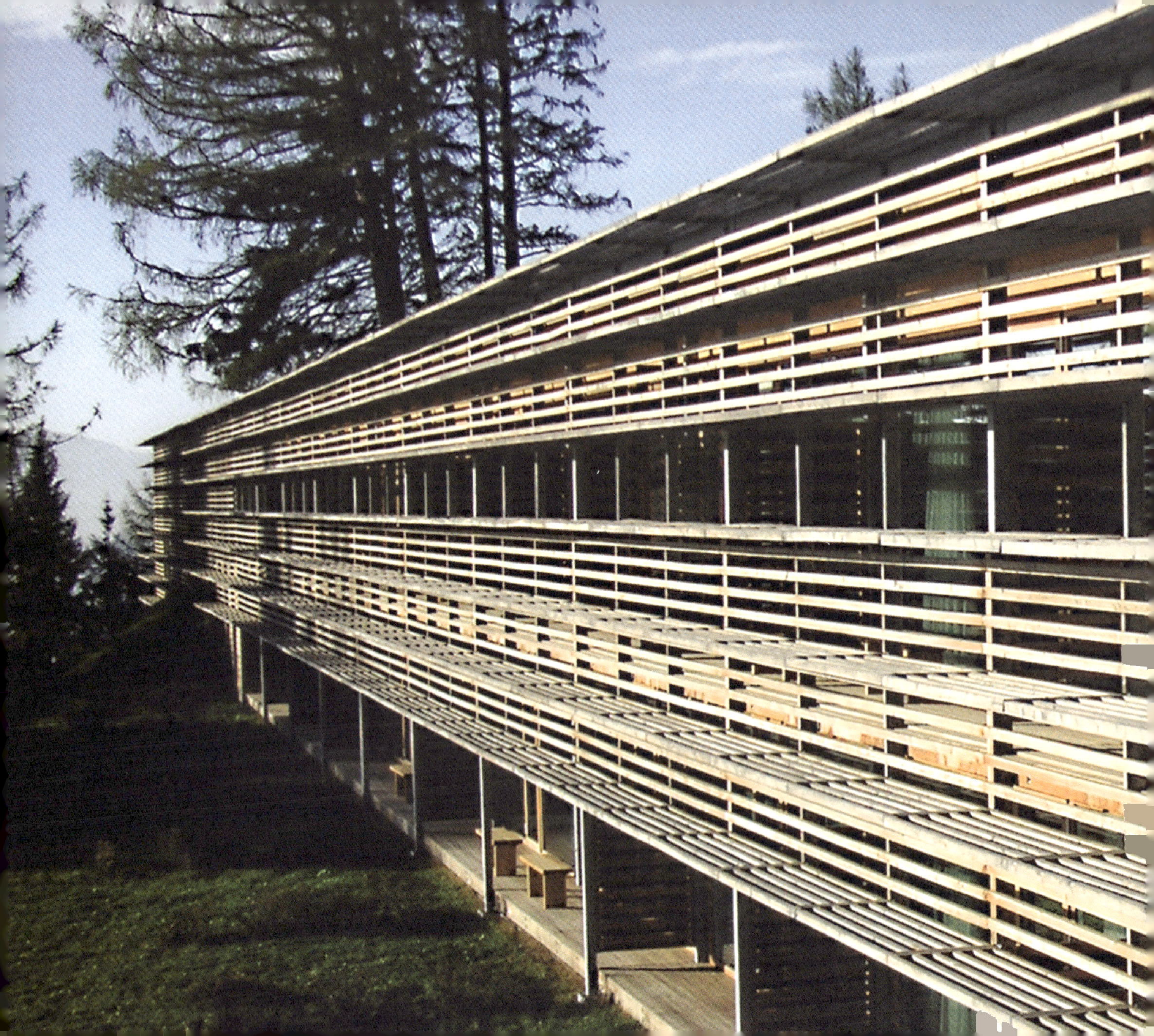

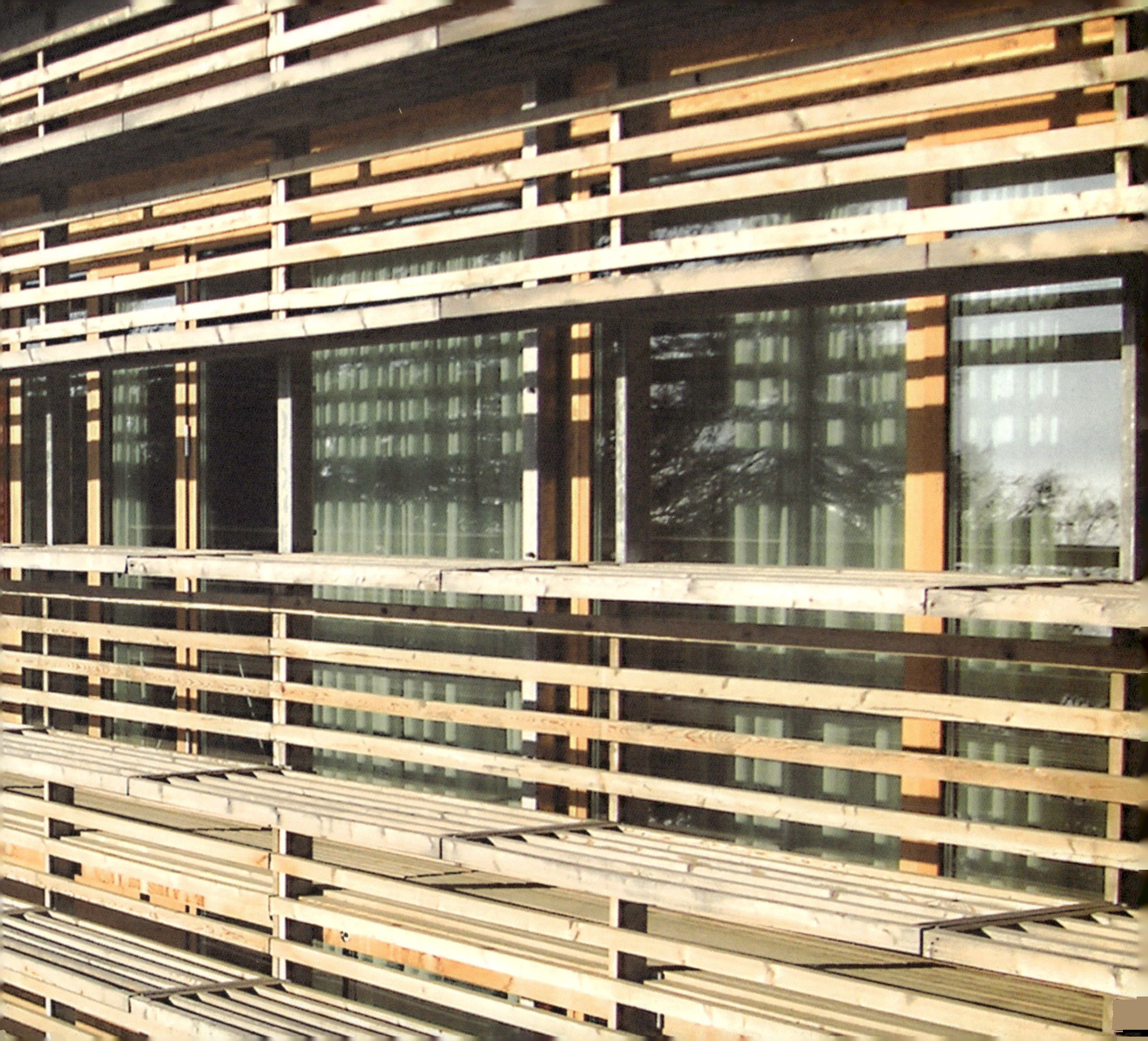

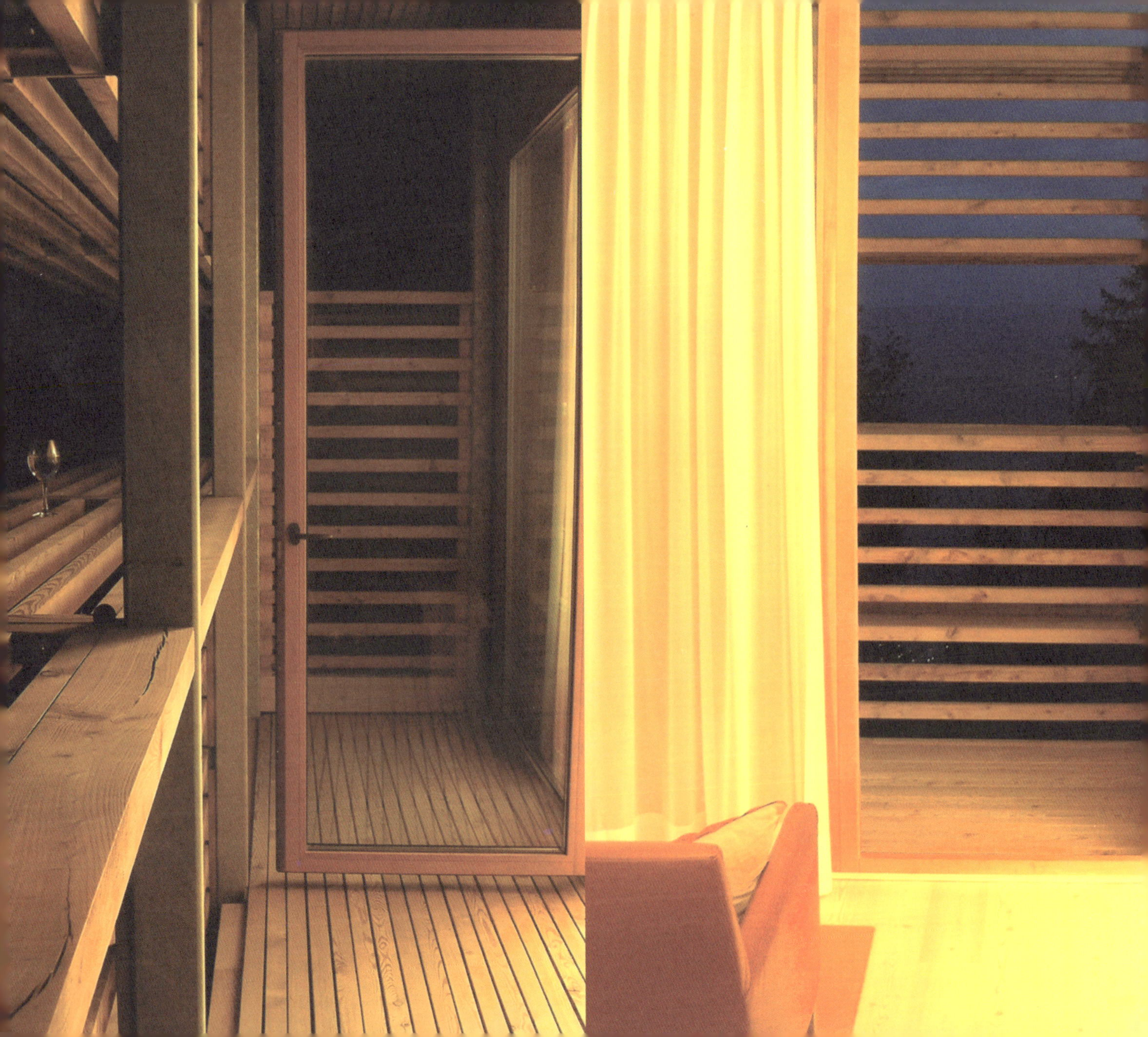

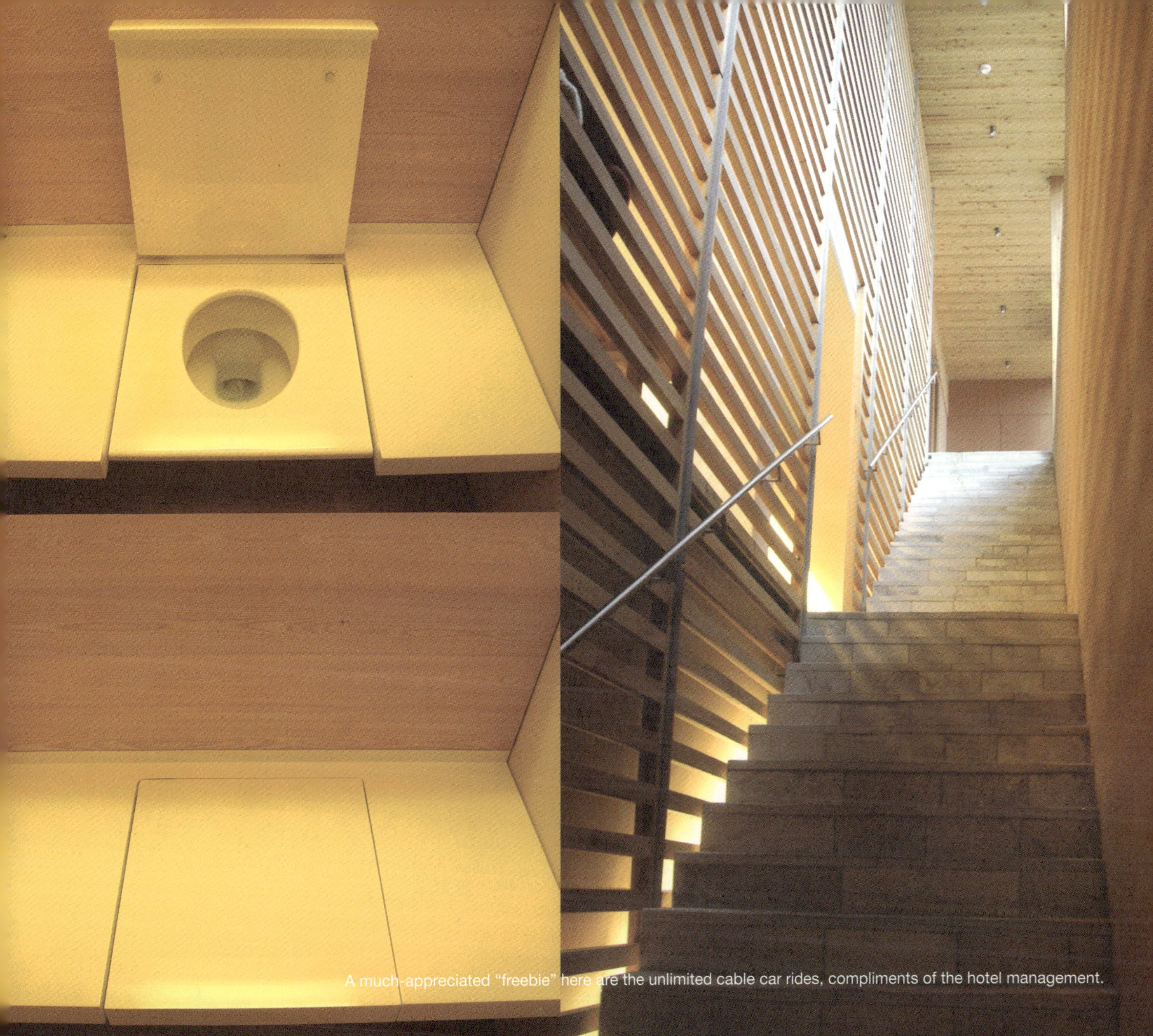

A much-appreciated "freebie" here are the unlimited cable car rides, compliments of the hotel management.

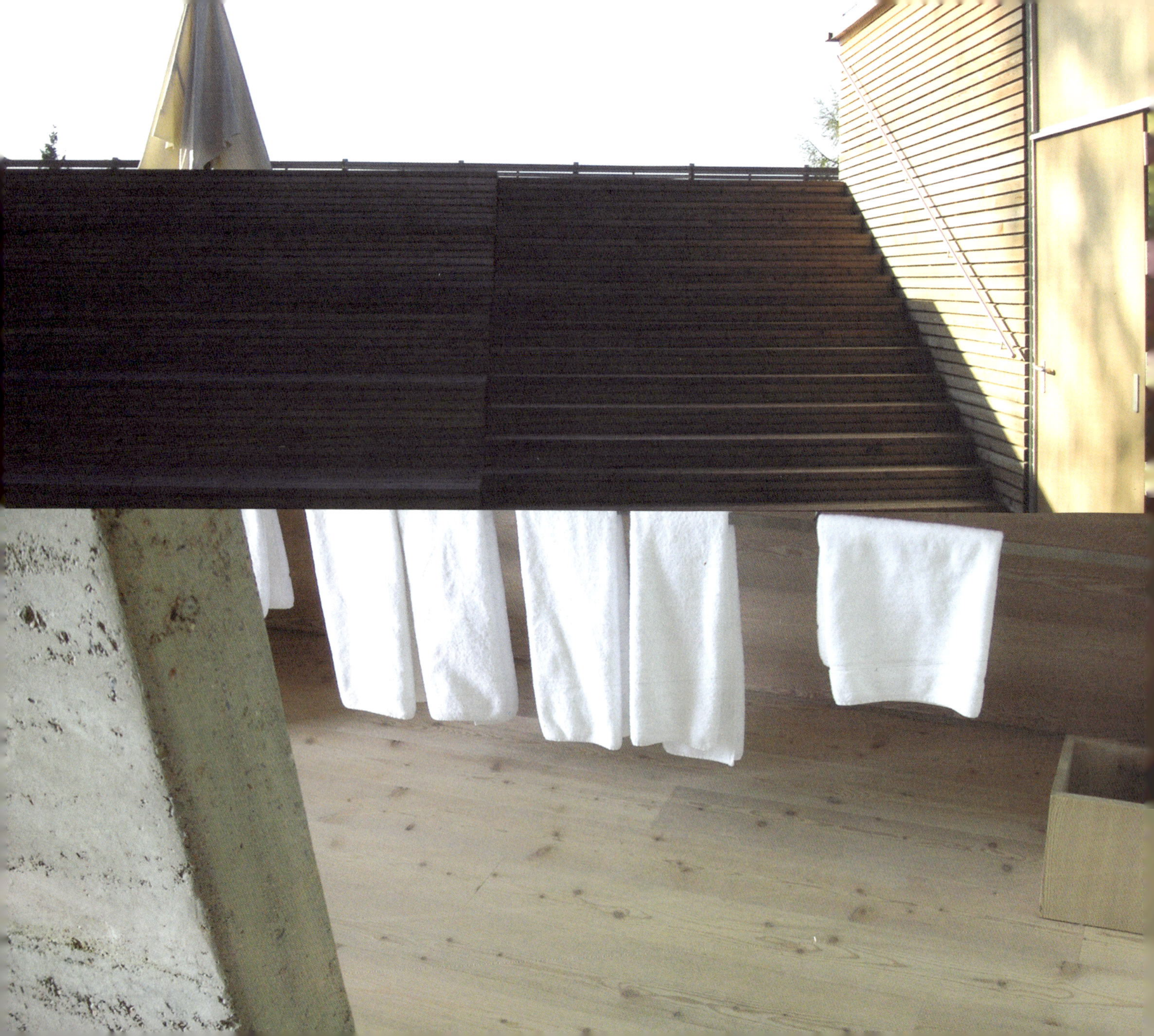

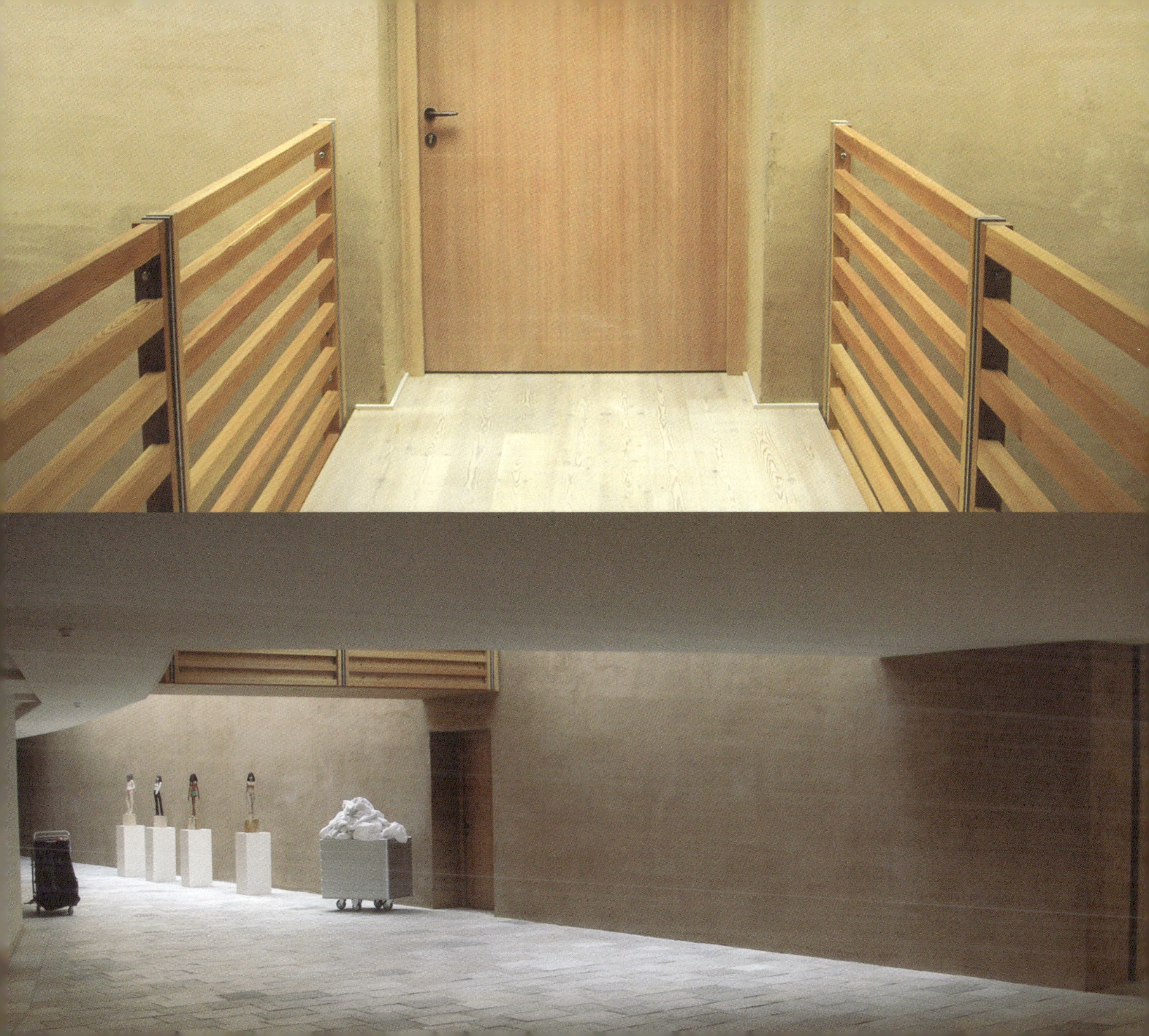

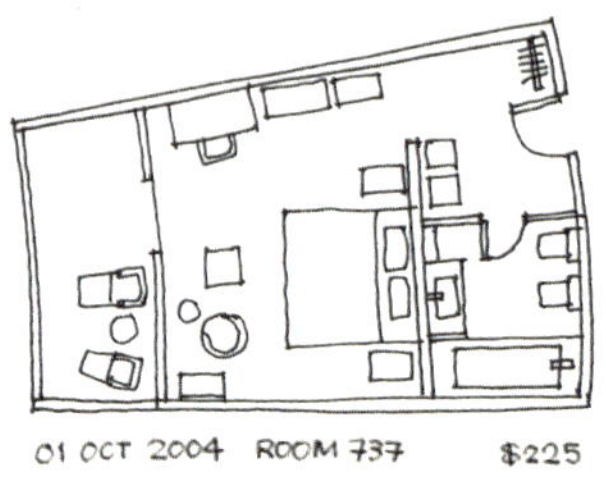

Hotel Therme Vals

OUT OF THIS WORLD

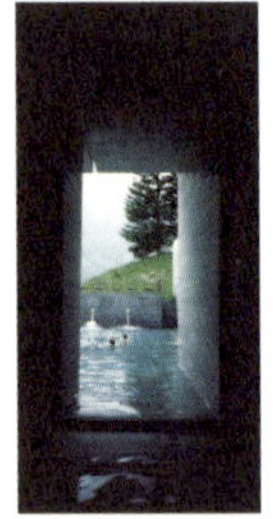

Many approach the long trip to this hot spring resort, designed by Peter Zumthor and nestled in a remote valley, with the piety of pilgrims. The austere spirituality of the place itself seems to encourage this. Zumthor, the carpenter-turned-designer, has always regarded all kinds of worldly ornamentation with blithe oblivion, preferring instead to concentrate on the physical and sensual experience that the structure itself imparts on its visitors. This he achieves through his choice of material and placement of facilities. Hotel Therme Vals is a prime example.

The hot spring baths are partitioned by rectilinear stonewalls of various sizes, all marked by numbers that represent the temperatures of the springs in Celsius. Interestingly, the wall colors also vary with the temperature, changing from charcoal grey to light tan. The stone has an almost mystical gleam in the gentle lighting, and when hit, makes a clear, ringing sound. The serene spaces and the gentle babbling of the springs transport the bather to a complete state of tranquility, otherwise found only in sacrosanct structures such as churches and temples. Fashioned completely from local granite, the resort is set into the side of the mountain, creating the illusion of being part of the mountain itself. In winter, bathing in the outdoor hot spring is like swimming in an unforgettable snow-covered, picture-postcard scene. After he designed the magnificent hot spring resorts, Zumthor also renovated the hotel rooms themselves. True to form, their design doesn't cry out to be noticed and is completely functional and optimal. The only noticeable thing about them is their actual *lack* of hotel clichés. Two small watches discreetly inlaid on a slim, brass pole located in the hallway remind you of the passing hours, just as you start losing track of time in the resort's relaxing atmosphere.

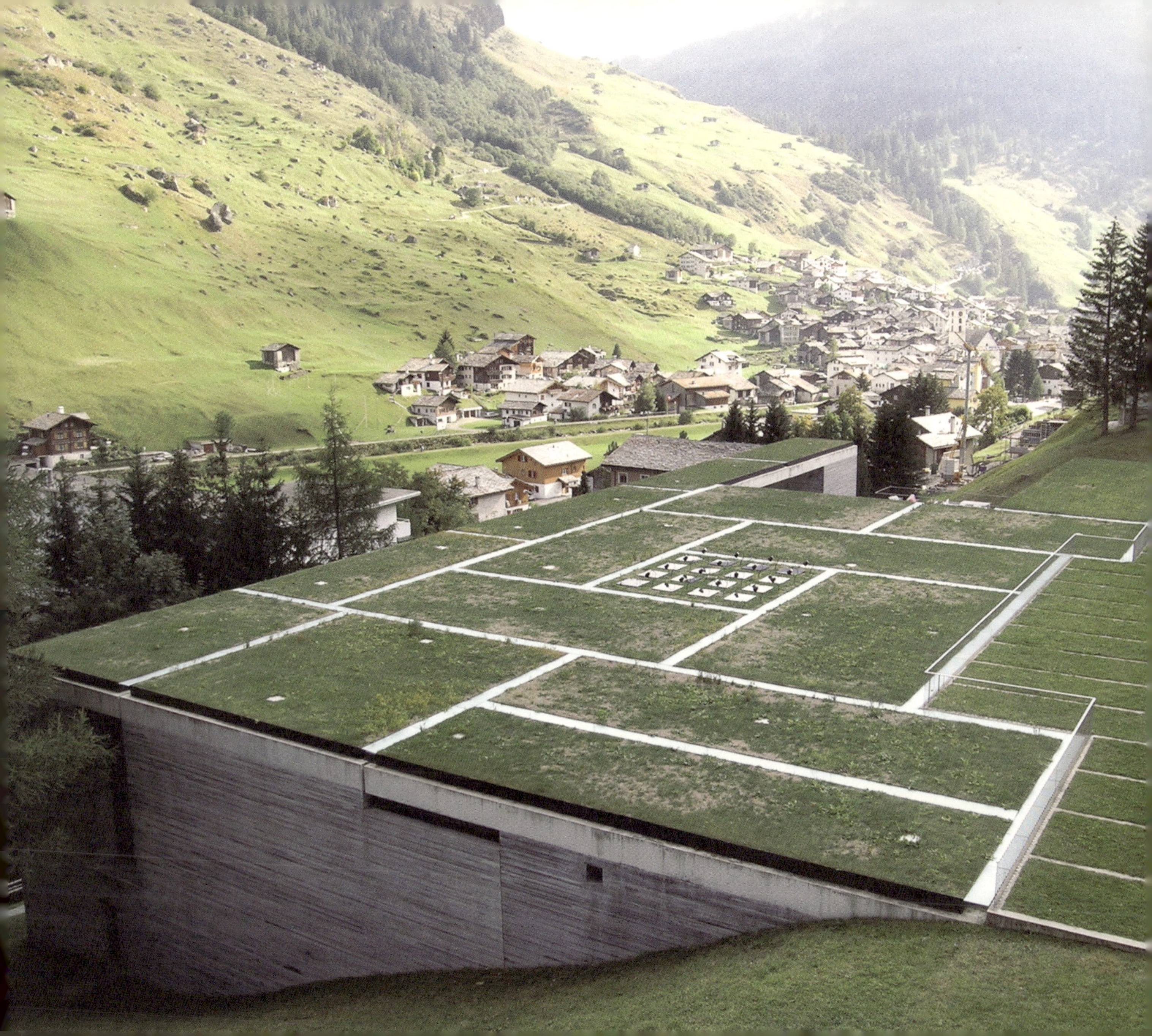

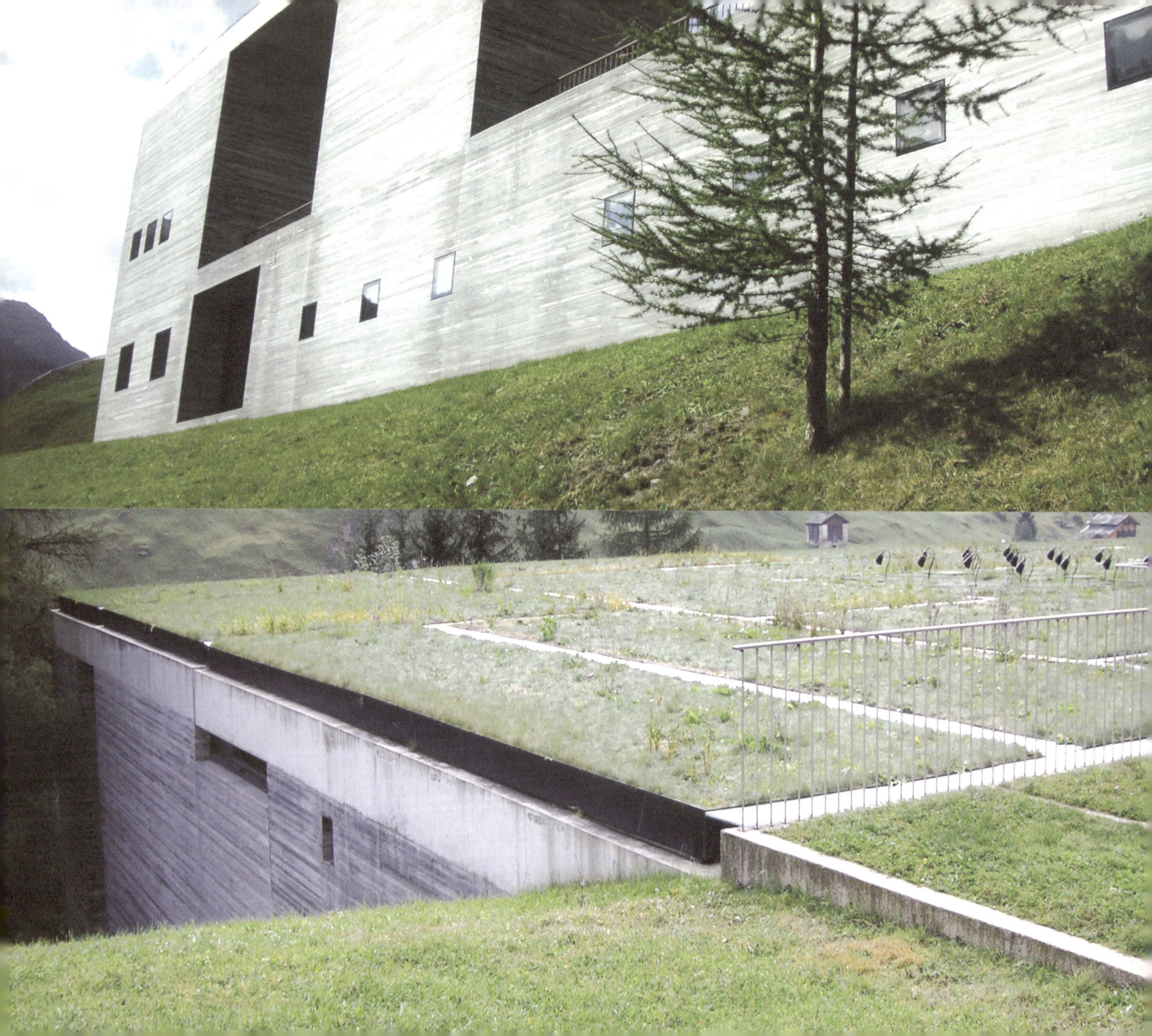

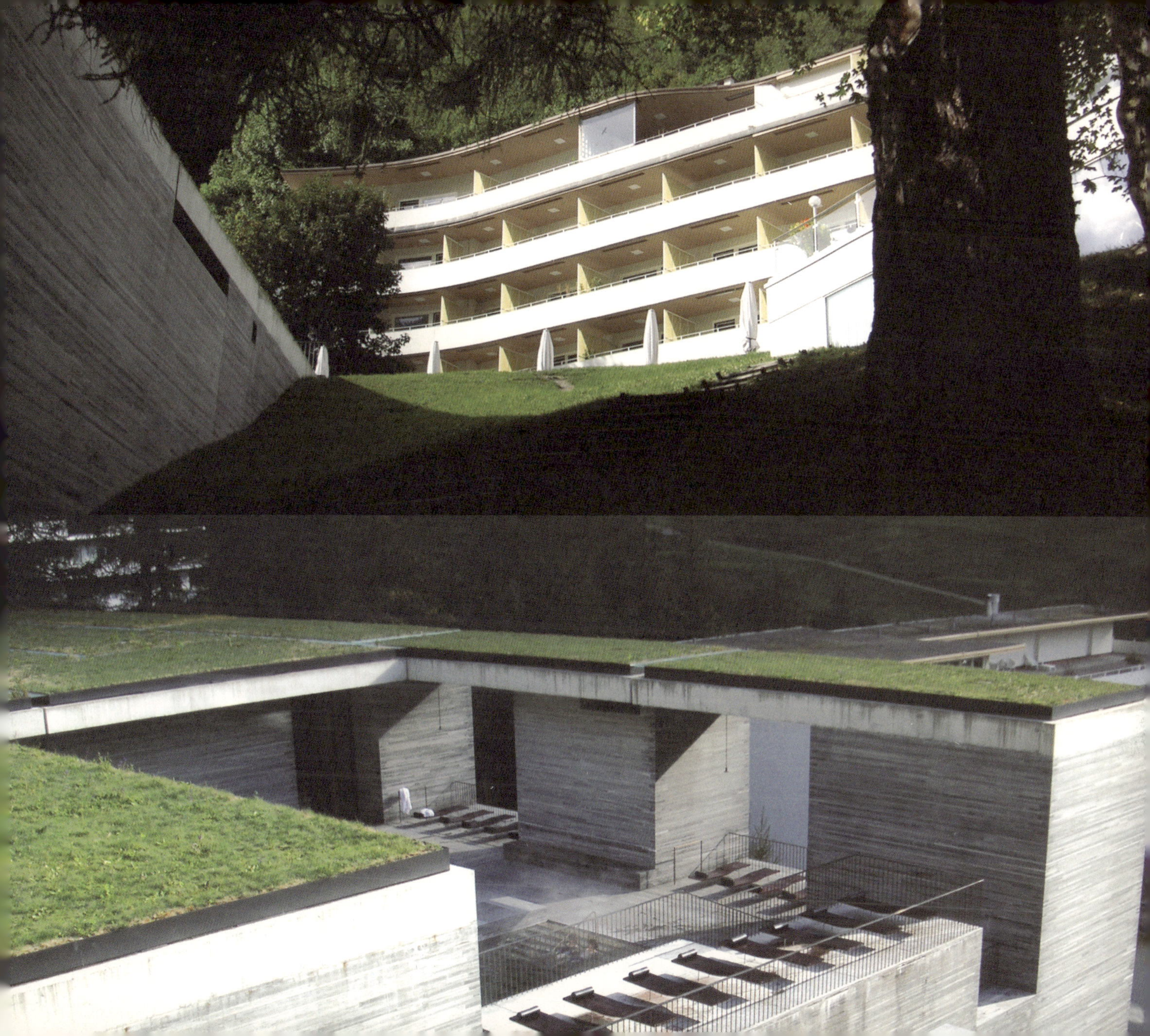

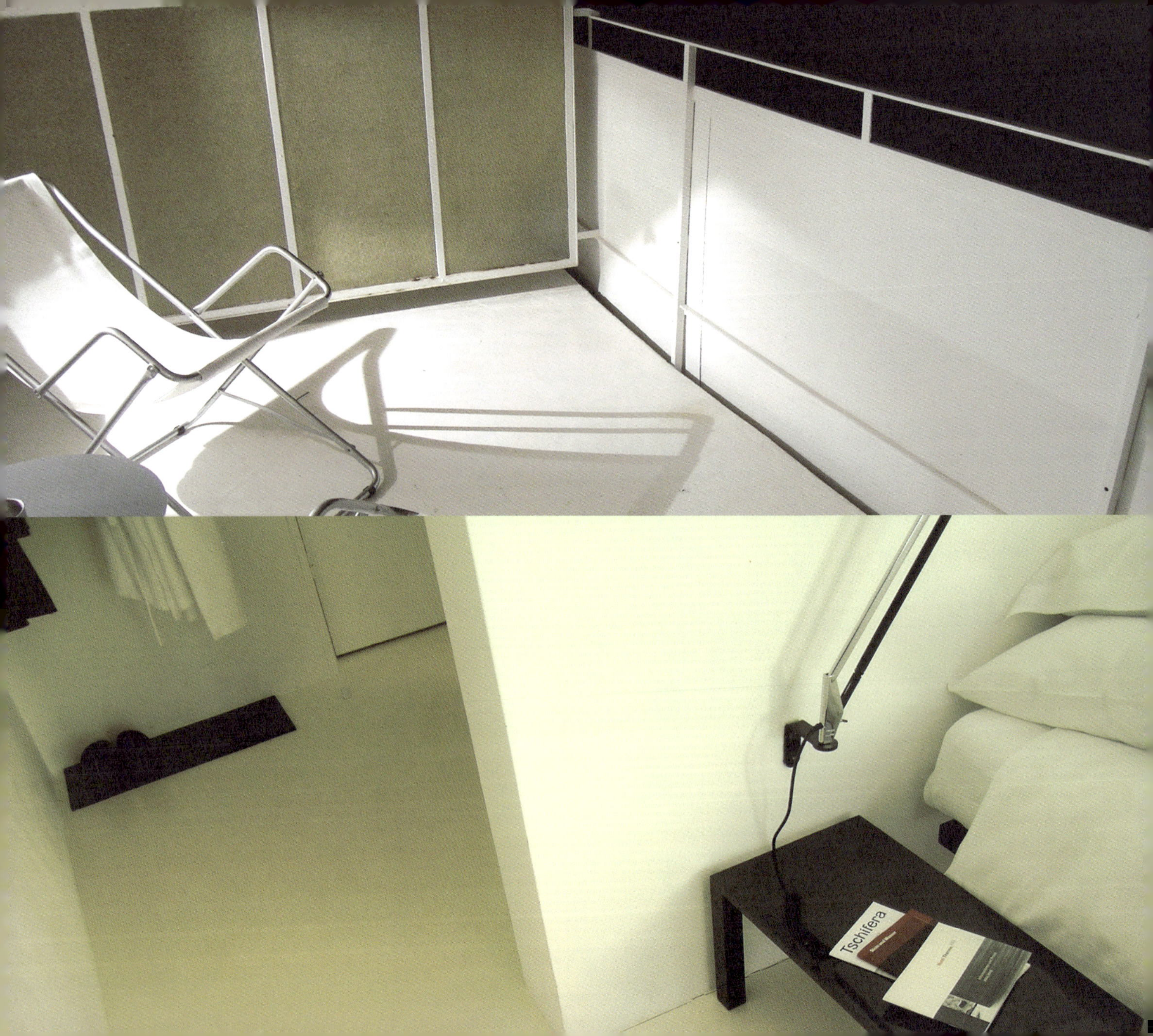
Tschifera

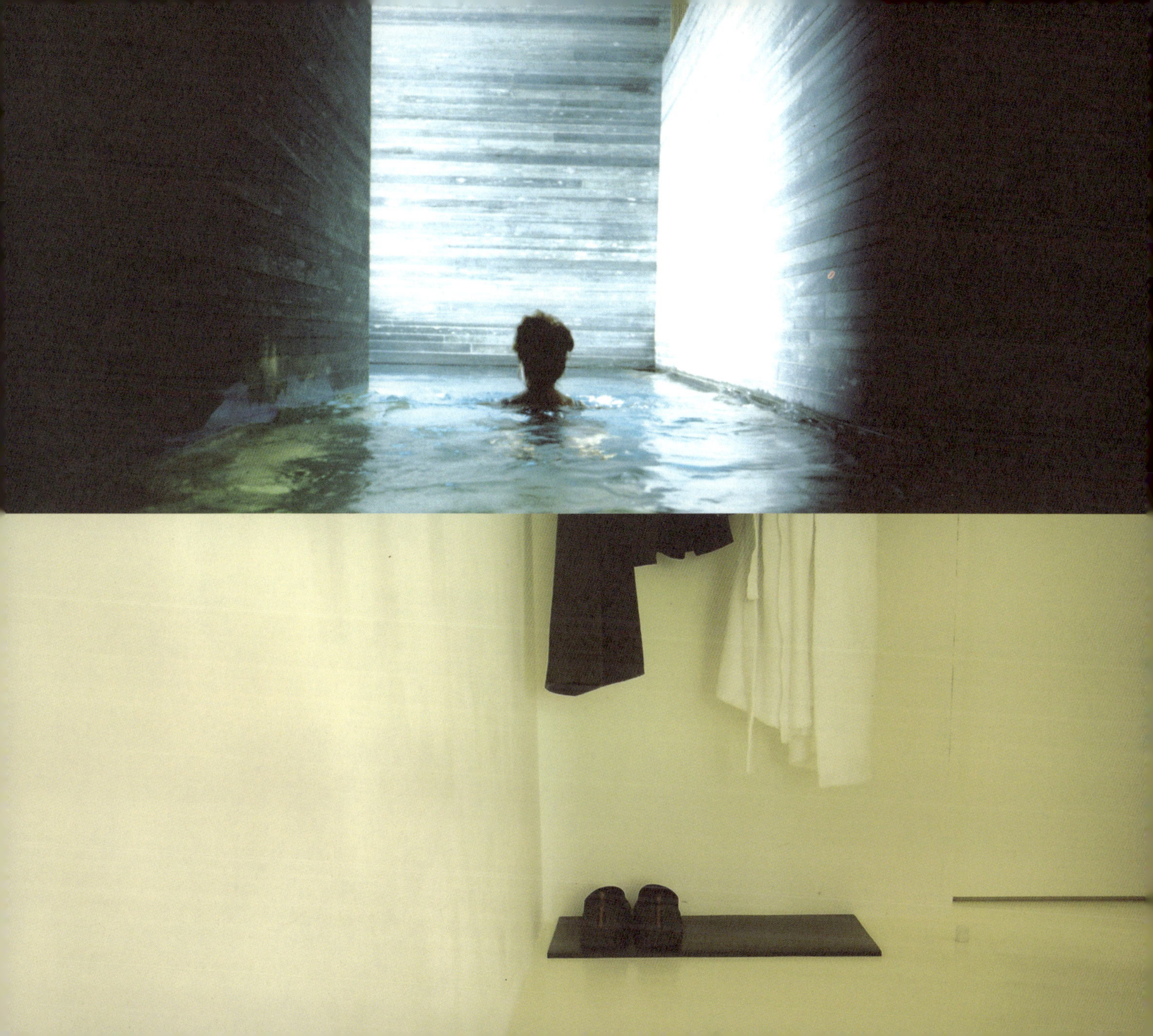

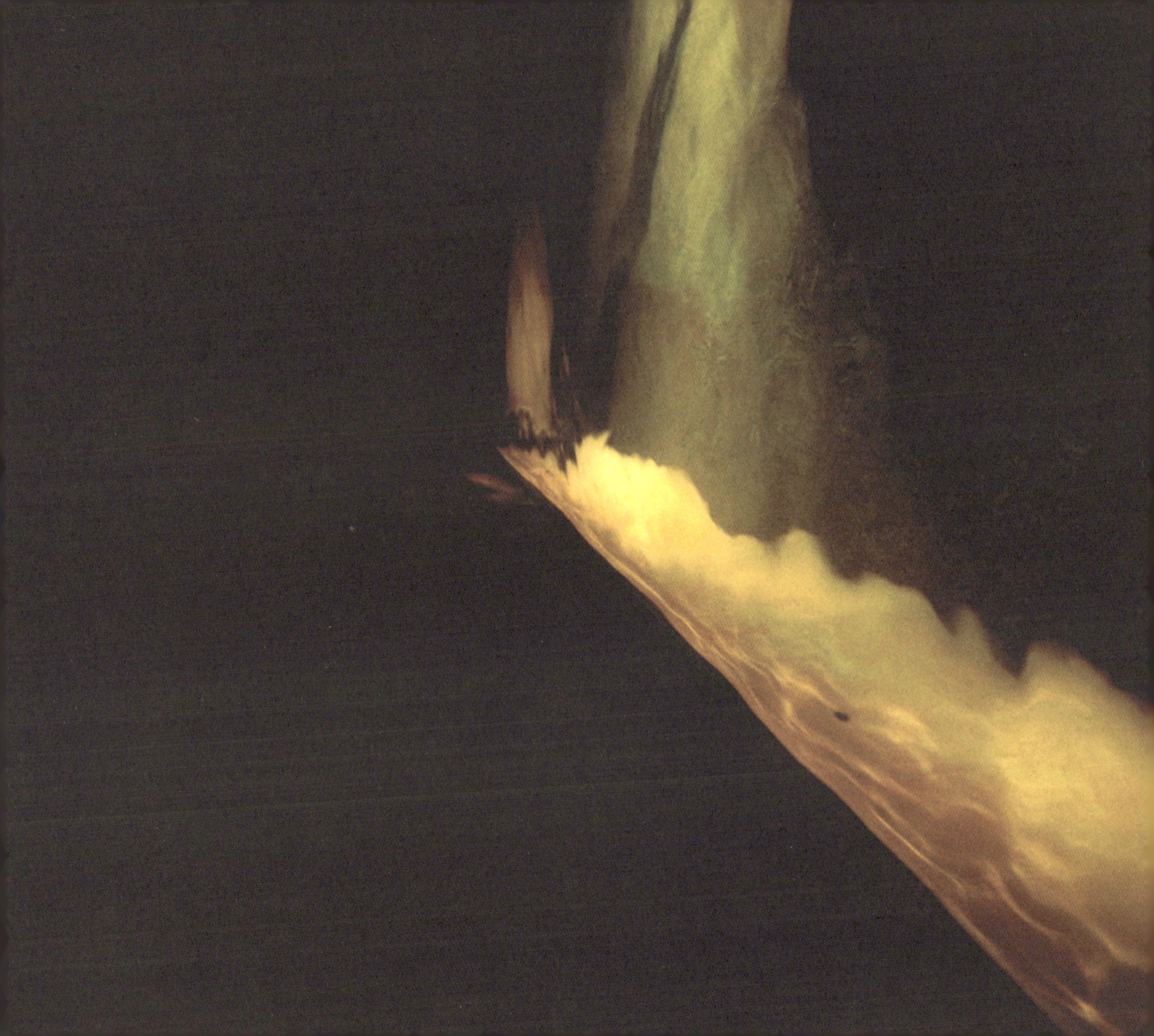

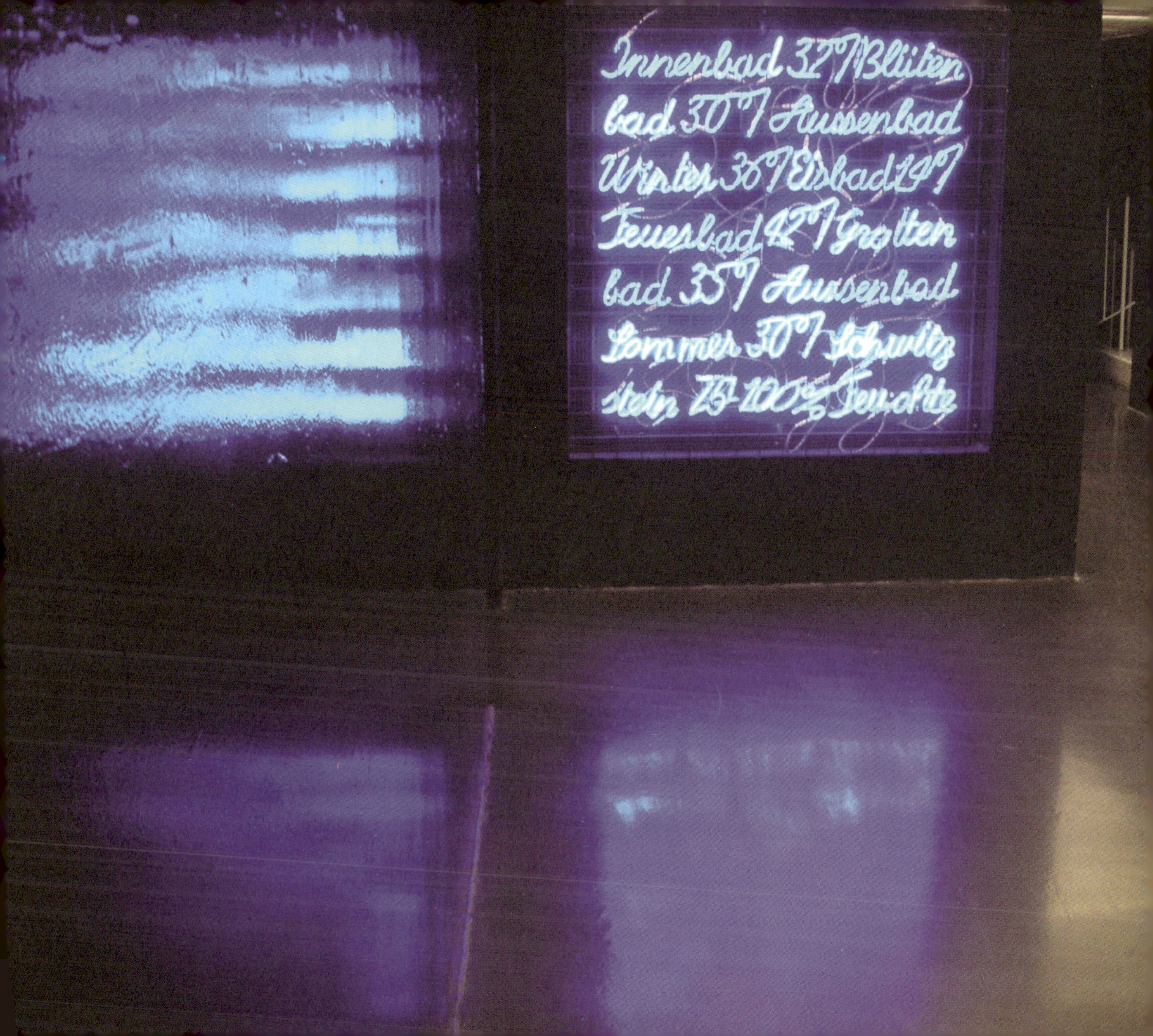

Innenbad 32° / Blüten
bad 30° / Aussenbad
Winter 36° / Eisbad 14° /
Feuerbad 42° / Grotten
bad 35° / Aussenbad
Sommer 30° / Schwitz
stein 75-100% Feuchte

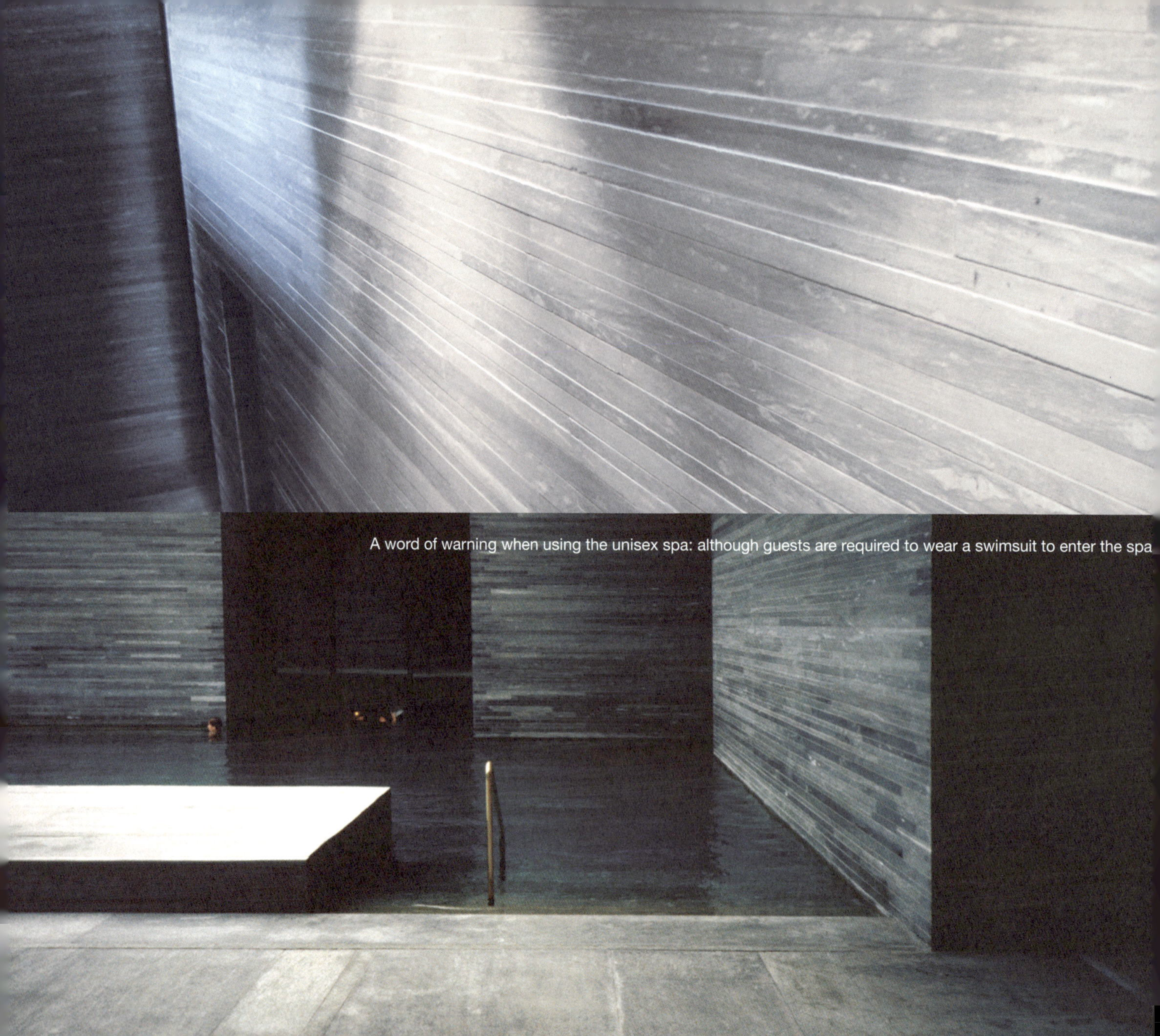

A word of warning when using the unisex spa: although guests are required to wear a swimsuit to enter the spa ome areas inside the steam room allow nudity. Look out for the signs in German on the door.

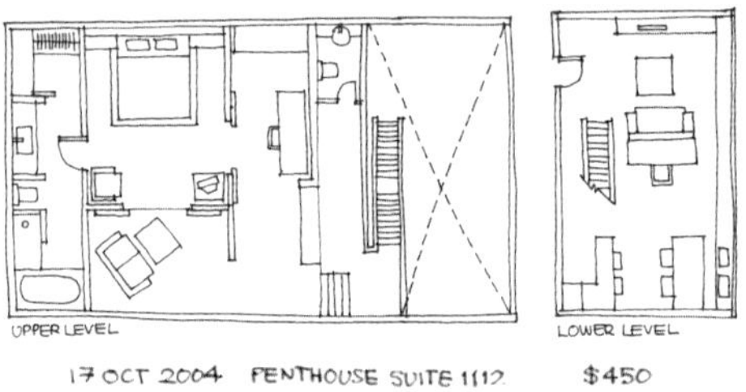

The Metropolitan

THEATER IN THE SKY

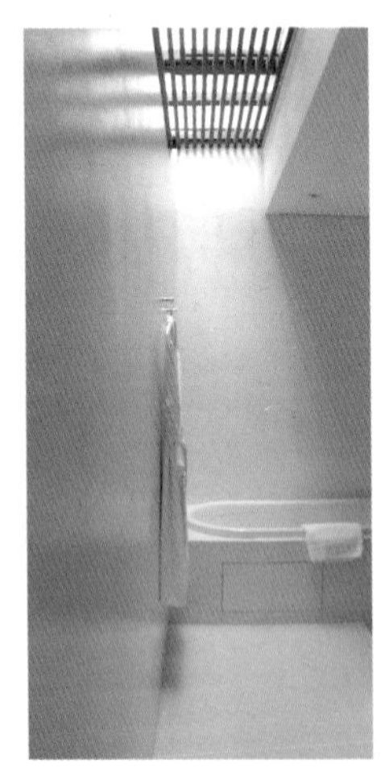

The Metropolitan Bangkok is unorthodox as far as chain hotels go. It clearly shows that corporate standardization doesn't have to mean faceless anonymity anymore, but can instead be a showcase of individual design talents. Its proprietor, the COMO group, has managed to build vastly different hotels in places as diverse as London, Bali, the Maldives, and Bhutan. Situated in Bangkok, one of the world's busiest cities, the Metropolitan used to be a YMCA, but is now renowned for its extraordinary comfort and the four 1,500-square-foot penthouse suites converted from the YMCA's old gymnasium. Originally a two-story unit, the penthouse perches high above the city of Bangkok, affording it a peerless view of the city. Its large windows allow it to be sun-drenched throughout the day, while the voluminous drapes that cover them have a cinematic touch. The penthouse's expansive size has not gone to waste under the designer's masterful touch. The immense sense of space allows a wooden staircase connecting the two levels to be situated right in the middle of the room without becoming an obstacle. After dark, the upper level becomes a stage on which the lights from the outside play out their poetic and mysterious phantasmagoria through the penthouse's larger-than-life windows.

BANGKOK

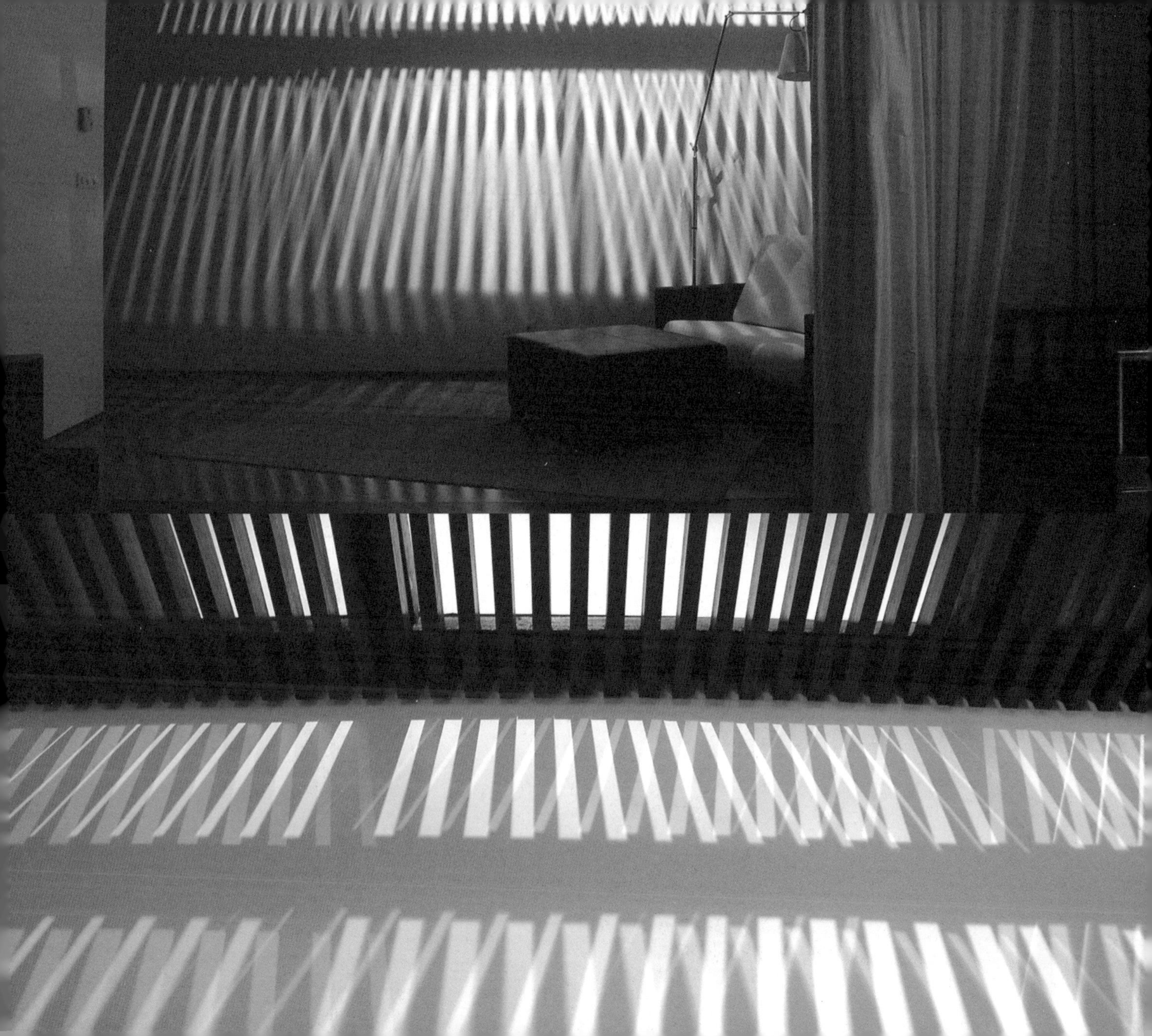

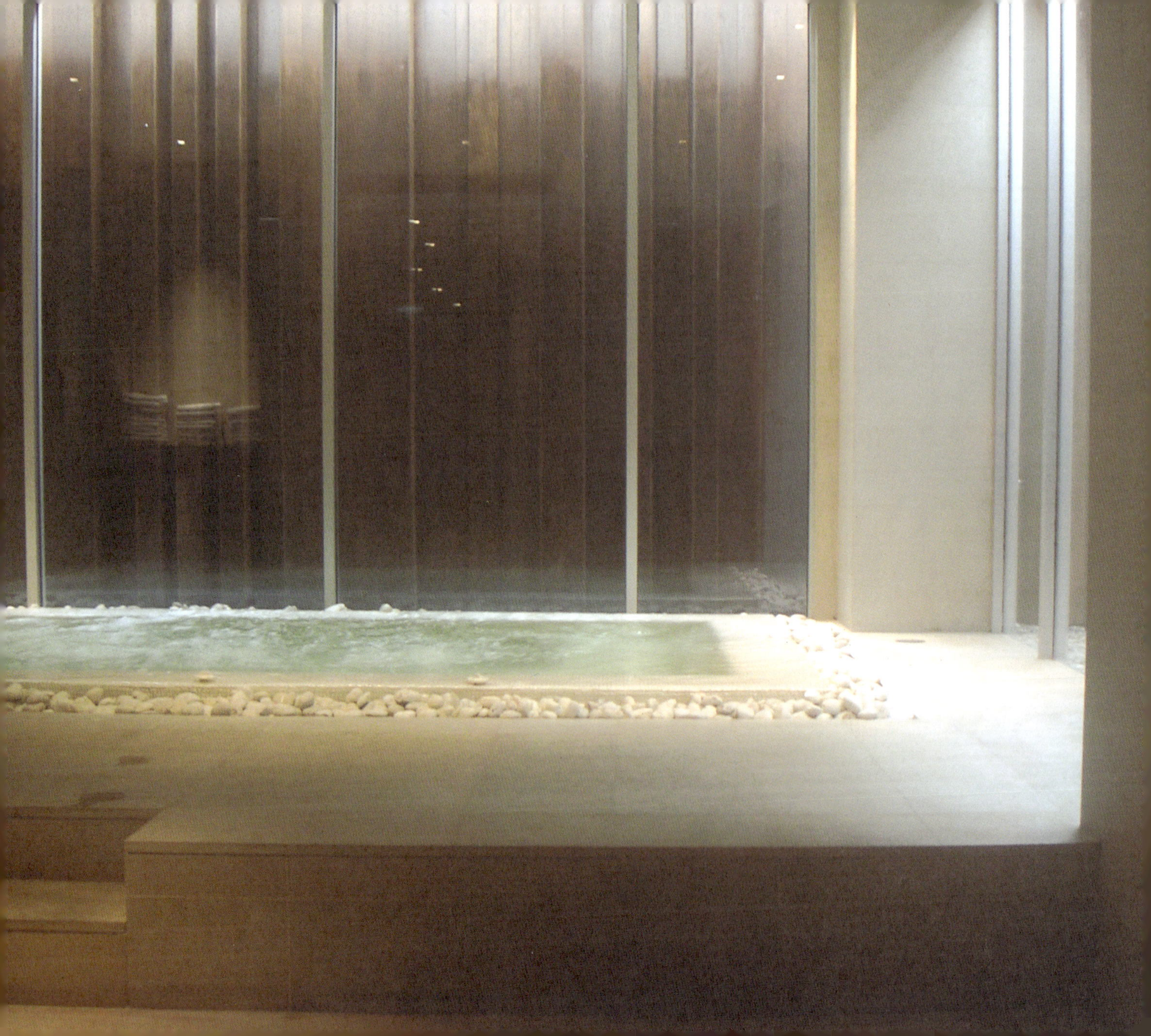

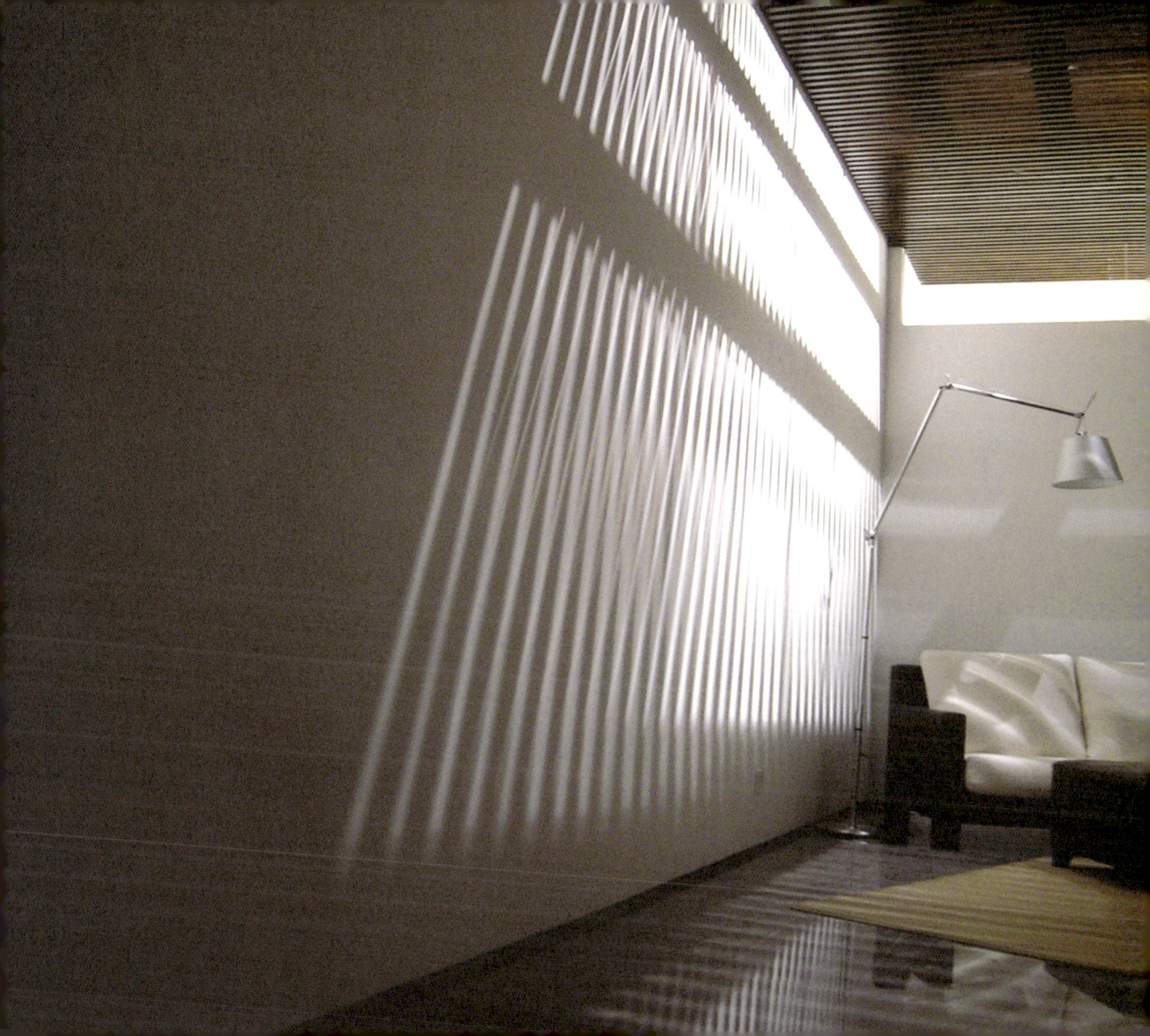

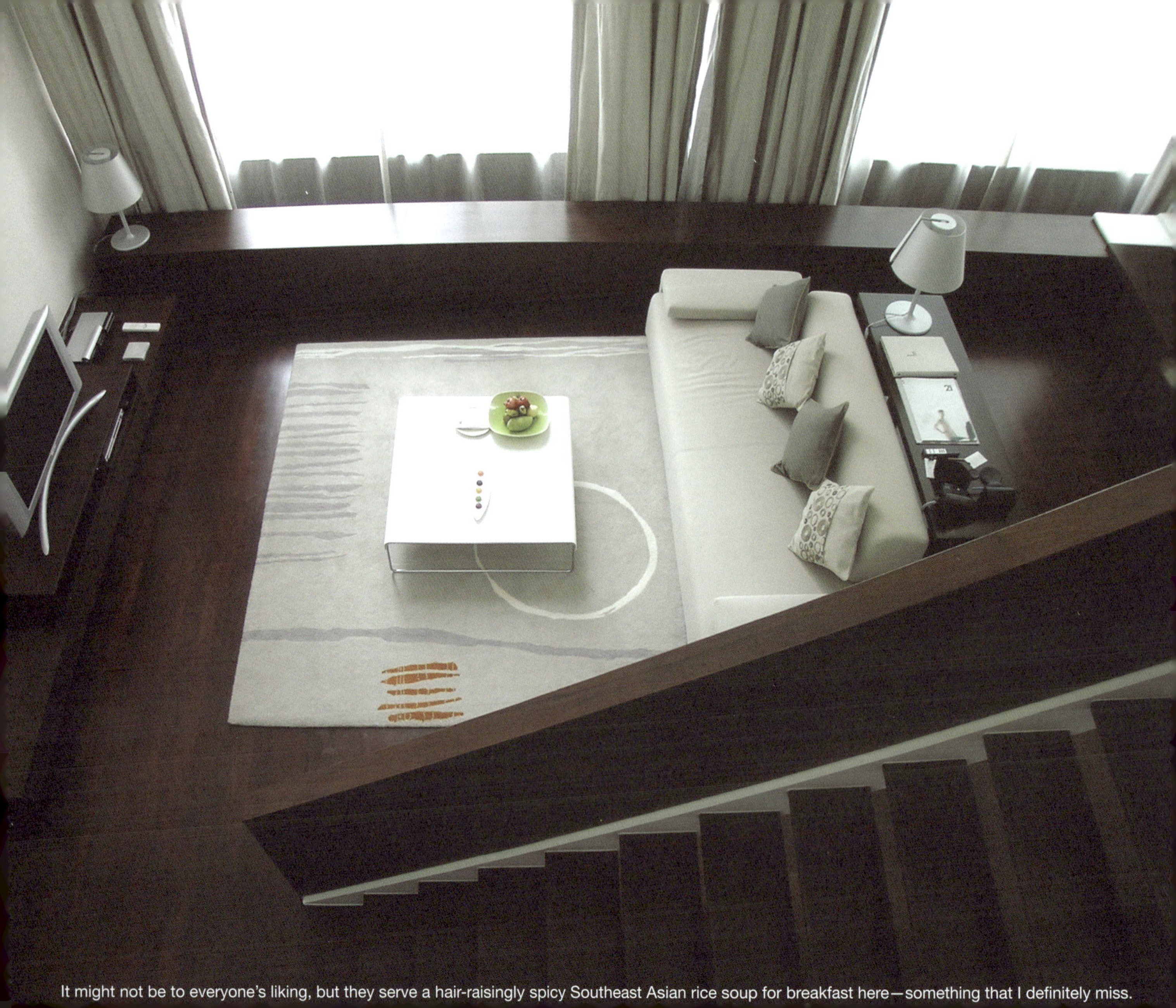

It might not be to everyone's liking, but they serve a hair-raisingly spicy Southeast Asian rice soup for breakfast here—something that I definitely miss.

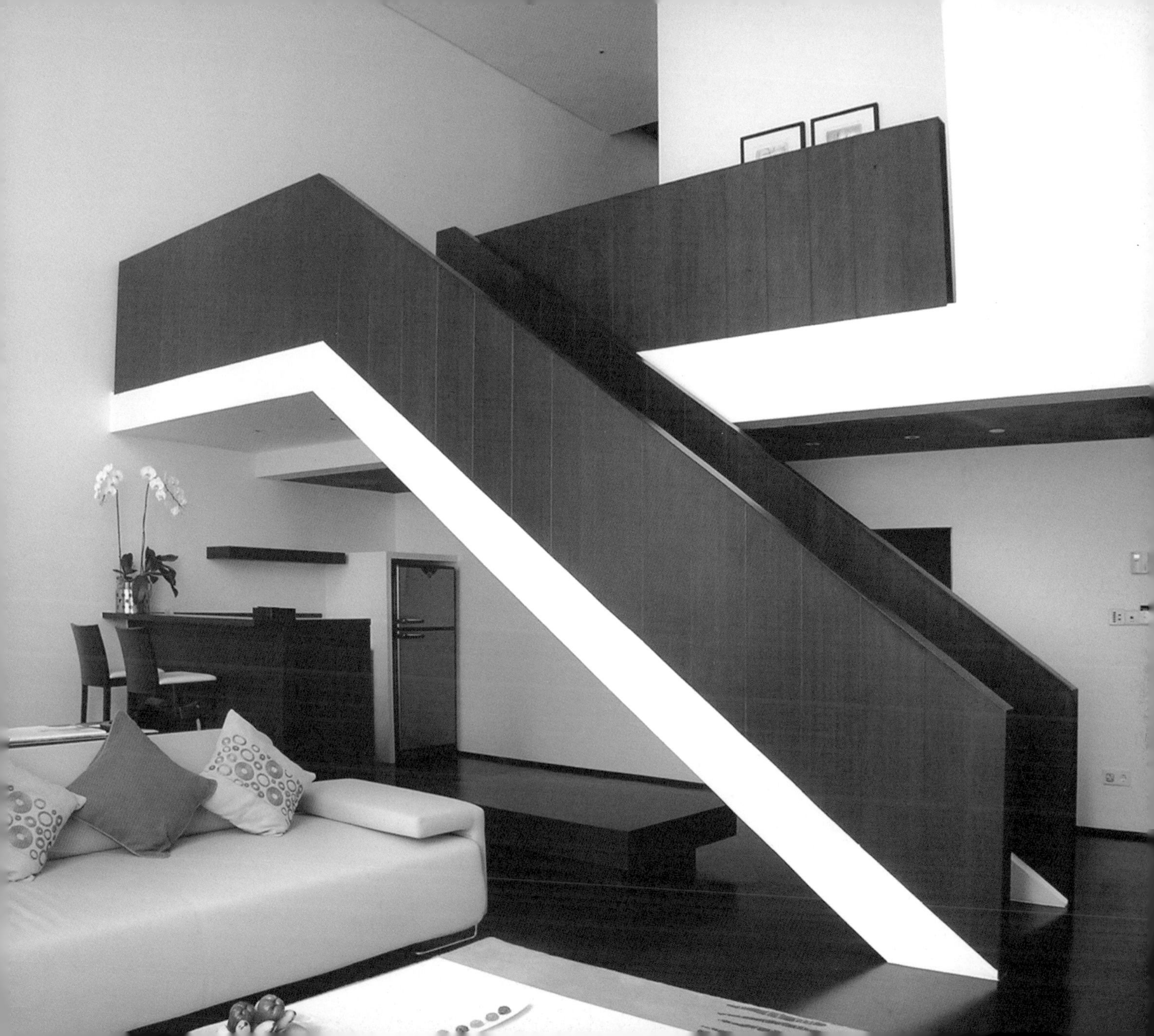

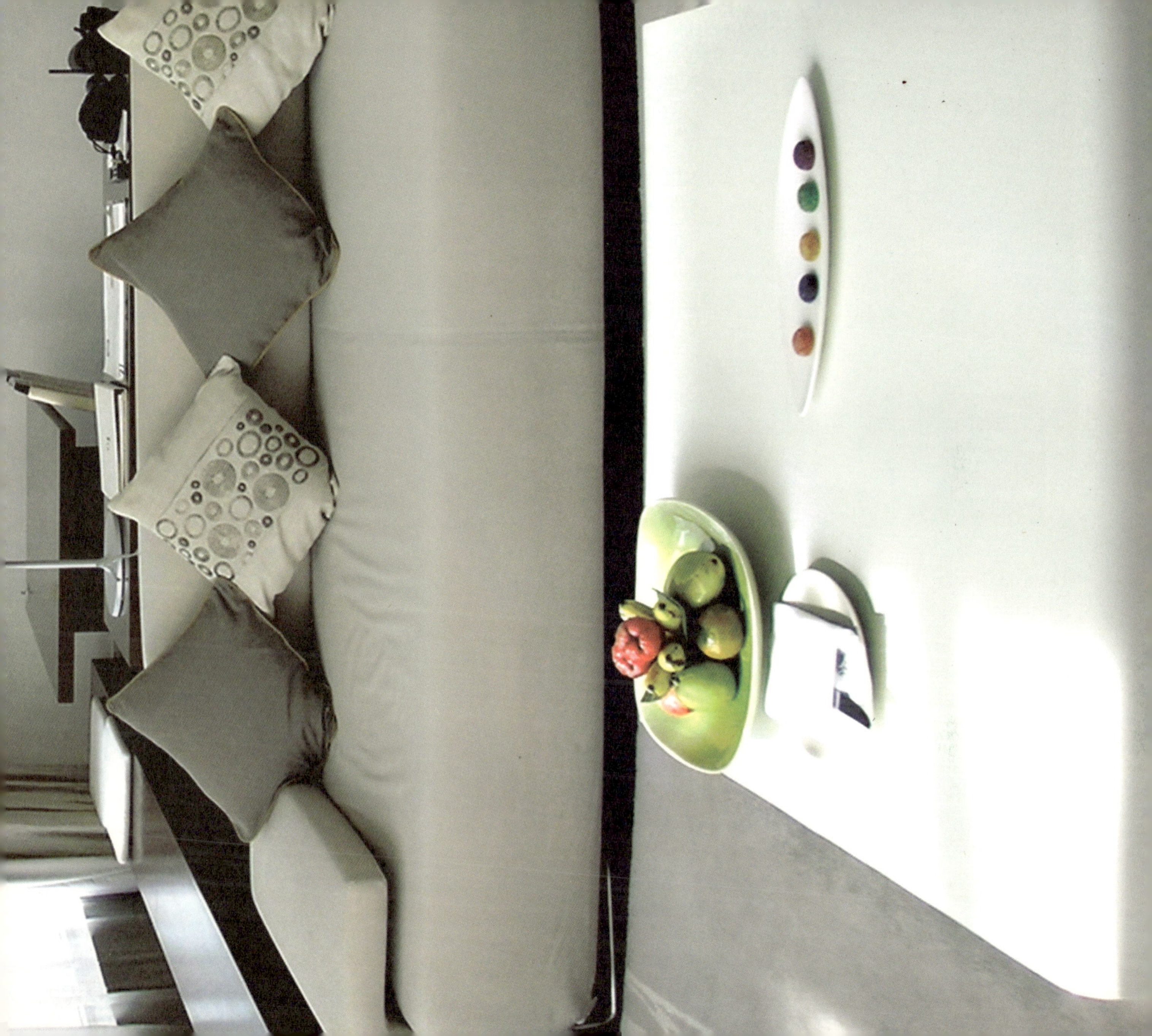

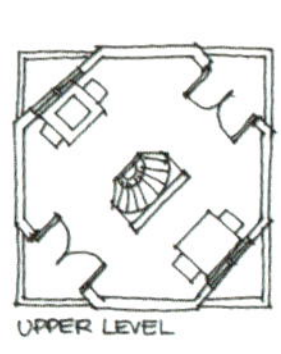

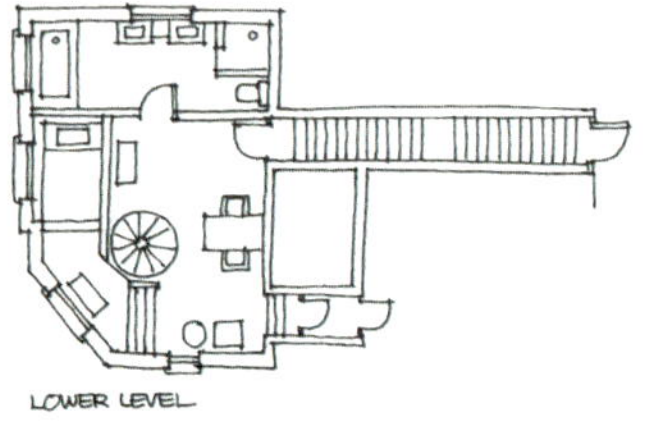

05 DEC 2004 TOWER ROOM 485 $242

Hotel New York

CHRONICLER OF A CITY

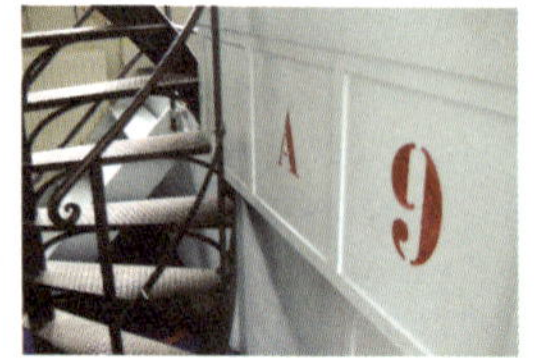

Hotel New York turns out not to be in New York after all, but in Rotterdam in the Netherlands. Rotterdam used to be the port of departure for numerous emigrants bound for New York on the other side of the world, hopeful and anxious for a new and better life. The migrant history began in 1620 and reached its high point in the early twentieth century. The building housing the Hotel New York was once the headquarters of a sea freight company by the name of Holland-Amerika Lijn, which built it over a century ago. The hotel with the history-laden name opened its doors in 1993. It overlooks the dark, brooding river of Maas and its busy harbor. Before the subway system was extended to this old industrial neighborhood, it could only be reached by water taxis converted from small pleasure boats. But even now, I still prefer the boats to the subway trains for shuttling between the hotel and the city center.

The hotel is three stories high and boasts seventy rooms—unexpectedly many for its small size. The sea-smelling air of Rotterdam wafts through the windows, bringing with it the sights and sounds of the port city. The well-lit bathroom reminds me of the splendor and insouciance of youth as captured in the 1998 movie *In the Heart of the Sun*. During one of my visits to Rotterdam I stayed in the clock tower at the top of the hotel. The room looked like an Edward Hopper painting. Intriguingly divided into three levels, the various parts of the room, including the four triangular balconies, are connected by a series of stairs, allowing the guest to view the room from various angles. The design is a prime example of mixing the old and new, and of sobriety and playfulness coexisting in perfect harmony. I keep thinking that the Hotel New York would be a perfect location for a movie, simply because it has such a cinematic feel about it; or perhaps it could be the setting of a novel. I, for one, find myself completely mesmerized by the play of light and shadow that can be found in the interior of the hotel, sometimes in the most unexpected nooks and crannies. The hotel has left its indelible mark on the old industrial neighborhood, which is undergoing its own fashionable renaissance. And the in-crowd of Rotterdam, which regularly frequents the hotel's huge, four-hundred-seat café-restaurant, agrees.

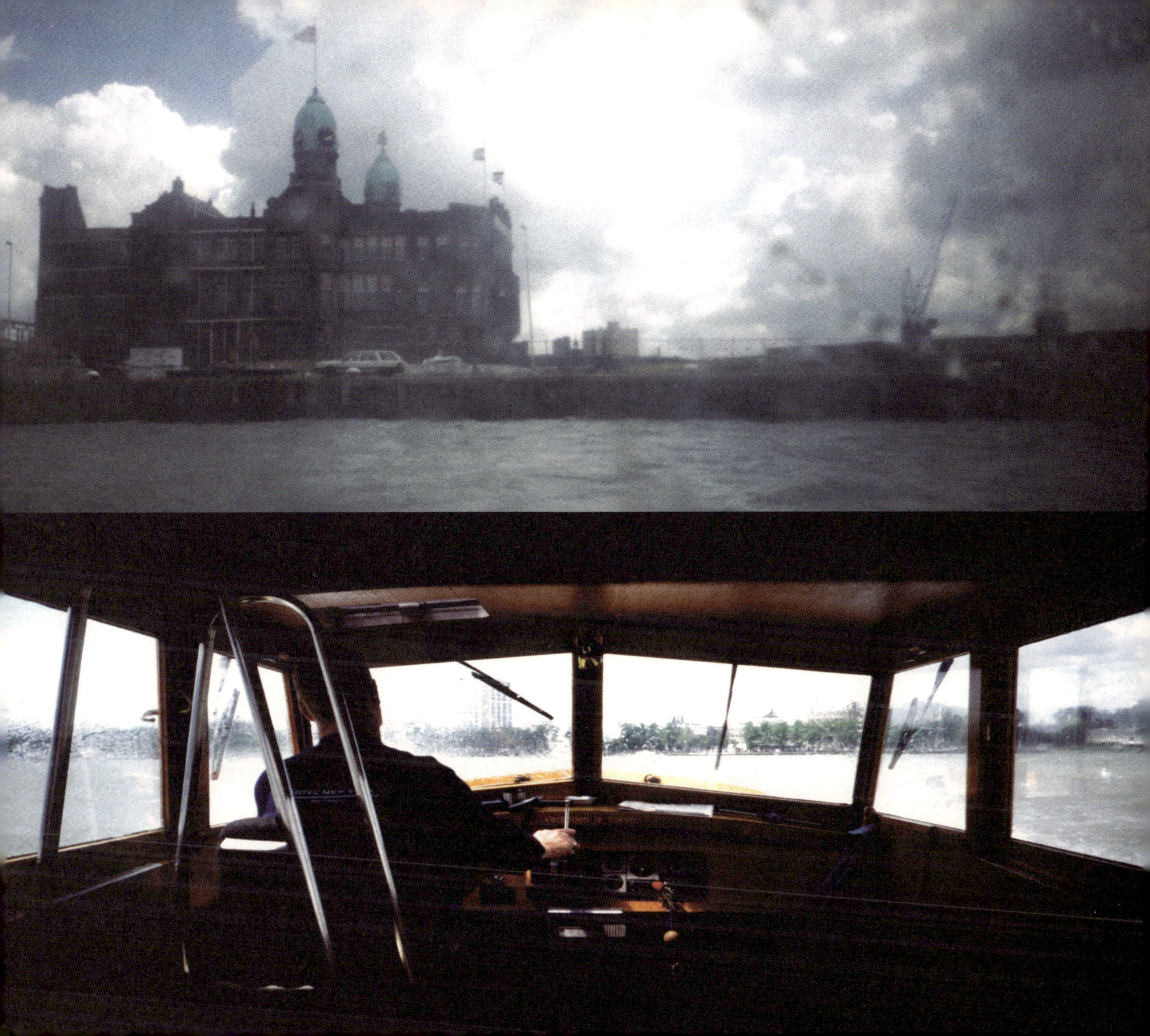

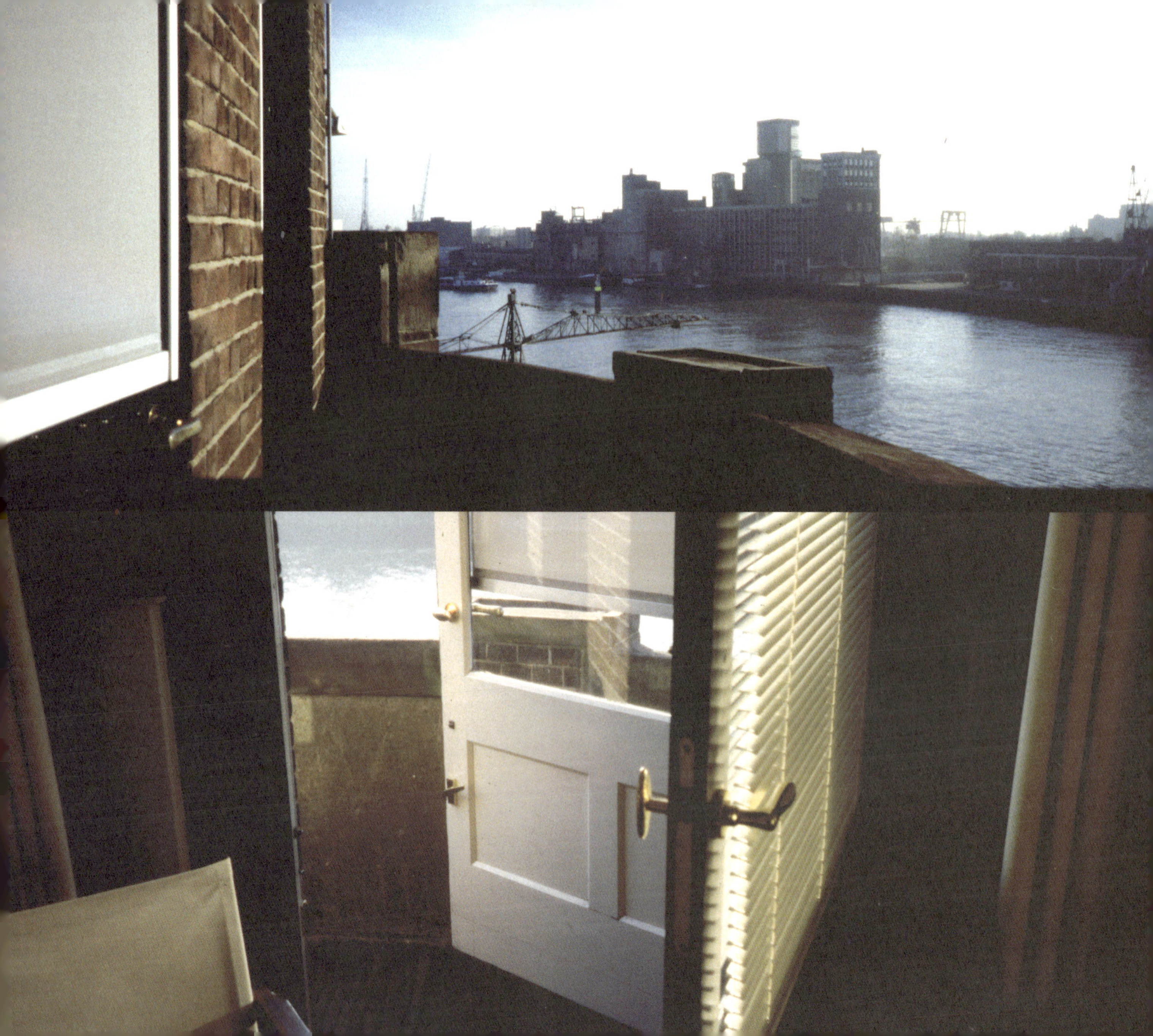

So much to explore, so little time . . .

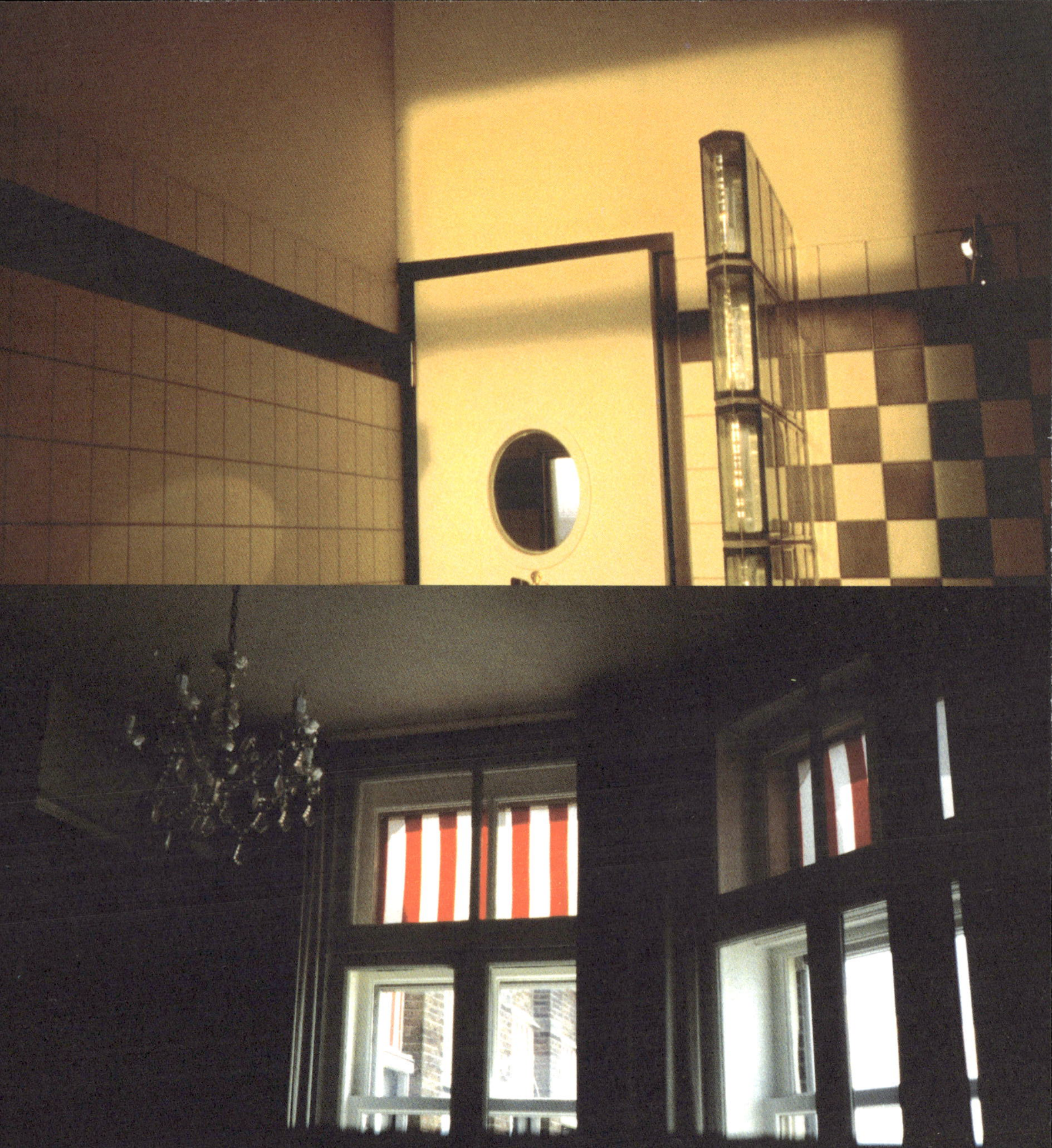

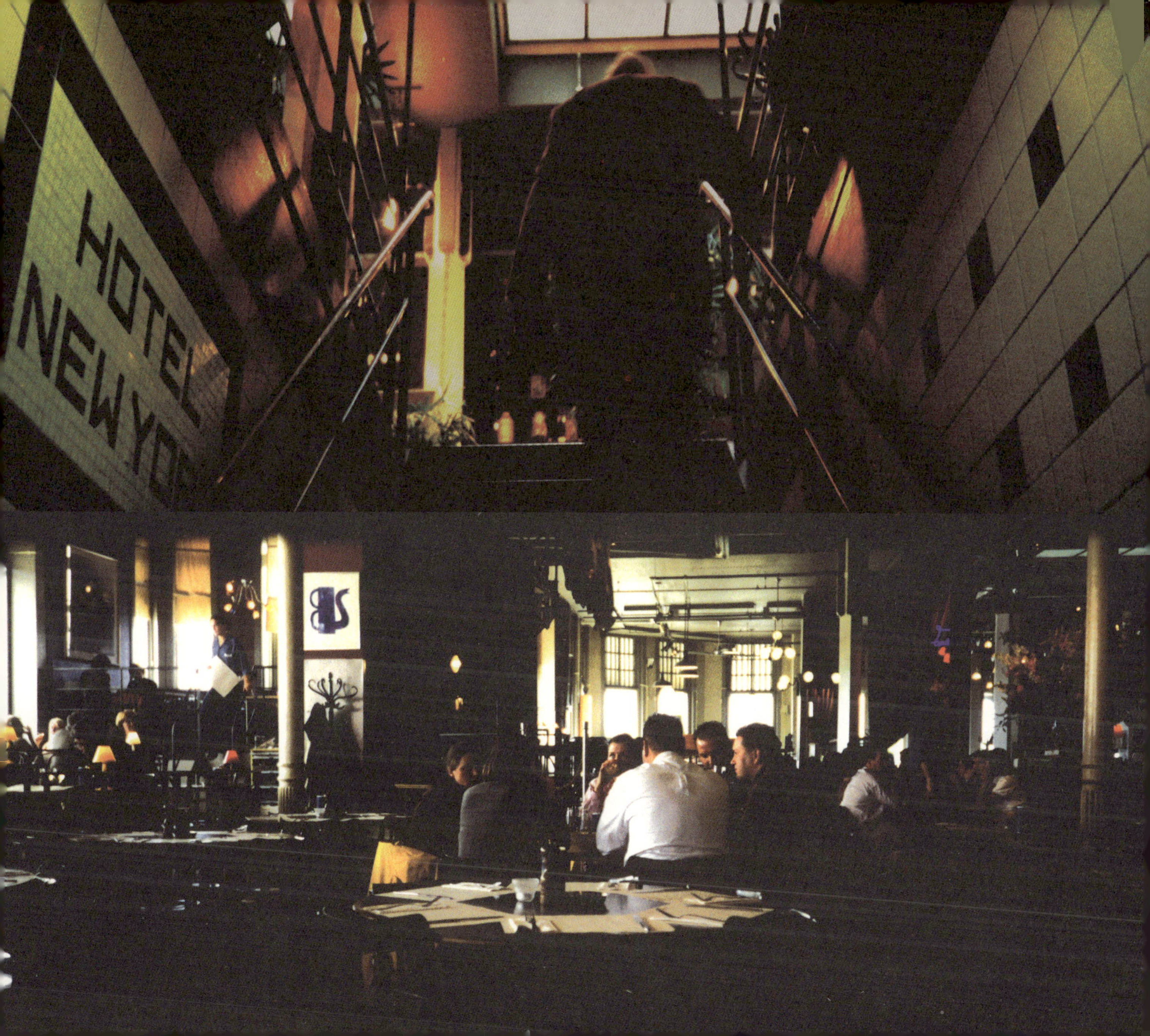
HOTEL
NEW YO

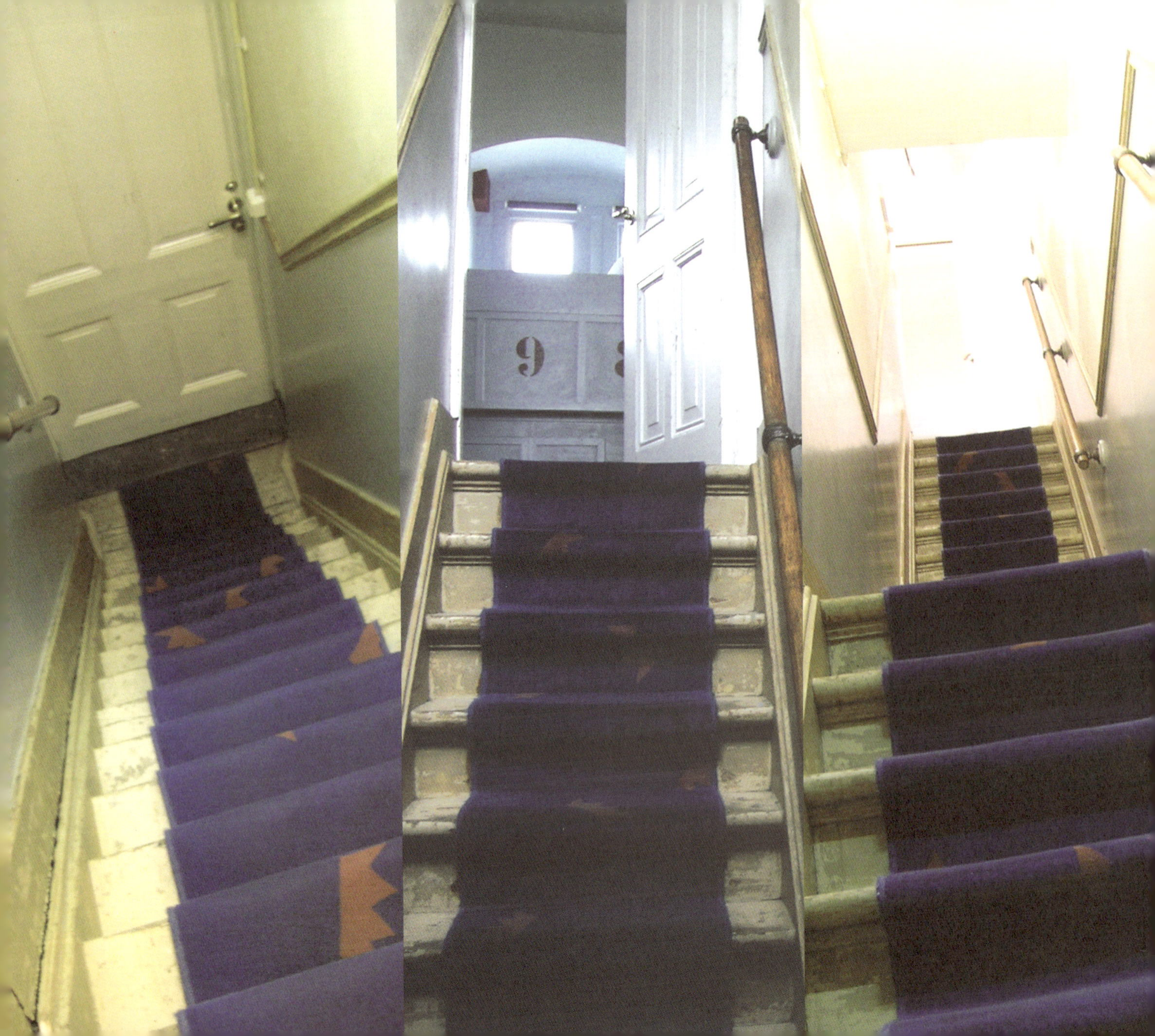
9

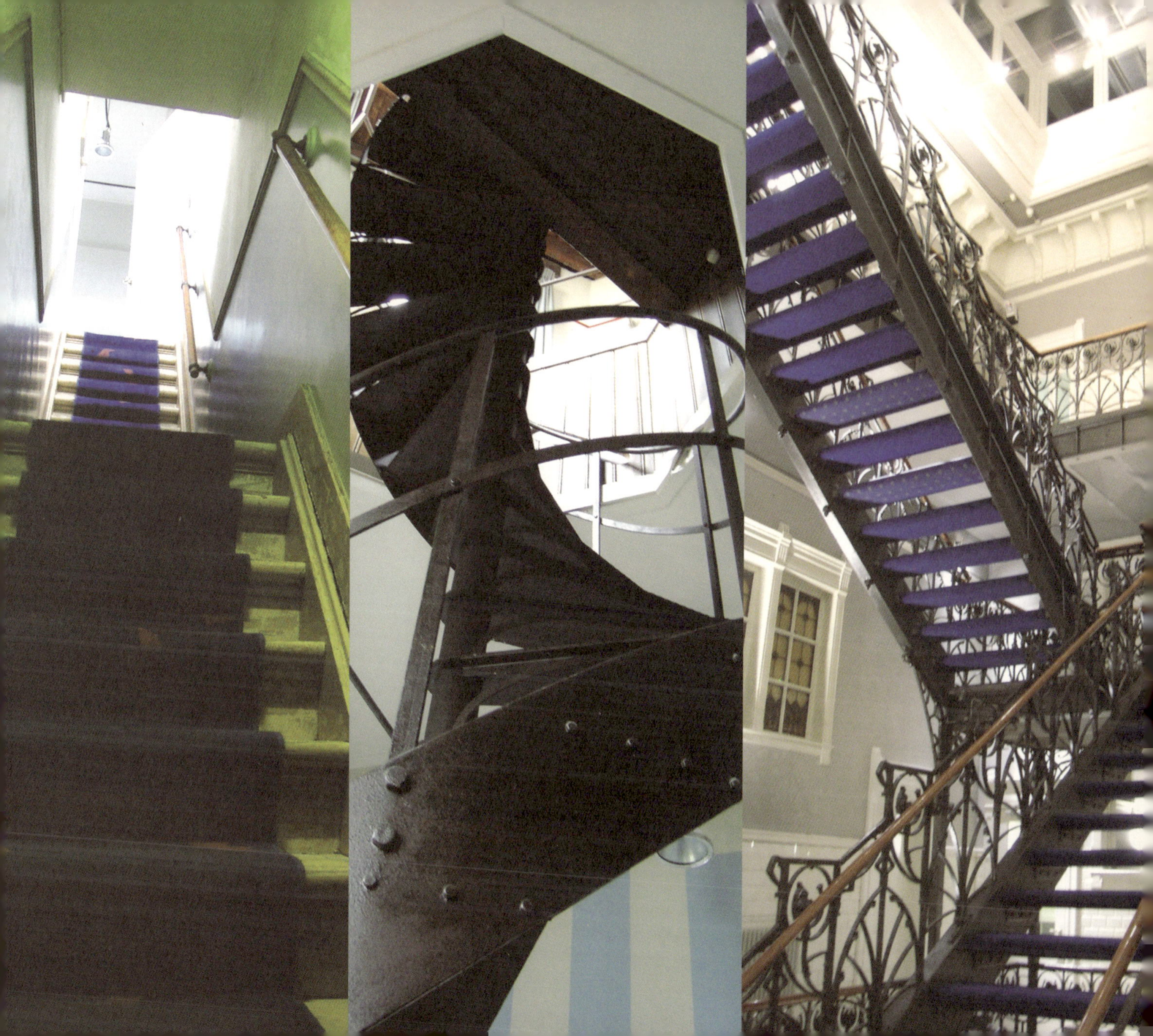

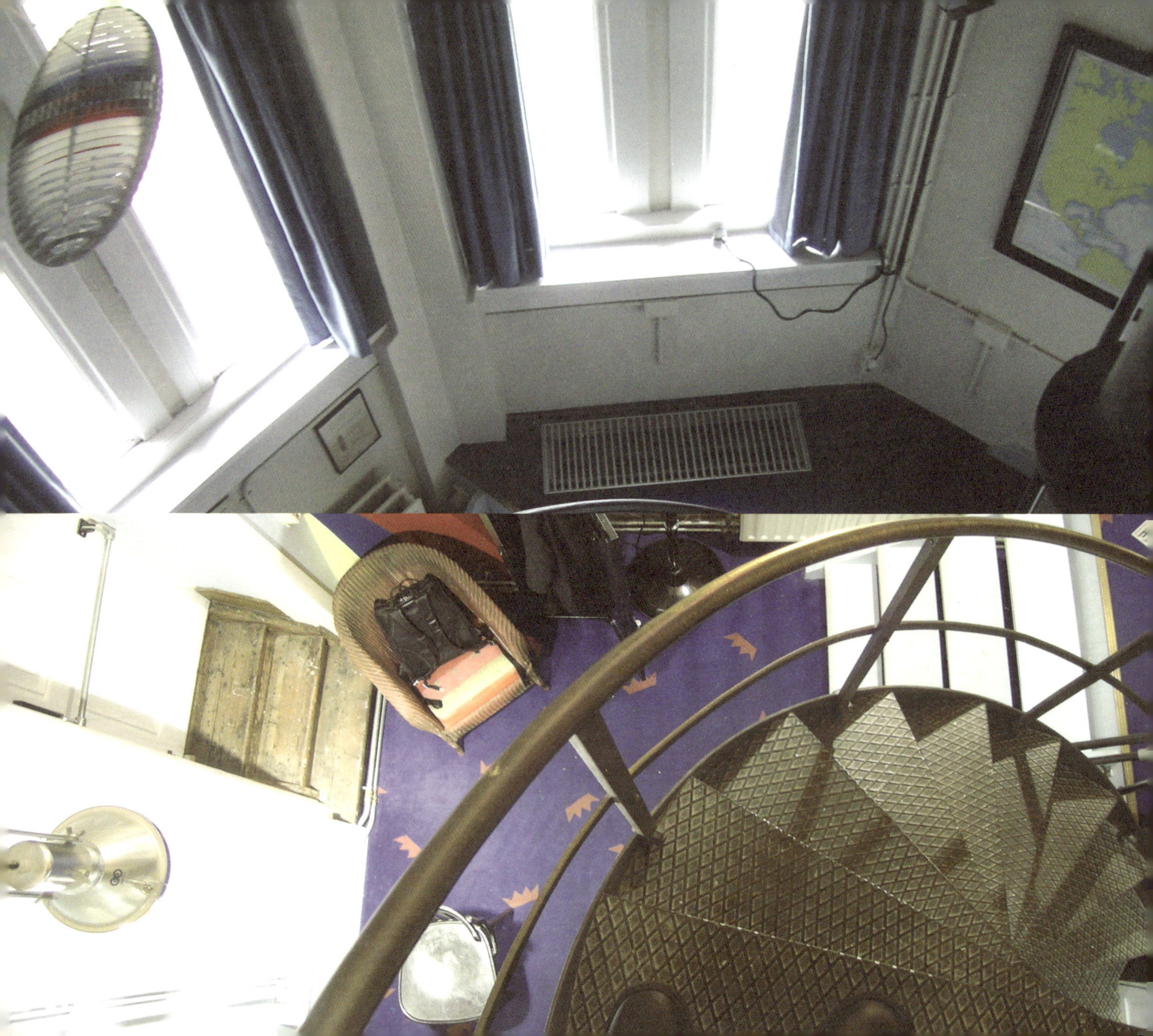

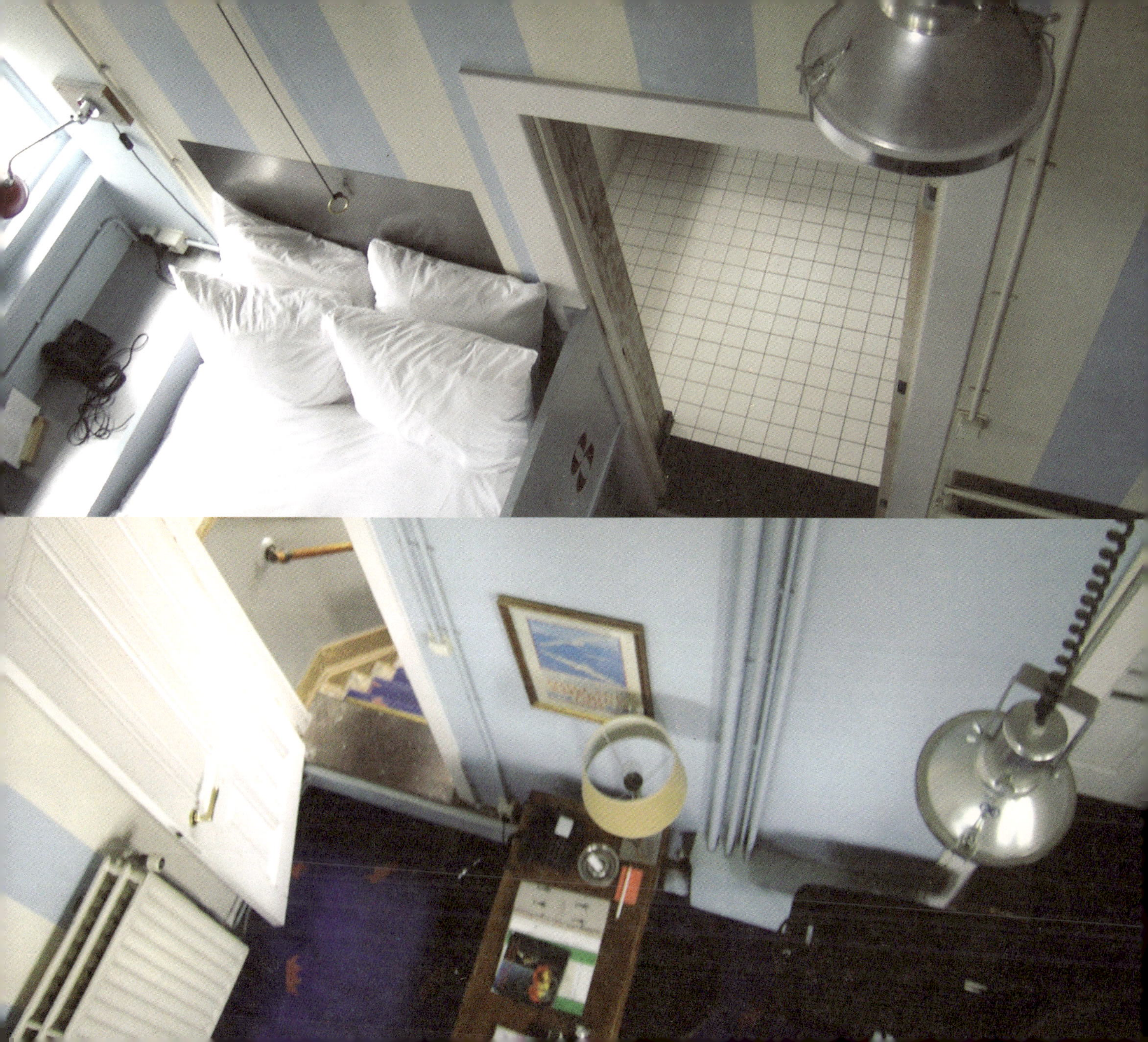

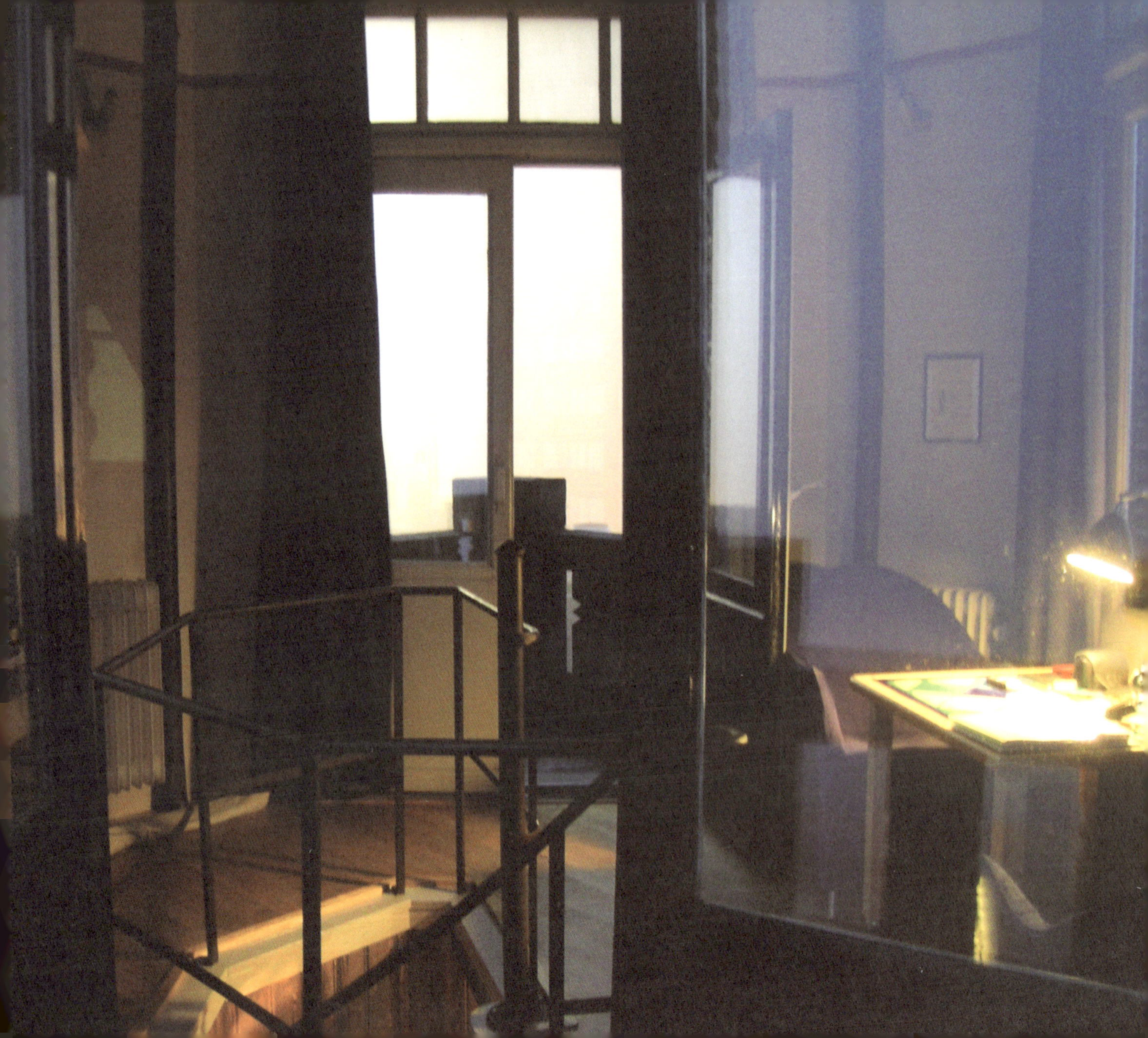

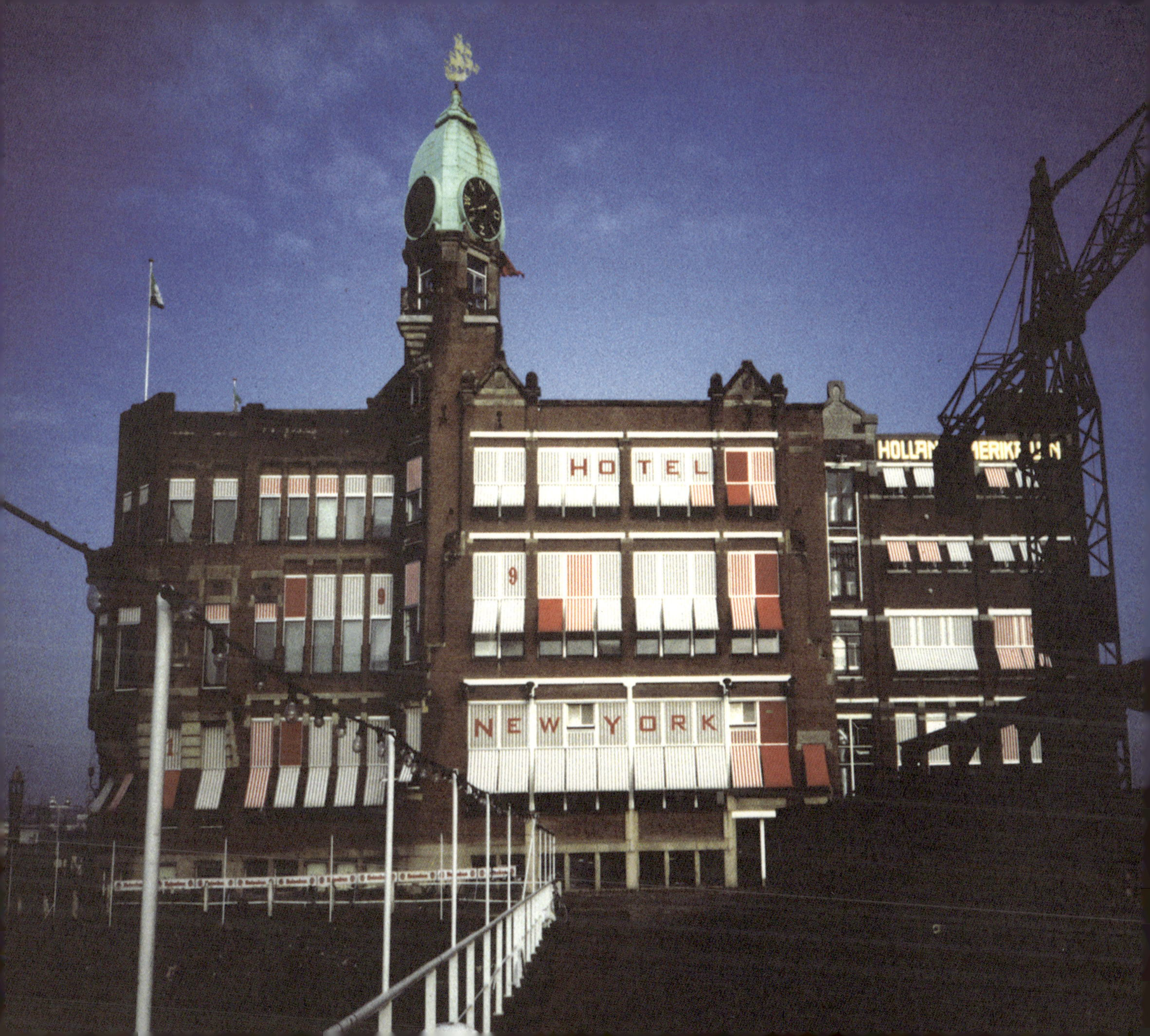
HOTEL
NEW YORK

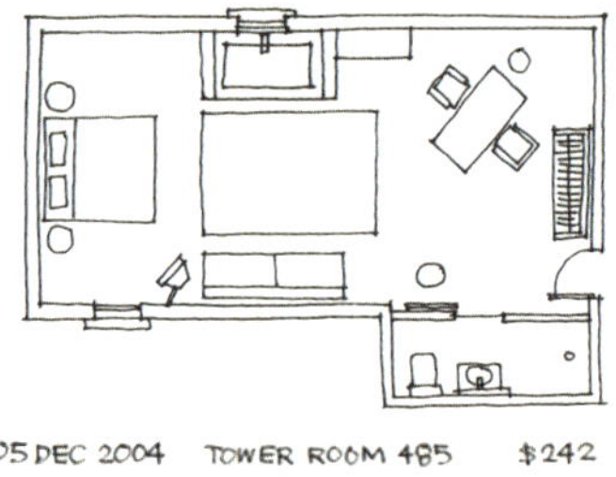

Lloyd Hotel

WHERE HISTORY WAS PAINTED

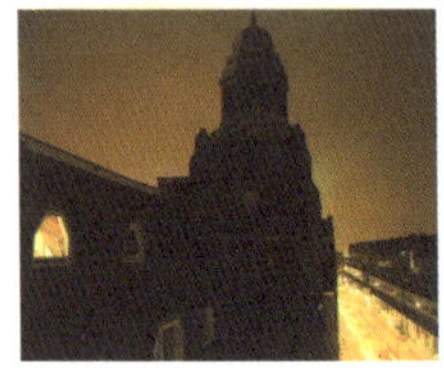

Back in 1920 an inn was built here, which served as a rest stop for Eastern European emigrants headed to South America. It was for that reason that a quarantine office was included in its east wing. The typically Dutch structure has survived two world wars, and the weather-beaten bricks of its exterior have the scars to prove it. At one time, it was adapted as a prison for underage offenders, until artists adopted it for themselves in the late 1980s and turned it into something of an artists' ghetto. In 2004, the designers of MVRDV reverted the building to its old hotel self, now grown all the more attractive with its share of history and worldliness. I chose to stay in one of the larger of the Lloyd Hotel's 120 differently designed rooms. Because it was situated on the top floor, its ceiling was triangular. The attic-like space reminded me of an artist's studio, with half-painted canvases and tubes and pots of paint strewn all over the floor because the artist is in too much of a creative frenzy to mind. The room itself seemed to have retained some of its spectral bohemian past in its not-quite-finished design and devil-may-care hybridism. In its use of space, the hotel emphasizes connectedness rather than partitioning. Its communal areas, wittily named *Cultural Embassy*, such as the library, the restaurant, and the kitchen are located in the center of the building, accessible by all via a system of corridors and staircases.

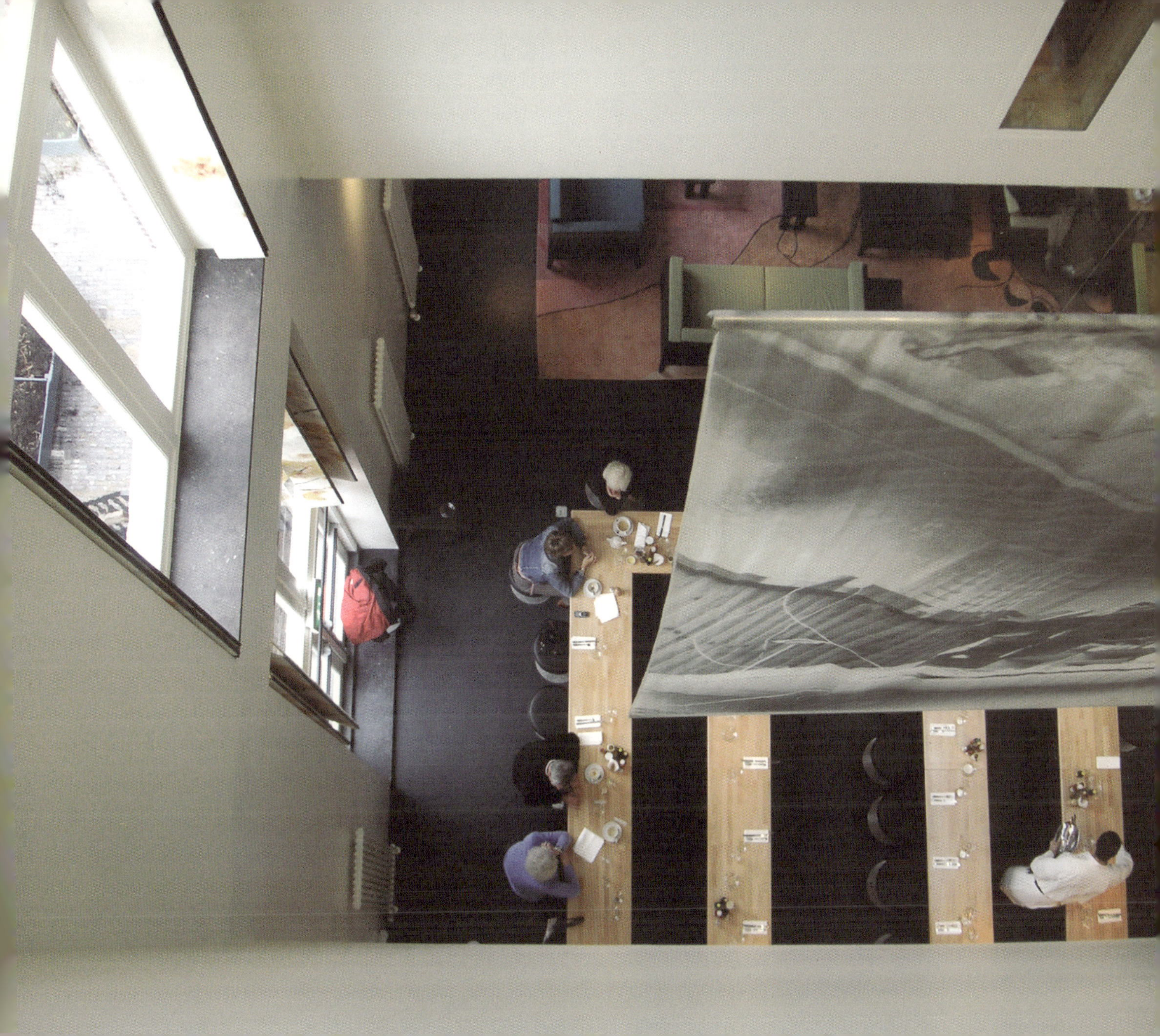

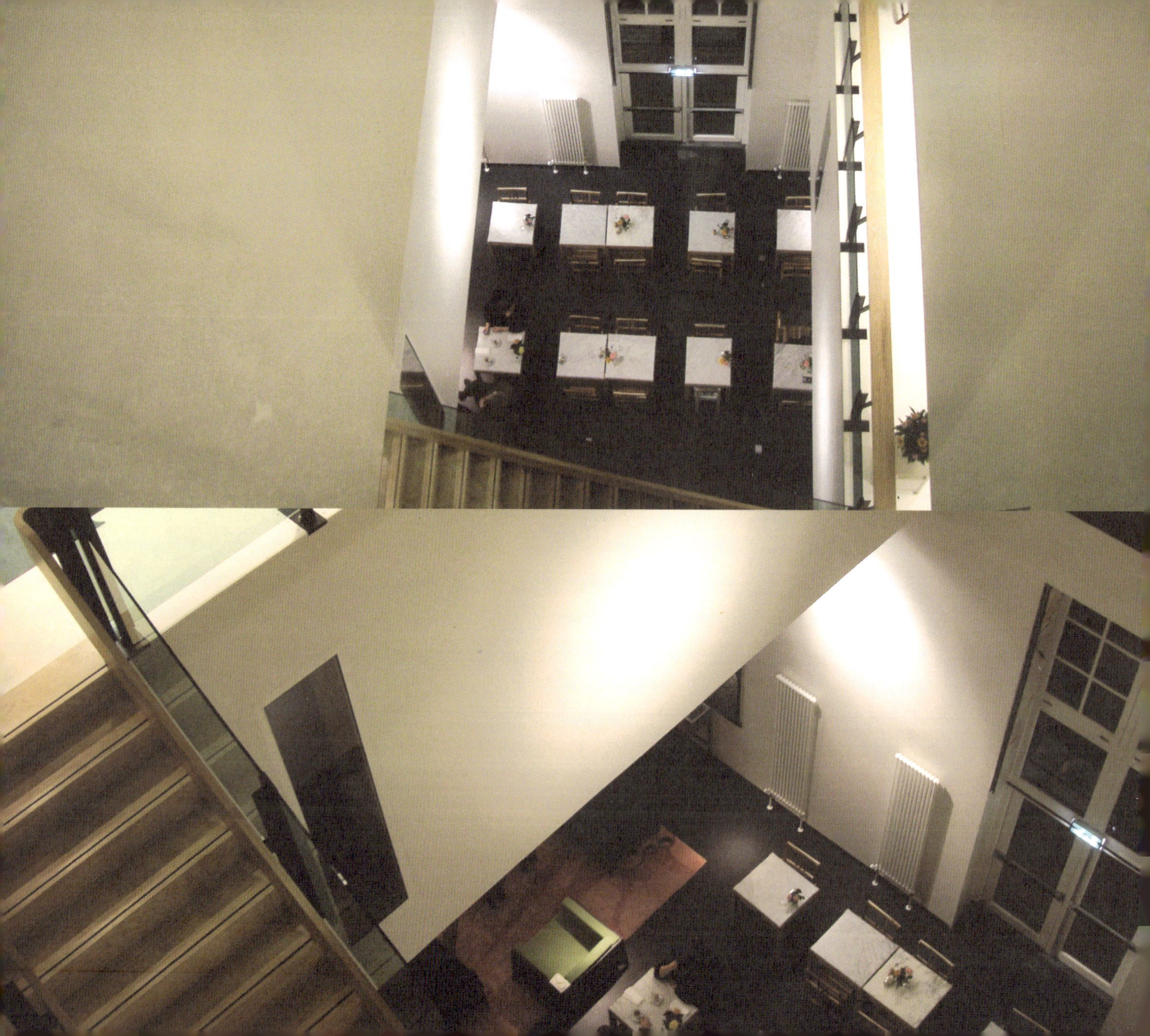

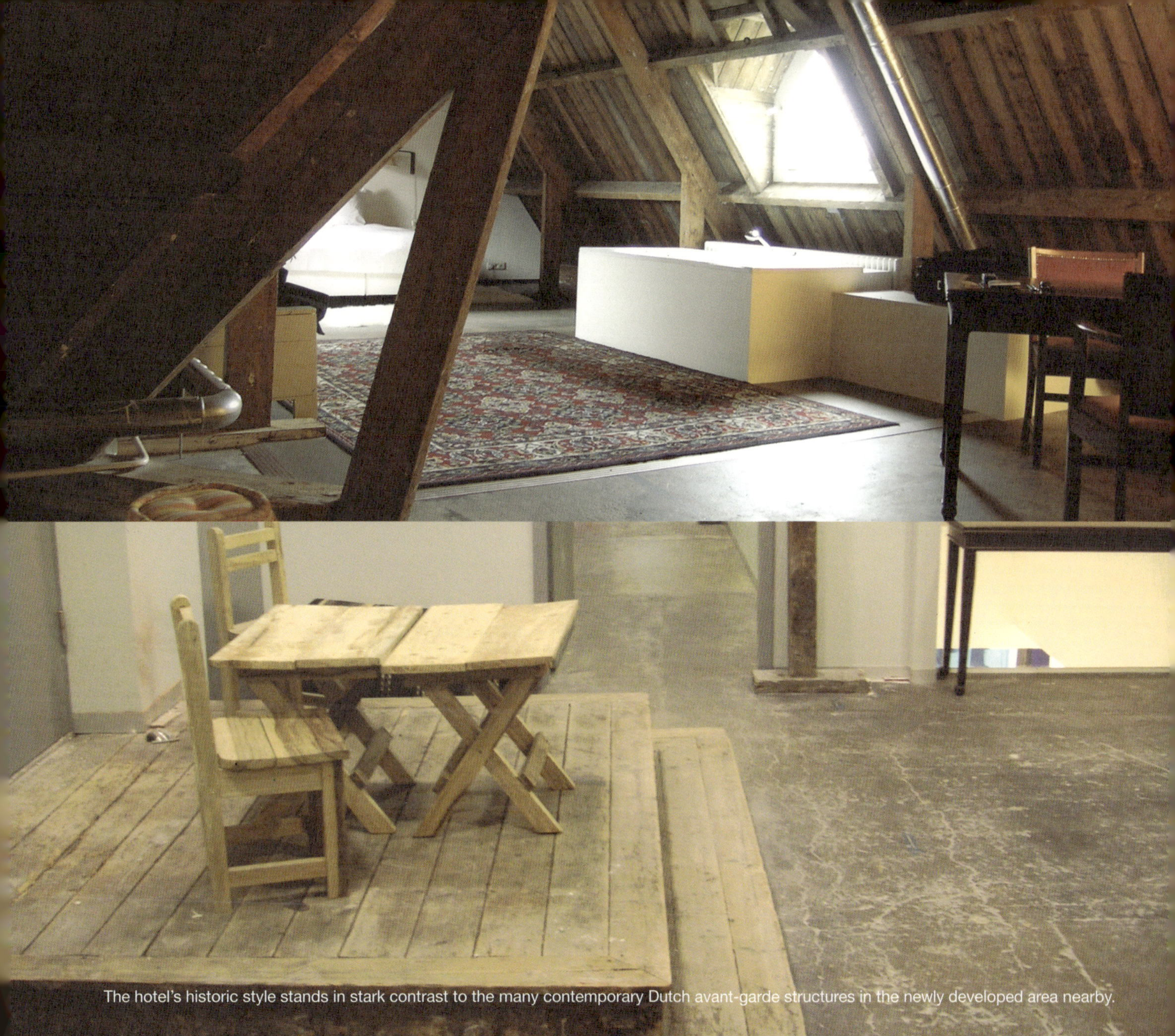

The hotel's historic style stands in stark contrast to the many contemporary Dutch avant-garde structures in the newly developed area nearby.

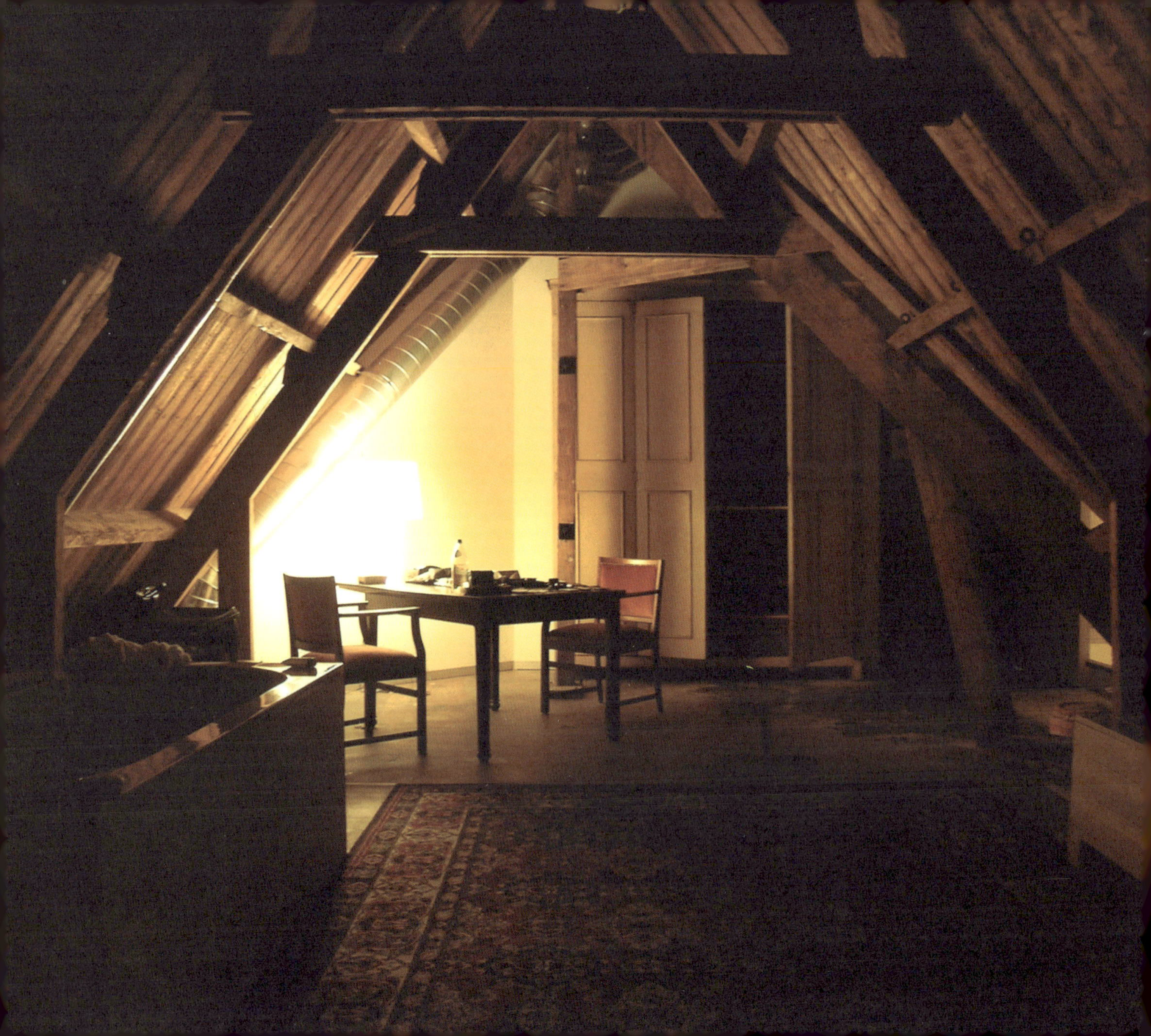

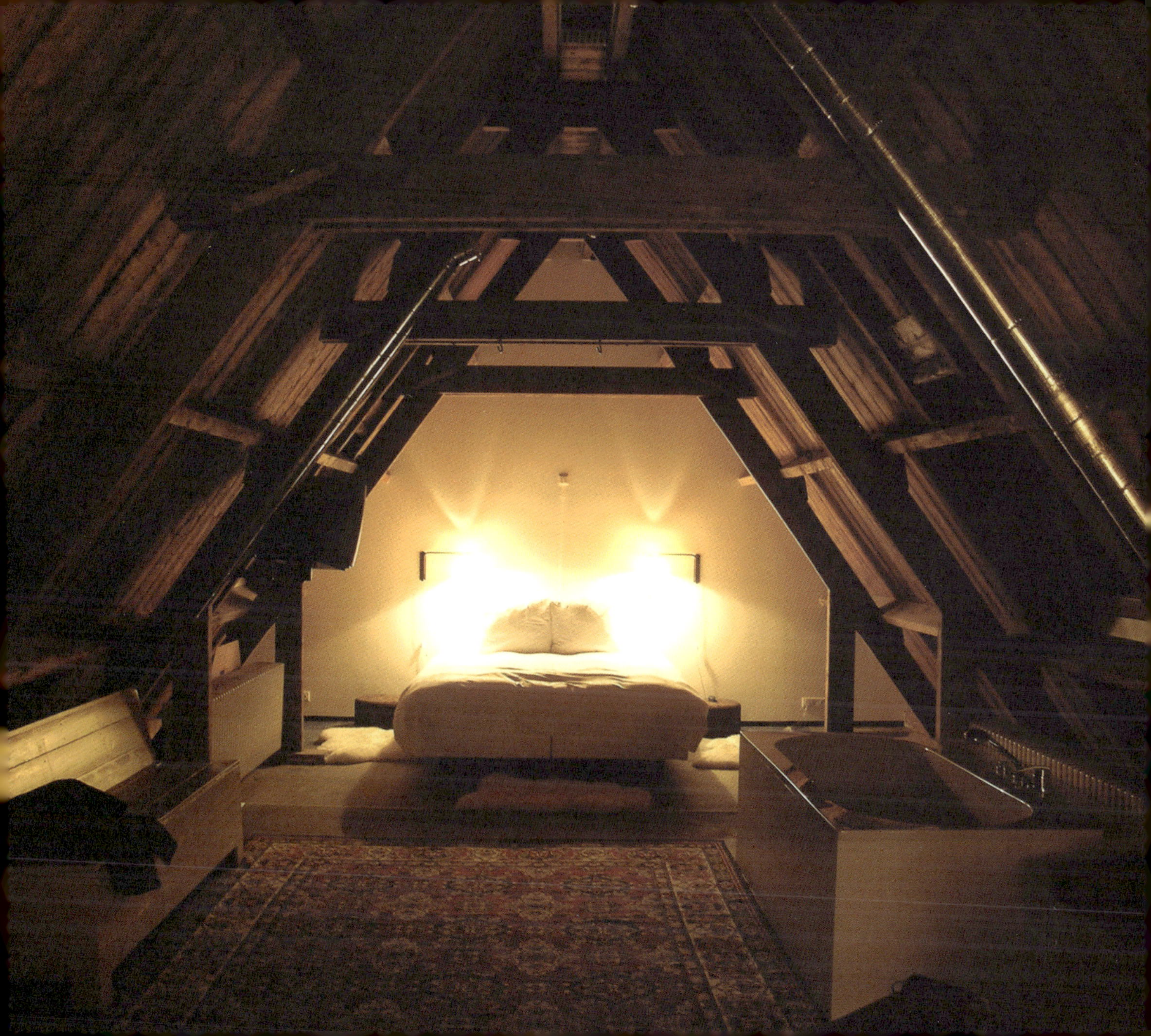

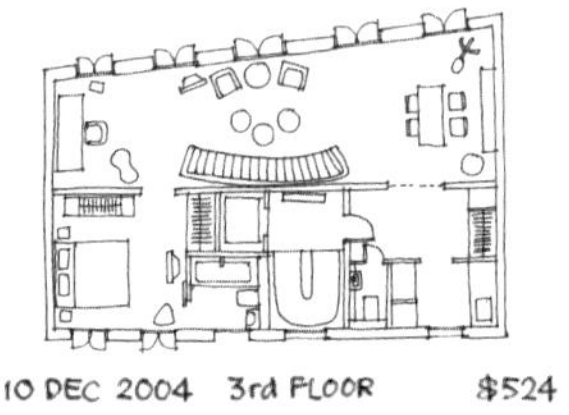

Hotel 5 Rue de Moussy

LUNCH WITH A FASHION MASTER

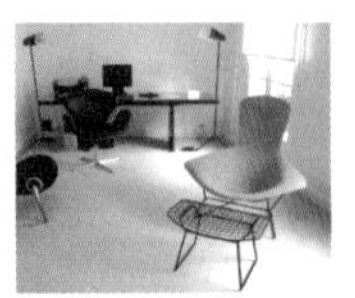

I must admit: ever since I stayed at the Hotel 3 Rooms in Milan, I have become a fan of Carla Sozzani's. At the time I thought that such a unique hotel could never be repeated elsewhere, which is why when I found out that Sozzani was going to design another 3 Rooms in Paris, I simply couldn't wait for it to open. I was even more intrigued when I learned that Sozzani's collaborator this time was none other than the Tunisian-French *haute couture* designer Azzedine Alaïa, whose boutique, atelier, and home all happen to be right next to the hotel itself. What I didn't know, however, was that I would have lunch with Alaïa on the day I checked in, prepared by the master fashion designer himself. Just like the one in Milan, the 3 Rooms at 5 Rue de Moussy also has only three "rooms," which, with their 1,200-square-foot area, look more like large apartments. When I arrived at the hotel, it was only nine o'clock in the morning. I left a copy of my book about the Suitcase House with Patrice the manager. Then around noon, Alaïa himself turned up in a Chinese suit and invited me to lunch with him. From the delicious salad and fish he prepared that day, I gathered that the personable designer probably enjoys cooking as much as he does designing.

Compared to Milan's 3 Rooms, Alaïa's tends more toward minimalism, but not at the expense of functionality. My largely white room belied its many hidden facilities, such as the floor heating system, the washing machine in the kitchen, the small but practical bathroom, and the bedside lamp large enough to light the entire bedroom. Nine large windows provided a view of the quiet courtyard below, as well as of Alaïa's atelier and an occasional glimpse of the designer himself just beyond.

In the furnishing Alaïa sensitively mixed and matched objects of contrasting textures and colors: Marc Newson's lamps and chairs, Jean Prouvé's apple-green wardrobe and desk, and a long, soft loaf-like settee. The result is spaces overflowing with details, possibilities, and puzzles, spaces that inspire solace and luxurious languor, as well as delight and sentimentality. But above all, beauty is found here, and when you leave, you leave a part of yourself behind, promising yourself to come back for it another day.

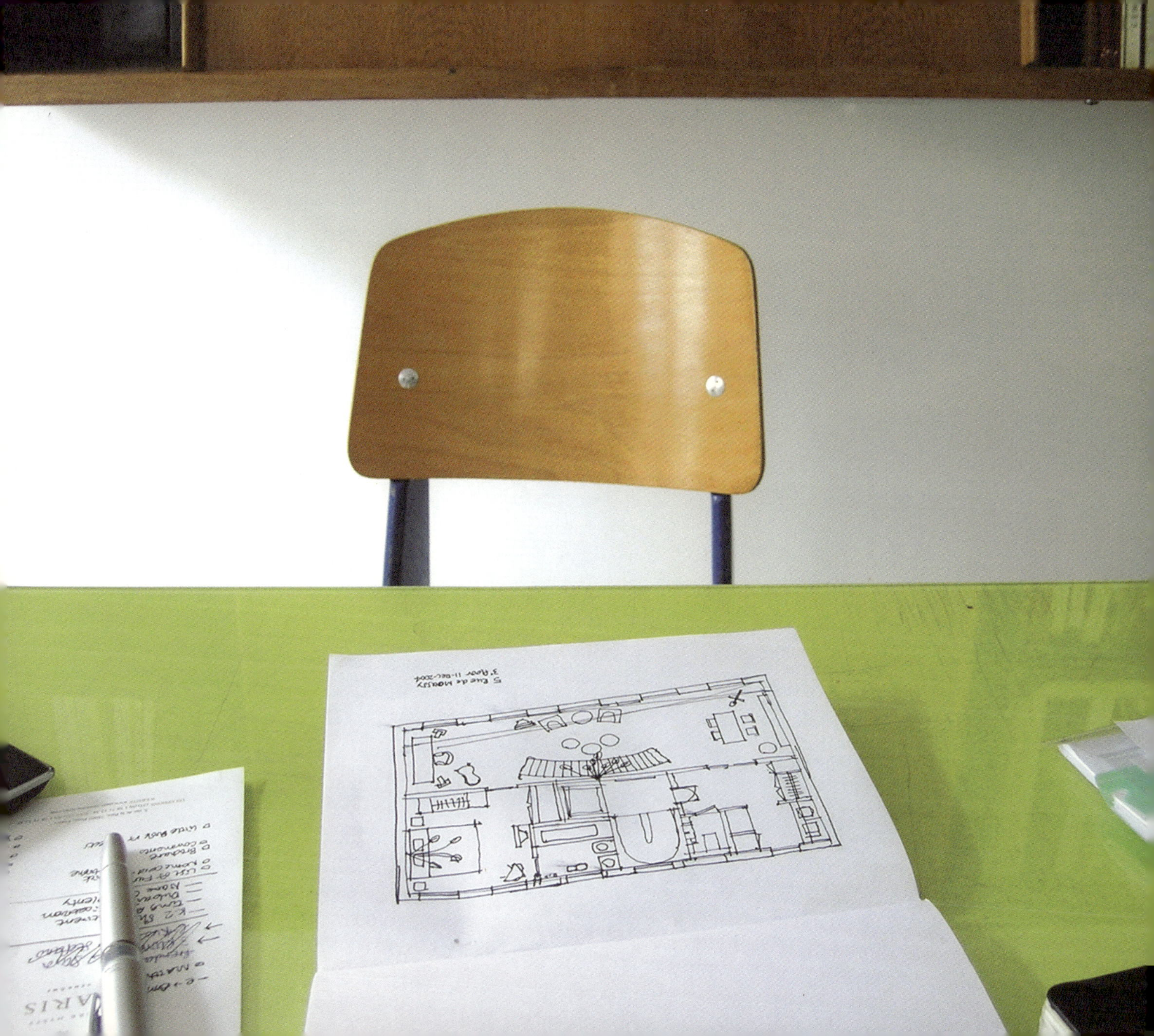

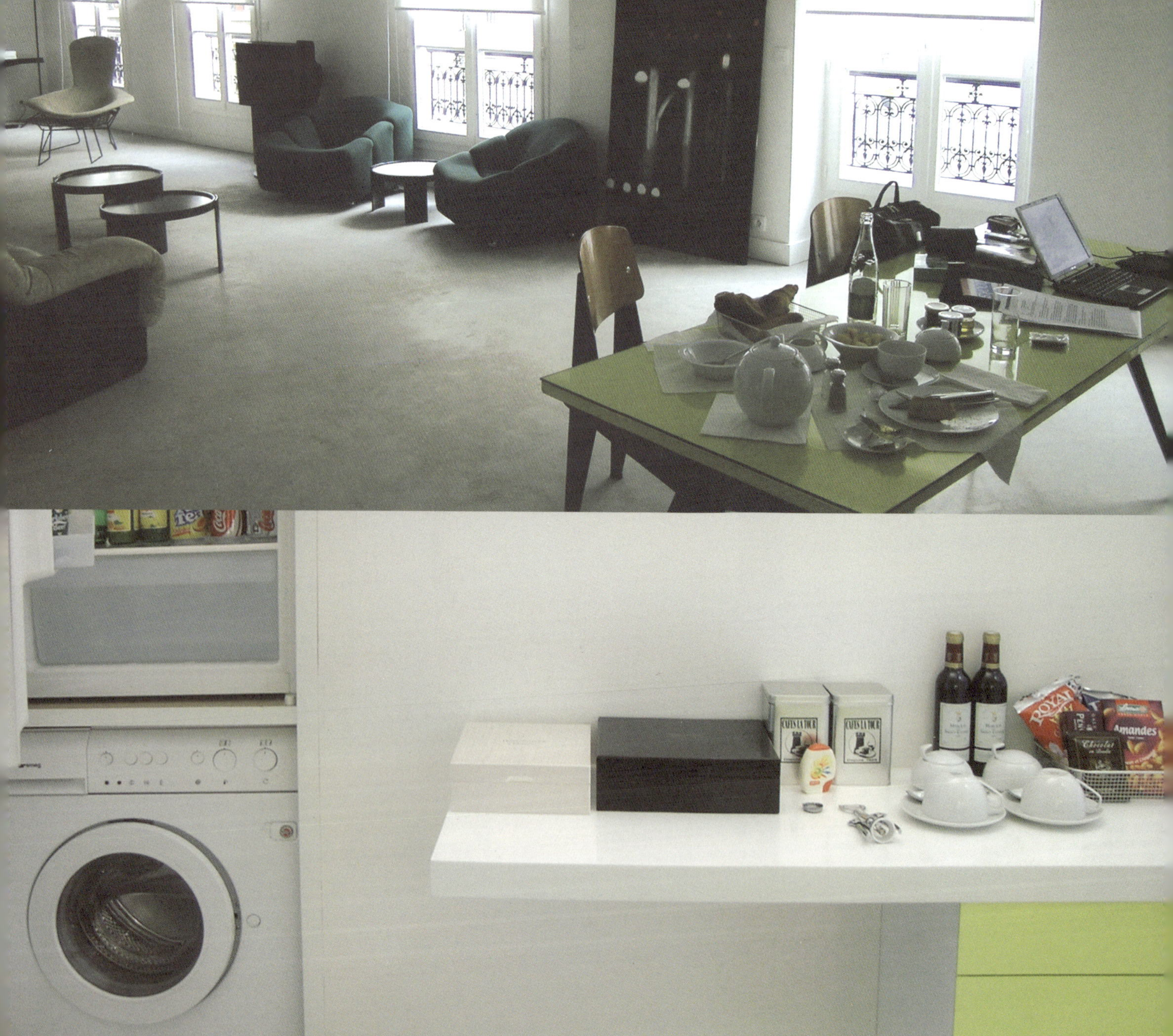
CAFES LA TOUR
CAFES LA TOUR
Amandes

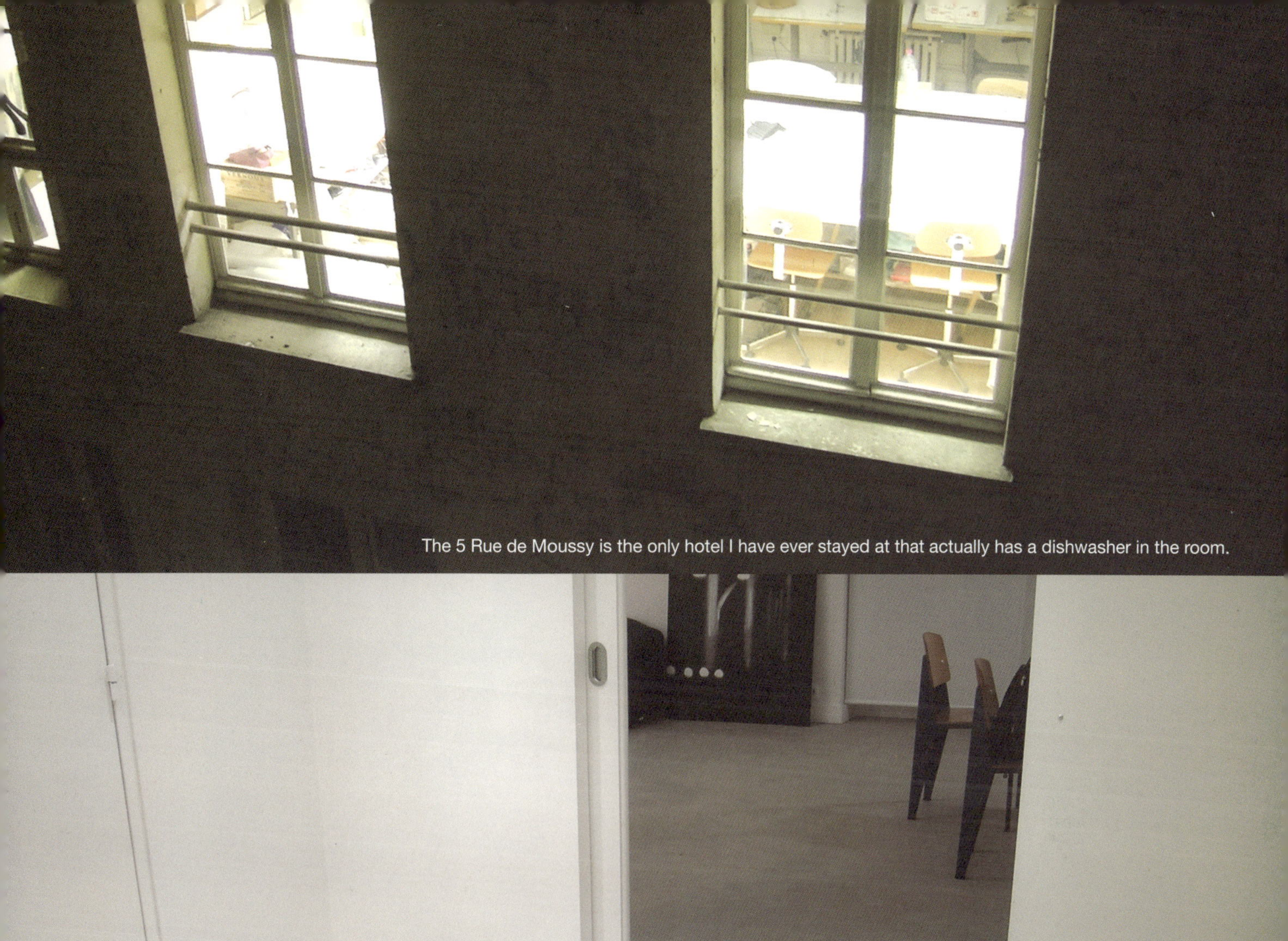

The 5 Rue de Moussy is the only hotel I have ever stayed at that actually has a dishwasher in the room.

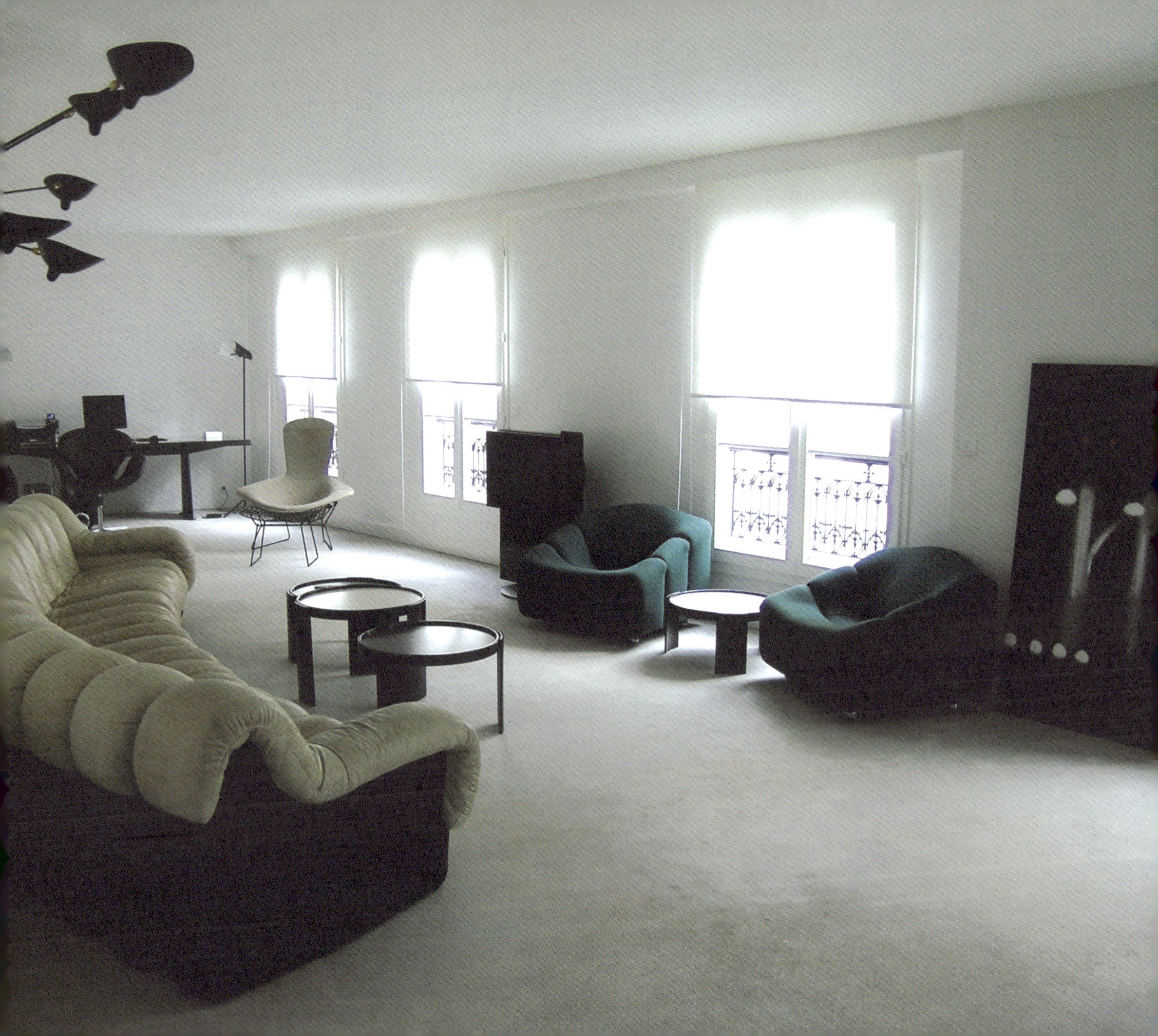

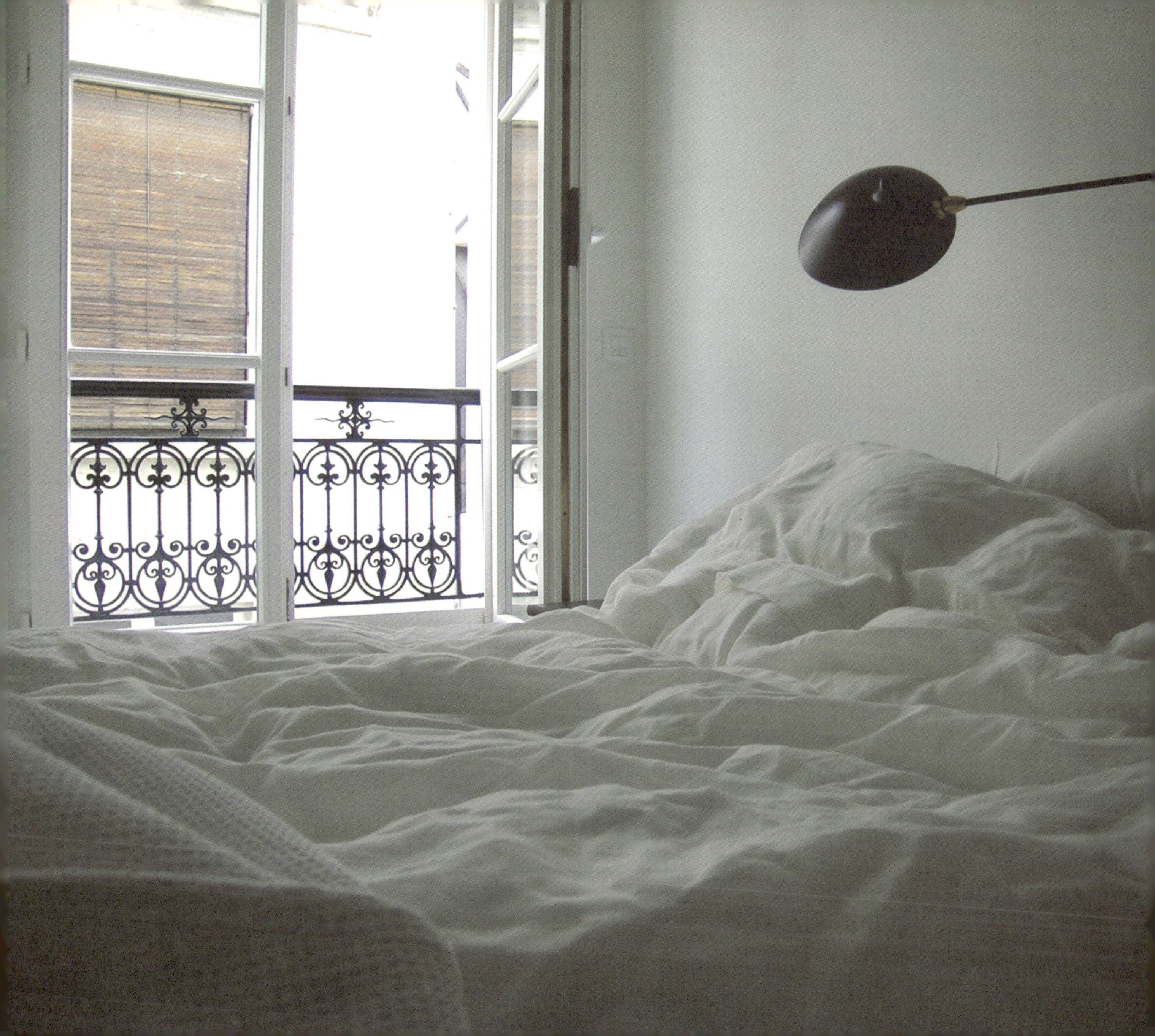

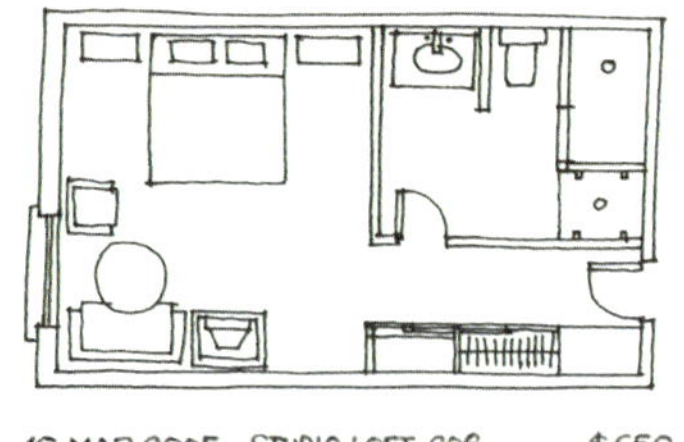

Mercer Hotel

THE BEST LITTLE REDBRICK SO(UTH OF)HO(USTON)

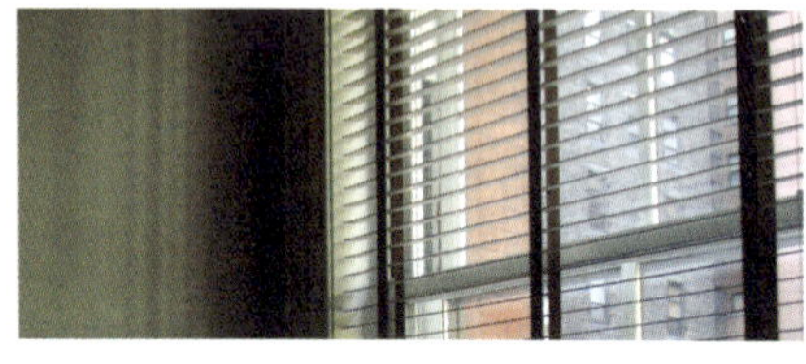

An informal survey ranks the Mercer as the best hotel in New York. But even when I'm not staying there, I make it a point to lunch at the Mercer Kitchen whenever I'm in town. Besides Jean-Georges Vongerichten's legendary culinary delights, the restaurant is also known for its ambience. In its design Christian Liaigre amply demonstrated the power of tapping into the character of a place. Although located underground, the hotel restaurant fully utilizes the abundant light of SoHo—one of the few areas in Manhattan free of skyscrapers. Its round glass bricks let in the sunlight and some of the hustle-bustle on the street, resulting in a phantasmagoric *son et lumière* for the benefit of the diners.

The Mercer was remodeled from one of the neighborhood's many old redbrick lofts and has retained its original high ceiling. The rooms' ingenious combination of lights and translucent fabrics results in a most tantalizing yet gratifying atmosphere worth every cent of the four-hundred-odd-dollar minimum charge.

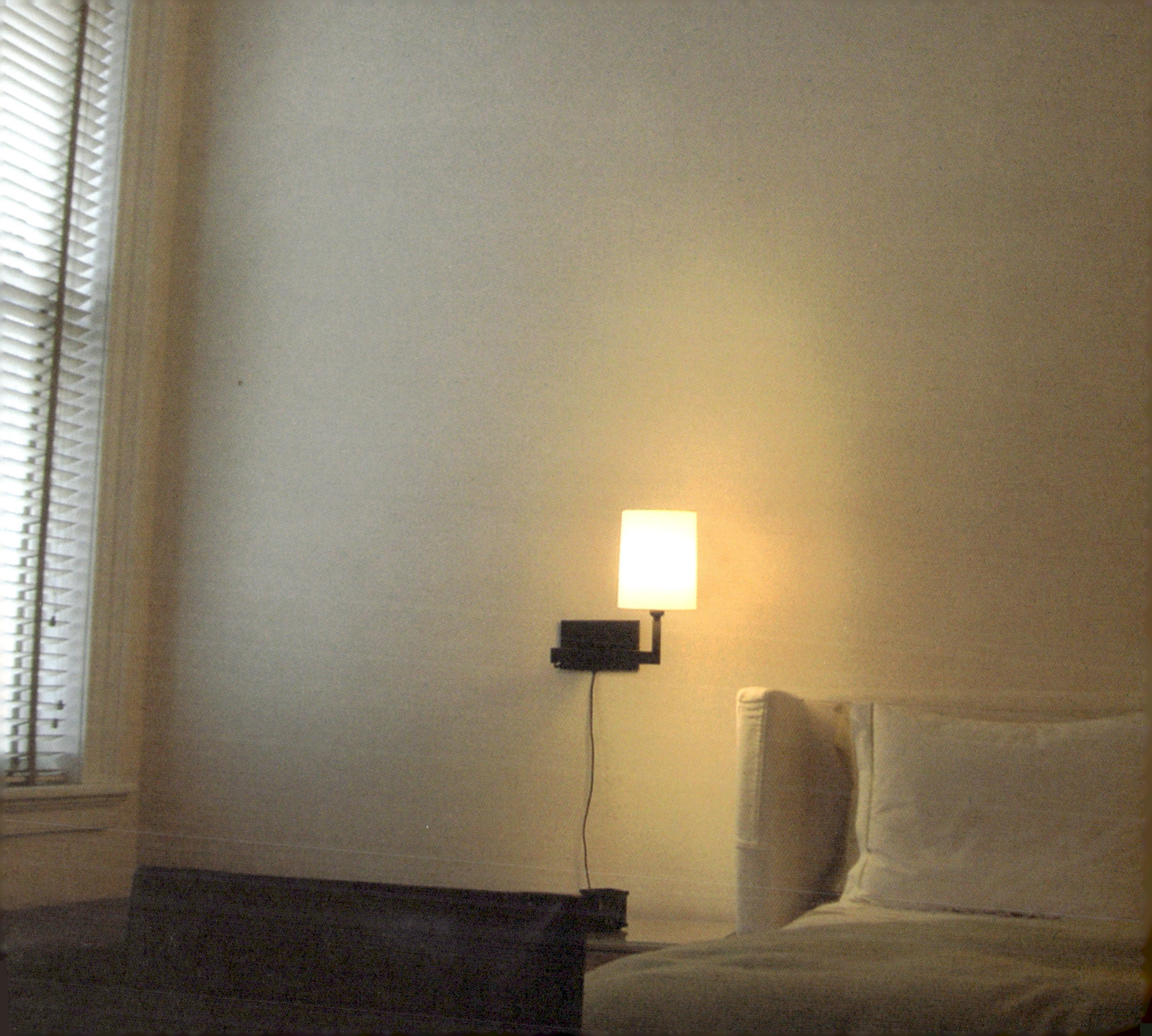

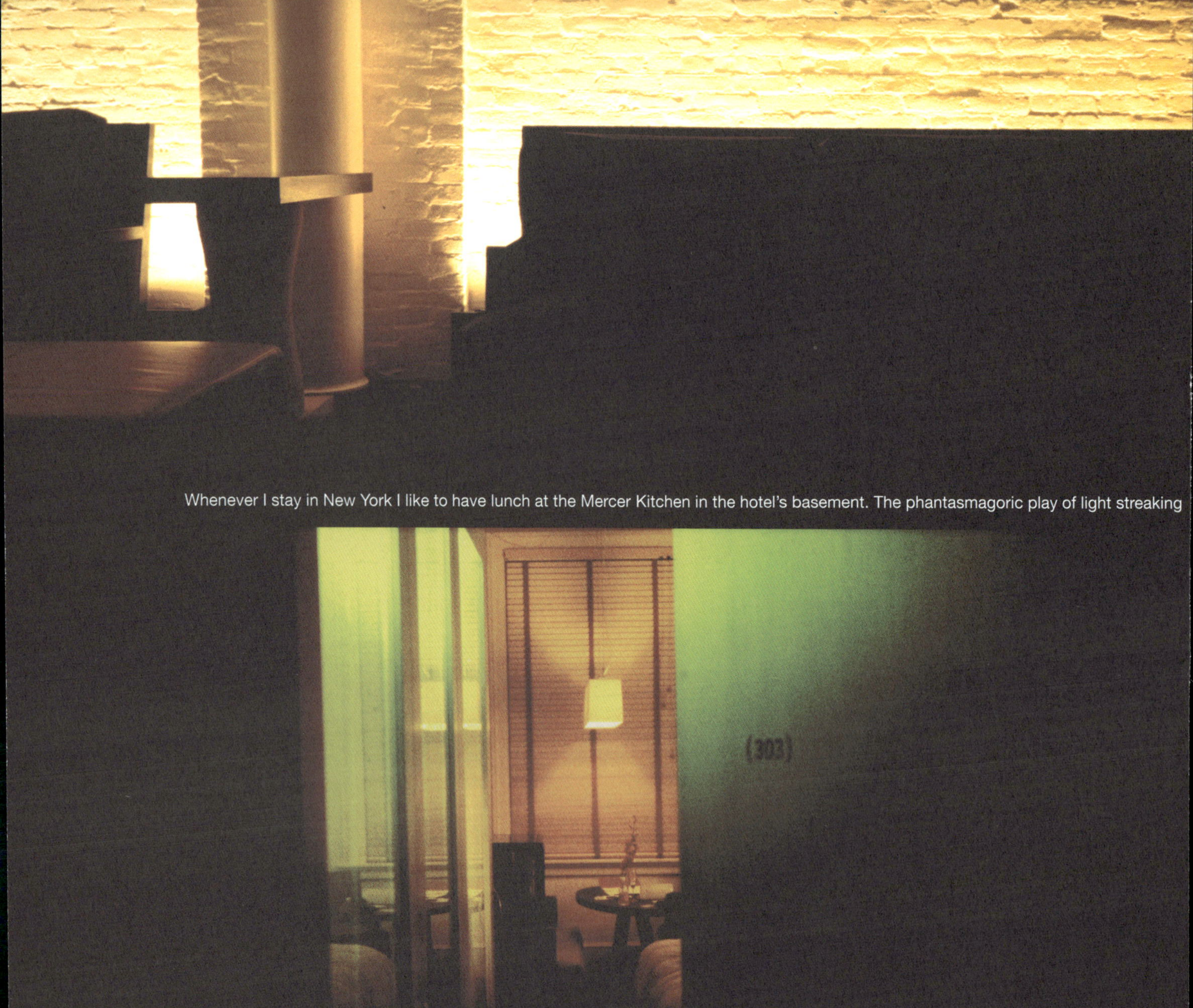

Whenever I stay in New York I like to have lunch at the Mercer Kitchen in the hotel's basement. The phantasmagoric play of light streaking

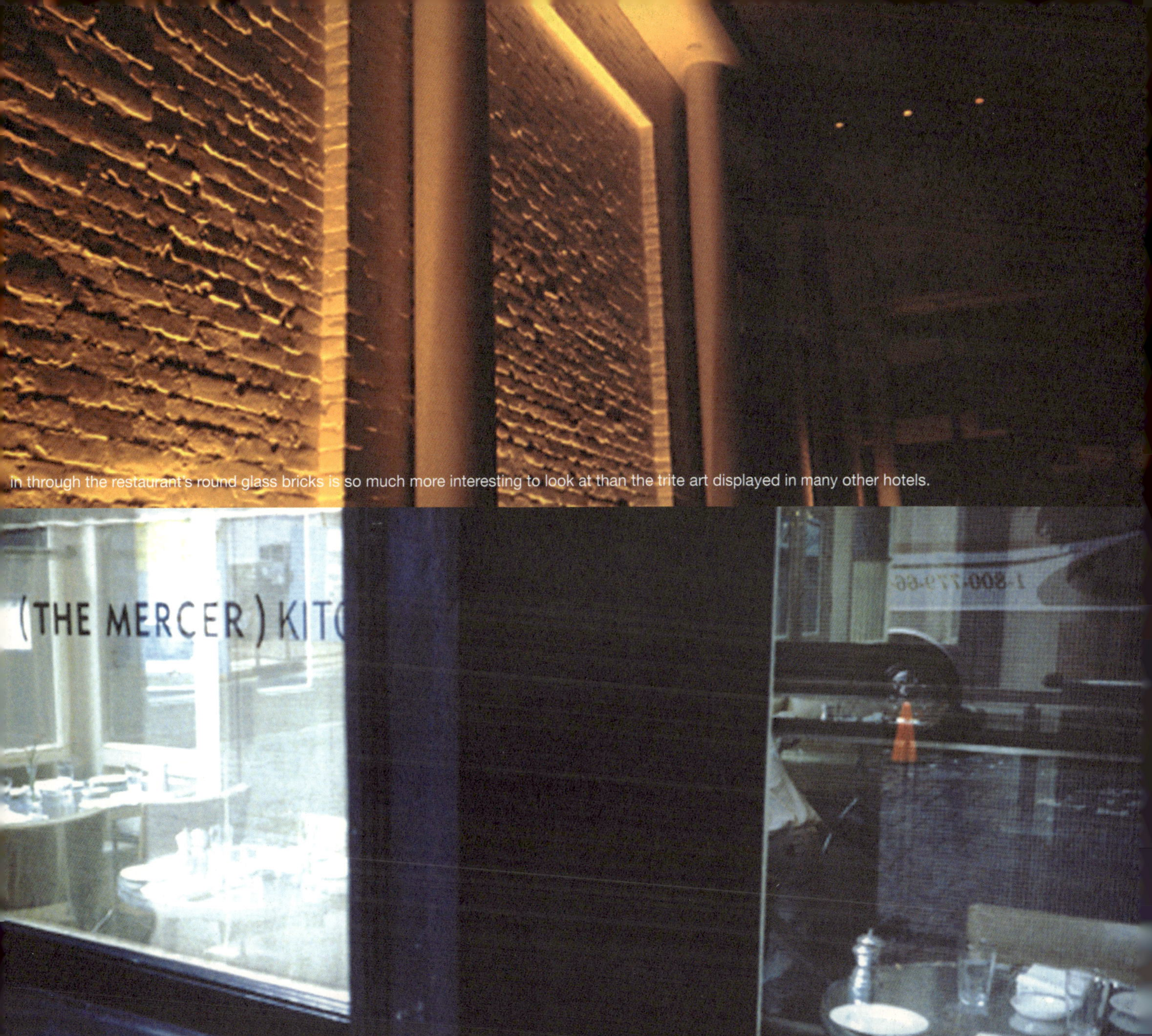

in through the restaurant's round glass bricks is so much more interesting to look at than the trite art displayed in many other hotels.

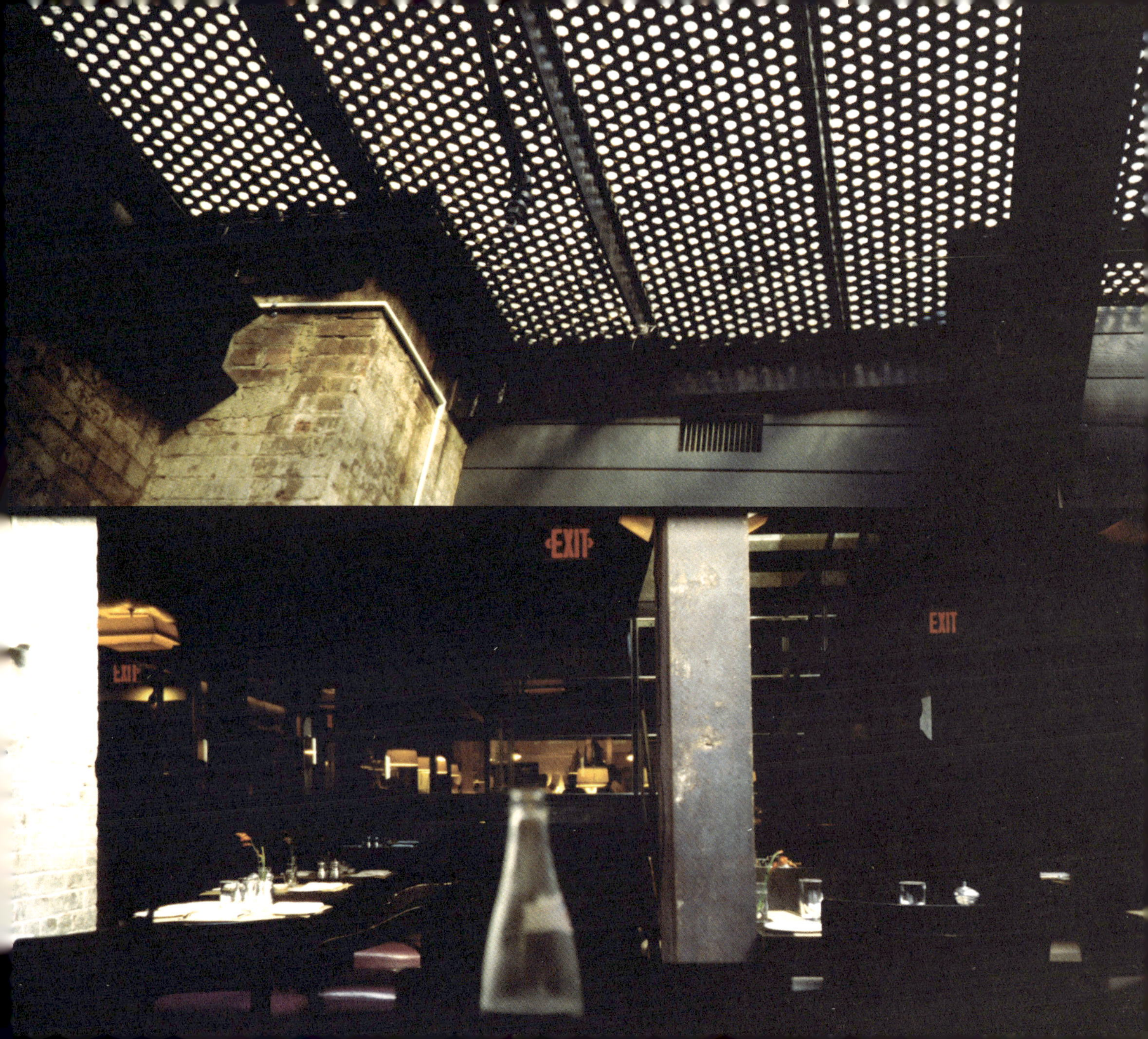
EXIT
EXIT

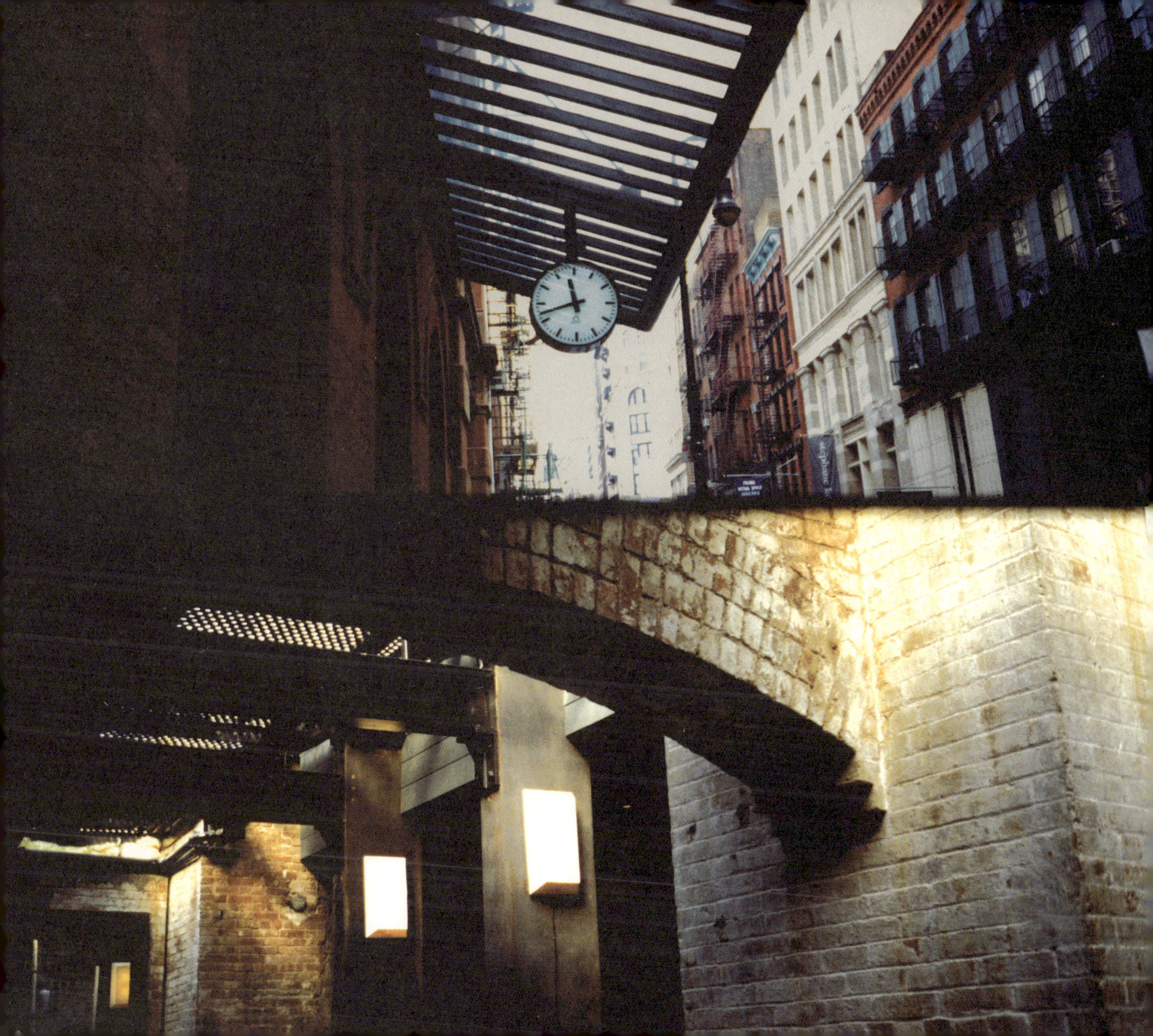

Hotel Information

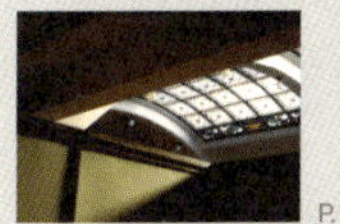
P. 14

Danubius Hotel Gellert

address: 1111 Budapest,
Szent Gellért tér 1.
HUNGARY
telephone: 36-1-889-5500
fax: 36-1-889-5505
e-mail: gellert.reservation@danubiusgroup.com
URL: www.danubiushotels.com/gellert
number of rooms: 234
room rates: $79–332

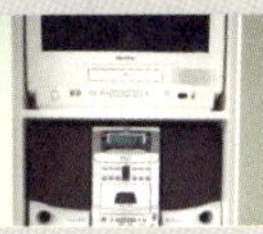
P. 18

Hotel Delano

address: 1685 Collins Avenue
Miami Beach, FL 33139
USA
telephone: 1-305-672-2000
fax: 1-305-532-0099
e-mail: bookings@morganshotel.com
URL: www.delano-hotel.com
number of rooms: 238
room rates: $360–1675

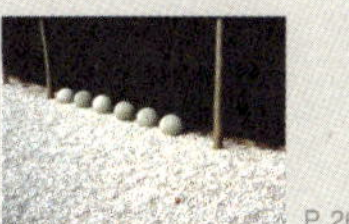
P. 26

Hotel Hempel

address: 31-35 Craven Hill Gardens
W2 3EA London
UK
telephone: 44-207-2989000
fax: 44-207-4024666
e-mail: hotel@the-hempel.co.uk
URL: www.the-hempel.co.uk
number of rooms: 40
room rates: $490–2600

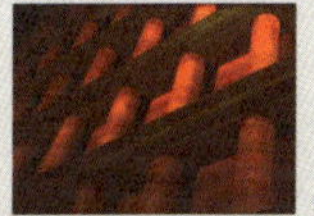
P. 30

Hotel Il Palazzo

address: 3-13-1 Haruyoshi, Chuo-ku
Fukuoka
JAPAN
telephone: 81-92-716-3333
fax: 81-92-724-3330
e-mail: stay@ilpalazzo.jp
URL: www.ilpalazzo.jp
number of rooms: 62
room rates: $150–730

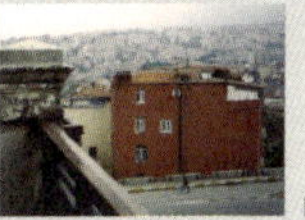
P. 34

Pera Palace Hotel

address: Mesrutiyet Cad.98/100
Tepebasi 80050
Istanbul
TURKEY
telephone: 90-212-251-4560
fax: 90-212-251-4088-89
e-mail: perapalas@perapalas.com
URL: www.perapalace.com
number of rooms: 145
room rates: $105–350

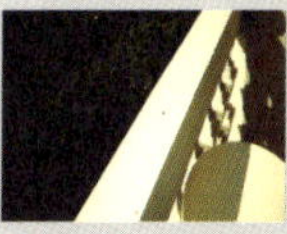
P. 38

Hotel Des Bains

address: Lungomare Marconi 17
Venice I-30126
ITALY
telephone: 39-415-265921
fax: 39-415-260113
e-mail: desbains@sheraton.com
URL: www.sheraton.com
number of rooms: 191
room rates: $240–342

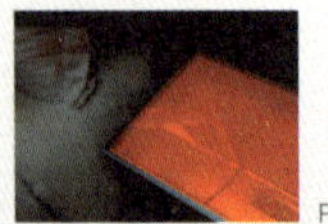

P. 44

The Hotel

address: Sempacherstrasse 14
CH-6002 Luzern
SWITZERLAND
telephone: 41-1-226-8686
fax: 41-1-226-8690
e-mail: info@the-hotel.ch
URL: www.the-hotel.ch
number of rooms: 25
room rates: $293–452

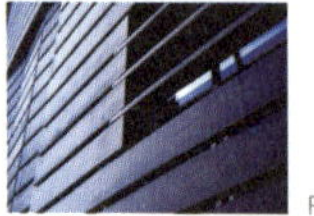

P. 50

Hotel Zurichberg

address: Orellistrasse 21
CH-8044, Zurich
SWITZERLAND
telephone: 41-44-268-3535
fax: 41-44-268-3545
e-mail: info@zuerichberg.ch
URL: www.zuerichberg.ch
number of rooms: 66
room rates: $169–546

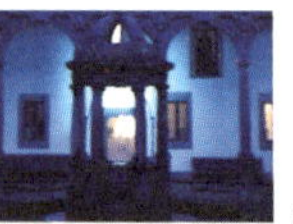

P. 54

Hostal de los Reyes Catolicos

address: Santiago de Compostela
Praza do Obradoiro 1. 15705
SPAIN
telephone: 34-981-582-200
fax: 34-981-563-094
e-mail: www.parador.es
URL: santiago@parador.es
number of rooms: 136
room rates: $254

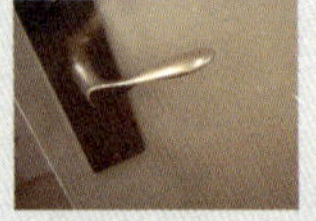

P. 58

Radisson SAS Royal Hotel, Copenhagen

address: Hammerichsgade 1
Copenhagen DK-1611
DENMARK
telephone: 45-33-426210
fax: 45-33-426300
e-mail: copenhagen@radissonsas.com
URL: www.radissonsas.com
number of rooms: 265
room rates: $215–371

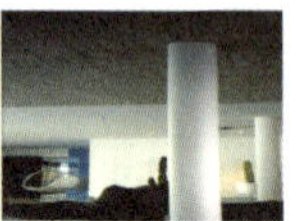

P. 62

Hotel Standard West Hollywood

address: 8300 W Sunset Boulevard
Hollywood CA 90069
USA
telephone: 1-323-650-9090
fax: 1-323-650-2820
e-mail: hollywood@standardhotel.com
URL: www.standardhotel.com
number of rooms: 139
room rates: $99–450

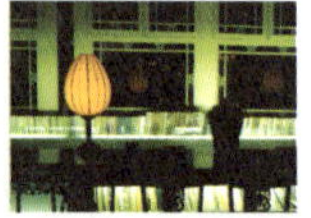

P. 66

The China Club

address: No.51 Xi Rong Xian Lane
Xi Dan, Beijing 100031
CHINA
telephone: 86-10-6603-8855
fax: 86-10-6603-9594
e-mail: tccbroom@public.bta.net.cn
number of rooms: 8
room rates: $158–238

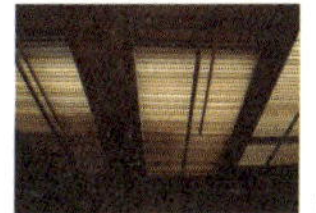

P. 72

Four Seasons Hotel at Sayan

address: Sayan, Ubud, Gianyar
Bali 80571
INDONESIA
telephone: 62-361-977577
fax: 62-361-977588
e-mail: FSRB.syan@fourseasons.com
URL: www.fourseasons.com
number of rooms: 60
room rates: $330–850

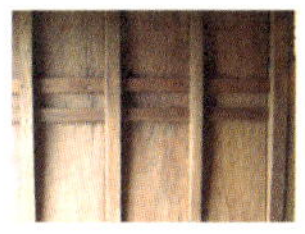

P. 76

Hotel Begawan Giri

address: Ubud, Gianyar
Bali 80571
INDONESIA
telephone: 62-361-978888
fax: 62-361-978889
e-mail: reservations@begawan.com
URL: www.begawan.com
number of rooms: 22
room rates: $495–3035

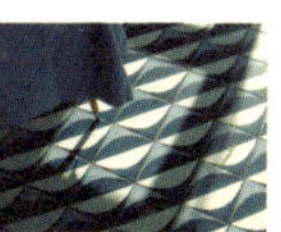

P. 82

Hotel Parco dei Principi

address: Via Rota 1
80067 Sorrento
ITALY
telephone: 39-081-878-4644
fax: 39-081-878-3786
e-mail: info@hotelparcoprincipi.com
URL: www.hotelparcoprincipi.com
number of rooms: 173
room rates: $240–715

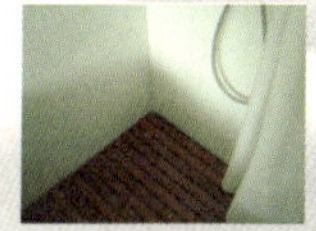

P. 88

Radisson SAS Hotel, Rome (formerly ES Hotel)

address: Via Filippo Turati 171
08185 Rome
ITALY
telephone: 39-06-444 841
fax: 39-06-443 413 96
e-mail: info.rome@radissonsas.com
URL: www.rome.radissonsas.com
number of rooms: 235
room rates: $298–1013

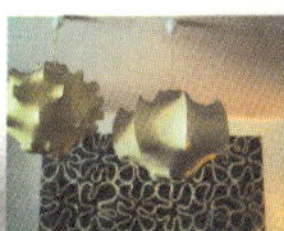

P. 92

Hotel 3 Rooms

address: Corso Como 10
20154 Milan
ITALY
telephone: 39-02-62-6163
fax: 39-02-2900-0760
e-mail: info@3rooms-10corsocomo.com
URL: www.3rooms-10corsocomo.com
number of rooms: 3
room rates: $383

P. 102

Northern Light Inn

address: Blue Lagoon Road
240 Grindavik
ICELAND
telephone: 354-426-8650
fax: 354-426-8651
e-mail: welcome@northernlightinn.is
URL: www.nli.is
number of rooms: 20
room rates: $165–330

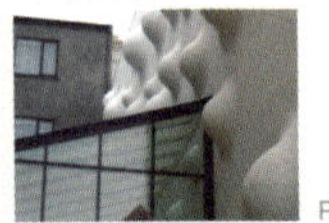

P. 108

Hotel 101

address:	Hverfisgata 10 Reykjavik 101 ICELAND
telephone:	354-580-0101
fax:	354-580-0100
e-mail:	101hotel@101hotel.is
URL:	www.101hotel.is
number of rooms:	38
room rates:	$394–988

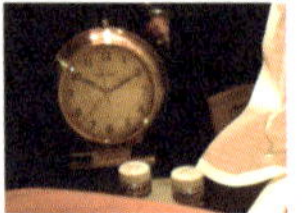

P. 114

Soho House New York

address:	29-35 9th Avenue New York, NY 10014 USA
telephone:	1-212-627-9800
fax:	1-212-627-4766
e-mail:	reception@sohohouseny.com
URL:	www.sohohouseny.com
number of rooms:	24
room rates:	$350–1150

P. 120

Hotel Le Corbusier

address:	280 Boulevard Michelet 13008 Marseille FRANCE
telephone:	33-4-9116-7800
fax:	33-4-9116-7828
e-mail:	contact@hotellecorbusier.com
URL:	www.hotelcorbusier.com
number of rooms:	21
room rates:	$62–69

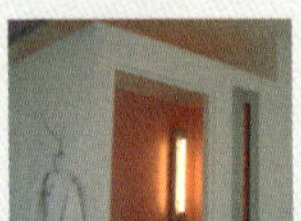

P. 126

Hi Hotel

address:	3 Avenue des Fleurs 06000 Nice FRANCE
telephone:	33-4-9707-2626
fax:	33-4-9707-2627
e-mail:	hi@hi-hotel.net
URL:	www.hi-hotel.net
number of rooms:	38
room rates:	$123–515

P. 136

Blue Woolloomooloo Bay, Sydney (formerly W Hotel)

address:	The Wharf at Woolloomooloo 6 Cowper Wharf Road Sydney NSW 2011 AUSTRALIA
telephone:	61-2-9331-9000
fax:	61-2-9331-9031
e-mail:	blue.sydney@tajhotels.com
URL:	www.tajhotels.com
number of rooms:	104
room rates:	$289–578

P. 142

The Maritime Hotel

address:	363 West 16th Street New York NY 10011 USA
telephone:	1-212-242-4300
fax:	1-212-242-1188
e-mail:	james@themaritimehotel.com
URL:	www.themaritimehotel.com
number of rooms:	124
room rates:	$295

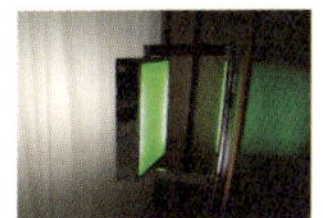
P. 146

Hudson Hotel

address: 356 West, 58 Street
New York, NY 10019
USA
telephone: 1-212-554-6000
fax: 1-212-554-6001
e-mail: hudson@morganshotel.com
URL: www.hudsonhotel.com
number of rooms: 1000
room rates: $175–475

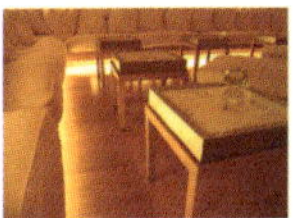
P. 152

Hotel Continentale

address: Vicolo dell'Oro, 6r
50123 Florence
ITALY
telephone: 39-055-27262
fax: 39-055-283139
e-mail: continentale@lungarnohotels.com
URL: www.lungarnohotels.com
number of rooms: 47
room rates: $330–568

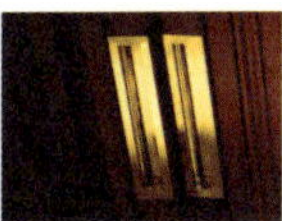
P. 158

Grand Hyatt Shanghai

address: Jin Mao Tower
No. 88 Century Boulevard
Pudong, Shanghai 200121
CHINA
telephone: 86-21-5049-1234
fax: 86-21-5049-1111
e-mail: info@hyattshanghai.com
URL: www.shanghai.grand.hyatt.com
number of rooms: 555
room rates: from $222

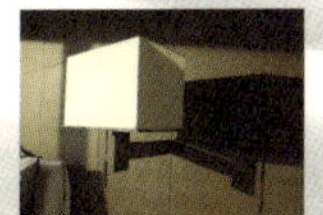
P. 162

Four Seasons Hotel at Marunouchi

address: Pacific Century Place
1-11-1 Marunouchi
Chiyoda-ku, 100-6277 Tokyo
JAPAN
telephone: 81-3-5222-7222
fax: 81-3-5222-1255
e-mail: reservation.mar@fourseasons.com
URL: www.fourseasons.com
number of rooms: 57
room rates: $563–1229

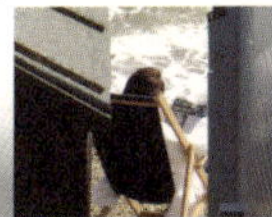
P. 166

Westover Hall Hotel

address: Park Lane, Milford-on-Sea
Lymington
Hampshire SO41 0PT
UK
telephone: 44-1590-643044
fax: 44-1590-644490
e-mail: info@westoverhallhotel.com
URL: www.westoverhallhotel.com
number of rooms: 12
room rates: $324–846

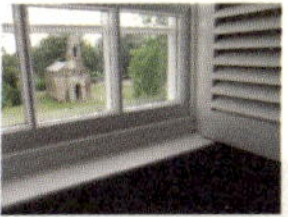
P. 172

Babington House

address: Babington, NR Frome
Somerset, BA11 3RW
UK
telephone: 44-1373-812266
fax: 44-1373-812112
e-mail: enquiries@babingtonhouse.co.uk
URL: www.babingtonhouse.co.uk
number of rooms: 28
room rates: $414–750

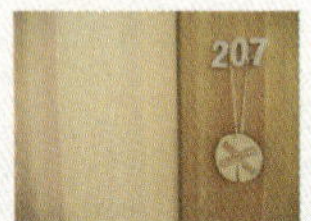
P. 182

Hotel Vigilius Mountain Resort

address: Vigiljoch Mountain
39011 Lana
Vigilius
ITALY
telephone: 39-0473-55-6600
fax: 39-0473-55-6699
e-mail: info@vigilius.it
URL: www.vigilius.it
number of rooms: 41
room rates: $273–735

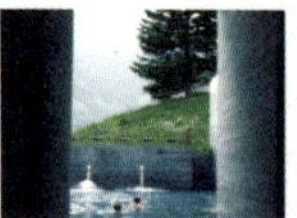
P. 190

Hotel Therme Vals

address: CH-7132 Vals/GR
Switzerland
telephone: 41-81-926 8080
fax: 41-81-926 8000
e-mail: therme-vals@bluewin.ch
URL: www.therme-vals.ch
number of rooms: 140
room rates: $87–215

P. 200

The Metropolitan

address: 27 South Sathorn Road
Tungmahamek Sathorn
Bangkok 10120
THAILAND
telephone: 66-2-625-3333
fax: 66-2-625-3300
e-mail: res.bkk@metropolitan.como.bz
URL: www.metropolitan.como.bz
number of rooms: 175
room rates: $240–2000

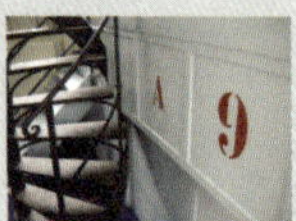
P. 208

Hotel New York

address: Koninginnenhoofd 1
3072 AD Rotterdam
THE NETHERLANDS
telephone: 31-10-439-0500
fax: 31-10-484-2701
e-mail: info@hotelnewyork.nl
URL: www.hotelnewyork.com
number of rooms: 72
room rates: $124–290

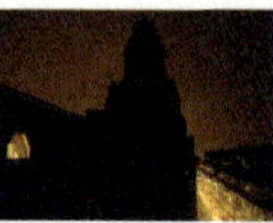
P. 220

Lloyd Hotel

address: Oosterlijke Handelskade 34
1019 BN Amsterdam
THE NETHERLANDS
telephone: 31-20-561-3636
fax: 31-20-561-3600
e-mail: post@lloydhotel.com
URL: www.lloydhotel.com
number of rooms: 116
room rates: $104–390

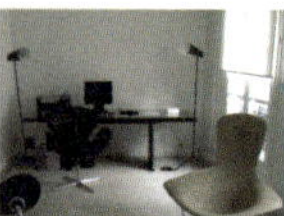
P. 226

Hotel 5 Rue de Moussy

address: 5, Rue de Moussy
75004 Paris
FRANCE
telephone: 33-1-4478-9200
fax: 33-1-4276-0848
e-mail: info@3rooms-5ruedemoussy.com
number of rooms: 3
room rates: $520

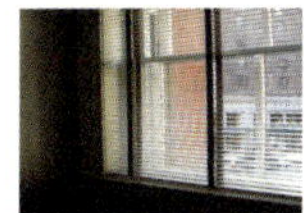
P. 232

Mercer Hotel

address:	147 Mercer Street New York, NY 10012 USA
telephone:	1-212-966-6060
fax:	1-212-965-3838
e-mail:	reservations@mercerhotel.com
URL:	www.mercerhotel.com
number of rooms:	75
room rates:	$410–2,300

All room rates are in USD. Hotels regularly update information, and the above is for reference only. Inquire directly at the respective hotel if necessary.

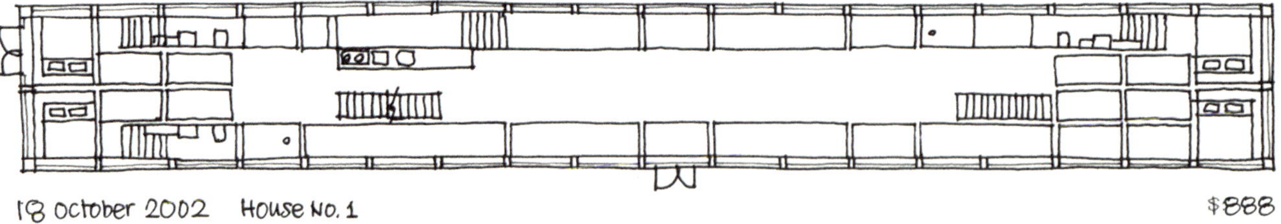

Everyone has their own idea of what an ideal house should look like. With hotels, the ideal can actually change depending on one's moods or needs. Sited in a valley in the Shui-guan section of the Great Wall near Beijing, the Suitcase House was designed with this flexibility in mind. It is a house at times and a hotel at others, which makes the building an interesting and rather pragmatic reflection of the transient times in which we live. The design was deliberately four-dimensional from the outset. Apart from the three spatial dimensions, future time was also factored into the equation. What make the Suitcase House's seemingly endless variations possible are its fifty pneumatically operated floor panels and the wide open interior. Free partitioning can create eight separate rooms. A space might be a living area at one moment and a conference room the next; bedrooms can become kitchens and the den can be turned into a sauna. It is the occupant and not the designer who decides the layout according to his or her needs.

Today, the Suitcase House has acquired a life of its own, far beyond my original expectations. People come to stay for various reasons and purposes. All this is possible because of the building's adaptability and the sense of exploration that it inspires.

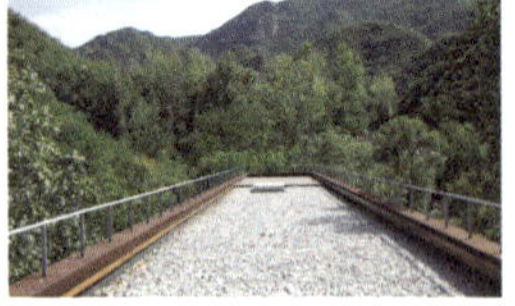

BEIJING

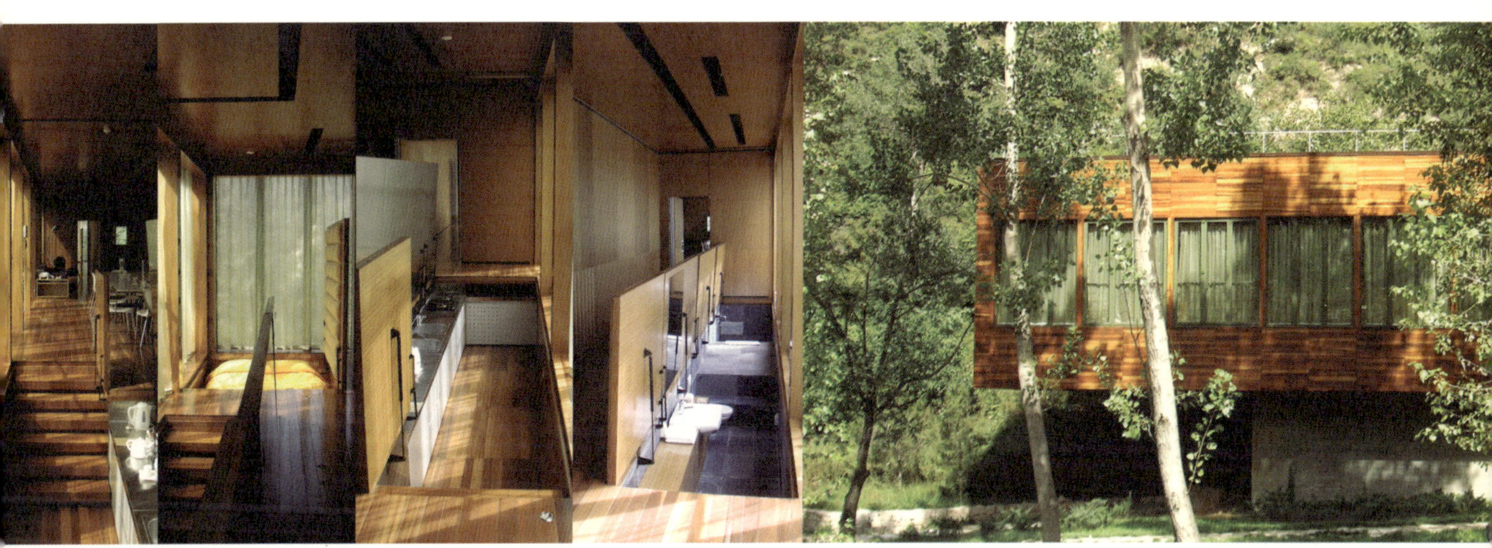

The Suitcase House stands at the entrance to the Commune by the Great Wall.

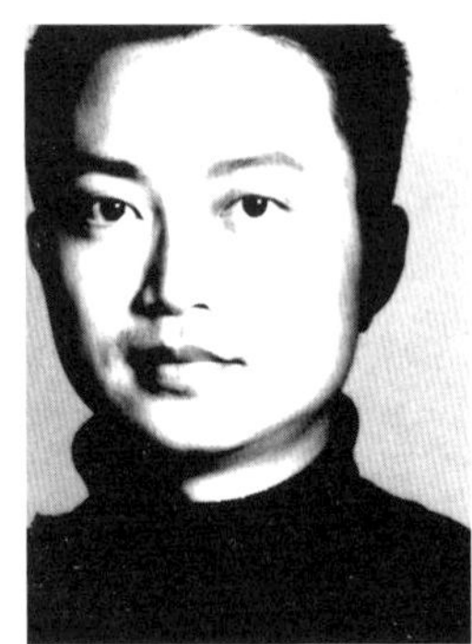

Gary Chang was born and raised in Hong Kong and received his degree in architecture from the University of Hong Kong. In 1994 he founded his design practice, Edge, later renamed Edge Design Institute. Since 1995, he has been on the faculty of various architecture departments of Hong Kong universities. Chang has received many prestigious awards, including First Prize at the 17th Triennale of Milan (1985), Second Prize at the 25th Central Glass International Architectural Design Competition in Tokyo (1990), the Hong Kong Young Architects' Award (1996), First Prize at the Vicenza Dedalo-Minosse International Architecture Competition in Italy (2002), and awards from the ar+d Design Competition (2002, 2003). Some of his best known works are the Suitcase House (built as part of the Commune by the Great Wall), the Kung-fu Tea Set (designed for Alessi's Tea and Coffee Towers project), Broadway Cinematique in Hong Kong, and the architect's own 355-square-foot apartment in Hong Kong.